ARMIES OF Bismarck's Wars

Dedicated to the loving memory of my father, Thurstan Bassett-Powell who, as an officer in the Royal Artillery, fought the last of the Prussians from 1939 to 1945.

ARMIES OF Bismarck's Wars

The Prussian Army, 1860–67

BRUCE BASSETT-POWELL

CASEMATE
Philadelphia & Oxford

Published in the United States of America and Great Britain in 2013 by
CASEMATE PUBLISHERS
908 Darby Road, Havertown, PA 19083
and
10 Hythe Bridge Street, Oxford, OX1 2EW

ISBN 978-1-935149-23-1

Cataloging-in-publication data is available from the Library of Congress and the British Library.

10 9 8 7 6 5 4 3 2 1

Printed and bound in the United States of America.

For a complete list of Casemate titles please contact:

CASEMATE PUBLISHERS (US)
Telephone (610) 853-9131, Fax (610) 853-9146
E-mail: casemate@casematepublishing.com

CASEMATE PUBLISHERS (UK)
Telephone (01865) 241249, Fax (01865) 794449
E-mail: casemate-uk@casematepublishing.co.uk

Photograph Acknowledgements

Images from Wilhelm Voss, *Illustriete Gesichte des Deutches Eingungskriege 1864–1866* on pages 29, 30, 31, 35, 36, 43, 46, 48, 52, 55, 56, 57, 58, 59, 64, 66, 67, 69, 70, 71, 72, 75, 77, 81, 86, 88, 91, 93, 94, 95, 96, 98, 101, 102, 103, 104, 105, 106, 107, 109, 110, 112, 113, 114, 115, 124, 164, 191, 199, 204, 206, 223. All other images are from the author's collection.

Contents

PART 4. UNIFORMS OF THE PRUSSIAN ARMY 1860–67

APPENDICES

Acknowledgements

THIS BOOK HAS BEEN MANY years in the making and the list of those who have helped me is long. Among the individuals and institutions which have provided me with valuable information are Dr. Winfried Münch at the Wehrgeschichtliches Museum in Rastatt, Germany; Elena Brosninsky at the Zeughaus in Berlin; the staff of the Rotunda, Royal Artillery Museum, Woolwich, London; and Peter Harrington at the Anne S. K. Brown Library in Providence, Rhode Island, USA.

I can only name but a few of the others whose assistance has been instrumental in bringing this work to fruition: Helmut Bauer, Sam Buhler, Larkin Connolly, Philip Cranz, Michael Embree, Zdenek Fink, Will Forester, Phil Hutchens, Rick Philips, Robert Ruman, Dennis Shorthouse, Peter Sorensen, Bruce Weigle, and most of all to my family who have put up with this project for all these years.

Introduction

THERE ARE RARE OCCASIONS WHEN the gift of political genius combines with that of military genius to produce an event that changes the course of history forever. One such event occurred on 3 July 1866 when, on one of the more pleasant of the River Elbe's wide valleys in Bohemia, a Prussian army defeated an Austrian army at the battle of Königgrätz. The geniuses in question and the architects of this victory were Otto von Bismarck and Helmuth von Moltke.

The relatively small kingdom of Prussia was no stranger to military genius. Forged at the battle of Fehrbellin in 1675, it was created from the Electorate of Brandenburg by Frederick William I (The Great Elector). He entered into a pact with the tough landowners of Prussia's eastern provinces to provide him with military officers in perpetuity. The landowners were known as Junkers, and the pact formed the basis of Prussia's military heritage. Less than fifty years after Prussia's birth as a nation, the Great Elector's grandson, Frederick the Great, stunned Europe with his strategic vision and the prowess of his armies on the battlefield. The battles of Rossbach and Leuthen (1757) alone provide testament to this. Despite the difficulties he faced in the latter part of the Seven Years War, Frederick's legacy survived intact. Most countries would not have been able to overcome a catastrophic defeat such as the one Prussia suffered in 1806 at Jena and Auerstadt, at the hands of Napoleon. However, within half a dozen years, the Prussian nation galvanized itself to take advantage of Bonaparte's own tragedy in Russia, and prevailed against him during the War of Liberation, 1813–14. The military luminaries of this era were Gerhardt von Scharnhorst, August von Gneisenau, and a theoretician whose work would alter the very concept of war, Karl von Clausewitz. Prussia would also share the glory at the climactic final clash of the Napoleonic Wars at Waterloo under the leadership of the legendary battlefield general, von Blucher.

The Congress of Vienna put Europe back together again, restoring most of the kingdoms, principalities and dukedoms to their former domains and, in many cases, enlarging them. The political skills of Prince Klemens von Metternich, Lord Castlereagh and Charles Maurice de Talleyrand-Périgord managed to place France, a monarchy once again, back into the ranks of the great powers of Europe along with Russia, Austria, Great Britain and Prussia, now the junior member of the five. The ensuing thirty years saw a period of relative peace as the great conflict that began with the French Revolution faded into memory. However, the liberal testament of that war had not been put to rest, and by 1848 it had fuelled a revolt that once again began in France, and spread throughout Europe in a matter of weeks. As it grew, the revolution began to encompass liberation movements against Austrian rule in Italy, Hungary and Bohemia. For more than a year, these movements held the Hapsburg armies at bay, but eventually they were bloodily and efficiently suppressed. In the final event, the conservative and authoritarian monarchies prevailed. Even in France where the king was ousted and replaced by an imperial dictatorship, the aura of liberalism faded. Prussia found itself in a war with Denmark over the Schleswig Duchy, and also allocating troops to deal with uprisings in Baden and Hesse-Kassel as well as on the streets of Berlin. The Prussian king, Frederick William IV, found himself in the awkward position of being offered the crown of all Germany, which he refused but nevertheless still encouraged a bid to become the dominant German power. This angered Austria who, in a test of military mobilizations between the two countries severely humiliated Prussia and forced her to recognize Austria's supremacy, with the Treaty of Olmütz in 1850.

At this low point for the Hohenzollern Kingdom, a cast of characters began to emerge on the stage that would transform the face of Europe within twenty years. As Frederick William IV descended into mental incompetence, his brother William, a military conservative, took up the reins, first as regent, and later as king. A political maverick, Otto von Bismarck began his journey to chancellorship and a military mastermind called Helmuth von Moltke began to take charge of the Prussian General Staff. They were not alone. General Albrecht von Roon, a brilliant administrator, set out to reorganize the army, taking it from a militia-based force of citizen soldiers (*Landwehr*) to a conscripted and efficient army fully ready for mobilization. The genius was not just military. Prussia seized on the weapons technology of two men; Nikolas Dreyse who invented the breech-loading needle rifle, and Alfred Krupp who developed steel, breech-loading, rifled cannon. Here was political will, strategic vision and a motivated military machine, all combined with the most modern weapons technology. With the legacy of Scharnhorst, Gneisenau and Clausewitz to draw on, all Prussia needed was a reason to act.

As all these ingredients came into play, they fed into a national paranoia that had been brewing since the time of Frederick the Great. Prussia was surrounded by very powerful neighbours: Russia to the north, Austria to the east, and France to the south. Any invading enemy could be in Berlin within hours, as there were no natural barriers. When Bismarck came on the political scene, his vision was that of a Prussia powerful and dominant in the region. Standing in the way of that vision was principally Austria, much of whose empire lay outside the German-speaking world it dominated. The humiliation of Prussia at Olmütz was the final straw, and from that moment Bismarck devoted himself to changing that equation. It is ironic that the first entity to get Bismarck's attention was not to the east, north or south but to the west in the small kingdom of Denmark. The Schleswig-Holstein question had not disappeared after the war of 1848–50. It erupted once again in 1864 and Bismarck took full advantage of it, engineering a war in condominium with Austria that, after a six-month campaign, wrested the two duchies from Denmark. The joint administration of the duchies by Prussia and Austria quickly led to friction that Bismarck again exploited. However, Austria was not Denmark, and any military adventure to the east was fraught with danger. Even so, Moltke had a plan and like any great military plan, it was bold and at the same time, a throw of the dice. Manipulating Austria into war was probably the easiest part of the plan. An ally was found in Italy, which would declare war at the same time, and force Austria to divert a large force southwards. Austria also had allies, as most of the south German states sided with them and they would hopefully draw off Prussian resources. The main theatre of the war was Bohemia, and as Moltke's plan went into effect the world looked on with the expectation that his gamble would fail and Austria would put Prussia in its place. In just seven weeks, that expectation was turned on its head and the world was looking at a Prussia now capable of dominating a much greater entity; a united Germany.

This work was originally planned to be a book about military uniforms. However, as so often happens with such projects, the fascination spread beyond its foundation, and I found it necessary to examine how an army whose dress was setting the pace for military fashion could also be an army which was pioneering the very way that war was fought. Finally, I was drawn to the great battle itself and its place in history, so it also had to be a substantial part of this endeavour. The first part gives an account of how Prussia progressed from 1815 to the middle of the century. It chronicles its social and political history, including the rise of Bismarck, from the revolutions of 1848 through the Schleswig war of 1864 and the Seven Weeks War, to the climactic battle of Königgrätz. The central theme of the book is about the Prussian army, and its military system, in the middle of the nineteenth century. It tells the stories of Clausewitz, Moltke, Roon and others. It explains how the General Staff evolved and how the army was organized. It describes how officers and men were recruited, how they were trained and how they lived. It traces the evolution of the needle gun, and its inventor Johann Nikolaus von Dreyse, and recounts the part that Alfred Krupp and his steel cannon also played in the story. The final part illustrates and describes in detail what every branch of the Prussian Army wore, as well as the fledgling Prussian Navy. Details about the Austrian and other armies are not given, except in the narratives of the battles and campaigns they fought alongside or against Prussia.

Königgrätz is often overlooked as one of the most decisive battles in history and does not always appear at all in many lists of such battles. History has allowed it to be overshadowed by the battle fought four years later at Sedan. This is probably because Sedan was the final major battle of the three of Bismarck's wars that led to the unification of Germany. However, I would argue that Königgrätz was a far more decisive battle for many reasons. It was the largest land battle to date involving more than 460,000 men on one battlefield. It was the first major conflict in which a quick firing, bolt-action rifle was the primary weapon of one of the armies. It was the first one where breech-loading, steel rifled artillery was used in numbers. Above all it was a battle that not only changed how wars were fought, but the course of history depended on its outcome. Had the Prussians failed, Austria would have remained the most powerful central European entity. They would have certainly impeded the unification of Italy by denying it much of Lombardy and Venice. The North German Federation may not have materialized, and German unity could have been a long way off. Bismarck himself would indeed have become "The biggest villain in Europe", as perhaps he was. Beyond that, it is pure speculation to suppose there would not have been a First World War, but absenting a war with France, and the loss of Alsace-Lorraine it is possible that Europe may have remained at peace for a long time.

Part One

Prelude

CHAPTER ONE

Europe 1815–50

AFTER TWENTY-SIX YEARS OF conflict, the upheavals wrought by the French Revolution ended in July of 1815 with Napoleon Bonaparte's departure to exile on the island of St Helena. The Congress of Vienna, work of which had been interrupted by the Hundred Days and its decisive conclusion at Waterloo, resumed its deliberations. Led by the charismatic Austrian statesman, Klemens von Metternich, the Congress would restore to Europe most, if not all, of its autocratic monarchies. The Bourbons again ruled in France, Spain and Naples; Austria recovered its Italian domains; and the hapless Poles were divided between Russia and Prussia. Even little Belgium became part of the Kingdom of the Netherlands.

The old Holy Roman Empire, swept from history by Napoleon in 1806, had become a German Federation (Bund) in 1816 consisting of thirty-nine kingdoms, principalities and dukedoms (along with four free cities) with a Federal Diet (Parliament) sitting in the free city of Frankfurt. By design, the dominant power in this new bund was Austria, as it had been before 1806 and, particularly in order to underscore its "German" nature, the Federation would exclude the non-German portion of its empire and the Polish provinces of Prussia. The Danish province of Holstein, almost entirely German speaking, was also included in a customs union that was begun in 1819 and which would give the federation an economic clout.

The architects of the new order were the Great Powers: Austria, Russia and Britain. As a major participant in the final defeat of Bonaparte, Prussia was accorded the same status. After France was accepted in 1818, the five would see themselves as the arbiters of European stability for years to come.

However, stability was not easy, and the Powers constantly found themselves forced to shore up the edifice they had created in Vienna. The liberation of Spain's South American colonies caused unrest on the Iberian

Europe in 1815.

Peninsula, prompting intervention by France, and problems in Naples and Sardinia also required Austrian military support. The tides of liberation had not ceased and Greece's struggle for independence from the Ottoman Empire was just beginning. Further east, the new tsar, Nicholas I, had to deal with the Decembrist Uprising before he was even crowned.

By 1830, the growth of trade and commerce fuelled by the Industrial Revolution in England had given rise to bourgeois prominence in European cities like Paris. This, combined with the equally swift growth of liberal ideals, would upset Metternich's finely tuned structure.

The fusion of bourgeois and liberal ideology erupted in Paris in July 1830. Within three days the last of the French Bourbons, Charles X, was gone and had been replaced by Louis Philippe, erstwhile Duc d'Orléans. The domino effect in Europe was almost instantaneous. The Belgians rose against the Dutch, the Poles against the Russians and several Italian duchies, including the Papal States, experienced revolts. The Belgians prevailed and won their kingdom but the unlucky Poles and Italians were suppressed.

Prince Klemens von Metternich (1773–1859).

Clearly the old absolutist order was under pressure, and although the bourgeoisie and liberals would somewhat diverge, the desire for constitutional reform would not die. Among the Great Powers, Britain stood alone. While Metternich fretted about the maintenance of monarchical authority, Britain, with its firmly entrenched middle class moved ahead with its own agenda including the Reform Bill (1832) and later Corn Laws. In addition, it was British volunteers who tipped the balance for independence in South America, Greece and elsewhere and it was Britain, with the help of the Royal Navy, that was emerging as the world's first superpower. To the liberals and middle class of Europe alike, this did not go unnoticed and within fifteen years, the pot would boil again, this time with indelible consequences.

The revolutions of 1848

By the late 1840s, a new word was gaining currency in a Europe used to what has become known as "The Long Peace" of the 1830s. The word was "socialism" and its mention gave rise to passion on both sides of the political spectrum. By February 1848, it was socialist pressure that gained the upper hand in a Paris seething with crime, poverty, and discontent. The ensuing violence led to bloodshed that included the slaughter of thirty-five civilians by a rash infantry volley. By this act, the reign of Louis Philippe I was unsustainable, along with the French monarchy itself. Months of wrangling and fresh socialist uprisings ended in December when a constitutional assembly elected Louis Napoleon, nephew of the great Bonaparte, president. The Second Republic had been born.

For Austria, the issue was not so easily resolved. Within days of Louis Philippe I's abdication, there was student unrest in Vienna, which by March became active rioting. In Bohemia also, there were clamours for reform and, before long Prague itself was in revolt. With Vienna almost ungovernable, both Metternich and the feeble-minded Emperor Ferdinand fled.

To make matters worse, the Italians saw the general situation as an opportunity to rid themselves of Hapsburg dominance and both Venice and Milan immediately exploded in revolt. In both places, and elsewhere in Italy, they looked to the king of Piedmont-Sardinia, Charles Albert, to champion their cause. Later that year the Hungarians, after three centuries as Austrian vassals, finally found a charismatic leader, Lajos Kossuth, to lead them in revolution.

Thus beset from all quarters, their empire aflame, their chief minister of over thirty years gone, and the emperor hidden in the Tyrol, the Austrians seemed to be in an untenable position. Two things saved Austria. First, the army – intensely loyal and led by two highly experienced, brilliant and ruthless military leaders, Field Marshal Alfred, prince of Windisch-Grätz in the north and Field Marshal Josef Wenzel Graf Radetzky von Radetz in Italy – rose to the challenge and came to the aid of the empire. Second, Metternich was replaced by Prince Felix zu Schwartzenburg, whose political deftness and astute diplomacy would trump the efforts of lesser men in Germany and elsewhere.

Field Marshal Alfred I, prince of Windisch-Grätz (1787–1862).

Windisch-Grätz quickly responded to the situation in Prague with a ferocious bombardment of the city with devastating results (his own wife was killed by a stray bullet during the uprising). Having tested the loyalty of his regiments, Windisch-Grätz moved on Vienna in October. With 60,000 men, he turned back an attempt by Hungarian Magyar forces to aid the rioting students. After taking the city, he had the insurgent leaders shot and imposed martial law. It would be some time before the lively Hapsburg capital would return to normal. Meanwhile the ineffective and feeble-minded Ferdinand had abdicated in favour of his nephew Francis Joseph, who would reign for the next 66 years.

In Italy, Charles Albert of Piedmont-Sardinia declared war on Austria and was able to keep Radetzky close to the Quadrilateral – the four fortresses[1] between the Mincio and Adige rivers. The old field marshal, however, finally defeated the Piedmontese at Custozza in July 1848. The king's renewal of the war in March 1849 was also quickly laid to rest at Novara later that month, forcing his abdication in favour of his son, Victor Emmanuel II. Radetzky then starved Venice into submission and restored the Hapsburg grand duke of Tuscany to Florence. The revolutionary Roman Republic in the Papal States was suppressed by French troops who returned the Pope to Rome. Although the Italian revolution was over, the lamp of liberty was not extinguished and would flare again within ten years.

The release of troops from Italy allowed the Austrians to turn their attention to the Hungarians, and with the help of a large Russian army pressing from the east, they were able to restore the situation there. A terrible revenge was exacted on the Magyars of Hungary, orchestrated principally by the infamous General Haynau, who also demonstrated his excesses in Italy.

Having faced collapse, the Hapsburg Empire had emerged victorious. Their ruthless generals had shown how a loyal army of such ethnic diversity as theirs could crush nationalist aspirations in regions that were foreign to them. Croat and Ruthenian soldiers had no more love for Italians or Hungarians than German and Slovenian soldiers had for Czechs. The final success for Austria, however, would be political and no man was better suited to wield that sword than Felix Schwartzenburg, the new chancellor.

Field Marshal Josef Wenzel Graf Radetzky von Radetz.

NOTES

1. The four fortresses in the Quadrilateral were Verona, Legnano, Mantua and Pesciara.

CHAPTER TWO

Prussia and Germany 1848–62

FOR THE GERMAN BUND, THE thirty years following the Congress of Vienna had passed rather uneventfully. The uprisings and revolutions on the fringes of their federation had largely passed them by. There were expressions of liberalism, including an attempt by Frederick William III (1797–1840), to form an assembly in Prussia, which was pounced on by Metternich, aided by the Junker squirearchy of the Prussian heartland and quietly quashed. Strong feelings of nationalism and a united Germany were everywhere, but seriously frowned upon by the absolutist princes and kings. In many of the principalities, the wearing of the German national colours of red, gold and black was proscribed. The Federal Diet sitting in Frankfurt was ineffective, even though their members were mostly of a middle-class and scholarly persuasion, they talked about everything and solved nothing, which was also to the liking of the ruling houses. The greatest achievement of the Bund was the Zollverein, the customs union that was formed by Prussia in 1819 and which was, within 25 years, joined by most of the states in the Bund. Foreign military adventures were rare: when the Greek Assembly chose Prince Otto of Bavaria to be their king in 1832, a Bavarian expeditionary force was sent with him, which remained for five years. There was a brief Swiss "Sonderbund" war of 1847, sparked by the revolt of seven Catholic cantons. It was almost bloodless, did not involve in any German troops, and resulted in Switzerland remaining united. However, "the long peace" was about to come to an end.

Frederick William IV and the Liberal collapse in Germany

The Paris Revolution of 1848 caused absolute consternation in Germany. It was like an earthquake with no warning. As early as March, unrest stirred in most of the principalities and states as well as in the adjacent Danish provinces of

Schleswig and Holstein. The people of Schleswig, mostly German-speaking, declared their own constitution and rose against the Danes, capturing the fortress of Rensburg on 24 March. The resulting reaction of Denmark led to a declaration of war between the Danes and the revolutionaries of Schleswig-Holstein. The German federation, led by Prussia, declared war on the Danes and sent 12,000 Prussian troops with 10,000 others from the federation. Thus began a three-year war on the Jutland peninsula.

In Berlin, Frederick William IV, who had succeeded his father in 1840, greeted word of the Paris uprising with alarm. The news, coupled with tidings of the student uprising in Vienna, caused angry crowds to fill the streets and the army, in an atmosphere of mutual distrust, reacted violently. When the king appeared on the balcony of his residence on 18 March to try and calm the throng, dragoons charged the crowds. This caused outrage, and the populace threw up barricades all over the city. Unlike the French soldiers in Paris, the Prussian troops obeyed their Junker officers with ruthless efficiency and volley after volley was loosed at the people of Berlin. To the soldiers' astonishment, the king made a proclamation that if the barricades came down, the troops would be withdrawn from Berlin. His angry army evacuated the city as the insurgents dragged in the bodies of their slain comrades for him to view and made him stand bareheaded while hymns were sung in honour of the dead. By the 21st, Frederick William was moving about the city, thronged by his now-adoring subjects who cheered as he proclaimed that "Prussia is henceforth merged with Germany", all the while decked out in the national colours of red, gold, and black.

Frederick William I.

However, the Junker backbone of Prussia was beside itself with anger. These tough country-bred noblemen who had supplied the officer class of the Prussian Army – and who would continue to do so – had been betrayed. Even the king's brother, William, left for England where he "wept for three days". The king's moral collapse in the face of the mob would earn him the enmity of his court and army to the end of his days.

In any event, an assembly was formed and a constitution drafted. The assembly was a weak affair populated by liberal professors relying, along with the constitution, entirely on the king's support of their labours. By September 1848 however, the king was beginning to wobble and upon the news of the astonishing recovery of the Hapsburgs in all parts of their Empire and the crushing of the student revolt in Vienna, he collapsed. He appointed a conservative ministry and quarrelled with the assembly, and by November, he ordered the army to remove it from Berlin to the small city of Brandenburg. The army delightedly complied and in December after finally dissolving the assembly outright, he granted a constitution that was anything but liberal. The blow to reform in Prussia was not over. In 1849, after battles with the elected chamber for which the constitution had provided, he dissolved that and modified the constitution again, leaving Prussia, and later Germany, with an autocratic system of government that would survive until 1918 and have disastrous consequences.

In the meantime, the parliament in Frankfurt had been dealing with their own agenda. For eight months, beginning in May 1848, the delegates occupied their days with fruitless debate and wrangling over the composition over a future German state. They talked about "fundamental rights" for Germans, the place of the church, the army and a myriad of details that in any other place and time might have been legitimate matters for discussion. But the elephant in the room was Austria. The ethnic diversity of the Hapsburg Empire was an obstacle to their leadership of a purely German state. Yet could such a state exclude the Germans of Austria proper?

As all this debate went on, the Austrian government, emerging from its difficulties more confident than ever, was beginning to lose patience. Time was not on the side of the Frankfurt Diet as Prussia was beginning to shed its liberal mantle and even the population of the city became restless and order had to be restored by Prussian and Austrian troops. Finally, on 28 March 1849, the Parliament adopted a constitution that created a German Federal Empire, with an upper and lower house. The crown of this empire however, was not to be offered to the Hapsburgs, whose attitudes had run so contrary to the enterprise that the delegates had lost any sentiment for their candidacy. Instead, it was to be offered to the king of Prussia, Frederick William IV. When word of this reached other rulers in the German states, there was consternation as many of them, especially the south German kings, Württemburg and Saxony, regarded the House of Hohenzollern as "newcomers" and would rather accept any other monarch. However, everything came to an abrupt halt when the king of Prussia, describing it as "a crown of mud and wood", refused to accept the imperial throne.

The disintegration of the Frankfurt Diet was now assured. No amount of pleading could save their work now. When the kingdoms of Bavaria, Hanover, Württemburg, and Saxony refused to consider the constitution, the lesser princes

GERMANY
1848-1866
DENMARK
SWEDEN
BALTIC SEA
NORTH SEA
SCHLESWIG
HOLSTEIN
POMERANIA
EAST PRUSSIA
WEST PRUSSIA
SCHWERIN
LÜBECK
MECKLENBURG
STRELITZ
HAMBURG
OLDEN BURG
BREMEN
HANOVER
PRUSSIA
VISTULA
SL
LD
BRUNSWICK
Berlin
BRANDENBURG
POSEN
RUSSIAN EMPIRE
HOLLAND
RHINE
WESTPHALIA
PRUSSIA
ANHALT
MAGDEBURG
WALDECK
HESSE-KASSEL
ODER
ELBE
SILESIA
BELGIUM
RHINE
HESSEN
THURINGIA
SAXONY
NASSAU
LUXEMBERG
DARMSTADT
FRANKFORT
MAIN
Prague
Koniggratz
(See Inset)
TO BAVARIA
BADEN
AUSTRIAN
FRANCE
WÜRTTEMBERG
BAVARIA
HUNGARY
Vienna
R. DANUBE
Munich
Buda Pest
EMPIRE
SWITZERLAND
R. DRAVE
R. SAVE
ITALY
THURINGIA
Sonderhausen
SR
SS
SM
PRUSSIA
SW
RS
Altenburg
Gotha
Weimar
SA
SG
SS
SA
Gera
SW
Rudolstadt
SW
SM
SS
SR
Greiz
Meiningen
SR
RS
RG
SAXE-MEININGEN
SAXONY
Coburg
BAVARIA
AUSTRIAN EMPIRE
Limits of German Bund until 1866
Prussian Territories
WALDECK Allied to Prussia in 1866
ABBREVIATIONS
LD Lippe-Detmold
SL Schaumburg-Lippe
SA Saxe-Altenburg
SG Saxe-Corburg-Gotha
SM Saxe-Meiningen
SW Saxe-Weimar
SR Schwartzburg-Rudolstadt
SS Schwartzburg-Sonderhausen
RG Reuss-Greiz (Elder Line)
RS Reuss-Schleiz (Younger Line)

Opposite: Prussia and Germany 1848–66.

and dukes followed suit and as the delegates dispersed ("fled" may be the better description), the revolution in Germany moved into its last act. Prussian troops were dispatched to quell last uprisings in the Rhenish Palatinate, Baden and, ignominiously for their king, Saxony. By the end of 1849, Prussian soldiers marched home from Baden having stamped out the last of the republican revolt in the city of Rästatt and restored its grand duke on 18 August. The Liberal revolution in Germany was now over.

The humiliation of Olmütz

Although the restoration of the old order had been accomplished, albeit with some not-so-liberal constitutions in place, there was one final drama to come. The vacillating Prussian king, although refusing the imperial crown of a united Germany, nevertheless wanted some semblance of a German union, preferably excluding, but in close association with, Austria. This limited federal system was proposed in May 1849 and was accepted by the smaller principalities as the best alternative to the failed effort in Frankfurt. However, as before, the larger kingdoms opposed it, especially in the face of scheming machinations by the Austrian chancellor, Schwartzenburg. A whole year of coming and going went on before, finally, in September 1850 a situation arose that played into Schwartzenburg's hands.

In the Electoral State of Hesse-Cassel a revolt erupted against the hated Elector (ruler), who fled to Frankfurt. In a provocative act, the Austrians trying to resurrect the old Bund and Schwartzenburg then offered to send Austrian troops to reinstate the Elector and crush the revolt. This was a direct affront to Prussia's sovereignty and an interference in her sphere of influence. As his Junker officers rattled their sabres and urged war, William Frederick IV did indeed mobilize, but he again hesitated to declare war. As Prussian troops marched toward Hesse-Cassel, the king agonized. Prussia was certainly not in a position to confront the rejuvenated Austrian Army aided by the south German states, largely because of the logistics involved. The recall of Prussian troops from the Schleswig-Holstein conflict, owing to a certain Danish victory, had not helped either as these troops, largely Landwehr, had been stood down.

Felix Schwartzenburg.

The armies did face each other and blows were struck causing the death of five Austrians and "one white horse" for the Prussians. Then, Nicholas I of Russia intervened and proposed an immediate conference, which was held on 19 November at Olmütz. The resulting resolution determined that the Prussians would demobilize and the Elector could return to Hesse-Cassel. It was also resolved that the new Union, such as it was, would be dissolved and the old Bund of 1815 would be resumed with Prussian delegates attending. Prussia, which, it could be argued, had been justified in its reaction to the Austrian action, collapsed in the face of reality. Schwartzenburg was triumphant and Frederick William IV, whose own weakness had led him to misjudge so many opportunities, had failed the cause he had wanted so much to support.

This "Humiliation of Olmütz" would resonate in Prussia for years to come and would be a rallying cry for reactionaries who wanted revenge. For one man, however, Olmütz was no shame – his devotion to his king, his staunch conservatism and his iron will would change the history of Germany and Europe forever – his name was Otto von Bismarck.

The rise of Bismarck

Otto von Bismarck was born on 1 April 1815, just as Napoleon was at the beginning of his final gamble. Prussia's considerable part in Napoleon's defeat at Waterloo less than three months later would help place it on the upper level of European nations and thus provide a milieu within which Bismarck could fulfil his destiny.

Born on the family's ancestral estate at Schönhausen, in Prussian Saxony, he was only a year old when the family moved to Kniephof in Eastern Pomerania. There he spent his childhood becoming an indifferent student at the local academy and at boarding school in Berlin. In 1832 he attended the very liberal University at Göttingen, returning to Berlin later to pass his exams by the skin of his teeth. His dislike of authority endangered his prospects everywhere, including service in the army (with the Guard Jäger) and the Prussian diplomatic service. At 24 years of age, on the death of his mother, he and his brother took over the farm and for ten years, he lived the life of the country squire – the Junker he so certainly was. He developed a local notoriety for drunken horse rides and wild partying, but did eventually marry, after a few unhappy relationships, in 1847.

That same year, he became a politician when he was apparently drafted to represent Magdeburg (in Prussian Saxony) in the Landtag in Berlin. His taste for politics was immediate and he took his responsibilities seriously although he returned to his estates regularly. He was there when the crisis of 1848 erupted and upon hearing of the riots, he hurried to Berlin to see what he could do. His feverish attempts to influence events at this time did not bring him much success,

Otto von Bismarck as a young man.

but he did come to the notice of the establishment. He was as appalled by Crown Prince William's decision to flee to England as he was by the vacillations of the king. His argumentative interview with William's wife, the future Queen Augusta, earned him her enmity for life. Later, however, Bismarck's brilliant speech in the Landtag, fully supporting William Frederick's conduct over the Olmütz affair, made him a favourite of the king from that moment on.

In 1852 he was sent to Frankfurt to temporarily replace the Prussian representative at the Federal Diet, a position that became permanent in 1854. Here, Bismarck would see the world beyond Prussia and it was here that he would develop his political genius for exploiting situations to his advantage before anyone else was aware that he was doing so. At the same time, his animosity towards, and mistrust of, Austria grew to the point where it became the centrepiece of his ambition to remove Austria from German affairs. The king's stroke in 1858 and his subsequent dementia brought about the regency of William, and the political manoeuvring in Berlin led to Bismarck's removal from Frankfurt. However, his new diplomatic posts as Prussian ambassador to St Petersburg in 1859 and to Paris in 1862 gave him the necessary international exposure and credentials for the next stage of his career.

William I, Bismarck, and Prussia 1858–64

The two principal objectives of Crown Prince William upon attaining the regency of Prussia were to uphold the constitution of 1848 and to maintain the integrity and efficiency of the army. The former presented no problem as he was a man for whom honour was almost a divine calling and he would do his duty come what may. The latter presented a problem as a certain General Albrecht von Roon had drawn up a memorandum in 1858 recommending a complete overhaul of the army, including the reduction of the Landwehr, which was not as committed to the crown as it was to the citizenry. This reorganization of the army required legislative support, which was not forthcoming from an assembly becoming more liberal as time went on. When Prussia reluctantly mobilized six army corps in 1859 to support Austria in its war with France, the exercise became a model of confusion and inefficiency.

In order to push through the reforms, which included almost doubling the regular army, William was forced to install Roon as war minister. When he came to the throne upon his brother's death in 1861, he faced an immediate crisis. The Landtag was refusing to authorize funds for his new army, which was already in being, and even Roon was about to concede to a two-year term of service in the ranks instead of three. William was prepared to abdicate rather than accept anything less than a three-year term. It was at this point that Roon urged him to recall Bismarck. Despite grave misgivings, not only his own but his wife's, William appointed Bismarck as minister-president.

William I of Prussia.

For ten years, Bismarck had forged his vision of the Germany to come. He was clear that some sort of federal entity was not in his imagination. He was a Prussian, first and foremost, and it was to Prussia and its monarchy that his loyalty lay. So his vision of a future Germany began with Prussia on equal terms with Austria and onward to a Germany headed by Prussia.

Now his hour had come, he used his unique combination of ruthlessness and persuasiveness to bring the political machinery into line. His speech of 30 September 1862 set the tone for the rest of his life. He reiterated that the money spent on the army was essential to Prussia's very existence; that the mistakes of 1848 and 1849 would not be remedied by speeches and "majority votes" but by "Iron and Blood".[1]

Bismarck's speech caused alarm, as it was expected to do and that, coupled with differences over length of service in the army, nearly brought him to a parting of the ways with his sovereign. However, in a first-class compartment on a dark train journey to Potsdam, the two men settled matters (or at least, Bismarck bemused the king into acceptance of his role). In October 1862, Bismarck furloughed the parliament and when it reconvened in January the following year, he laid down the law. From that moment on, he was a virtual dictator, answering only (and devotedly) to his king.

NOTES

1. "Eisen und blut" has always been translated by English-speaking historians as "Blood and Iron".

CHAPTER THREE

The Second Schleswig War and the Final Crisis

FROM JANUARY 1863 ONWARD, BISMARCK, not only as minister-president, but also as foreign minister, devoted himself to the removal of Austria from German affairs. On the issue of German unification, he was not alone: most Germans and their leaders in both north and south recognized that, as a people they were one. As usual, Austria was the complication. One of the most unifying systems in Germany at the time was the Zollverien (customs union), which excluded Austria, and Austria's control of the Bund precluded a political extension of the Union while Austria was not a member.

The year 1863 was a pivotal year for Bismarck as events within and beyond Prussia's frontiers challenged his grip on the reins. When the Poles rose against the Russians in the spring of 1863, he sent troops to patrol the border and overrode any sympathy for them that surfaced in the Landtag. He continued to be in conflict with the Landtag over everything from annual budgets to his limitations on the press, but he always prevailed through force of will and through the king. Bismarck was also able to prick Austria's balloon in September when Franz Joseph I of Austria called a Congress of Princes in Vienna. Bismarck persuaded William not to attend, even threatening resignation if he did so, an action which essentially invalidated the Congress despite its high-minded declarations. This was followed by an even more unlucky congress of European sovereigns in Paris, a suggestion of Napoleon III, which never took place. Finally, on 15 November 1863, there came an event for Bismarck to exploit. King Frederick VII of Denmark died suddenly.

The Second Schleswig War

No account of the "Schleswig-Holstein Question" is ever written without reference to the witty comments of Lord Palmerston, prime minister of Britain:

"Only three men have ever understood it. One was Prince Albert, who is dead. The other is a German professor who became mad. I am the third and I have forgotten all about it."

The basic essentials are these: The duchies of Schleswig and Holstein, at the bottom of the Jutland peninsula, often called the Elbe Duchies, did not belong to Denmark proper. They, along with the tiny Duchy of Lauenburg, were the personal property of the king of Denmark, awarded in 1815 by the Congress of Vienna. To complicate matters, Holstein (almost entirely German) was part of the German Bund and Schleswig (approximately half Danish, half German) was not. Their relationship to each other, and to their neighbours either side were further complicated by ancient proclamations that they be undivided. The revolutions of 1848 had encouraged Holstein to try and establish its independence by force, but this fell apart when Prussia's support wavered and led to the London Protocol whereby it was agreed that in the event of Frederick's death (he had no heirs), the duchies would become the property of Prince Christian of Glücksburg. A counter-claim by the supporters of the Duke of Augustenburg, although it was a strong one, was negated.

Denmark and the Duchies, 1864.

To further add fuel to this very complicated fire, there came the Danish Council of State (Rigsraad) which, in October 1863, had come up with a constitution which effectively annexed Schleswig to Denmark. Frederick died before he could sign it and Christian IX, when he came to the throne, was under enormous pressure to do so, which he did. Thus, with the London Treaty breached, the Federal Diet in Frankfurt announced support for the Augustenburg claim and enacted a "Federal Decree of Execution" upon Denmark. Hanoverian and Saxon troops marched into Holstein on 15 December to enforce the decree and the Danes wisely evacuated the Duchy and moved into Schleswig.

For Bismarck, the whole issue of the succession to the duchies was moot. Long before the death of Frederick VII, he had set his mind on Prussian annexation. This was partly to aggrandize Prussia but mainly to establish a naval

Field Marshal Ludwig von Gablenz (1814–74).

base at Kiel for a growing Prussian Navy. To enforce the Augustenburg claim was not an acceptable solution, so he engineered a necessity for both Prussian and Austrian troops to "support" the Hanoverians and Saxons. He knew this would lead to a war with Denmark, which would do two things; it would test the capabilities of Prussia's new army after Roon's reforms and it would also manoeuvre Austria into a situation that he could manipulate to Prussia's advantage.

On 16 January 1864, the Austrian and Prussian governments presented an ultimatum to Denmark, demanding withdrawal of the constitution within 48 hours. It was rejected. So on 1 February, while the Hanoverian and Saxon troops stood by as onlookers, the Austrian and Prussian armies crossed the River Eider into Schleswig.

Types of Prussian and Austrian Troops in Schleswig in January 1864, by Richard Knötel. (Voss)

The Austrian force consisted of four infantry brigades (five battalions each), one cavalry brigade, and 48 guns totalling about 25,000 men. The Prussians marched with six infantry brigades (six battalions each), including a combined Guards division and two cavalry brigades, along with 110 guns totalling about 45,000 men. The Austrians were under the command of Lieutenant-Field Marshal Ludwig von Gablenz and the Prussians were under Prince Frederick Charles. The unfortunate choice of overall commander was an 80-year-old Napoleonic veteran, Field Marshal Frederick von Wrangel. Bismarck had insisted on a Prussian commander, and the Austrian condition was that it had to be an officer who had seen active service. The ensuing war was to be longer than it needed to be partly due to this decision. Cuts since 1848 had left the Danish army with about half its normal strength of around 25,000. The current crisis had added 30,000 to 40,000 largely untrained reservists to the colours. On paper there were 23 infantry regiments, eight cavalry and approximately 150 guns, of which about 40 were fortress pieces of 36-, 84- and 168-pounders and some additional mortars.

The Danes had set up defensive positions on the River Schlei along a line roughly corresponding to fortifications known as the *Dannewerke*, built to repel a German invasion in the medieval period. Offensive action

Frederick von Wrangel (1784–1877).

began on 2 February with a Prussian assault on the Missunde redoubts which was repulsed with almost two hundred casualties. Prince Frederick Charles immediately ordered an artillery bombardment while his infantry lay low. The Austrians on the other hand, with considerable élan, launched their Brigade Gondrecourt against the Danes at the village of Ober-Selk the next day, ejecting the Danes and subsequently pushing them off the nearby heights of Königsberg.

Despite stopping the Prussians, the Danish commander, Christian de Meza, and the rest of the high command decided upon an immediate retirement to Flensburg and on 5 February, a general retreat of 40,000 men with guns begins. The Austrians, although surprised by this move, acted quickly and engaged the Danish rearguard near a village by a lake called Oerversee on 6 February. Despite serious hand-to-hand fighting, including the use of rifles as clubs, the Austrian Brigade Nostitz carried the position at the point of the bayonet. The Danes then split their forces, with 28,000

Prussian piquets in Denmark, February 1864. (Voss)

men going to more permanent and secure fortifications at the town of Düppel and the remainder, some 14,000 men, pushing into Jutland and making defences at Frederica.

The suddenness and speed of the Danish repositioning took both the Austrians and Prussians aback. The Prussians themselves had been somewhat stung by the success of the Austrian forces, especially when compared to their own fizzling efforts at Missunde. Their discomfiture was further compounded by the fact that the Guards Division had been mere spectators at Oerversee as the Austrian commander had not required their assistance.

Bismarck, aware of the political implications of this, and the fact that Wrangel had neither foreseen nor prepared for the Danish move, immediately sought to reassure the Powers (Britain and France). The stated intent of both Austria and Prussia had not included the invasion of Denmark proper and the Austrians in particular were unwilling to move into Jutland. The chief of staff of the Prussian Army himself, Field Marshal Helmuth von Moltke, had been dispatched to Schleswig to assess the situation and even Crown Prince Frederick joined the debate. Wrangel was reluctant to start a formal siege on the formidable defences of Düppel and had allowed the Austrians, along with the Guards Division, to pursue the Danes while Frederick Charles masked Düppel. Despite orders to the contrary, and mostly due to poor maps, advanced parties of the Prussian Guards actually moved into Jutland, occupying the village of Kolding on 18 February. At this point, both France and Britain were considering intervention,

Danish commander General Christian de Meza (1792–1865).

Prussian Battery No. 3 before Düppel. (Voss)

and explanations for the error were hastily dispatched. Bismarck struggled to keep control of the situation and dispatched the soldier/diplomat Lieutenant-General Edwin Freiherr von Manteuffel to Vienna to persuade Franz Joseph I that an assault on Düppel was the only course. This was the opinion of Moltke himself, and despite calls for a prior seaborne assault on the nearby island of Alsen, he insisted Düppel should be the first objective. Manteuffel succeeded in his mission and preparations were made for a Prussian attack on the Danish bastion.

The main line of defences rested on a line from the Alsen Sound to the sea and was strengthened by ten redoubts. There was a line of trenches behind this front with lunettes at intervals and, to cover the bridge between Alsen and the mainland, a small redoubt was placed opposite the Sonderburg.

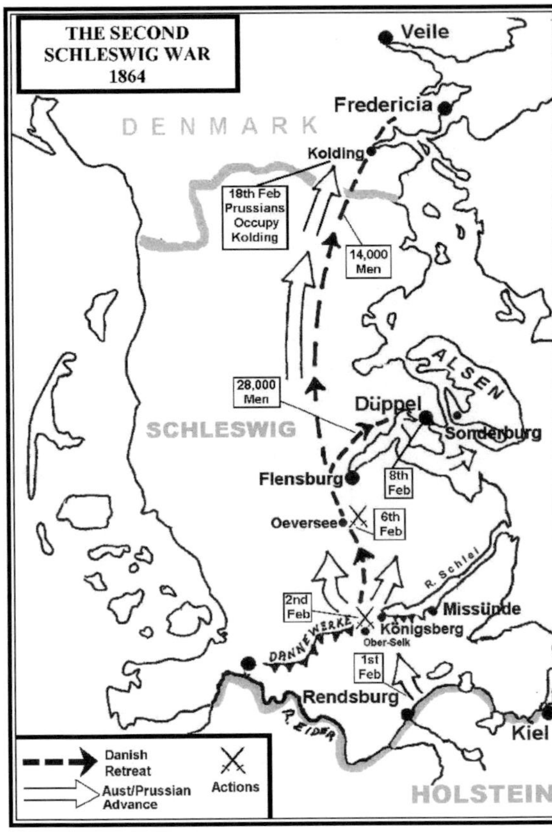

The Second Schleswig War 1864.

Sporadic raids, counter-attacks and artillery activity had been taking place since mid-February and battery fire started on 15 March. An additional Prussian division arrived at the same time, along with some heavy artillery. With the fresh troops dug in and the increased artillery, Frederick Charles tested the defences more intensely and among the pieces firing on the Düppel redoubts were the new rifled cannon built by a company known as Krupp. However the results were mixed as the impact of the shells merely threw dirt in the air without causing many casualties. The main bombardment began on 2 April, as one more Prussian brigade arrived. At dawn on 18 April, the infantry went in, attacking redoubts I to VII in separate columns. The fighting was intense and the Danes resisted valiantly but the redoubts fell one by one. Before 10:00 a.m., the VI redoubt was overrun by the Elizabeth and Queen's Guard Grenadier regiments and the others succumbed soon after; II and III redoubts fell to the 35th, 8th and 18th regiments and IV and V fell to the 24th and 64th regiments. At the same time the Prussians were bombarded from the sea as the Danish armoured monitor *Rolf Krake* used the guns from its two revolving turrets to good effect from the Sound. By 2:00 p.m., the Sonderburg redoubt had fallen and the siege was over. The Danish losses included 672 killed and 3,600 taken prisoner. The Prussians suffered over 1,000 casualties.

If the land operations had been a foregone conclusion for the Austro-Prussian forces, the naval side of affairs was quite different. Even before its operations against the Prussian storm troops at Düppel, the *Rolf Krake* had been in action as early as 18 February against a pontoon bridge the Prussians had built at Egernsund at the mouth of Nüpel River.

Prince Frederick Charles (1828–85).

Prussian Infantry Regiment No. 53 storming Redoubt No. IV at Düppel. (Voss)

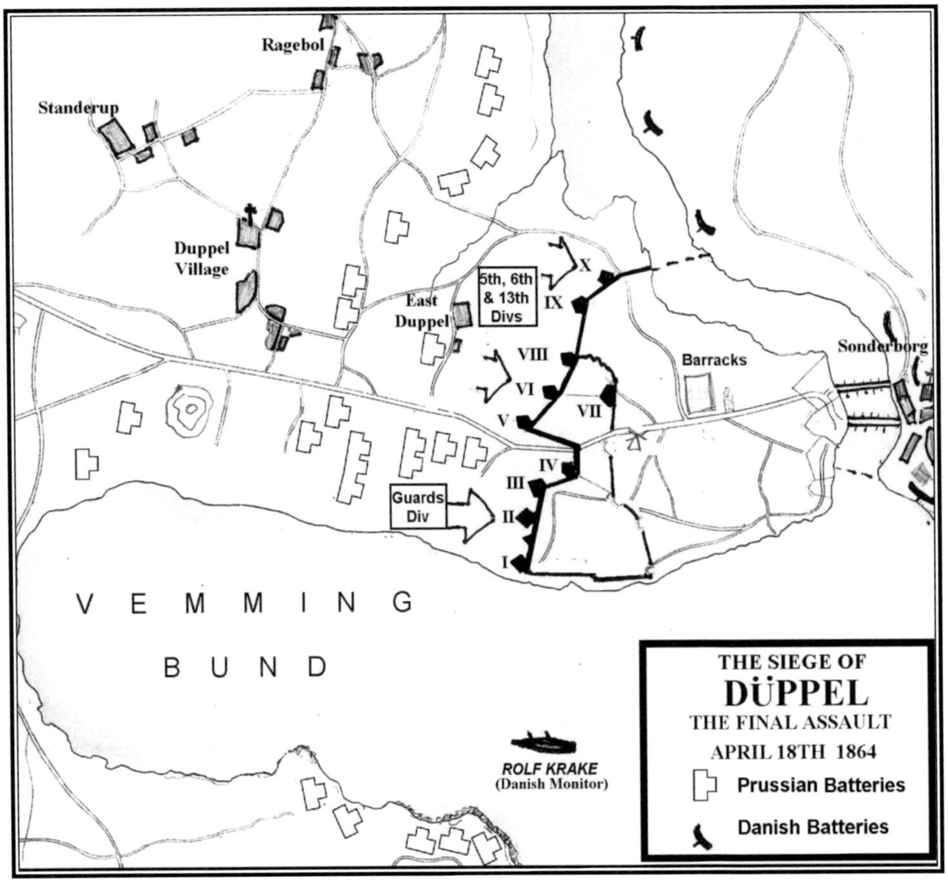

The siege of Düppel, the final assault 18 April 1864.

Shallow water and enemy artillery fire prevented destruction of the bridge but the Prussian artillery had failed to do serious damage to the *Rolf Krake.*

In March a Danish squadron prevented a Prussian naval force from breaking the blockade set up from the start of the war. In a fierce exchange of fire on 17 March off Jasmund, the ship of the line *Skjold* with the steam frigates *Sjælland* and *Tordenskjold* forced the Prussian corvettes *Arcona* and *Nymphe*, with six other vessels, to withdraw to Swinemünde. After the collapse of Düppel, a Danish squadron, including the frigate *Niels Jue* and the corvettes *Dagmar* and *Hejmdal*, was sent to counter an Austrian squadron threatening them from the North Sea. On 9 May, while negotiations were ongoing in London to end the war, this squadron made contact with the Austrians under command of Rear-Admiral Wilhelm von Tegetthoff in the flagship *Radetzky* off Cuxhaven in the Heligoland Bight. In the short but fierce battle that followed, the Austrian *Schwarzenberg* caught fire after a shell exploded in a magazine, and with the three Prussian gunboats that had joined the squadron, Tegetthoff broke off the engagement. An attempt by the Danes to cut off the retreat was partly hindered by the presence of the British frigate HMS *Aurora*.

As the Prussians prepared to follow up their victory at Düppel, the now-usual debate began as to how best to achieve success. It seemed unlikely the Danes would continue to resist much further but Moltke insisted that since they hadn't sued for peace, the allies should occupy Jutland. Finally, after a visit to the front by a delighted King William, it was decided that Moltke should be appointed chief of staff to a disgruntled Wrangel. On 20 April, a London conference was called and a cease-fire was agreed. After weeks of Danish intransigence and Austro-Prussian pressure, the war resumed on 26 June. Moltke's long-planned invasion of the island of Alsen took place on 29 June and the resistance of the Danes, who had only six regiments of infantry, was insignificant. The action was over before lunch with 300 Danes dead and wounded with 2,800 captured or missing. The total Prussian losses were fewer than 400.

While the allies continued the occupation of Jutland and began landing on the North Frisian Islands, King Christian decided that further resistance was

The amphibious landing at Alsen by Prussian troops on 29 June 1864. (Voss)

futile and a new Danish government sued for peace on 8 July. However, the Danes held no cards as their British and French support had evaporated and the Germans were in no mood to compromise. In Vienna on 1 August 1864, the king of Denmark ceded all rights to the duchies to the emperor of Austria and the king of Prussia. The peace was ratified by treaty on 30 October.

Militarily speaking, the war was judged by foreign observers as a better showcase for Austrian arms than Prussia. The efficiency and élan of the Hapsburg troops had outshone their allies especially at Oerversee, whereas the siege of Düppel, with its inevitable outcome, had been seen as rather indecisive and lengthy. This was a misperception that, two years later, would see the Austrians falsely endowed with qualities they didn't have. Prussian leadership under Wrangel was indeed sorely lacking and contributed to this erroneous assessment. However, lost in the analysis was the performance of the Prussian individual weapon, the Dreyse needle gun (*Zündnadelgewehr*), of which much more will be written later. If observers had sought statistics they would have concluded that this rifle, in the hands of a trained soldier, would dominate the battlefield of the future.

The Gastein Convention

On 2 August, the day after the king of Denmark ceded his rights to the duchies, William I of Prussia and Franz Joseph I of Austria met for breakfast at the Palace of Schönbrunn outside Vienna. Also present were Bismarck and his opposite number in the Hapsburg government, Rechburg. Franz Joseph wondered aloud what was to become of the duchies and asked whether they were to become Prussian provinces. Bismarck, with typical shrewdness, declared that he would be delighted to know his sovereign's thoughts on the matter. William, with great hesitance, announced he had no rights to the duchies. Thus playing into Bismarck's hands was a situation that precluded an Austro-Prussian "deal". He was now free to manipulate Austria as he saw fit and acquire the duchies for Prussia outright.

Christian, Duke of Augustenburg (1798–1869).

The only agreement settled initially was the removal of the Hanoverian and Saxon troops from the duchies, which was accomplished by December 1864. With three Prussian brigades and one Austrian, the allies had about 12,000 men in the duchies, which were being controlled by a joint military government

All parties now moved to support the Augustenburg claim to the duchies; all that is except for Bismarck. By manipulation, negotiation, and a host of other unprincipled acts, he was able to sideline the issue by introducing possible counter-claims from Oldenburg, Hanover, and even Russia. When pushed by the king to address the Duke of Augustenburg's claim, he proposed a set of conditions which basically made the duchies a vassal entity to Prussia including Prussian control of the duchies' foreign and military affairs plus the permanent annexation of Kiel as a naval base. The Duke, naturally refused. By this time, frustrated and outmanoeuvred, Austria found itself forced to enter into a compromise that, whilst not satisfying the original intentions of the Danish war, would leave her with some dignity and avert a war, which many considered, inevitable.

In early August 1865, the king of Prussia and the emperor of Austria met yet again; this time at the small village of Gastein, south of Salzburg in Austria, accompanied by their respective senior ministers. The so-called Convention of Gastein was meant to lay the fractious issue of the duchies to rest. The document signed on 14 August essentially turned Schleswig-Holstein into an Austro-Prussian condominium. Austria was to administrate Holstein, while Prussia administrated Schleswig. Other provisions of the agreement established a federal fleet to be based in Kiel with the Prussians in control of the harbour and the building of a canal to link the Baltic and the North Sea. Rendsburg became a federal fortress, and the duchies were admitted into the Zollverein with the usual minor paragraphs concerning financial reparations and administrative issues. Finally, the tiny Duchy of Lauenburg was sold to the king of Prussia, who paid for it out of his own pocket.

Thus was the Schleswig-Holstein question resolved. At least for the time being. At least for Austria. Perhaps. In fact, nothing was settled except that another part of Bismarck's complicated jigsaw puzzle had been slotted into place. Bismarck described it best himself as an agreement that "merely papered over the cracks".

Preparations for war

If Bismarck had wanted to win a popularity contest, he had gravely miscalculated. By the end of 1865, he had not only exasperated the Austrians, the Frankfurt Diet and most of the informed population of Prussia (no less than in the rest of Germany) but he had incurred the displeasure of his own sovereign. The prospect of an open break with his brother monarch was not a thought that King William relished. Any policy, even with the potential reward of a dominant Prussia in all of Germany, was fraught with risk.

Bismarck certainly had allies, especially in the army, and he was able to rely on Moltke and Roon to support him when it came to the king. They had been crafting one of the world's most efficient military machines and Moltke assured the minister-president that he could field 200,000 men in a Bohemian theatre and crush the Austrians, provided Italy could be neutralized.

Italy, whose independence had been largely won for her at Solferino in 1859, still needed to incorporate the province of Venetia to complete the Risorgimento[1] as well as the city of Rome, which was still under Papal control (underwritten by a French garrison). Prussian overtures to King Victor Emmanuel's government in early 1865 were rebuffed. A Prussian guarantee of Venetia in return for Italian support in a conflict with Austria, was felt to be too risky, not only because it would leave the Italians beholden to Prussia, but also because they wanted to approach the matter peacefully. However, later that year, an Italian offer of one billion lire made directly to Franz Joseph was predictably rejected. An interesting interchange considering both nations were near bankruptcy.

King Victor Emmanuel II of Italy (1820–78).

In October 1865, Bismarck decided he needed a rest and went to Biarritz.[2] By somewhat less than a coincidence, he met up with Louis Napoleon. The French emperor was probably the man Bismarck needed the most in his pocket. France, with the largest and most experienced army in Europe, could trump any move that Prussia made at this time if it wished and so French neutrality was essential. As no-one else was present, it is not known exactly what was discussed, but it seems that by his usual combination of flattery, veiled threats, and implied promises, Bismarck managed to convince Napoleon to sit and watch events, while urging the Italians to ally themselves to Prussia's cause. Bismarck had placed another piece in the jigsaw puzzle.

The end game was now in sight but the hurdles facing Bismarck still remained high and, for lesser men, practically insurmountable. Although he strongly felt that Prussia had the military assets to win a war over Austria, he still had to convince his king and the crown prince (who would be commanding an army in the event of a war) to see things his way. Only Bismarck had the arsenal of political skills, innate cunning and raw nerves to accomplish such a feat.

Within Prussia itself, he converted the royal circle and the political establishment one by one to his view. Eventually the king himself was brought around to the opinion that war under the circumstances would be just, as well as winnable. Only the crown prince remained unconvinced, describing such a conflict as "a crime".

By contrast, Austria was easier to deal with. The Prussian minister-president moved quickly to place the Hapsburg government in the most uncomfortable position he could contrive. In Holstein, the Austrians, led by Gablenz, were trying hard to govern their portion of the condominium fairly. This was not to Bismarck's liking and he continuously protested that their methods of administration ran counter to the agreement at Gastein. The differences between Austria and Prussia in the duchies was to remain a catalyst for harsh exchanges between the two countries for the early part of 1866.

In March the king finally consented to an alliance between Italy and Prussia, secretly concluded later that month and signed on 8 April. It would take effect only if Prussia went to war, and then only for a period of three months. In another provocative (and for Bismarck, astounding) move he proposed to the Frankfurt Diet that a parliament should be elected by universal suffrage throughout Germany. This was meant to assuage liberal fears of Prussian autocracy spreading throughout Bund. However it did the opposite, especially in Austria, where it was seen as another move to isolate the Austrians. When Franz Joseph got wind of the Italo-Prussian treaty it was almost the last straw. Feeling threatened from all sides, he called a military council. The realization that Prussia could mobilize in just over three weeks, compared to the seven weeks that Austria required, prompted the military council to suggest a discreet troop movement toward the border.

All along, Bismarck had needed the Austrians to make the first move. The "discreet" troop movements were denounced as an aggressive act, and diplomatic notes flashed between Vienna and Berlin. Despite Prussian outrage, the feeling against Prussia in all of Germany was high and demands came from Munich and elsewhere for Berlin to lower the temperature. On 7 May, an attempt was even made on Bismarck's life in the Unter Den Linden, with the failed assassin later taking his own life. But Bismarck kept his nerve. With complete confidence in the Prussian Army and the General Staff, Bismarck decided to force the issue.

A last-ditch attempt by the three neutral powers of Britain, France, and Russia ran aground. Their proposal of an international conference to settle the Schleswig-Holstein question was shrewdly accepted by Bismarck, although he did not welcome the prospect. It was a non-starter however, as the Austrians again blundered, and instead of accepting this face-saving initiative, they imposed a set of conditions on the proposal that were unacceptable to all parties.

On 8 June, Prussian forces crossed the Eider from Schleswig into Holstein. Gablenz ordered an immediate Austrian withdrawal; a move intended as a forlorn hope to keep the peace. It was not to be. The following Monday, 11 June, Austria called upon the Diet to vote against Prussia. With the full knowledge that a vote on behalf of Austria meant war, a narrow majority of mostly south German states did so. Bismarck immediately announced that "the Federal Compact is broken". His hour had come. The die was cast and the fate of Germany would now rest on the outcome of a battle near a remote village in Bohemia.

NOTES

1. The Risorgimento, or Wars of Italian Unification, are generally considered to have begun around 1803 and continued through the 1848 revolutions and the 1859 war, and were not actually considered completed until the taking of Rome in 1870.
2. He had planned to meet up with his beloved Kathy Orlov, with whom he had been infatuated since 1862, but she had cancelled, probably because he had brought Johanna and the family. He would never see her again.

Part Two

The Seven Weeks War

CHAPTER FOUR

The Advance to the Elbe

THE VOTE IN THE FEDERAL Diet on 11 June 1866 was initially a procedural motion, proposed by Bavaria to halt warlike preparations, including the demand that both the Austrian and Prussian armies demobilize. It was also intended to reverse the Prussian eruption into Holstein and prevent a war. As Prussia had already declared that a vote for the motion would break up the confederation, no one really had any illusions that a war could be averted. After some early confusion, including an accidentally cast vote, the states lined up on the side of the party they would support in case of hostilities. Voting for the Austrians were the kingdoms of Saxony, Bavaria, Hanover, and Württemburg; the Electorate of Hesse-Cassel; the grand duchies of Baden and Hesse-Darmstadt; the duchies of Nassau and Saxe-Meiningen; the Principality of Reuss-Grez (of the elder line); the Landgraviate of Hessen-Homburg; and the Free City of Frankfurt. Voting against the Austrians were the grand duchies of Mecklenburg-Schwerin, Mecklenburg-Strelitz, Oldenburg, Luxemburg, and Saxe-Weimar; the duchies of Anhalt, Saxe-Altenburg, Saxe-Coburg-Gotha, Brunswick, and Lemburg; the principalities of Waldeck, Lippe-Detmold, Schaumburg-Lippe, Schwartzburg-Rudolstadt, Schwartzburg-Sonderhausen, and Reuss-Schleitz (of the younger line); and the free cities of Bremen, Lübeck, and Hamburg.

Prussia's representative at Frankfurt had left the assembly in an uproar after delivering Bismarck's plan to reform Germany based on the 1849 proposal. It was universally ignored. On 15 June, the Prussian ambassadors to the kingdoms of Hanover and Saxony, and Electoral Hesse (Cassel) presented ultimatums requiring that they demobilize immediately and accept the Prussian reforms unconditionally. All three refused, and the following day, Prussian armies crossed their borders. All three armies withdrew rapidly before them. The Hanoverians, who had just completed annual manoeuvres, moved southwards to Göttingen, hoping to link up

Helmuth von Moltke (1800–91).

with VII Federal Corps and the Bavarian Army, while the Hessians, completely unprepared, retired on Frankfurt. The Saxon army, fully mobilized and ably led by their own Prince Albert, marched into Bohemia to join their Austrian comrades.

As the Prussian armies moved toward the borders of Bohemia, the last preparations for war were being made. It is remarkable to note that it had been only two weeks since King William had finally been convinced that a war was not only inevitable, but necessary. On 20 June, Italy, which had been mobilizing since late April, declared war on Austria. Four days later, they were defeated at the Battle of Custozza. Meanwhile, Prussian troops had occupied Hanover by 19 June and overrun Hesse-Cassel on 22 June. They were now poised for an imminent clash with the Hanoverian army between Eisenach and Erfurt.

The Prussian armies of Prince Frederick Charles and Lieutenant-General Karl Herwarth von Bittenfeld had now reached the Saxon–Bohemian border, and on the night of 22 June Frederick Charles issued an order of the day to his troops which began "Soldiers! Austria, faithless and regardless of treaties . . .", going on to accuse the Hapsburg government of numerous violations of borders and calling upon his men to rely on God for victory. In the last sentence, he included the legend that appeared on all soldiers' helmet plates ". . . With God for king and Fatherland . . ." It was, he said, a declaration of war. Early on the morning of 23 June, the Prussian armies crossed the frontier into Austria.

The Prussian war plan

Ever since he had collaborated with Roon on the reformation of the Prussian Army, the chief of the General Staff, Helmuth von Moltke, had defined the imperatives of Prussia's war philosophy. With Russia to the east, France to the west and Austria to the south, Prussia could not adopt a passive stance but must be prepared for an aggressive posture to counter any threat and have the military assets to support it. Moltke's view, shared by Bismarck, was that in order to survive, Prussia would inevitably have to face a war that must not only be anticipated, but provoked – on Prussia's terms – before a potential enemy could organize. Above all, the seat of such a war must be as far from Prussia's borders as possible, as a conflict on Prussian soil would already presume failure and be impossible to manage. Bismarck left no doubt about this philosophy in his "Iron and Blood" speech.

Moltke employed all the resources available to him, both material and intellectual. The emerging strategic importance of railways and the telegraph were uppermost in his mind; he well understood their use during the American Civil War, having received many accounts from attached military observers. He factored in tactical changes required of the infantry using a repeating rifle capable of firing six shots compared to one for a musket, and its ability to be fired while a soldier was lying down. However, many of these innovations would prove too radical for many in the army to have been effectively implemented, and traditional tactics had to be melded with new ones in order to be accepted. The Danish war had been somewhat of a dress rehearsal, and many deficiencies found then needed to be addressed. Finally, as with any military plan, the political imperatives were to prove more arduous to navigate than the military ones, and Moltke had to revise his scheme constantly to accommodate them.

At the core of Moltke's plan was the philosophy of annihilation. He envisioned his own "Cannae" in which his armies enveloped the enemy and destroyed them. He expected the Austrian commander, Benedek, whom he respected, to move aggressively to link up with his allies (particularly the Saxons and Bavarians) in Bohemia and make a thrust through Lusatia. In line with Moltke's thinking, it would be necessary to move first, initially overrunning Saxony. He knew this would be possible as Prussia could mobilize far faster than Austria. Having either neutralized the Saxons or forced them to withdraw, he would meet the Austrians north of Prague and defeat them. In order to concentrate his forces for such a blow, he also knew that he would have to arrange his armies to bring the main thrust in the centre, and the envelopment from the east, in Silesia. He would therefore place the larger component in Lusatia with a second army in Silesia.

Although the Austrians began their mobilization on 21 April, Moltke was restrained from following suit by his reluctant king until 12 May, when initial orders to secure mounts and equipment were sent out. The formation and command appointments were made for the two main armies: The First Army, based in Lusatia, consisted of III and IV Army Corps, under the command of Prince Frederick Charles, nephew of King William; while the Second Army of V and VI Corps was headquartered in Silesia, and led by the king's son, Crown Prince Frederick William. Satisfied with this structure, Moltke moved to the next phase of his plan.

There were still frustrations for him however. King William would have preferred to mobilize in increments so as not to provoke a complete rupture while a peaceful solution was still possible. He flatly rejected Roon and Moltke's plea for a general advance to Dresden on 5 June. It proved difficult for Roon and Moltke to impress upon William the complicated logistical problems associated with the movement of large numbers of troops by train. Moltke was now forced to adjust his plan, not only because of the king, but also due to surprising news from Bohemia. It seemed the Austrians were concentrating near their fortress of Olmütz for a possible drive on the capital of Silesia, Breslau. He decided to move the Second Army east to Neisse and dispatched I Corps and the Guard Corps to Silesia. A third army, designated the Army of the Elbe, was formed from VII and VIII Corps and deployed along the Saxon border, subordinate to, and in support of, First Army. The Army of the Elbe was placed under the command of General Herwarth von Bittenfeld.

By 14 June, it appeared that Moltke's envelopment plan was at serious risk, with his armies stretched in a wide arc and separated at some distance from each other. Criticism was inevitable and one comment suggested that the armies

The army commanders. From left, Prince Frederick Charles, First Army; Crown Prince Frederick William, Second Army; Herwarth von Bittenfeld (1796–1884), Army of the Elbe.

were strung out, "like beads on a string".[1] Moltke, however, understood the risk and considered it mitigated by the fact that the Austrians had not done as he expected and joined their allies near Prague. He now predicted their convergence near the town of Gitschin on the Cidlina River and was confident that the enemy, concentrating as it should to meet the advancing armies, would not have the advantage many assumed. Moving to defeat one Prussian army, the Austrians would always have the fear of a flank attack should the other advancing Prussian force remained less than a day's march away.

Moltke also seemed so sure of his adversaries among Austria's south German allies that he only designated a single corps, along with some Landwehr units, to deal with them. This force was commanded by General Vogel von Falckenstein. Moltke hoped that Falckenstein would act with speed to roll up the Hanoverians and Hessians north of the Main, leaving the Bavarians and the rest of the south Germans too disorganized to do much more than give up the fight. Whatever the implications, the hour was at hand and the Prussians ready to move. At noon on 22 June, Moltke telegraphed Prince Frederick Charles and the crown prince to inform them that the king had commanded that both armies march into Bohemia the following day and, "seek a junction in the direction of Gitschin". He also ordered VI Corps to remain on the Neisse.

Austrian preliminaries

Had the Prussians had been aware of the true state of Austrian readiness, they would have slept much easier in their beds. Emperor Franz Joseph had entrusted the defence of his nation to Feldzeugmeister Ludwig von

Benedek, the world-famous "Hero of San Martino", and other campaigns, mostly in Italy. Benedek's appointment to command the armies in Bohemia was made before the Italian declaration of war, so the emperor had dispatched Archduke Albrecht, a member of the Imperial family, who was unfamiliar with the plains of Lombardy, to deal with that threat. Whatever the mismatch in milieu, both men were able commanders.

By the end of May, Benedek had disposed the seven corps of his North Army in a defensive funnel spreading from Vienna north to the Silesian border in the east, and to the Saxon Lusatian border in the west. The III and VIII Corps were around Brünn, II, IV, VI and X Corps in a screen around the fortress city of Olmütz, in Moravia, and I Corps north of Prague in Bohemia. These dispositions were the work of his chief of staff, Major-General Gideon Krismanic, who despite all sorts of pressure from Vienna had refused to move them further into Bohemia until all the reserves and other mobilized troops had arrived.

Major-General Gideon Krismanic (1817–76).

This revealed the bankruptcy of the Austrian mobilization system. Even having begun mobilization weeks before Prussia, it was now lagging far behind. It was true that the Austrian rail system was not nearly as advanced as that of Prussia, but no contingencies had been included in the plan to accommodate this. The swift concentrations of the Prussians on the borders of Saxony and Bohemia surprised the Austrian staff. Franz Joseph, concerned that the North Army was not moving fast enough into Bohemia, sent an adjutant from his Imperial Staff, Lieutnant-Colonel Beck. This unusually far-sighted and gifted officer urged Benedek and Krismanic to swiftly move into Bohemia to counter the developing threat. Krismanic's jealousy and Benedek's indecision nearly brought Beck's mission to naught but he was able to persuade Benedek to move I Corps north toward the Saxon border. Beck, who had mentally prepared for this war, personally strongly favoured a concentration in western Bohemia, linking with the armies of the south Germans and Saxony and a march directly on to Berlin. His trip to Dresden on 10 June dismayed him even further, as no decision had yet been made for Saxon support in case of war.

It is now evident that Benedek's decision-making apparatus, both personal and within his staff, was deeply flawed. Competent as he may have seemed, there appears to be no doubt that Benedek was a reluctant commander, out of his depth.

General Ludwig von Benedek (1804–81).

He seemed paralyzed to act in the face of Prussian moves clearly designed to outflank him. As he and his staff learned more about the Prussian positions, instead of exploiting them, they reacted to them. The next few days, before hostilities began, the Austrian troops were subjected to a series of marches and counter-marches that had exhausted them. By the time the Prussians were ready to move across the border, Benedek had been bluntly ordered by Franz Joseph to move his headquarters to the fortress of Josephstadt on the Elbe, and his armies into Bohemia. Moltke's move of the Guard to Neisse, however, concerned him enough to retain a corps near Olmütz.

If Benedek thought that his allies were mobilizing rapidly, or even at the leisurely pace of his own armies, he was to be sorely disappointed. None of the south German states had even started mobilization, except for Saxony which had, as mentioned, mobilized fast enough to be ready to extricate itself from the Prussian advance. The Bavarian army was concentrated near Würzberg but in no condition to meet any aggressive action. The Hessen-Cassel forces arrived in Frankfurt without ammunition for their Prussian-supplied needle guns and few even wore uniforms. Only two Hessian cavalry units were able to join VIII Federal Corps, which comprised the remaining south German forces. This formation was proving difficult to assemble. The Baden government was very pro-Prussian but didn't want to upset its neighbours, so its forces were reluctantly dispatched. The remaining units were all in various states of unpreparedness. The Hanoverian army, having retired from Göttingen, was now taking up defensive positions around the town of Langensalza, north of Thuringia, hoping to link up with the Bavarians to the south.

The road to Königgrätz

Early on the morning of Saturday 23 June, Prince Frederick Charles, astride his horse, positioned himself near the raised yellow and black gate-pole that marked the frontier between Saxony and Austria. The temperature was already beginning to rise, promising a suffocatingly hot day. Frederick Charles watched as the first column of his army marched past, seeing the dust clouds of the other four columns filling the air to the east. His first major objective was a crossing of the Iser River, near Podol, which he expected to be strongly defended. He then planned for a junction near Münchengräz with Herwarth von Bittenfeld and the two columns of his Army of the Elbe, which had crossed into Bohemia the day before, for the final push to Gitschin. In order to understand better the sequence of events as they occurred on all fronts, the narrative will now take the form of a chronology.

Sunday 24 June

The question of supply and provisioning affected both First and Elbe armies from the start. For the Army of the Elbe, the assumption was that the countryside through which they marched was a poor one, providing few supplies. Much of the population melted away and the conscripts, in this case from the Rhenish provinces, were unskilled in living off the land. For the First Army, supply problems slowed down the advance considerably. Problems with hastily employed civilian wagon-drivers, timid at the prospect of warfare, were among many of the issues to be dealt with. In the driving rain that had replaced the dusty heat of the previous day, the army of Prince Frederick Charles marched on Reichenburg, reaching it in the evening. Here he decided to stop and make headquarters in the local Schloß.[2] A brief skirmish took place between the Thüringian Uhlans of the advance guard and a body of Austrian Hussars, in which some horses were killed.

To the east, in Silesia, the corps comprising the crown prince's Second Army assembled at their start positions – I Corps at Landshut and Libau, V Corps at Lewin, VI Corps at Neisse, and the Guard Corps at Frankenstein and Silberburg.

Near the Thüringian forests in the western theatre, the Hanoverians, having reached Langensalza, may have been surprised that the Prussians were not on their heels. In fact, by dawdling in Minden and Hanover City, Falckenstein had almost let King George and his army escape to join the Bavarians. However, urgent messages from Moltke in Berlin and a final order from King William himself finally propelled him to rush a scratch force of Landwehr and some regular troops to intercept them.

Neither the Great Headquarters in Berlin or the army commanders in Bohemia would know of the greatest catastrophe of this day for nearly 48 hours. Far to the south, by the small Italian village of Custozza on the River Mincio, the Austrian Army of the South had crushed an Italian army. The defeat was a combination of good generalship by Archduke Albrecht and abominable leadership on the part of the Italian General, La Marmora.[3] This event had the potential to knock Prussia's Italian ally out of the war at an early stage, and allow a victorious Austrian army to march north to Bohemia to support Benedek's North Army.

Monday 25 June

Moltke's entire plan, like all good plans, relied on speed and he was constantly anxious about the progress of the armies. Frederick Charles, although a solid and dependable commander, was cautious and despite being a cavalry officer, his tactical use of this arm during the war would jeopardize the course of events several times. In the current situation, instead of using his cavalry in force for reconnaissance and to probe at the enemy, keeping them off guard, he placed his mounted troops at the rear of his columns. He therefore decided to remain at Reichenburg on 25 June to rest the infantry and allow the cavalry to catch up. He also wanted to be sure that the Army of the Elbe would be in place for the planned link-up at Münchengräz.

The Saxon army, having reorganized itself after the retreat from Dresden, was at Jung-Buntzlau, ready to defend the line of the River Iser with the Austrian I Corps, commanded by General der Kavallerie Eduard Count von Clam-Gallas. Overall command for this operation was given to the Saxon Crown Prince Albert who ordered Clam-Gallas to take up positions between Münchengräz and Turnau to the east, with the Saxons to the west.

Because Frederick Charles had no proper cavalry screen he was unaware of the Austro-Saxon positions. He had expected to meet them in force at Reichenburg, but was now not sure in what strength they would be along the Iser.

The Second Army, in Silesia, was now ready for its passage through the mountains into Northern Bohemia. Moltke's plan called for it to move only when Benedek's forces were heavily engaged, trying to repulse the invasion of the Army of the Elbe and the First Army from Saxony.

Prince John of Saxony (1801–1873).

For the Hanoverian army at Langensalza, it was the beginning of the end. Although the faltering pursuit by the Prussians had allowed them to get this far, they were tired, hungry and poorly equipped for battle. Their Bavarian allies to the south, who could have been in a position to reach them, failed to muster the will to do so. On 25 June, Prussian General Friedrich Gustav von Beyer's combined division arrived at Eisenach, cutting off any retreat to the west. That evening, General Eduard von Flies arrived with his division at Gotha and Falckenstein, and with Lieutenant-General August von Goeben's troops moving down from Göttingen, the Hanoverians were essentially surrounded on three sides, their only exit to the east and Prussia itself. The King of Prussia had dispatched Lieutenant-General Gustav von Alvensleben to negotiate an armistice with the Hanoverian king, and Prussian troops were instructed to hold their positions until 26 June.

Action between Prussian Jägers and Austrian Hussars, Podol 26 June 1866. (Voss)

Tuesday 26 June

The Prussian First Army's rest day on 25 June would likely have turned into another on the following day had not an urgent telegram, sent three days earlier, arrived from Moltke, reading: "Only a vigorous advance by the First Army will disengage the Second". This spurred Prince Frederick Charles to send Lieutenant-General Heinrich Friedrich von Horn with his 8th Division to secure the Iser crossings at Turnau and Podol. Early on the morning of 26 June, as Horn's advance guard moved toward Liebenau, they met the first outposts of Clam-Gallas' I Corps, and a sharp artillery duel ensued. As the Prussian cavalry pursued the infantry retreating to the hills, largely without result, Horn's infantry moved on

toward Turnau. By about 4:30 p.m., a force of Austrian cavalry at Sichrow, led by Baron Leopold von Edelsheim of Solferino fame, offered more obstruction with their mounted batteries. This caused Frederick Charles to dispatch General Eduard von Fransecky with his 7th Division to support Horn. As the 8th Division dealt with Edelsheim's effective resistance, Fransecky's division rushed down to Turnau to find the village empty and the two bridges burned, with the Austrians on the other bank disappearing into the dusk.

Further west, at about 6:00 p.m., two battalions of Austrian infantry commanded by Major-General Leopold Gondrecourt had crossed the Iser at Münchengräz and shortly afterwards bumped head on into the Army of the Elbe's advance guard of the 14th Division at Hühnerwasser. The ensuing battle, short as it was, would become a harbinger of the terrible harvest that would later be reaped by the Prussian needle gun. As Austrian jägers and infantry advanced with the bayonet after a volley, the aimed, continuous fire from a few companies of Prussian infantry decimated them and put the survivors to flight. Gondrecourt had no choice but to retreat the way he had come.

The Saxon crown prince, now in Münchengräz, received orders from Benedek to "Hold the Iser at all costs", which surprised him. He had understood his instructions were to only slow the passage of the First Army as best he could, so that the main weight of North Army could be deployed near Gitschin.

At 8:30 p.m., the Austrian Brigade Poschacher, led by Colonel Franz von Bergou, advanced to Podol accompanied by the brigade artillery. The fight that took place among the small houses on the winding street that ran from the stone bridge across the Iser was a bloody one. Again the needle gun took its toll and, despite a desperate resistance, the Austrian battalions were broken apart by the murderously accurate rifle fire. The full moon, occasionally obscured by the smoke and flames, shone upon the fierce hand-to-hand fighting which failed to stop the Prussians pushing the Austrians out before midnight. Prussian losses were about 130 officers and men while the Austrian casualties exceeded 1,000. It was now impossible for Prince Albert and Clam-Gallas to regain the Iser crossings, and it was decided that their combined forces would retire toward Gitschin the following day.

At Langensalza, the negotiations between Alvensleben and blind King George had collapsed, and the cease-fire expired at about 10:00 a.m. The rest of the day, as the Prussians prepared their assault, the faithful Hanoverian soldiers could do little more than await their fate.

Late in the evening to the east, the armies in Silesia were stirring for their march through the mountains. Next day, the thunder of battle would erupt from Thuringia in the west to the River Aupa, far away in eastern Bohemia.

Wednesday 27 June

Prince Frederick Charles, having driven the Austro-Saxon forces from Turnau and Podol, decided that instead of pushing with his available forces to secure Münchengräz immediately, he would consolidate and wait for the Army of the Elbe to join him. Again, his lack of urgency infuriated Moltke, whose whole objective was to keep the enemy off balance by continuous pressure. As it was, Prince Albert and Clam-Gallas had already decided not to make a do or die defence at Münchengräz but instead to fall back on Gitschin.

Before dawn, in the Silesian mountains, the forces of the crown prince began their marches down into Bohemia. In the east, V Corps, led by Prussian General Karl Friedrich von Steinmetz, a grizzled old veteran of the Wars of Liberation, entered the border town of Nachod. In the pre-dawn darkness, Steinmetz and his staff were stuck in a traffic jam of wagons and artillery caissons in the narrow gorge leading down into the town, listening to the early skirmishes without being able to make decisions. As he emerged from the throng, he directed his advance guard to make for the plateau of Wysokow where the first troops of the Austrian VI Corps, led by Lieutenant Field Marshal Wilhelm Freiherr von Ramming, had reached the field after a forced march from Opocno.

By 9:00 a.m. a full battle was developing on the plateau, as Ramming's 1st Brigade advanced up the heights. Despite energetic and courageous attempts, especially by Ramming's jägers, to push them back, the rapid fire of the Prussians told quickly and by 10:00 a.m. the brigade was in tatters. Before the Prussians could advance, another Austrian brigade was thrown into the fight but sadly, their fate was similar. They were mown down in ranks and many simply sank into the tall grass and brambles as the needle-gun bullets and shrapnel ripped above them. Ramming misjudging the result and thinking the Prussians were on the run, sent in his cuirassiers. They were met by Steinmetz's dragoons and uhlans who held them while more Prussian infantry and artillery poured into the fight. Between 1:00 p.m. and 2:00 p.m., despite almost suicidal charges led by gallant, but often insubordinate officers, Ramming ordered a retreat to Skalitz. He may not have had to give an order; his demoralized infantry were streaming from the field in disarray.

The duke of Saxe Coburg with the Prussian artillery at Langensalza, 27 June 1866. (Voss)

These troops, many of them disaffected Poles and Hungarians, would tell stories of the battle that would spread rapidly, soon all would know that the needle gun was a terror weapon that couldn't be resisted, and many would question what their generals were going to do. The casualties told a more succinct story. For the Austrians the cost was 5,719 including 2,197 dead and missing. On the Prussian side casualties were just 62 officers and 1,060 men of which 283 were dead.

While Steinmetz was telegraphing the news of his victory to Berlin, his brother officer, General von Bonin, was having a very different experience. His I Corps, forming the right wing of the Second Army, had descended into the Aupa Valley en route for the town of Trautenau, the first stage on his march to Gitschin for Moltke's proposed junction with the First Army. His first objective that day was the small village of Pilnikau. As his advance guard of the 1st East Prussian Grenadiers pushed into Trautenau from the mountain passes they ran headlong into a fusillade from the hills on his left flank. This fire came from the forward battalions of Lieutenant Field Marshal Ludwig von Gablenz, of Danish War fame, who had conducted an exhausting march from Josephstadt early that morning. The startled Prussian troops endeavoured to restore the situation as best they could, but Bonin's lack of reconnaissance would cost him dear.

As Gablenz's Mondel Brigade pulled back – to await reinforcements that were still over three hours away on the road from Josephstadt – the Prussians

Storming the farmhouse at Wisakow, near Nachod, 27 June 1866. (Voss)

continued to move through the town. Bonin's 2nd Division attacked Mondel's rearguard on the Hopfenberg heights. These troops resisted valiantly until overwhelmed. By this time, Bonin felt he had secured the town and when an officer from the 1st Guards Division, making its way down through the Eypel Pass a mile or two away, offered assistance, he declined it. His troops were still slowly emerging from the narrow defiles above Trautenau three hours later when Gablenz's divisions finally reached the field. Again, Bonin was to be punished for a lack of reconnaissance. This time he was unable to prevail and despite the grievous losses his infantry inflicted upon the advancing Austrians, he was in danger of being surrounded, so he began his retreat back up the Aupa valley, all the way back to Landshut, where he had started at four in the morning.

General Albert Ferdinand Adolf Karl Friedrich von Bonin (1803–72).

Bismarck called this action "The slap that rocked the whole Prussian Army", but as much of a setback as it was, it could have been worse. The Austrians had again suffered tremendously, taking nearly four times as many casualties as the Prussians. Five thousand were dead, wounded, captured or missing including 191 officers that the Hapsburg army could not afford to lose. Again however, Benedek failed to see the opportunity presented to him. With Steinmetz exposed to the east and the crown prince, unaware of Bonin's misfortune, forging ahead with the Guard Corps in the middle, the Austrian Feldherr should have seized the day. However, instead of turning his full might against this army emerging onto the Bohemian plateau, he

Austrian and Prussian cavalry clash at Nachod. (Voss)

stuck to his original plan to confront the First Army with six army corps before turning on the crown prince.

This was not the only defeat of the day for the Prussians. Away to the west at Langensalza, the Hanoverian army had held up its honourable and ancient military reputation. Having decided to fight it out, they had prepared relatively effective defences around the town. The Prussian general Flies, with his mixture of garrison troops and Landwehr, had decided to move instead of waiting for Goeben and the larger part of the army to get into position. It was a costly mistake. The Hanoverians easily put his troops to flight, especially the Landwehr who covered themselves with dishonour by shamming wounds and skulking behind trees. A final charge by one of the regular regiments was thrown into disorder by a magnificent cavalry charge from the Hanoverian Lifeguards and only with some steady work by a Prussian ally, the green-clad troops of Saxe-Coburg-Gotha, was the line restored.

Once again, the Prussians were to benefit by circumstance. The Hanoverians' successful last stand would bring them no relief. The Prussians had completed their encirclement and the exhausted defenders had no resources. They spent the night of 27 June resigned to capitulation and perhaps incarceration for the remainder of the war.

Despite the uncertainties of the day, the Prussian armies had progressed. The First Army had united with the Army of the Elbe, and Trautenau notwithstanding, the Second Army was emerging successfully into eastern Bohemia. Moltke and headquarters nevertheless remained anxious. Would Frederick Charles pick up speed tomorrow? Would the Austrians prevent the crown prince from reaching a climactic battle in time?

General August von Goeben (1816–80).

Thursday 28 June

The Prussian Guard Corps, under the command of General Prince August von Württemburg, had camped for the night just beyond the Eypel defiles. In the middle of the night, he received the news of Bonin's misfortune at Trautenau from the crown prince. He was ordered to cross the Aupa and cut off Gablenz's retreat from Trautenau the next morning. Gablenz had hoped to prevent the Guards from debouching from the Eypel passes, but a combination of low morale and lack of reinforcements changed his plans. Instead, he placed his artillery in a line between Burgersdorf and Neu-Rognitz, supported by three infantry brigades. The 1st Guard Division, led by the Guard Jäger and Guard Fusiliers, and supported by the Guard Hussars, advanced upon this formation, taking heavy losses from the artillery fire. The only Prussian battery's six guns gave ineffective fire support. At this point, the Prussians also

Prussians and Hanoverians clash on the Unstrut River near Langensalza. (Voss)

made a bayonet charge, and began to suffer similar losses to their enemy. However, with the remainder of their division coming up on their left, the Austrians were soon retreating to Soor.

The 2nd Guard Division had swung right to meet Gablenz' Grivicic Brigade to the north at Alt-Rognitz. The contest was unequal. Within an hour the brigade had almost ceased to exist. Those who were not killed, wounded, or taken prisoner managed to make their way westward over the top of Burgersdorf to join their comrades decamping from Soor. Remarkably, Gablenz managed to extricate his remaining forces without further mauling. He was extremely angry. Why had Benedek cancelled an order that would have allowed reinforcements from Lieutenant Field-Marshal Tassilo Count Festetics' IV Corps to support him at Prausnitz to the south?

Further along the Aupa River at Skalitz, 22 miles to the east, General Ramming was also frustrated with Benedek. The Austrian Feldherr, who had arrived at Ramming's headquarters at the railway station there at 10:00 a.m., had assumed that Steinmetz would consolidate in Nachod, and wait for VI Corps to come through the mountains. He then put the rearguard in the charge of the incompetent

The Prussian crown prince comforting Austrian officers after the battle of Nachod.

General Karl Friedrich von Steinmetz (1796–1877).

Archduke Leopold after ordering the bulk of the troops under Ramming to proceed west for the projected battle at Gitschin. Even as he and his staff rode away from the town back to Josephstadt, he must surely have heard the sound of battle as the Prussians erupted on the road from Nachod.

Old General Steinmetz had decided not to wait for VI Corps. Unlike the caution displayed by the First Army, the crown prince's corps commanders acted with decisiveness. Although Bonin's attack had failed, Steinmetz reckoned that at the very worst, he would be pushed against the Guard Corps on his right, and felt he had nothing to lose by pressing on to Skalitz. He was right. Instead of organizing a fighting retreat, Leopold's brigade commanders led reckless assaults, against orders, on the advancing Prussians. After pushing back Leopold's left flank, the advance guard of the 9th Division comprising the 37th Fusiliers and the 58th Regiment, met the Austrian Fragnern Brigade in Dubno Wood, north of the railway line. The carnage was inevitable. Half of the Fragnern Brigade was cut down by the Prussian fusiliers and as more troops of both sides were fed in from opposite ends of the wood, the Austrians were reduced to heaps of dead, or wounded and screaming men. Fragnern was killed, along with most of his officers. Because of these unauthorized attacks, the Austrians again were reduced by overwhelming casualties. The Prussians swept forward, and by 3:00 p.m., with Steinmetz at their head, they took the railway station in Skalitz. Leopold's brigades were now a leaderless rabble. They streamed out of Skalitz, mixed up with wagons and artillery caissons, many without weapons, shakos and equipment. As they overtook Ramming's columns retreating to Josephstadt, they infected them with the same hysteria. Behind them they left nearly 3,000 dead plus an additional 3,000 prisoners, over half of them unwounded. Steinmetz, pleased with his success, decided to secure Skalitz then wait for the Guard Corps to come up on his right from Eypel, and VI Corps to finish their march out of the mountains, before he took any further action.

While the forces of the crown prince were making good their recovery from the reversal at Trautenau, Prince Frederick Charles and his two armies were finally securing the Iser River crossings. Having stationed himself with his chief of staff, General Konstantin von Voigts-Rhetz, Frederick Charles directed the battle that was unfolding toward Münchengräz. Herwarth von Bittenfeld, bringing the Army of the Elbe up from Hühnerwasser, sent his advance guard – led by the 17th, 20th

The campaign in Bohemia.

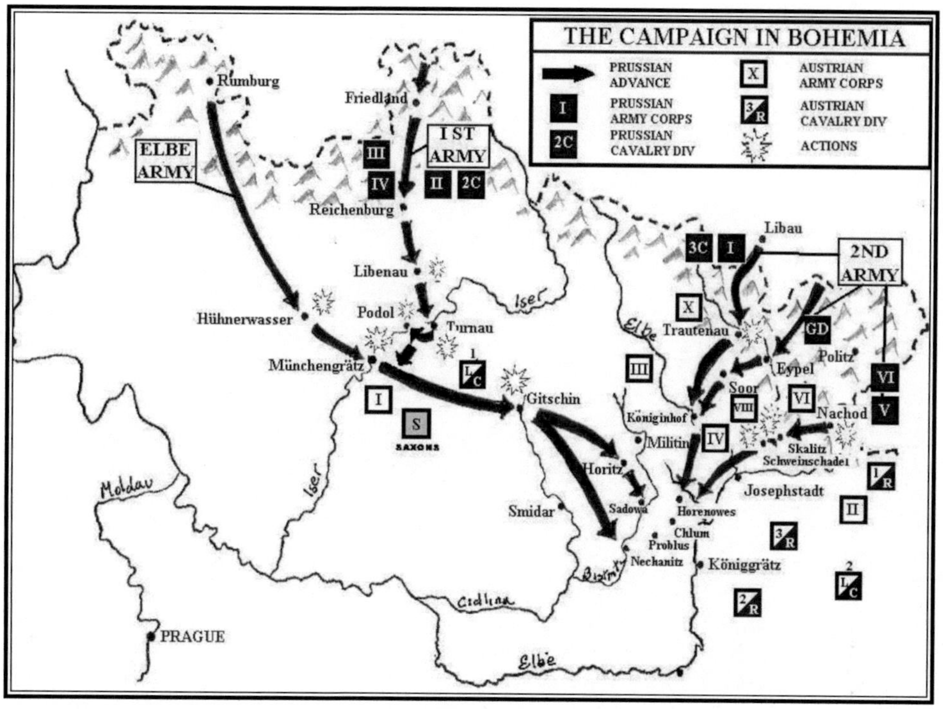

and 56th regiments, and supported by three artillery batteries – against the weak Austrian force west of the Iser. They were quickly forced from the field, but burned the last bridge over the river as they departed. From Podol, the advancing divisions of Horn and Fransecky were fired upon by an Austrian battery atop a hill known as the Muskey Berg. This battery was also silenced by Fransecky's troops. At this point Frederick Charles had the fantastic idea that he had surrounded the whole of Prince Albert and Clam-Gallas' army. He was to be sorely disappointed. In fact, Prince Albert had made good his escape, and the massive preparations that had been made for two Prussian armies to crush him came to naught. This proved another lesson for the Prussian prince, demonstrating the virtues of risk versus caution.

With Münchengräz taken, the Iser crossings were in Prussian hands and the way open to Gitschin. As Frederick Charles headquartered himself in one of Wallenstein's castles, his men raided the cellars for wine and beer. For the remaining thousands of soldiers of the Army of the Elbe and the First Army, now crowded into a small area by the bend in the Iser, there would be no beer and not much food, as the logistical nightmare continued. This would cause the Army of the Elbe to again be left behind to re-victual as the prince, with more prompting from Moltke, prepared to move on Gitschin.

General Steinmetz at the Battle of Skalitz, 28 June 1866 (Voss)

In many ways, the day had dawned somewhat bleakly on the Prussian enterprise. The defeat at Trautenau the day before had been followed by news of another Prussian defeat at Langensalza. At the same time, the disaster that befell their Italian allies at Custozza had just filtered down, and caused additional worry as the prospect of a reinforced Austrian army loomed. The actions of Soor, Skalitz and Münchengräz, however, although not definitive, proved that the enemy was retreating on all fronts. Whether the decisive battle would fall where Moltke had indicated was uncertain, but it was becoming quite clear that the Austrians now had to be caught before they could escape. At headquarters, Moltke knew little of these developments as telegraph communications in eastern Bohemia were not yet set up, and the mounted couriers still took over 24 hours to get to Berlin. He was, though, encouraged late in the night by one piece of good news. The Hanoverian king at Langensalza, his army surrounded and with no hope of help from the Bavarians, had decided to save his men from certain destruction. He sent an emissary to Falckenstein to say he would surrender the next day.

Friday 29 June

Early in the morning of 29 June, the crown prince, mounted, and with his staff alongside him, watched as the somewhat chastened General Bonin, at the head of I Army Corps, marched past him through the town of Trautenau. The general's new task was to advance with his corps to Pilnikau, along a road cleared for them by the Guard Corps.

The Guards themselves were moving toward Königinhof on the Elbe where their advanced party of fusiliers and Jäger were already engaged with the Austrian outposts. In the town itself was a single brigade, that of Fleishhacker, which was dispatched east into the cornfields to deal with the advancing Prussians. A short bombardment from the accompanying Guards artillery and a few companies of the Fusiliers made quick work of this brigade and the single battalion left to cover the retreat in the town itself. The survivors of this battalion joined its shattered brigade retreating across the Elbe to the town of Militin. A few miles to the east, General Steinmetz, advancing from Skalitz after his action of the previous day, bumped into three brigades of Festetics' IV Corps at Schweinschädel, on the road to Gradlitz. The ensuing artillery cannonade lasted almost three hours, but succeeded in convincing Festetics to retire on Josephstadt thus avoiding the otherwise inevitable decimation of his troops at the hands of the needle gun.

The commander of the First Army received two telegrams that morning from Moltke; one informing him of the victory at Nachod and the defeat at Trautenau, the other urging him to continue his drive in order to support the Second Army's advance. This time Prince Frederick Charles needed little egging on. The previous evening, he and Voigts-Rhetz had decided to move the 5th Division, with six cavalry squadrons toward Gitschin, so at about 9:30 a.m. he sent Lieutenant-General August von Werder's 3rd Division as the advance guard for the main attack.

For the Austrians, the defensive possibilities of Gitschin were well known, and some of the natural features to the northwest of the town were ideal for defensive purposes. Clam-Gallas and his deputy, General Gondrecourt, deployed 56 of their 96 guns on the Privysin Heights, and the remaining 40 between the heights and Eisenstadl, where General Eugene Piret's brigade was positioned. Clam-Gallas had every expectation, given the favourable terrain, that he could hold the heights with the Brigade of Abele to the west and the Brigade of Poschacher, by Brada village in the centre. Between the Privysin position and

Eisenstadl, was the village of Diletz where the Saxons were meant to have been in position. Unfortunately, because they had taken a circuitous route from Münchengräz, the first Saxon Brigade had not arrived by late afternoon. South of the Münchengräz–Gitschin road was the Ringelsheim Brigade, already badly cut up from the day before. Clam-Gallas and Prince Albert had every expectation that at least three corps from North Army would be joining them before the night was out.

It was General Tümpling's 5th Division from Turnau that first appeared before Privysin at about 3:30 p.m. They had rested about two hours' march from Gitschin on the previous evening and were fully fit for action. Tümpling's guns opened fire first, and after an hour or so, his forward battalions advanced on the heights by Brada after clearing the small village of Podultz. By now the effects of the Prussian needle gun[4] were well known and Austrian jäger, well hidden behind

The Prussian Battery of Captain Blotnitz at Langensalza, 27 June 1866. (Voss)

trees, were continually handed loaded rifles by their comrades in the rear. This had the result of blunting the attack and the fusilier battalions of the 8th, 12th, and 48th regiments began falling as fast as their enemies had done in previous actions. This turned out to be the most difficult time for the Prussians at Gitschin, and Tümpling's 10th Brigade were even pushed back by Poschacher after intense hand-to-hand fighting. But these actions, effective as they could be, were rare and Austrian commanders, as they so often did in this campaign, flung densely packed formations against rapidly firing Prussians while many units were held back as idle onlookers. Although wounded, Tümpling soon found his enemy's weaknesses and relentlessly pushed his troops onward. Saxons, hastily coming into position near Diletz were confronted by the 8th Grenadiers and 48th Regiment who had moved along the Cidlina stream to cut them off. They suffered badly and the banks of the small river were soon littered with their cornflower-blue-clad bodies. Edelsheim's cavalry fared no better and a gallant but useless charge against the Prussian 8th Grenadiers near Zames Village emptied many a saddle.

As the Austro-Saxon centre began to collapse, the forces of General Werder were beginning to roll up the Ringelsheim Brigade on the Münchengräz Road. The 3rd Division's spearhead, comprising the 2nd Jägers with the 14th and 42nd Infantry regiments, had heard the guns of Tümpling's artillery opening up on the Privysin Heights and ran headlong into the Austrians at Unter-Lochow about a mile from Gitschin. Ringelsheim's defences were sound and for three hours the Prussians were unable to make a dent. While the rest of Werder's division came up to make a flank attack, Ringelsheim was suddenly ordered to retire upon Gitschin. The reason for this soon became clear. Albert and Clam-Gallas had been informed by Benedek that there would be no relief from North Army. They were ordered to break off the engagement and retreat to the Elbe.

The disengagement of fighting troops from a battle in progress is difficult and fraught with danger. Unfortunately, the retreat order had already reached most of the units, who were only too happy to move to the rear. The result was chaotic disorder in Gitschin; men, wagons, ambulances, and frightened civilians jammed the main road. The Prussians, exploiting this situation, quickly overcame the Austrian rearguard and only the decisive action of the Saxon Life Brigade prevented a catastrophe. They held the Prussians at bay until the last unwounded Austrian had left Gitschin and at around 1:00 a.m. on 30 June, they melted away, to form up on the Smidar Road and march off in proper ranks and good order.

General der Kavallerie Eduard Count von Clam-Gallas (1805–91).

Pursuit was not an option for the Prussians. Their exhausted troops fell down where they stood and slept, thankful that they had survived while so many had not. This was the toughest battle that had been fought so far and Prussian losses were severe: 71 officers and 1,482 men, along with 56 horses. Unsurprisingly, the Austrian casualties were much higher at 181 officers, 4,714 men, and 222 horses. The Saxons, whose soldiery were of a higher calibre than their Austrian ally, had lost 27 officers, 586 men, and 58 horses. As well as all this, approximately 7,000 prisoners had been taken, some of them at the last moment when two Hungarian battalions got lost during the retreat and surrendered.

The battle fought at Gitschin had not been the decisive one. Perhaps Prince Frederick Charles had harboured the thought at one point, but the rapid Austrian retreat from Münchengräz had convinced him otherwise. By the end of the day, however, the situation for the Prussian armies was satisfactory on all fronts. The First Army was secure at the critical junction point of Gitschin, and the Second Army of the crown prince was firmly established at Königinhof on the left bank of the Elbe, threatening the important Austrian fortress of Josephstadt.

The Battle of Gitschin, 29 June 1866 (Voss)

In the west, the Hanoverian Army, after surrendering, handed over all their weapons and war stores to the Prussians although their cavalry were allowed to keep their sabres. Then, as their king and his son departed into exile, they were sent home from Langensalza by train. Thus ended the history of a proud army whose service over nearly 200 years, largely for the British Crown, had been honourable and courageous. They had held the line at Minden during the Seven Years War and stoutly defended Gibraltar twenty years later.[5] As the King's German Legion, they had marched and fought with Wellington's army, from the Iberian Peninsula to Waterloo. At least their story had ended with the credit of winning their last battle.

So, as Prussian troops slept fitfully in hard, rutted fields around Gitschin, or sheltered among the pine trees on the banks of the Elbe, the Austrian army of Clam-Gallas shuffled slowly through the night towards the fortress of Königgrätz, on the Elbe. Their thoughts may have been of defeat at the hands of the dreaded needle gun, but it is more likely they were focused on hot food, wine, and shelter, especially, as somewhere on the road near Horitz, it began to rain.

Lieutenant-General August von Werder (1808–88).

Saturday 30 June

At the Great General Staff Headquarters in Berlin, the news of the events of 29 June was most welcome. The Hanoverians had been eliminated, the Bavarians and their allies were offering no immediate threat north of the Main, and, most importantly, the Austro-Saxon forces were now retreating on all fronts. Such progress, felt Moltke, justified the move of Great Headquarters to the Front. The vast retinue of the king, including not only Moltke and Bismarck, but also huge numbers of staff, aides-de-camp, foreign attachés and attendants, left Berlin by rail in six trainloads during the day. The journey was preceded by a congratulatory and somewhat pompous order of the day from the king to the army, telegraphed ahead as they began the journey.

Wellington's aphorism comparing the sadness of a battle lost to a battle won was well suited to the sights at Gitschin on the morning of 30 June. As far as the eye could see men men lay in heaps. The grey Austrian greatcoats mingled with Prussian and Saxon blue, the latter of a cornflower shade. Shakos, Pickelhaubes, hats, rifles, valises, and other equipment were strewn amongst the maize, and littered on the banks of the Cidlina river. The wounded still moaned or shouted for help, their cries contrasting with the occasional whinny of an injured horse. The town itself was packed with wounded and prisoners, not to mention abandoned wagons, carts, and stores. The treatment of the wounded was a problem. On the Prussian side, the situation was more organized as Prussia had signed the Geneva Convention in 1864 and their stretcher bearers and some medical staff wore the Red Cross on a white brassard round the left sleeve. The stretcher-bearer corps (Krankenträger) was established on a corps basis, and performed a critical service on the battlefield. For the Austrians, things were less happy. They had not signed the convention and although they possessed a hospital orderly corps, they did not have a proper stretcher-bearer unit, and the wounded had to rely on their comrades to carry them to the rear. With no Red Cross armbands they were as vulnerable as any other soldier. Thus, as in warfare throughout history, many of the injured succumbed to their wounds. The lessons of the Crimean War had not been learned in Vienna, and the field hospitals were not well equipped, nor could they keep up with the traffic.

Despite their string of victories, the exhausted Prussian troops were not altogether happy. The chronic supply problems had never really been solved, so the rank and file were increasingly required to fend for themselves. Discipline was becoming harder to maintain as officers found it more difficult to prevent the looting of houses, farms, and palaces. For the Army of the Elbe, still at Münchengräz, the problems were at their worst, and quartermasters were frantically telegraphing Berlin for re-supply, to no avail. In some cases, dysentery had appeared and fears rose that a typhus or cholera epidemic would decimate the ranks while thirst and hunger weakened them. To make matters worse, the rain had spread all over northern Bohemia and become a steady downpour, compounding the difficulties of the Prussian soldiery for whom, without tents, conditions became miserable.

Prince Frederick Charles and his staff moved headquarters to Gitschin, while the crown prince stayed at Königinhof. Both commanders failed to use their cavalry to probe the Austrian rearguards, to establish their whereabouts. In fact, there was no communication between the two headquarters, even though they were less than a day's march apart. Thus, Frederick William had no idea of the results of the battle at Gitschin until late in the evening. What was to disappoint Moltke the most was that their plan, especially on behalf of Frederick Charles, was to unite both armies before a final assault on the Austro-Saxon Army. This was in complete contradiction of his own master plan. On the evening of 30 June, however, the argument was academic. None of them had any idea where Benedek was.

An aerial view of the area east of Gitschin to the Elbe would have revealed as chaotic a scene as ever there was in the annals of 19th-century warfare. The best part of seven Austrian army corps were milling about in total disorder. Five corps alone had become completely mixed up on the Dubenec plateau, as they had attempted to retreat to Josephstadt on roads that had become quagmires in the pouring rain. In the town of Dubenec itself, the Feldzugmeister himself had been "holed up" since the morning of 29 June. He was as demoralized as his army. Under other circumstances, Dubenec was a natural fortress, but with the Prussian Second Army ensconced on the east bank of the Elbe and the First Army within striking distance to the west, it was indefensible. Benedek, therefore, gave orders on 30 June for the army to retreat to Königgrätz, the southernmost of the Elbe fortresses. At the same time, he composed a long message to Emperor Franz Joseph that was full of self-pity, excuses, and blame for all around him. It concluded with a plea for the emperor to sue for peace and avoid a disaster. The reply on the following day was abrupt: capitulation was impossible, but a retreat was acceptable and there followed the famous taunt in the form of an annex from the adjutant-general, Crenneville: "Has a battle been fought?"

Adjutant-General Crenneville.

Sunday 1 July

In the hopes of further denying Benedek the chance to defeat First and Second armies separately, Frederick Charles moved his divisions forward during the day. By evening, the 6th Division, supported by the 5th, were in Militin, the 7th and 8th in Horitz, and the 3rd and 4th, with the reserve cavalry and artillery park, on the Gitschin–Horitz road. On his right wing, Herwarth von Bittenfeld's Army of the Elbe had moved down to Smidar, north of Sadowa on the Bistritz River. The Prince made his headquarters at Kammenitz, a small village halfway between Gitschin and Horitz. The crown prince's Second Army had also probed across the Elbe, but he and his headquarters remained at Königinhof.

The king's train reached Gitschin in the morning, and almost immediately Moltke issued an order for the Second Army to remain firmly on the left bank of the upper Elbe, while the First Army was to advance "without pause" towards Königgrätz. The Army of the Elbe was to protect their right flank. Although Moltke, like his army commanders, had no idea where Benedek was, his intuition told him that keeping the crown prince on the opposite bank of the Elbe would still enable him to outflank the Austrians and hit them in the rear. At any rate, he called for a war council the next day to make his wishes understood.

By now Benedek, installed at Königgrätz, may well have been on the verge of a nervous breakdown. He remained indecisive, as his troops struggled to overcome the massive logistical chaos that his orders had caused. Apart from the fact that reaching their appointed destinations presented a great challenge by itself, the securing of food and supplies had become impossible. His staff were in no better shape. Many of them despaired of making any sort of stand against the Prussians. Colonel Beck arrived back from Vienna again, and was stunned at the inactivity at headquarters. He met with Benedek's chief of staff, Krismanic, who seemed to have washed his hands of the whole situation.

Gustav von Alvensleben (1803–81).

The supply problems for the Prussians were scarcely better. Although large quantities of stores were now mounting at the railheads at Reichenberg and Franckenstein, it appeared impossible to move them forward even though the railway was operating at least as far as Gitschin. The wagon trains got stuck in the mud and those that made it further down the line were held up by the vast numbers of troops choking up the roads. Still, the Prussians at least passed a tolerable night, as many of them found shelter from the rain in the villages.

Leonhard von Blumenthal (1810–90).

Monday 2 July

Moltke's council of war was somewhat hindered by the fact that no one knew exactly where the Austrians had gone. The general, and logical, wisdom was that they had crossed the Elbe to take up positions behind Königgrätz so as to more easily fall back on the fortress of Olmütz. The crown prince was represented by General Alvensleben and Major-General Leonhard von Blumenthal, who, with Prince Frederick Charles and Herwarth von Bittenfeld, pressed Moltke to allow them to unite to ensure the defeat of Benedek's forces. Moltke was unmoved, and determined to stick to his plan. The armies would remain where they were until the morrow. Then, the Army of the Elbe would move down toward Pardubitz to secure the bridgeheads on the lower Elbe. Bismarck, who was also at the meeting, offered another element of urgency. Napoleon III of France was pressing for a cease-fire, and unless the Austrians were soon defeated, diplomacy might intervene and undo their success so far. The Austrians must be found immediately.

Benedek, meanwhile, had held a war council of his own. His spirits had revived somewhat, and he seemed to think he could offer battle with more confidence, including some "soldier's luck" as he had suggested in a more upbeat note to the emperor. Present were Beck, Krismanic, army Chief of Staff Alfred Henikstein, Ramming, Clam-Gallas, Gondrecourt, Count Thun, and the other corps commanders. Having gathered them together, Benedek inquired if their supply problems had been solved, and announced that the army would remain camped between the Bistritz River and Königgrätz. No battle was mentioned, and apparently no discussion of one was held. As the meeting adjourned the lacklustre staff simply returned to their units. Later, this meeting was castigated by many of the officers present and called a farce.

Whatever the Austrian feldzugmeister had indicated, the Army of the North was preparing for battle. The excellent Engineer Corps were organizing fieldworks. Battery positions were being prepared on the Chlum and Lipa heights facing across the Bistritz, and, finally, the various brigades and corps were settling down in their designated areas.

The city of Königgrätz.

Back at his headquarters in Kammenitz, Prince Frederick Charles had received reports from forward units, that Austrian patrols and campfires had been seen in the Bistritz Valley on the previous night. A prisoner had told his captors that the Austrian III Corps was at Chlum. The prince immediately dispatched a Major Unger with a cavalry detachment to investigate. After a series of hair-raising escapes including a lance wound from an Austrian uhlan, Unger returned with an amazing report. He had managed to reach a hill above the village of Dub and had seen that large numbers of Austrian troops were bivouacked there.

General Constantin von Voigts-Rhetz (1809–77).

For the first time since the campaign started, Frederick Charles was galvanized into action. He decided to attack at dawn the following day, and made his plan that night with Voigts-Rhetz. At about 10:00 p.m., he sent Voigts-Rhetz to Gitschin with the news. There, Voigts-Rhetz found the king asleep, and had him woken by an aide. The king immediately sent him to Moltke, who awoke with the words, "Thanks be to God!" Moltke also learned that the prince had sent a message to the First Army, asking that the Guards be sent down to assist. Moltke knew that should Benedek truly have the Elbe to his back, then his "pocket battle" (*Kesselschlacht*) was at hand. He immediately sent another officer, to order his entire army to march as fast as possible, down along the right bank of the Elbe, and take Benedek in the flank. This officer, despite considerable risks, placed the message in the hands of the crown prince at about 4:00 a.m.

NOTES

1. Geoffrey Wawro, *The Austro-Prussian War*, p.55.
2. Ironically, this castle was the property of Prince Frederick Charles'Austrian opponent, Count Clam-Gallas.
3. La Marmora was also the Italian prime minister. His military career began in 1823 and he distinguished himself at the siege of Pescheria in 1848. He led the Sardinian Army in the Crimean War of 1854–55 and the Franco-Austrian War of 1859. His brother Allessandro raised the famed Bersaglieri Regiment.
4. See Chapter 9.
5. After their absorption into the German army the Hanoverian troops were eventually allowed to place the battle honours "Waterloo" on their helmet plates (The 73rd Regiment and 10th Jager added "Peninsular"). In addition the 10th Jager Regiment wore the cuff title "Gibraltar".

CHAPTER FIVE

The Battle of Königgrätz

Benedek's initial dispositions

Feldzeugmeister Benedek chose to make his stand between the Bistritz River and the Upper Elbe, which flowed in parallel in a southwesterly direction, roughly six to eight miles apart. His position was bounded to the north by a line of villages, from Benatek in the west to Trotinka near the Elbe. His left flank was six miles to the south marked by a line from Nechanitz on the Bistritz, to Königgrätz itself. Topographically, the land sloped gently down to the west bank of the Bistritz and rose more sharply on the east. Several hills overlooked the river, the highest of these being Lipa and Chlum in the north, and further to the south, the hills of Prim and Problus. It was heavily forested along the river; the largest woods being those of Sweip (Sweipwald) near Benatek, and Hola (Holawald) behind the village of Dohalitz.

This was a prosperous part of the Austrian Empire and the area was liberally dotted with villages, mills, small factories, and country houses. From Nechanitz on the east bank of the Bistritz going north were the villages of Popowitz, Tresowitz, Mokrowous, and Dohalitz. The village of Sadowa was on the west bank. Through it passed the main road between Gitschin and Königgrätz, which bisected Benedek's position from northwest to the southeast. A mile or so behind this was another line of villages from Hradek in the south through lower and upper Prim, Problus and Stresetitz, to Lipa on the Gitschin road.

Benedek centred his defences around the hills of Chlum and Lipa, which his engineers had fortified with redoubts and entrenchments. The plan drawn up by Krismanic and his staff positioned North Army as follows: in the centre was Archduke Ernst's III Corps with Gablenz's X Corps on his left, covering Dohalitz and Mokrowous (44,000 men and 134 guns). The right wing, between Chlum and the village of Nedelist, was to be secured by IV Corps, led by Festetics and Thun's

II Corps (55,000 men and 176 guns). This would block an envelopment by the Prussian Second Army. That, however, was not anticipated before the First Army had been dealt with. To the south, on the left wing, were the Saxons of Prince Albert along with VIII Corps, now led by General Weber in the place of the inept Archduke Leopold, (40,000 men and 140 guns). These were ranged along the heights of Tresowitz and Popowitz, by the Bistritz. Edelsheim's Light Cavalry Division stood behind the Saxons at Ober Prim, and the 2nd Light Cavalry Division on the northern flank at Nedelist. In reserve, along the Main Road by Wsestar and Rosnitz, he placed I Corps, now commanded by Gondrecourt, with Ramming's VI Corps and three divisions of cavalry, as well as the artillery reserve. This formidable reserve force totalled nearly 60,000 men (11,500 cavalry), with 320 guns.

In addition to making his dispositions, Benedek had to deal with disruptions in his chain of command, coming directly from Vienna. Army Chief of Staff Henikstein had been recalled to the capital the previous day after an angry emperor received a telegram from him claiming that all was well, which he flatly didn't believe. Benedek refused to let him go, and pleaded with Franz Joseph to rescind the order. Late on the eve of battle another order was received replacing Krismanic as operations chief with the bearer of the message, General Alois von Baumgarten. All this created confusion at headquarters and surely contributed to the débacle that was to follow. On the morning of 3 July, Benedek had to spend time bringing Baumgarten up to speed, so the battle itself was well under way when he and his staff finally arrived on the scene at the late hour of 9:00 a.m.

The Prussian advance to the Bistritz

Neither the First Army or the Army of the Elbe had enjoyed much sleep on the night of 2 July. By midnight, most formations were breaking camp and within a few hours were on the move to what, in later years, would be called their "start lines". The plan, hastily crafted by the Prince and Voigts-Rhetz, called for the 7th Division, under Fransecky, to advance to Cerekwitz, just above Benatek, and for Horn's 8th Division to advance down the main road toward Sadowa in the centre. To Horn's right, the 3rd and 4th divisions were to place themselves opposite Dohalitz and Mokrowous, while on the extreme right, the Army of the Elbe's 14th, 15th, and 16th divisions were to effect a river crossing down by Nechanitz and advance on Problus. In reserve, on the Gitschin–Königgrätz Road behind Horn,

The Prussian 49th Regiment crosses the Bistritz, 3 July 1866. (Voss)

came the 5th and 6th divisions. The cavalry division, under Alvensleben, was placed between the Army of the Elbe and the 3rd Division, a mile or so from the Bistritz opposite Popowitz. The driving rain that began just after dawn complicated things a little, especially for the artillery, whose limbers got stuck in the mud or slid off the flattened wet barleycorn into ditches.

The prince would make his first headquarters on the hill at Dub, a mile from Sadowa, and he arrived there shortly after 6:00 a.m. as most of his units were getting into position. His initial apprehension that the enemy had slipped away was banished by reports to the contrary, although the thick mist and rain prevented any visual assurance. Typically, Frederick Charles' first thought was to pause before launching the offensive, and get his men fed because few of them had eaten much in the last twenty-four hours. However, as his cavalry began to probe across the Bistritz, at about 7:30 a.m., the Austrian artillery opened up and the battle began. Fifteen minutes later the king and his retinue, including Moltke and

Bismarck, arrived on Dub Hill. His arrival was greeted by a salvo from an Austrian battery across the river, which just missed him but swept a troop of his uhlan escort off the heights, killing four.

Moltke immediately took control of the agenda. Bismarck, who would remain close to Moltke for the duration of the battle, asked about the size of the enemy force. The chief of staff's vague reply belied his real thoughts – that they had the entire North Army before them. He was now convinced that his original plan of envelopment could prevail. The prince had been enjoying the thought that he could claim the glory for himself by defeating whatever enemy forces were before him before his cousin arrived with the Second Army. He was quickly disabused of this notion, as Moltke made it clear that he was only to fix the Austrian Army where it was, and allow the Second Army and the Army of the Elbe to defeat them on the flanks. In addition, Frederick Charles' idea of a pleasant breakfast for the men before the attack was destroyed as Moltke ordered (via the king, of course) an immediate general advance by all forces across the Bistritz.

By 8:30 a.m., the artillery of both sides, about 300 guns in total, were heavily engaged in a duel of a magnitude not seen on European soil since Leipzig in 1813. Suddenly, all along the riverfront from Benatek down to Nechanitz, dark-blue Prussian forces erupted from the earth and swarmed down the banks of the Bistritz. In the centre, Horn's batteries continued to trade fire with the Austrian defenders as his 8th Division moved on Sadowa alongside the 3rd Division on their right, while they attempted to cross the river at Dohalitz and Mokrowous. The defenders refused to yield easily and the rifle fire increased in intensity, proven by growing clouds of white smoke that eventually hid the river from view. The Prussian guns turned their fire on the villages. In these villages only a few buildings were built of stone; most of the cottages were made of pine so they were soon ablaze, and black clouds now mingled with the white gunpowder smoke.

The initial surge of the Prussian Army in the centre was quickly slowed by the Austrian resistance. Benedek's soldiers had learned lessons from the earlier Bohemian battles and made good use of cover and dispersal, especially among the jäger, and drastically reduced the force-multiplying effects of the needle gun. By 10:00 a.m., however, despite severe casualties caused by cannon fire as much as musket, the courageous efforts of Werder's 3rd Division, led by the 14th and 54th regiments, had cleared the villages of Dohalitz and Mokrowous. However they were now stopped in their tracks as they came under fire from the massive concentration of artillery based on the Lipa heights. With their ranges well marked, the Austrian gunners forced the attackers to keep their heads down for the next four hours.

On their left, Lieutenant-General Herwarth von Bittenfeld's 4th Division and Horn's 8th, were already through Sadowa and across the Bistritz where, on the edge of the Hola forest (Holawald) they were checked by the Rumanian Border Regiment of Archduke Ernst's 5th Prohaska Brigade. The Rumanians didn't hold for long, though and began an orderly retreat through the forest where, had it not been for the guns on Lipa finding the range of the Prussians in the wood, their retreat would have become a rout. This Austrian bombardment was intense and accurate and the discomfiture of the Prussians was exacerbated by wood splinters flying from the pine trees, shattered by the shellfire, and often more lethal than shrapnel. It was not long before the young men of Pomerania and Thuringia had had enough, and Horn sent back a few of his battalions, who had borne the brunt of the fighting and suffered severe losses, to the rear. The king of Prussia, on seeing

The Prussian 26th Regiment on the outskirts of Cistowes, 3 July 1866. (Voss)

these troops, angrily admonished them and accused them of cowardice, threatening to return them to the front. Prince Frederick Charles had to remonstrate with his Sovereign and explain that they had bravely done their duty, and had earned a respite. The Royal contingent had moved from Dub at around 10:00 a.m., and was now upon the heights of Roskosberg, right behind Sadowa. The mood was anxious as they began to see the advance stalled all along the front. Moltke himself was trying to get a handle on events taking place on his left since 8:30 a.m. – he had very good cause to be worried.

The battle in the Swiepwald

As the Prussian efforts to cross the Bistritz began to gain momentum, Count Festetics of IV Corps had made a decision that would have profound consequences later in the day. Festetics was persuaded by his chief of staff, and second-in-command, General Anton Mollinary, that the Maslowed heights obscured the terrain beyond, and their position would be difficult to defend. So upon the urging of his chief of staff, Festetics moved his troops westward from Benedek's intended position, east of Chlum, to the village of Maslowed and the edge of Swiepwald. Count Thun's II Corps, whose orders were to support IV Corps, naturally moved forward with them and took up a position just north of Maslowed. Unfortunately, the two corps, now facing the Prussian First Army in the west, had opened up a gap, now poorly defended, to an incursion from the north. The decision would, in the short term, cost the lives of many in both armies, and possibly cost Benedek the battle itself.

The vanguard of General Fransecky's 7th Division had forded the river opposite Benatek, and entered the village with little resistance. At about 8:00 a.m., as these fusiliers of the 27th and 67th regiments consolidated their positions and prepared to move forward, a large force of the enemy appeared at the end of the Swiepwald to the south of the village. The fusiliers decided to wait until the rest of the division came up before advancing. The forest was occupied by the Brandenstein Brigade of Festetics' IV Corps and when, at about 8:30 a.m., the now complete 7th Division hurled themselves forward in a charge from Benatek, the mostly Italian and Hungarian regiments were put to flight easily. The cheering Prussians, their commanders yelling "Vorwärts!" and other Blücherian encouragements, hurdled over the prostrate bodies of their unfortunate foes, as they chased the backs of their comrades out of the forest and into the village of Cistowes, a few hundred yards further south towards Lipa. They

The fighting on the edge of the Swiepwald. (Voss)

were now, however, in for a surprise. The village was occupied by the Appiano Brigade of III Corps, led by Archduke Ernst, a unit with more backbone than their brothers in the Brandenstein Brigade. From the surrounding woods and the village a devastating fire was poured into the Prussian ranks, not only by the infantry, but also the four batteries of 4- and 8-pounders situated in the village and on the Maslowed heights. The Austrian jägers decimated the 27th Magdeburg Regiment, killing the commander and most of his officers. The gallant charge might have been ended there and then, had not the 66th Regiment entered the fray and together they and the other four battalions pushed the Austrians out of Cistowes.

Fransecky's men flung themselves down, their chests heaving from their exertions, but they had barely begun to sort things out before the enemy's horns sounded to their front and III Corps batteries, repositioned before Maslowed, began raining shells upon them again. What they did not know was that, because of Festetics' repositioning, their single division was facing the better part of three Austrian corps comprising 46 battalions of infantry, plus the attendant guns. Now Festetics, angered by the destruction of his Brandenstein Brigade, had ordered two more brigades to advance into the Swiepwald as the artillery bombardment intensified. Suddenly Prussian counter-battery fire bracketed his own position and the resulting explosions killed his chief of staff and tore off Festetics' foot. Field Marshal Mollinary, with as much zeal as his boss, took over the command of IV Corps and urged the Fleischhacker and Poeckh brigades forward with their bands playing and colours flying.

Like a grey tide, the Austrian battalions, in columns, streamed into the wood to the strains of the *Radetzky Marsch* and the *Kaiserhymne.* Their eyes glistened, not only with fear, but the effects of a double ration of schnapps as they surged forward to certain death because their commanders had forgotten the lessons learned so recently on the banks of the Aupa and Cidlina rivers. Fransecky's battalions were waiting for them and must have marvelled at the sight briefly before they pulled their triggers and began the slaughter. The Hapsburg troops fell as if cut by a scythe, but they came on, clambering over their fallen comrades and levelling their bayonets for the kill. At this moment, the sights and the sounds in the Swiepwald must have been at their most horrific with smoke swirling around in the steady rain, shrapnel and bullets cutting the air and ricocheting off the tree trunks. Explosions cracked against trees causing limbs and splinters to cartwheel through the air, striking bodies with no regard to friend or foe, and the shrieks and cries of men locked in mortal combat blended weirdly with the music of the bands, now more subdued as bullets found musicians just as easily as riflemen.

Courage was not lacking on either side, as the fight began to descend into local struggles. Men on each side contested small clearings or clumps of bushes, often to the last man, but despite the carnage wrought by the needle gun on their ranks the Austrians, by sheer weight of numbers, pushed the Prussians further back toward the edge of the wood, and out of the village of Cistowes. Mollinary had persuaded Count Thun to commit II Corps to the battle, and his leading brigades were already arriving on the scene. At about midday, Fransecky was just reading a message from the king, denying reinforcements for his hard-pressed division. He knew he had to hold his position until the arrival of the crown prince with the Second Army. But where was the crown prince? His casualties mounting and his options diminishing, Fransecky well understood that if his division collapsed, the Prussian left wing would be snapped off, offering the Austrians an opportunity to outflank the First Army. So, grimly determined to hold at all costs, he urged his dwindling band of men to stand.

The battle on the Prussian right wing

Prince Albert of Saxony had reconnoitred his area of command on the afternoon of 2 July. His orders had been to place his Saxon Corps upon the heights overlooking the Bistritz, by the villages of Popowitz and Tresowitz. He correctly

The Austrians try to retake the Swiepwald. (Voss)

surmised that if the Prussians came in force across the bridge at Nechanitz, a large village at a southerly turn of the river, he would not be able to react quickly enough to prevent them enveloping his wing. He sent an officer from his staff to ask the feldzeugmeister if he could pull them back to the Problus–Prim line, where he could more effectively deal with the threat. Benedek accepted Prince Albert's judgement without question, and the change had a significant effect on the ensuing battle.

Herwarth von Bittenfeld's Army of the Elbe, three divisions strong, began its move across the river at 8:30 a.m., led by the advance guard. These were the fusiliers of the 28th Regiment, who attacked Nechanitz in the centre, where the retreating Saxon pioneers had attempted to fire the bridge. The Prussians dealt with this by dumping their field kettles on the flames and throwing torn-up boards, doors, and gates across the charred gaps. Their comrades in the 33rd and 17th regiments had taken the villages of Lubno and Hradek on each flank and linked up with the 28th across the river. Despite these ferocious assaults from the veterans of Hühnerwässer and Münchengrätz, the Saxons were able to make a fighting withdrawal in good order to Prim and Problus. Since the only supporting cavalry were the squadrons of the 7th Hussars, there was little additional offensive pressure that the Prussians could bring to bear, especially when General Edelsheim, one of Benedek's most competent cavalry commanders, was hovering nearby with his light cavalry division.

The Saxon and Austrian batteries now poured down heavy fire upon the Prussian advance guard, who took up positions along the Lubno–Hradek ridge to await reinforcements. But Herwarth von Bittenfeld, the most unsuitable of Moltke's army commanders, was not an aggressive general, and held back his reserves as he feared a Prussian collapse in the centre would leave him exposed. Even though he requested, and obtained, a large portion of Alvensleben's reserve cavalry, he failed to use them and for nearly four hours, left his forward troops to suffer. These brave men attempted to take the woods below Prim, but were repulsed with heavy losses. The 15th and 14th divisions did finally cross the repaired bridge at Nechanitz, the latter well after 11:00 a.m., but were forced to lie down in the pouring rain and wait for the bombardment to let up before further advances could be made. Given Herwarth von Bittenfeld's hesitance, and the Saxon stubbornness, this would not happen until nearly 3:00 p.m.

An astute observer on the heights of the Roskosberg at about midday might have judged the mood of the king and his entourage matched the damp and gloomy weather that hung upon the fields, woods, and villages that lay before them. That smoky gloom was constantly punctured by flashes and bursts of shot and shell that revealed the intensity of the fighting. The fires from blazing villages pierced the darkened depths of the valley and whenever the black smoke cleared, there could be seen thousands of blue and grey bodies of men whose days as farmhands, carpenters, or shop-workers were now over. The king's face showed troubled concern as he squinted through his glass to see any signs of progress, or the arrival of the crown prince. His nephew was also worried about the First Army, which he feared would break soon if the Austrian pressure was not lifted.

Perhaps Moltke, sniffing and dabbing his nose with the red handkerchief that remained in his hand all day, was still confident. He had, after all been the one who had strongly urged the king not to send reinforcements to Fransecky. "I must seriously advise Your Majesty to send not one single man of Infantry to support

General Fransecky," he had said, adding, "We must watch for an Austrian offensive which will be beaten off as long as we have III Army Corps in reserve." He further assured his Sovereign: "Fransecky will stand, I know him."

However, Fransecky was not at all sure he could stand. Mollinary was about to send two more fresh brigades from Thun's II Corps into the Swiepwald, having ignored a direction from Benedek to return to his former position. The feldzeugmeister had received a disturbing message that the Prussian Second Army was approaching, so he was torn between allowing Mollinary to finish off Fransecky, which had the chance of turning the Prussian Left, or shifting those forces to meet the growing threat from the north. As usual, he made no decision.

For the Prussians, the most serious peril lay in the centre in that other forest of horror, the Holawald. The early afternoon had brought serious questions of withdrawal but Lieutenant General Albrecht Gustav von Manstein of III Army Corps was determined to, at least, commit his final reserves before making any rash determinations. Not so his brother commander of II Army Corps, Major-General von Schmidt who was, by all accounts, close to a nervous breakdown. The scene on this front was much the same as in the Swiepwald and the murderous artillery fire was taking a similar toll.

To many upon the Roskosberg that bleak afternoon, the tide seemed to be turning against them. For Count Bismarck, the thought was unbearable, and he, more than any, knew what a defeat, or even a stalemate here would mean to the future of Prussia and, needless to say, to himself. So, it was with more than a little apprehension that he frequently scanned the ridges across the Bistritz with his telescope. It was upon one of these scans, that he saw what seemed to be a line of trees moving, with Austrian guns shelling them. This ridge was a prominent one on the battlefield, dominated by what looked like an enormous tree (but was in fact two smaller ones), and remained a feature remembered by many on that fateful day. Bismarck mentioned his observation to Moltke, who immediately trained his own glass upon the ridge. Without saying a word, Moltke rode over to the king, and in his usual deadpan manner said "The campaign is decided, and in accordance with Your Majesty's wishes." If it had been a hot sunny day, the king would have imagined his chief of staff was suffering from sunstroke, and his immediate comment suggested that. However, Moltke persisted "The success is complete Sire, Vienna lies at your feet."[1] It would be a while yet before most of the officers on that hill were actually convinced that the crown prince had, in fact, arrived on the battlefield.

The Second Army joins the fight

When, at about 4:00 a.m. that morning, the brave Count Finckenstein had delivered Moltke's message ordering the advance of the Second Army against the Austrian flank, the crown prince and his chief of staff hastily drew up the necessary marching orders. By 7:00 a.m., the troops were beginning to stow their valises and non-essential gear in the wagons (which would remain in Königinhof until after the battle). Although their troops were less than twelve miles or so from their objective, even a mid-19th-century army could move at little more than three miles per hour, and it was after 8:00 a.m. that most of the army was on the move. Like their counterparts in the First Army, they had to contend with driving rain and muddy, slick tracks on their line of march, much of it worsened by the Austrians in retreat. Artillery and ammunition columns were badly delayed with their wheels becoming entangled in the barleycorn stalks, often having to be hacked away by swords and pick-axes.

For the crown prince and Blumenthal, the issue of how and where they would come into contact with the enemy was somewhat moot. They had no idea of who they were up against: the whole of Benedek's army or part of it? Should they move to shore up the First Army's left wing, or should they get behind the enemy by staying close to the Elbe? In many ways, neither man actually expected to fight that day. They shared the opinion of a number of their adversaries that this was unlikely to be a one-day affair. However, there was no lack of urgency, for between 8:30 a.m. and 9:00 a.m., they could hear the constant rumble of artillery fire in the distance before them.

The commander of the forward elements of the Guard Corps, Major-General Konstantin von Alvensleben, had received an urgent dispatch at about 9:00 a.m. requesting assistance to the hard-pressed 7th Division of General Fransecky. His troops had been encamped forward of the main army at Dobrowitz, so he immediately pushed his 2nd Guard Brigade rapidly toward the village of Jericek and the Prussian left flank. This response rippled through the Second Army and especially the reserve artillery, under Colonel Kraft zu Hohenlohe-Ingelfingen, who got his batteries on the move behind the 1st Guard Division. Unsurprisingly (for many), the only element that was not imbued with this sense of urgency was Bonin's 1st Army Corps, which left its bivouacs long after 9:00 a.m. and were not completely on the march until about 11:00 a.m.

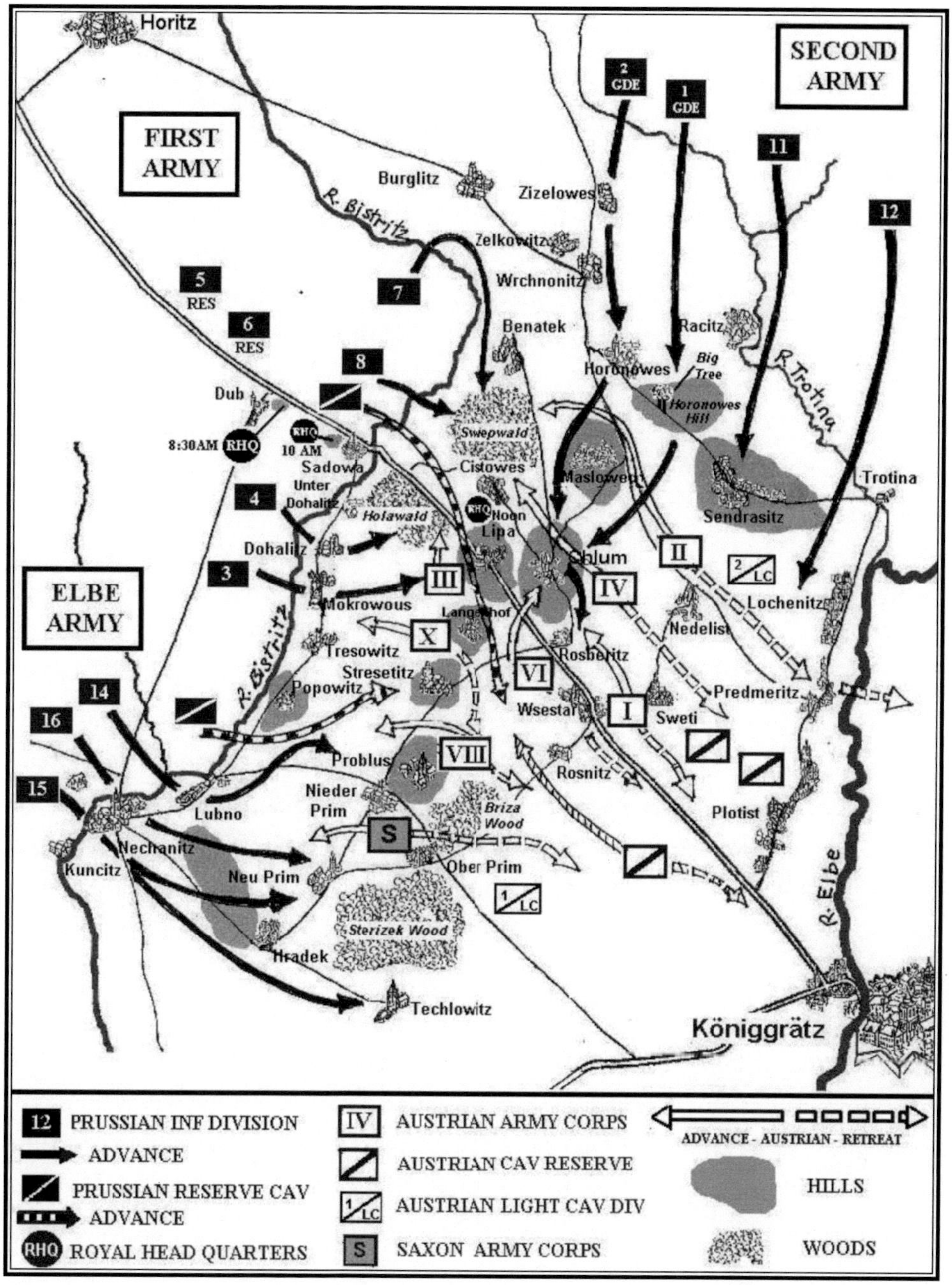

The weather continued to be a major problem and certainly helped to delay the advance of the crown prince. However, the closer they got to the actual fighting, the more it began to dawn on the Second Army staff that this was no rearguard action. At about 10:00 a.m., Prince Frederick William and his chief of staff agreed that this was not only a major battle, but the decisive one. At about this time, the reserve artillery commander, Hohenlohe-Ingelfingen, had managed to overtake the 1st Guards with his guns, and paused at Chotoborek to assess the situation. As he surveyed the fire of Austrian batteries before him, the crown prince rode up and quickly ordered him to focus his attention on the "big tree" on top of the ridge by Horonowes. He told him to keep the tree on his right and, "Bang away smartly!" in order that his cousin would know he was on the field.

By 11:30 a.m., portions of the Second Army were making themselves felt on the Austrian right wing. Part of the 2nd Guard Regiment and Guard Jägers were already at Benatek, although they were halted and redirected east to be in line with Alvensleben's advanced guard. On the far left flank, the Silesians of General Louis von Mutius' VI Corps were marching down the right bank of the Elbe from Josephstadt (no longer deemed a threat), toward the Trotina River and the village of Lochenitz beyond. In the centre, the artillery duel was an unequal affair. The Austrian batteries had changed front as soon as Hohenlohe had opened fire from Jericek, and their superior guns and gunnery were taking their toll on the Prussians. However, Hohenlohe had skilfully used his mobility to move his guns around, so as not to be completely destroyed. It was infantry fire that became the Hapsburg gunners' downfall: without Thun's II Corps where it should have been, they were without infantry support of their own and gradually their guns began to fall silent as the Prussian needle guns felled their crews, forcing the remainder to limber up and retire. Urged on by their crown prince, the Guards swept past the big tree and fell on the village of Horonowes beyond. Fransecky's relief was now assured.

Until this moment, Feldzeugmeister Benedek had been assuring himself that the battle was going his way. He might have even entertained the thought that the insubordination of Festetics and Mollinary was becoming an advantage, especially if it led to the demise of the Prussian left wing. However, he needed to make a decision immediately: whatever the merits of Mollinary's move, if it were to have any effect it must be now, before the Prussian Second Army appeared. An all-out assault using the vast Austrian reserve and cavalry might just turn the tide in time to allow II and IV Corps to wheel right and take on the crown prince. At this critical juncture, Benedek permitted events to override his decision-making process once more. This may have been the most fatal in the long catalogue of errors made by the Austrian commander since the day he took over North Army. Baumgarten was aghast at the situation but was powerless to influence events and

The Prussian 22nd Regiment advances on Trotina, 3 July 1866. (Voss)

his predecessor, Henikstein, and the deposed Krismanic, although present, had nothing to contribute. The news of the appearance of the Second Army at about noon therefore, forced Benedek to return to his original plan. He ordered Mollinary to extricate II and IV Corps from the Swiepwald battle, and move to face the Prussian assault on the right wing. Even on a parade ground it is not easy to turn twenty or thirty battalions on a sixpence, to face another way: In the full heat of battle, with casualties mounting, morale dropping and recalcitrant commanders in charge, it is almost impossible. The result would be more catastrophic than the Austrian leader had feared. Even as he and his staff were digesting the current situation, at about 1:30 p.m., a messenger brought news of a disaster developing on the left wing.

The collapse of the Austrian left

Crown Prince Albert of Saxony had not only held back the Army of the Elbe for the best part of the morning and early afternoon, but with a local counter-attack at about 11:30 a.m., pushed them out of the forest by Neder-Prim, and almost back to Nechanitz. He therefore decided to advance his Saxon brigades against the junction of the Prussian 14th and 15th divisions before they could fully connect. He requested assistance from General Weber's Austrian VIII Corps with two brigades of infantry to his right and Edelsheim's light cavalry to support the Saxon cavalry brigade and horse artillery in the centre. Soon after 1:00 p.m., in a state of high optimism, he began his descent from Ober-Prim toward Hradek with the Saxon Life Brigade in the van, their green and white colours flapping in the wind, and bands playing. But his plan was to run into trouble almost immediately.

The 68th Regiment outflanks the Austrians and Saxons at Ober-Prim, 3 July 1866. (Voss)

At the same time that the Saxon crown prince had decided to renew his offensive, Herwarth von Bittenfeld had received a dispatch from Moltke, advising him of the arrival of the Second Army on the battlefield, and stressing the importance of an immediate advance by the Army of the Elbe against the Austrian left. Herwarth von Bittenfeld immediately ordered the commander of the 15th Division, Lieutenant General Philip Karl Frieherr von Canstein, to develop an attack in accordance with these instructions. Canstein sent his 29th and 30th brigades right round the Austrian left, toward Hradek and the Stezirek wood, to take them in the flank. The 30th Brigade, led by the 28th Regiment, performed its task with great efficiency, and surprised the Austrian Schulz Brigade which, completely demoralized by the ferocity of the Prussian attack and the hailstorm of needle-gun bullets, ran for their lives. As they did so they ran headlong into their Saxon allies who, despite a great degree of discipline, were unable to continue their attack. This disruption was not the only effect on the Saxon push. The collapse of the Schulz Brigade was followed by the disintegration of the remaining Austrian troops who, desperately trying to reorganize themselves, were felled in their hundreds by the rapid rifle fire of the Prussians. The Saxons frantically attempted to restore their front, but to no avail as the 29th Prussian Brigade was already nagging at their other flank by Neder Prim. Prince Albert now ordered a retreat, which the Saxons performed with courage and discipline. At the same time, Herwarth von Bittenfeld dispatched the 14th Division across the Bistritz, at Nechanitz, toward Problus. As the artillery of this division began to bombard their right wing, the Saxons and the remains of VIII

Corps began to pull back to a line anchored on the Briza wood, behind Ober Prim. He also sent his cavalry round behind Stezirek wood to harry the Prussian infantry, but without Edelsheim's light cavalry, now being used to cover the retreat of VIII Corps, there was little they could do. Any doubts that Prince Albert may have had that his order was necessary were eliminated when he was informed that the Austrian X Corps on his right near Langenhof had also begun to retire.

Here now was a chance for the ancient Herwarth von Bittenfeld to cover himself with glory and roll up Benedek's North Army from its left flank. However, his front-line troops were exhausted, and he had failed to bring up the 16th Division and Alvensleben's cavalry reserve, for which he had begged earlier, and which he could have used to pursue the retreating Saxons. So the wary old man chose to sit upon his laurels for the time being and leave the decisive blow to someone else.

Chlum and the breaking of the Austrian right

One can only imagine the confusion and disappointment of the ordinary soldiers of the Austrian IV and II Army Corps. In the bloody maelstrom that was the Swiepwald, they had suffered staggering casualties from the dreaded needle gun. Their sacrifices had appeared to be paying off as their commanders promised them that one more attack, one last effort, would succeed in shattering the Prussian left wing, causing it to collapse like a pack of cards. Now they were pulling back, before finishing their job. They were retreating to face a third Prussian Army, which was attacking from the north. They had had no idea there even was a third army and as they stumbled back to reorganize a new front between Maslowed and Horonowes, their morale disintegrated completely. The rain was letting up and a pale sunlight was struggling to emerge as, down the misty hills and valleys, like a pack of hungry wolves, the army of the Prussian crown prince descended on them with a fury.

The divisions of Frederick William's army had been advancing on a wide front, hinged upon Alvensleben's advanced guard at Horonowes, with the intention of slamming the door shut on an Austrian escape. To the left of Alvensleben was the 11th Division under the command of Lieutenant-General Alexander Freidrich von Zastrow, whose immediate objective was Nedelist. On the left wing was Lieutenant-General Conrad Wilhelm Prondzynski's 12th Division, which had just crossed the Trotina River and was making its way to Lochenitz. The resistance they encountered was minimal, as the Austrian redeployment had yet to stabilize, and given the relentless Prussian advance, it is unlikely it ever would do so sufficiently to stem the tide.

At Horonowes, the Guards had paused to take a breath, but despite orders not to do so, the commander of the 1st Guards Division, Lieutenant-General Hiller von Gartringen[2] moved his troops through Alvensleben's, and began an advance on Chlum. Quickly moving through the now quieter Sweipwald and village of Cistowes, the Guards' battalions ran into heavy artillery fire from the heights, and it was down to Hohenlohe and his reserve batteries to come to the rescue again, as the Guard artillery had not yet come up. Although severely outgunned, Hohenlohe-Ingelfingen once more shifted his gun positions frequently, to reduce the Austrian effectiveness. This action allowed the 1st Guards Brigade to advance up the heights with only token casualties, and as their drummers beat the time the first elements of the 1st and 3rd Foot Guards regiments crested the hill.

In the village of Chlum itself, where, because of the hill, the only visible building was the church spire, just a single Austrian battalion had been posted. They were Hungarians of the Appiano Brigade and characteristically, they were stunned at the sight of Prussian troops in their midst. Their commanding officer was so confused that he insisted they were Saxons! The firefight in the village was brief and devastating, and despite exhortations and threats from their officers, the Hungarians fled in every direction. Now in possession of Chlum, however, the Guards faced the rest of the Appiano Brigade, which the commander had feverishly deployed as best he could. The brigade was in a chaotic situation; not only was it being decimated by the needle guns of the Guards who had taken good cover on the edge of the village, but they were bowled over by fleeing Austrian hussars who were wildly evading similar gunfire from the Prussian Guard Jäger. The Appiano

The fight for the churchyard at Chlum, 3 July 1866. (Voss)

Brigade was now joined by what was left of its sister 4th Brigade, of III Corps. Although much cut up in the Holawald earlier in the day, the 4th Brigade now fought with great ferocity, including an unexpected bayonet charge which pinned the Prussians to the southern edge of Chlum. The tide quickly turned back, however, and this courageous brigade crumbled as volley after volley slammed into them. Of all the valiant last stands that day, the sacrifice of the Horse Battery of III Corps Reserve is the most notable. Having moved their guns forward to within 150 yards of the village, to prevent further Prussian advances and cover the retreat of their comrades, they began to bombard the enemy positions. It was a suicidal move. Their rate of fire could not match the Prussian breech-loading rifle and they fell like ninepins, as they steadfastly worked their guns. Within five minutes the battery was silent. A monument now marks the spot where these gallant gunners perished, known as the Battery of the Dead.

Benedek was still on the Lipa heights when a staff officer galloped up announcing the loss of Chlum. The feldzeugmeister was thunderstruck and immediately ordered Baumgarten to investigate, but before the chief of staff could move, Benedek spurred his own horse in the direction of Chlum and, followed by his staff, galloped off. As they neared the village, the news was confirmed when they had to force their horses through fleeing soldiers. In an act of desperation, Benedek put himself at the head of the 52nd Regiment, to retake Chlum. In spite of his reckless bravery, the charge foundered quickly. Colonel Neuber, an aide, took Benedek by the arm and led him back to the waiting staff and together they galloped away. Ironically, as they rode down the hill they were mistaken for Prussian cavalry and fired at by their own troops. Several staff officers were dismounted, and one was killed. For Benedek, as he glanced behind him at the flaming ruins of Chlum, he knew that any hope of restoring the situation had passed. Defeat was now inevitable and he must soon get Ramming's reserve in action to prevent a rout.

Ramming's counter-attack on Rosberitz and Chlum

It was now about 3:00 p.m., and the 1st Guards Brigade was joined by the 2nd. They began, with their comrades in the 11th and 12th divisions, to consolidate the position between Chlum and Lochenitz. As the assault on Chlum was in progress, a few companies of the Guard Fusiliers had bypassed them, and pushed on to Rosberitz village on the Sadowa–Königgrätz Road. As the Austrian counter-attacks had developed, the fusiliers had become more isolated in their salient position, and found it more difficult to defend. Ramming had been in possession of Benedek's order to attack the Prussian positions at Chlum and Rosberitz for a critical fifteen minutes before he took any action. Even then, he ordered a bombardment of the Guards in these two villages by 120 guns, which more than keeping their heads down, enabled them to prepare for the attack to come. Prince Hohenlohe was back in the picture with his batteries again, but for once, was less effective with his tactics of shifting positions when some of his gun teams overreached themselves and suffered for their mistake.

At about 3:30 p.m., Ramming unleashed his assault, beginning with Rosberitz. It was led by his 3rd Brigade which included the elite 4th Regiment, the ancient and celebrated "*Hoch und Deutschmeister*" from Vienna. As they advanced, the fusiliers in the village were joined by a battalion of the 2nd Guards Regiment, which took cover behind every pile of rubble, every shattered window, and every low wall they could find in the burning hamlet. The volley they let forth shattered the front companies of the Deutschmeisters' formation, but they still came on. Fortunately for the Prussians, a Ukrainian regiment to the Deutschmeisters' left disintegrated after receiving a similar volley, but the Viennese drove on into the village, despite their

Austrians fighting their guns to the barrel at Chlum, 3 July 1866. (Voss)

The Battery of the Dead. (Voss)

casualties and soon the fight for Rosberitz became as vicious as that in the Swiepwald. After a half hour's fighting, the Prussians were forced from the village. Their retreat was covered by the 3rd Foot Guards, who had come up in time to share the casualties, but enabled the survivors of the attack to make an orderly extraction as well as allowing the fusiliers to save their colours from Austrian capture.

Now Ramming sent in the final reserves of VI Corps. Later he was to say that his actions saved the army, but at the time, he was desperately trying to restore the front and prevent a further Prussian advance, in hopes of turning the battle around. For the next 45 minutes, battalion after battalion of Austrian infantry sacrificed themselves against the constant stream of fire from the needle guns in the hands of the Prussian infantry in Chlum. As each column reached the front, they dissolved into writhing grey masses, with the survivors streaming to the rear, abandoning their equipment, and making for the road to Königgrätz and safety. Ramming led one charge himself, miraculously coming through unscathed and still mounted.

Elsewhere on the battlefield, the general collapse of Austrian fortunes was everywhere evident. As the rapid advance of the Prussian Second Army accelerated, the remnants of Count Thun's II Corps, last seen in the Swiepwald learning lessons from the needle gun which they would wish to forget, spread out to defend the Austrian right wing. Joining them were a fresh infantry brigade and the Taxis Cavalry Brigade, but instead of even attempting to stem the Prussian advance on Nedelist and Lochenitz, Thun simply marched his corps of 25,000 men across the Elbe at Predmeritz and out of the battle. In any other army his action would have been deemed an act of cowardice of the grossest kind.

By 4:00 p.m., the Saxons and the Austrian VIII Corps were in full retreat from Problus. In the centre, King William had ordered a general advance at about 3:30 p.m., and the bruised but unbowed battalions of Fransecky and Horn were finally on their way forward from the holocaust that was the Swiepwald and Holawald, followed by the reserve 5th and 6th divisions. Before them Gablenz and his X Corps simply melted away, joining the thousands of Austrian troops struggling to depart the battle. The roads to Königgrätz and the Elbe were now clogged with disbanded and leaderless units, hopelessly entangled despite frantic efforts by officers of all ranks to instil some semblance of order, but all relentlessly heading for salvation. Although Rosberitz remained clear of Prussian troops, Ramming's attempt to retake

Prussian Guards defend the village of Rosberitz, 3 July 1866. (Voss)

Chlum was flagging, and much of his fine army corps lay in heaps before the village defence lines. It was now that Benedek sent orders to Gondrecourt to attack Chlum with his I Army Corps. The order itself was characteristically confusing as it had been crossed out once and rewritten illegibly. As usual, both the timing and the objective revealed the feldzeugmeister's failure to grasp the course of events. Had he coordinated Gondrecourt's attack with Ramming's, and made a concentric assault on Chlum and Rosberitz, they would have had a fairer chance of throwing the Prussians out of both villages, and restoring the centre. Now, however, with Ramming's corps decimated, there was little chance of achieving anything. But, with their bands playing, the brigades of Poschacher, Leiningen, and Ringelsheim shouldered their Lorenz rifles, formed column and began their ascent to Chlum. It must have been an extraordinary experience because, if they glanced down the hill to their left, they would have seen masses of their comrades fleeing in the opposite direction, along the main road toward the Elbe.

Fransecky's 7th Division finally retakes the Swiepwald, 3 July 1866. (Voss)

The final throes: the battle lost and the flight across the Elbe

Half an hour after the king had given the general advance order on the Roskosberg, the Royal Headquarters arrived on the heights of Lipa. From this vantage point they could view almost the whole battlefield, which was now more visible as the rain had stopped, and the sky was clearing. As Moltke surveyed the field with the rest of the field, he must have felt a deep satisfaction as he watched his army advance toward the southeast. It is often curious to the modern student of Prussian military history to imagine the constraints placed on this architect of the victory. His desires, however urgent, often had to be sent as suggestions or advice through the king, or the princely army commanders, to be turned into orders. His direct countermanding of one of Frederick Charles' orders, to the reserve corps commander General Manstein, was greeted with "And who is General Moltke?"! The prince now placed himself at the head of his cavalry reserve, and led them toward Wsestar, on the Königgrätz road, hoping to cut off the retreating Austrians and strike the final coup-de-grâce.

After riding away from Chlum, Benedek had been galloping around the battlefield, which was now shrinking rapidly, trying to rally troops, and giving orders left and right. The staff following him on these almost mindless dashes were also dwindling as they carried off his orders or found urgent tasks to perform, often in the direction of Königgrätz. At times, Benedek was seen struggling, almost being borne along by the crowd on the main road. He would gesticulate and threaten, then spur his horse with difficulty out of the throng. At one stage, he confronted a squadron of cuirassiers as they tried to escape, and almost convinced them to turn around when a shell burst on their flank, beheading their commanding officer. Benedek burst into tears as they gave him no further heed, and fled off the battlefield. There was speculation, then and now, that he himself was searching for a bullet. Again, however, events overtook him, as it appeared that Gondrecourt's last frantic assault was failing.

Although it was fully accepted that his was a holding action to allow some order to the Austrian retreat, Gondrecourt's brigades, who had distinguished themselves in the recent war against Denmark, boldly stormed up the heights of Chlum. The result was now predictable. First Poschacher's "Iron" Brigade disappeared into the storm of the Prussian fusillade, which as the smoke cleared, became a confused mass of the dead, the dying and the captured, with the remainder wild eyed and racing for the rear. The same fate awaited the two other brigades, as, after only a few volleys, they tumbled down the hill en masse, their survivors doffing their equipment and skipping to join their comrades in the great retreat. The Piret Brigade of I Corps had been sent by Benedek to stem the advance of the Army of the Elbe from Problus, on the left. Despite awful casualties, they had in fact forced the leading elements of Herwarth von Bittenfeld's army to go to ground momentarily, thus relieving the pressure on the south side of the road. Chlum was now once again safely in Prussian hands, and as the victorious Guardsmen gathered in their prisoners, their officers paused to smoke cigars and congratulate themselves. At this moment of triumph, Hiller von Gartringen, the man whose insubordination had got them here, was struck down and killed by a shell burst.

Amazingly, it was only at this time that the headquarters of the Second Army caught up with events. So swift had been the Prussian advance that the crown prince had remained mostly in the dark about the battle's progress. Now staff officers and runners began to arrive at Maslowed with news of the success at Chlum, and Frederick William knew that the field was theirs and the battle won. Their anxiety was relieved, and the prince may have reflected that he had indeed played the part of Blücher at Waterloo.

Prince Albert and the Saxon Army prepare to leave the battlefield.

At the same time as the final assault on Chlum collapsed, the last dramatic action of the battle drew to a close on the plains between Stresetitz and Rosnitz. It must be said here that neither the Austrian or Prussian cavalry arms were put to effective use during the battle. The bulk of the Prussian reserve cavalry had only crossed the Bistritz at about 4:00 p.m., and the Second Army's cavalry division had "disappeared" for almost four hours.[3] Now that their moment had come, it was too late to have much effect on the outcome of the battle. The Prussian cavalry, even if unopposed, could have done little but harry the retreating army. The Austrians could have done some handy work on the Saxon flank, and possibly wrecked Herwarth von Bittenfeld's tentative progress. Now, however, they could slow down a Prussian pursuit and they were to use their cavalry arm more skilfully than their enemy.

The first elements of Frederick Charles' cavalry, led by Major-General Georg Reinhold Count von der Groeben, had spread out between Langenhof and Rosberitz, and were busy getting amongst the Austrian infantry and artillery, who were trying to pull out of Rosberitz. Suddenly, as the 3rd Dragoons and the 12th Hussars neared Wsestar, they collided with the Austrian Reserve Cavalry Division of Lieutenant-Field Marshal Wilhelm, prince of Schleswig-Holstein. The 3rd Dragoons were easily put to flight, and the 12th Hussars pushed back almost to Langenhof. All might have met total disaster, without the arrival of three squadrons of uhlans. As the remaining squadrons of Holstein's other brigade approached Langenhof, they came under fire from Prussian artillery and infantry, followed by a charge of the remaining cavalry from Groeben's division. In the melée that ensued, the stronger Austrian formations were able to extricate themselves but, perhaps infected by the panic all around them, galloped wildly toward Rosnitz, trampling a field hospital as they fled.

It was now the turn of Major-General Karl Maria, Count Coudenove, and his division of 25 squadrons, to advance on Stresetitz. This was the action witnessed by observers on the hill at Lipa, and history has endowed it with many more romantic superlatives than it deserves. As they advanced at the trot near the eastern edge of Stresetitz village, they encountered the three fugitive squadrons of 3rd Dragoons, who had galloped south after their brush with Holstein's cavalry. The fight was predictably unequal, and the 3rd Dragoons suffered the largest loss of any Prussian cavalry that day. Coudenove, however, was not finished, and moved toward a mass of cavalry from Alvensleben's reserve, "lent" to the Army of the Elbe. They had just crossed the Elbe, and were unready when Coudenove's squadrons smashed into them. In the short but vicious bout of hacking and slashing that ensued, the Austrians got the better of the Prussians, As with almost every Austrian–Prussian clash of the war, though, the infantry and artillery of the Prussian army intervened, with devastating fire from Problus, Langenhof, and Stresetitz, and the effect was shattering. The Hapsburg cuirassiers and uhlan regiments whirled around, and began leaving the field. If the initial advance had not quite been a charge, their flight definitely was. The cornfields around them were littered with dead and wounded and as the sound of the horscs' hooves reached the frightened men, a low moan rose across the stricken field. The men made pathetic efforts by waving strips of cloth to warn off the panicked horsemen but it was all in vain and the moan became a shriek as the squadrons thundered through towards Königgrätz.

By now, the last of the survivors from Gondrecourt's I Corps had left the Chlum heights and joined the river of refugees heading for the Elbe crossings. By 5:00 p.m., Benedek had not one single effective infantry or cavalry formation. As he watched his shattered army stream by, he turned once more to the only arm that was worthy of any credit that day: the artillery. He bade the commander of his reserve artillery, Lieutenant-Colonel Hofbauer, cover his retreat. Hofbauer promised that he would work his guns to the last man, which he did. He poured fire onto the advancing Prussian infantry and did, for a little while, hold them back.

The scenes at the Elbe crossings by the fortress of Königgrätz were forever etched on the memories of those that witnessed, or participated in the retreat. The commander of the garrison had closed the gates of the city fearing a Prussian assault. Now, between fifty thousand and sixty thousand terrified troops swirled around the walls, convinced that the Prussian army would appear at any minute and complete the slaughter. At the actual crossings there was pandemonium; wagons and caissons blocking the bridges were turned over with their drivers; men swarmed into the river down its muddy banks, and many were drowned by the weight of their equipment. Many tried to grab the stirrups of cavalrymen fording across, and were often hacked off. To add insult to injury, the garrison commander ordered the sluice gates of the city opened to raise the water level causing even more men to drown. But the Prussian threat never materialized, and later that night, the garrison commander opened the gates. As Benedek and a few staff officers crossed the Elbe a mile south of the fortress at about 6:30 p.m. (oblivious to the chaos around the walls of

Königgrätz), they could hear the guns of Hofbauer's batteries doing their work. They would not be silenced until well into the night.

As all three Prussian armies finally converged on the plain where the cavalry fights had taken place, just an hour earlier, it became evident that the victory was something less than a Cannae. A large portion of the Austrian Army – nearly 180,000 men – had escaped across the Elbe, and most of the Prussian high command had no idea that it was nothing more than a rabble, without a single effective unit. However, the enthusiasm for pursuit was tempered by the fact that the Prussian armies themselves were disorganized, and, at the moment, somewhat unmanageable. So, as the Austrian guns before the Elbe barked their final defiance, the corps and regimental commanders tried to bring some order to their units, amid a general air of congratulation and relief. At about 6:30 p.m., Moltke had decided that a general pursuit within the next 24 hours was impractical. He surmised, correctly, that Benedek's army would not be an effective fighting force any time soon, and that the road to Vienna would remain open. He therefore directed that the morrow would be a day of rest, and gave various

Prussian Uhlan Regiment No. 11 charges the Austrian cavalry on the plain of Stretetitz, 3 July 1866. (Voss)

dispositions and marching orders for 5 July. Accommodations had been made for the king and his staff at Horitz, and as they made their way back during the twilight, a light drizzle began.

For the rest of the exhausted soldiers, accommodations were less formal. They began to make their bivouac in the fields between the villages. Around them the wounded lay in their thousands, many of them continuing to cry out for help. Prussian stretcher-bearer units would work through the night and into the following morning to bring them to the improvised dressing stations in the buildings that remained standing in the villages. The dead would remain where they lay for another 12 hours. There were no Austrian hospital orderlies as, without the protection of the Red Cross, they had retreated with the rest of the army. In addition to Prussian doctors were the Knights of St John who, with their own nurses plus wagons and equipment, were of valuable assistance.

King William is cheered by his troops toward the close of the battle.

Victory!

As the sounds of battle died away, and the gathering dusk spread across the plain, the victorious soldiers settled down around their campfires and lit their pipes, most marvelling at their luck in pulling through unscathed. The regimental bands entertained them with victory marches and tunes while the glow from the burning villages still played upon the scene. Presently, after the bugles sounded the evening call, echoing over the fields could be heard the strains of the old German hymn, *Now Thank We All Our God.*

NOTES

1. Gordon Craig. *The battle of Koniggrätz*, Ch. 6; the Official History.
2. Hiller was unfortunately hit by a shell splinter that dismounted him. He died before he could receive medical attention.
3. Major-General von Blumenthal was horrified at the mishandling of the cavalry reserve. "Of the cavalry division almost nothing on earth was to be seen. It could have disappeared into the earth". Later, "I comforted myself with the reflection that it would turn up somewhere, however nothing was seen of it again".

CHAPTER SIX

The Final Weeks of the War

After the battle

The following morning dawned somewhat gloomily, as there was still occasional drizzle, and the mist lay fairly heavy. There was a promise of brightness to come, however, as the sky began to lighten on the horizon in the west. The Prussian soldiers on the field had either slept soundly or lain awake, listening to the sounds of agony around them. Already, as they stoked their campfires and ate what little rations they could find, the ghastly task of burying the dead had begun. Burial parties were drawn mostly from the Austrian prisoners and the reserve battalions which had crossed the Bistritz late on the day of battle. Many men wandered the field looking for fallen comrades, to collect whatever mementoes they could find to send home to loved ones, and often to bury them separately from the mass graves dug by the fatigue parties. These graves were mostly unmarked save for a crude plank bearing the number of slain and the respective regiment. Officers, of course, were buried together in separate trenches. The Prussian losses, although severe, were about a quarter of those sustained by the Austro-Saxons. Prussian casualties amounted to 99 officers and 1,830 men killed, 260 officers and 6,688 men wounded, with 276 men missing. Needlessly to say, Fransecky's division had suffered the most, with over 2,000 casualties, while the Guard Corps sustained 1,338.

As the men waited for the wagons to bring up their valises and other personal gear from the rear areas, teams from the ammunition columns of the artillery were recovering what they could in the way of damaged cannon and other equipment. Remount units scoured the field for riderless horses, putting many of the poor beasts out of their misery. The Austrians had left behind over 6,000 horses, a third of which were dead, adding to the 900 horses killed on the Prussian side. Austrian and Saxon prisoners were being marched to the rear in long columns, after spending a miserable night on the field. There were over 21,000 of them and – except for the Italians, who would be soon going back to a unified country – they were apprehensive about their future. Enemy officers, as was the custom of the time, were immediately paroled and could move freely about the battlefield. Some were quartered with their Prussian captors and given writing materials so that letters could be sent home through the Austrian lines under a flag of truce. That afternoon, King William returned to the battlefield, to spend some time inspecting the troops and visiting the wounded. He also would attend funerals for some of the more senior officers who had fallen the previous day. As he and his staff proceeded, they passed a carriage occupied by a blindfolded Field Marshal Gablenz,[1] sent by Feldzeugmeister Benedek to treat with the Prussians regarding an armistice. Gablenz was directed to Moltke's headquarters in Horitz.

Benedek himself had spent the day attempting to bring some order to his retreating army. His losses in men and matériel made it impossible to contemplate any resistance, bar a skeleton rearguard. Apart from the loss of 21,000 or more unwounded prisoners-of-war, there were over 23,000 dead, wounded or missing, including nearly 1,400 Austrian and Saxon officers. Around Königgrätz itself there was still chaos. Individual soldiers, many unarmed, fruitlessly searched for their units before giving up and simply following the stream of refugees heading east. Benedek could do little more than point them in the direction of Olmütz, where they could re-form under the cover of the fortress's guns. His despair was compounded by the arrival of the foreign minister, Alexander Count Mensdorff, on 5 July, who reported a worst-case scenario back to Vienna. On the evening of that day, as Benedek prodded the demoralized remnants of North Army in three straggling columns toward Olmütz, he could hear the Prussian guns begin again, this time against the fortress of Königgrätz itself.

General Vogel von Falckenstein (1797–1885).

Moltke received Gablenz at Horitz, with extreme courtesy and promptly informed him that there could be no armistice without the agreement of Prussia's ally Italy, as the treaty signed before the war prohibited a separate peace. As the Austrian field marshal left to inform his chief of his failure to secure a truce, Moltke made his dispositions. He ordered the crown prince and the Second Army to follow Benedek toward Olmütz, and the First Army and the Army of the Elbe to proceed towards Vienna, via Brünn. Although elements of all three armies began their movements late on 5 July, it wasn't until 7 July that they were all fully on the march. In addition to this main pursuit, Moltke dispatched the Guard Landwehr Division, newly arrived in reserve, to occupy Prague and other parts of Bohemia, while the 1st Landwehr Division remained in Saxony. The guns that Benedek had heard from the other side of the Elbe had long fallen silent as an atmosphere of melancholia fell upon the battlefield by the Bistritz, where the grizzly work of the surgeons would continue for many more days. Meanwhile, a few hundred miles to the west, there was still a war going on.

The western theatre and the actions on the River Maine

The atmosphere of military incompetence that engulfed North Army in Bohemia lay just as heavily on the armies and commanders of their allies in the western theatre of the war. The mobilization of the two army corps, the 7th Bavarian and the 8th Federal, was not even complete before the Austrian defeat at Königgrätz. Prince Charles of Bavaria's feeble attempt to link up with the unfortunate Hanoverians, at Langensalza, was a portent of things to come. His belated forced march petered out near Meiningen on 30 June, just as King George's dispirited troops were getting their tickets for the express train back to Hanover. There was more hesitation before he decided to turn back and retreat to Wurzburg. He then changed his mind again. On 1 July, he decided upon a union with Austrian General Prince Alexander of Hesse, in command of the 8th Federal Corps, at the town of Fulda, forty miles or so to the west.

Charles of Bavaria.

As we have seen, the leadership of the Prussian forces arrayed against the south Germans was hardly of the first quality. Falckenstein's tardiness in pursuing the Hanoverians, and the mismanagement of the Langensalza battle by his subordinate General Flies, should have produced a windfall of opportunity for any enemy. However, given their even more inadequate opponents, fortune once more smiled upon the Prussian enterprise. The speedy capitulation of the Hanoverians had allowed Falckenstein's forces to concentrate at Eisenach and Gotha, and on 1 July, this force of three divisions was given the title of Army of the Maine. The 1st Division was commanded by Lieutenant-General Goeben, the 2nd by General Beyer, and the 3rd by General Manteuffel. On the morning of 2 July, Falckenstein began his march south to drive the Bavarians further east and so prevent any link with the 8th Federal Corps, now moving west from Frankfurt. By 3 July, Goeben's division had met Prince Charles and his Bavarians at the town of

Wiesenthal, just north of Meiningen. The short, sharp combat that followed the next day put the Bavarians in full retreat.

Although Prince Alexander of Hesse had pushed his 8th Federal Corps east from Geissen to link up with the Bavarian VII Corps, he was still struggling to bring his forces up to strength. On paper, the order of battle for this army corps included four divisions; the 1st contained the army of Württemburg, the 2nd that of Baden, the 3rd Hesse-Darmstadt, and the 4th was a combined Austrian and Nassau division, with two detached squadrons of Hesse-Cassel Hussars. The nominal strength of this corps was 49,800 men, with 134 guns, but by 27 June he had only assembled 39,000 men and 80 guns. To this was added an under-strength brigade of infantry and cavalry from Bavaria to act as a reserve. On 30 June, he received the message from Prince Charles to effect the junction with VII Corps, in Fulda, by 3 July. It was not to be. By that time, Alexander's forward patrols had run into vedettes from General Beyer's right wing of Maine Army. Late the next day, he received news of Königgrätz and the Austrian defeat. At the same time, his Bavarian cavalry reserve, sent to make contact with Prince Charles, ran into the Prussians at Hünfield, above Fulda and, in a brief skirmish, were sent packing. With the news of

Bavarian cuirassiers wade into Prussian troops at Hünfeld, 4 July 1866.

the Bavarian defeat of Wiesenthal, Alexander needed little more encouragement to turn his forces around and head back to Frankfurt.

The wedge driven by Falckenstein between Prince Alexander's VIII Corps and Prince Charles and his Bavarians, was decisive. The rest of the campaign, lasting some three weeks, consisted of a series of running skirmishes with the two disparate armies, as they retreated south of the Maine. Fights ensued with the Bavarians at Hammelburg on 10 July, and at Bad Kissingen, the celebrated spa town on the upper Saale. The ferocity of the battle there surprised the townspeople and visitors.[2] The Bavarian infantry, unlike their Austrian cousins, used their Podewils rifled muskets with good effect, and many a Prussian infantryman was taken down by their accurate fire. Bavarian leadersip, however, was not up to the task of winning battles, and they soon withdrew toward Wurzburg.

Prussian hussars and Bavarian chevaulegers battle it out at Helmstadt.

As they retreated back to Frankfurt, the VIII Corps battled with the Prussians at Laufach and Aschaffenburg where, on 13 July the Württemburg and Hessian divisions were defeated. The next day, Prince Alexander evacuated Frankfurt, along with what remained of the Germanic Diet. They headed for the ancient city of Augsburg near Munich, where they set up shop at their last official establishment, the Three Moors Inn. As they left, they declared Frankfurt an open city. On 16 July, with bands playing and colours flying, Falckenstein and his army marched down the Hanauer Landstrasse and, by the evening of that day, had established his headquarters in the city.

Prince Alexander was now south of the Maine, with the Bavarians nearing Wurzburg. The Army of the Maine, now commanded by General Manteuffel, as Falckenstein had been called away by the king to govern Bohemia, received reinforcements from the North German duchies of Oldenburg, and a reserve

The fighting in Aschaffenburg on 13 July.

division from Mecklenburg, as well as contingents from Anhalt, Waldeck, Lippe, and the Hanseatic cities. His forces now numbered over 60,000 men, and they were able to occupy Wiesbaden on 18 July. On 24 July, with the Bavarians camped on the outskirts of Wurzburg, the Prussians caught up with the 8th Federal Corps at Tauberbischofheim after a couple of brushes at Hundheim and Werbach. By that evening the south Germans were in full retreat and the next day, as they approached Wurzburg, the Bavarians were entering that city from the east after reverses at Gersheim and Helmstadt.

Mercifully, there would be no more fighting on the Maine. On 26 July, word came of an armistice, signed the previous day, between the king of Prussia and the king of Bavaria and other south German leaders. The Army of the Maine then occupied Franconia while the terms of the truce and the positions of the various states were made clear in the new German order that had been thrust upon them. In the dining room at the Three Moors Inn at Augsburg on 28 July, the last remaining ministers of the Federal Diet voted themselves out of office forever.

Italy and the close of the war

Archduke Albrecht's victory over La Marmora at Custozza on 24 June was so decisive that the Italian Army virtually disintegrated. A vigorous pursuit would have rendered the remnants of that army incapable of any action in the foreseeable future, and may have destroyed Italian dreams of total unification. Instead, Albrecht hesitated and fell back into the Quadrilateral, making his headquarters in Verona on 26 June. There he stayed for another week before venturing back to Custozza. By then, a renewed Italian Army, now under the leadership of Count Cialdini, was assembling. On 4 July, news arrived of Königgrätz, and within hours Albrecht was ordered to move with V and IX Corps of his South Army, back to defend Vienna. That same day, the Emperor Franz Joseph, in order to remove an immediate bone of contention, ceded Venetia to Napoleon III of France.

Albrecht's failure to pursue the Italians after Custozza was not in any way capitalized upon by King Victor Emmanuel and his advisors, to begin another offensive. Two weeks had passed before Cialdini had mustered his 14 divisions, including the somewhat reinvigorated troops mishandled by La Marmora at Custozza. Meanwhile, Garibaldi and his volunteers had mounted an abortive invasion of the Tyrol on 23 June, where he was still embroiled in fruitless skirmishes[3] with the better-trained Austrian Tyroler Kaiserjäger when Cialdini began his pursuit on 7 July. It would be another two weeks until Cialdini even reached Udine, where he was forced to halt with massive supply problems.

Further south, another disaster had befallen Italian fortunes. Its much-vaunted fleet had been confidently prepared for operations against Austrian assets since early in the war. However, after hearing of the battle of Custozza, Admiral

The Austrians charge at the battle of Custozza, 24 June 1866.

Persano decided to leave his fleet in the port of Ancona until further orders. On 17 July he was ordered to attack Lissa, an island at the mouth of the Adriatic where the Austrians had two fortified ports. At the same time, the Austrian Admiral Tegethoff sailed from Fasana, with a squadron half the size of the Italian fleet assembled by Lissa. In the action that followed on 20 July, Tegethoff bested the Italians with a brilliant display of seamanship. In doing so, he also confirmed the role of the armoured ship in modern naval warfare. By use of the ram, Tegethoff's ironclad flagship, *Ferdinand Max*, destroyed the flagship of the Italian fleet, the *Re D'Italia*. The defeat was so humiliating for the Italians that the news was kept from the populace for more than three days.

By 22 July Cialdini was still stuck at Udine and although he had probed forward toward Rovereno and Belluno, Archduke Albrecht's dispatch of reinforcements by train from Vienna prevented him from crossing the frontier in force. That same day, a cease-fire was agreed upon following the announcement of a truce in Austria. The Italians pressed the Prussians not to agree on a peace with Vienna so that they could, with Prussian help, annex the southern Tyrol. This request Bismarck happily refused, as Italian vacillation after Custozza rendered joint Italo-Prussian operations against Vienna unworkable. However, events had already moved far beyond that issue, as will be seen. Nevertheless, Italy still clung to more profitable terms in separate negotiations with the Austrians, and the truce was extended several times before a treaty was signed. By this time, however, attention had long been focused away from Italy and everywhere else toward the final act, played out in a hunting lodge ninety miles north of Vienna.

The march to the Danube

By the time the Prussian armies had begun their march toward the Austrian capital, the weather had improved dramatically; it was now hot and more like a central European summer. Warm weather, though, does not always help an army on the march and as the great dark-blue columns snaked across the Bohemian plains, huge dust clouds rose in the air and many a plodding *soldat* grew parched. The Prussian supply system was now incapable of keeping up with the armies, and the men had to requisition their necessities on the march. Consequently, much of eastern Bohemia and Moravia was turned into a wasteland. The king and the Royal Headquarters left Pardubitz on 7 July, and travelled with the First Army on its drive to Vienna via Brünn, while the Army of the Elbe took a westerly route

Lissa, 20 July 1866.

through Iglau. On the same day, the crown prince and Second Army also crossed the Elbe at Pardubitz, and proceeded east in pursuit of Austrian North Army. On 10 July, near Neustadt, advanced patrols fell in with Benedek's straggling rearguard just over a day's march from Olmütz. A few miles further on the next evening there was a skirmish between Prussian uhlans and Austrian hussars at Saar. By 12 July however, Benedek was safely in Olmütz.

From the moment the battle of Königgrätz had ended, the Hapsburg emperor, Franz Joseph, had determined to make peace. His cession of Venetia to France was the first move, with the hopes of some armed demonstration by French forces on Austria's behalf. Napoleon III however, had no stomach for military intervention, although Austria did secure the good offices of the French emperor in the peace process. As the Prussian armies relentlessly tramped toward the Danube, a flurry of diplomatic activity was gathering momentum in European capitals. Lines of communication had, for some time, been open between Bismarck and Count Mensdorff, but as the Royal Headquarters arrived

in Brünn on 13 July, a day after the troops of the First Army had occupied the city, there was little mood for anything but the harshest terms for their recently defeated foes.

The victorious king would settle for nothing less than the humiliation of Austria. Apart from financial and territorial concessions on a vast scale, a victory march through Vienna was seen as an essential symbolic demonstration of Prussia's superiority. The two Prussian princes were of a similar mind, and Moltke, despite the somewhat belated pursuit of North Army, was devising strategies that would reduce Austria's military potential indefinitely. In fact, he had spotted Benedek's error in making for Olmütz, for now the feldzeugmeister could be trapped in that fortress city. Critically, however, by the First Army's march to Brünn, Benedek would be cut off from the Austrian capital. Benedek had managed to dispatch portions of three corps – III, IV, and VI – by rail to Vienna on 14 July. This infusion of some 40,000 men was added to Archduke Albrecht's forces, which had been sent from Italy to defend the city. Now however, Benedek was forced to make a decision; the direct route to Vienna had been cut at Lundenburg near Brünn, so the only route open to Vienna was the long one eastwards and then south over the Lower Carpathians through Hungary. He left one corps on the west bank of the March River, upon which Olmütz stood, to slow a Prussian pursuit. The battle that followed at Tobitschau on 15 July was a large one involving Prussian General Bonin's three divisions, and resulted in yet another defeat for the Austrians. However, since Benedek's line of march seemed to be removing his forces as a threat, the Second Army was ordered south to join the rest of the army, which on 17 July had occupied Nikolsburg, some 90 miles north of Vienna.

Franz Joseph I of Austria (1813–1916).

The French ambassador to Berlin, M. Benedetti, had been flitting between the two armies in a small carriage, since 13 July. His attempt to organize a cease-fire at Brünn on 14 July had been rejected out of hand and, by 17 July, he had left Vienna with revised proposals, only to find the king's headquarters had now been established in the castle of Prince Dietrichstein,[4] in Nikolsburg. By this time, Bismarck had formulated his own set of conditions for a peace, conditions that were in direct conflict with the wishes of the king and his generals. Bismarck knew that a humiliated Austria, forced to suffer huge losses in land and treasure, would always be a thorn in Prussia's (or a North German entity's) side. Exclusion from German affairs plus the imposition of a reasonable war reparation fee would reduce the likelihood of Austria becoming a hostile state friendly to a Prussian enemy. The king, naturally, would hear none of this, and stubbornly held out for his pound of Hapsburg flesh. Bismarck was similarly resolute, and pressed vehemently for his point of view.[5] By 21 July, Benedetti had arranged for a meeting at Count Mensdorff's hunting lodge, at Nikolsburg, where a temporary truce was announced for that day.

Both armies were now facing each other for what, in the absence of a cease-fire, would have become an all-out assault on the Austrian capital. When the armistice was announced, the Prussian troops of the First Army were largely camped at Marchfeld, near the old Napoleonic battlefield of Wagram, while units of their 8th Division had moved toward the March River, near Pressburg, to prevent the now exhausted remnants of North Army effecting a passage. The crown prince's Second Army had passed through Brünn on 18 July, and was approaching Lundenburg by the time of the truce. The cease-fire found advanced patrols of Herwarth von Bittenfeld's Army of the Elbe only 15 miles from Vienna at Stockerau, from where they could see the spires of St Stephen's Cathedral in the city. It should be noted here, that poised as they were for the final assault on the enemy's capital, the condition of all three armies was far from perfect. Lack of proper provisions had led to large outbreaks of dysentery and in many cases, cholera had appeared, and was claiming lives daily. The commissariat department of the Prussian Army was beginning to clear its backlogs, but not without the destruction of tons of spoiled rations and ruined clothing. Replacement provisions were on their way, but if the army fought a great battle, these stores would not arrive in time to supply them, victorious or not.

It finally befell the crown prince to convince his father that he must concede to Bismarck's wishes. Despite the glorious visions of humbling his enemy, William realised that the minister-president was probably right. The two parties spent four days on the details of a peace to come and on 26 July, a permanent armistice was announced from Nikolsburg. The fighting was over.

Epilogue

"The world has ended!" were the words of the Pope's state secretary when the news of Königgrätz arrived at the Vatican. "Thirty dynasties have been swept away!" declared a London newspaper, and the French press lamented that Vienna could no longer be regarded as arbiter of central European affairs. This universal

Negotiations at Nickolsburg, which led to the permanent armistice announced on 26 July.

astonishment was not unfounded. Indeed, the political and diplomatic face of Europe had been changed so dramatically that leaders and politicians everywhere were largely at a loss for suitable responses. As the weeks following the battle unfolded, and the world watched as Austria's western allies were trounced and Prussian armies plunged toward the Danube, everyone fully expected that the war would only end when (as King William wished) they triumphantly paraded through Vienna.

The truce at Nikolsburg, therefore, was greeted with universal relief. Not that the absence of a parade had made that much difference to the outcome. The agreements made at Nikolsburg were finally codified by a treaty signed on 23 August at the Blue Star Hotel in Prague. The essentials included Austria's acceptance of the dissolution of the old German Bund, and her exclusion from all German affairs in the future. In addition, there was a harsh indemnity of forty million Prussian dollars,[6] as well as the recognition by Austria of an entity, later known as the North German Confederation, which included Saxony and most of the states north of the Maine River. The south German states would be allowed to form their own union, and be permitted a free association with the north German states if they wished. Finally, the Schleswig-Holstein issue was solved forever as those duchies, along with the Kingdom of Hanover, and the duchies of Hesse-Cassel and Nassau, were annexed by Prussia outright.

The previous day, treaties had been signed in Berlin between the south German belligerents and the Prussian minister-president. For Italy, her separate treaty with Austria was more difficult. Austria's successes at Custozza and Lissa, along with her prevention of an Italian invasion allowed her some bargaining power. Temporary armistices were established while negotiations persisted. Italy failed to gain much more than Venice and the Quadrilateral forts, with very little financial gain when, on 3 October, the final treaty was concluded in Vienna.

By the time the treaty was signed in Prague, there was not a Prussian soldier to be seen anywhere on Austrian territory. The last of them had left Prague by train on 18 August and they were happy to leave, because the cholera had continued to claim more lives than expected, including those of three generals. On arrival in Berlin, Prince Frederick Charles was greeted by a near-empty capital, and signs everywhere of mourning for the dead, and help for the wounded. However, plans for parades were well under way by the middle of September, and massive crowds turned out for the troops as they marched in triumph down the Unter-Den-Linden, on 21 September. Bunting and flags in the Prussian colours flew everywhere, and King William took the salute with the pride and gratitude of a victorious sovereign.

Gratitude was also extended to the victors. As well as a myriad of medals and awards bestowed upon thousands from general to gefreiter, special honours awaited the two architects of the victory. Among many handsome rewards he received, Moltke was awarded the Order of the Black Eagle, plus the colonelcy of the 9th Infantry Regiment. Bismarck himself was made a major-general, much to the discomfiture of the regular army, along with countless other acclaims of greatness. A mere three months earlier, he had been regarded as a heavy-handed politician whose recklessness would plunge Prussia into the abyss. He may well, therefore, have reflected wryly on the words of the staff officer who rode up to him on the Lipa heights after the battle. "Congratulations Excellency, we have won a great battle and you have become a great hero. But if the crown prince had not come in time, you would now be the greatest scoundrel in Europe!"[7]

NOTES

1. Gablenz had little chance of success. Moltke demanded that the three fortresses of Theresienstadt, Josephstadt and Königgrätz should be surrendered to Prussia to sustain even a three-day truce. These conditions were beyond Gablenz's authority to negotiate, so he returned to the Austrian lines empty-handed.
2. The mayor had assured the inhabitants that there would be plenty of notice of the Prussian advance and not to panic. His assurances were in vain. The sudden arrival of the Prussians and the reception given by the Bavarian infantry astonished the inhabitants. None understood the intensity of a modern battle with quick-firing weapons.
3. Garibaldi was amazed at the strength of opposition by local Tyrolean inhabitants who went out of their way to hinder the progress of his troops. Having been badly mauled at the border town of Cassarobach, they retreated to Bogolino where they were again beaten and Garibaldi himself was wounded.
4. Napoleon Bonaparte had slept in this castle (and in the same room as King William) after his victory at Austerlitz in 1805.
5. The argument between king and minister-president became so intense that at one point (according to Bismarck himself) he contemplated running out of the room and jumping out of the window.
6. Estimated at more than half a million US dollars by early 20th-century standards.
7. Emil Ludwig. *Bismarck.*

Part Three

The Prussian Army and Navy 1860–67

CHAPTER SEVEN

The Roon Reforms and the General Staff

THE BATTLE OF JENA, FOUGHT on 14 October 1806, destroyed the army forged by Frederick the Great over sixty years before. To be sure, apart from the structure, uniforms and regimental names, it was not an army he would have recognised. Following his death in 1786, years of poor leadership and decay had shorn it of its efficiency and left it ill-equipped to face the French revolutionary armies at the end of the century. Despite superior numbers, the Prussian army was no match for Napoleon and his Grande Armée on that fatal field in Thuringia. Nevertheless, the defeat and accompanying humiliation would be regarded as a catastrophe of unbounded proportions, and the memory of it seared into the minds of Prussian and German soldiers for over a century. Arising out of the ashes came able commanders such as Ludwig Yorck, August Neidhardt von Gneisenau, Gerhard von Scharnhorst and Gebhard Leberecht von Blücher. Under their leadership a new Prussian army was created that was able to reassert itself on the battlefield during the Wars of Liberation in 1813 and 1814, and to share decisively in the final victory at Waterloo.

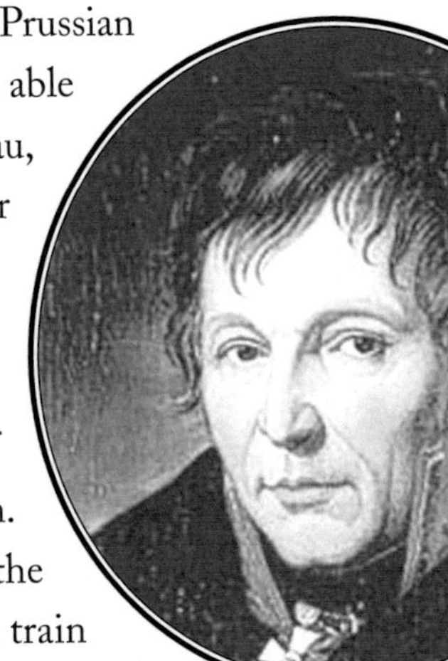

Gerhard von Scharnhorst (1755–1813).

The treaty that followed Jena[1] included French occupation of much Prussian territory and limited the size of her army to 42,000 men. Between 1806 and 1813, Scharnhorst devised a scheme, called the *Krümper* system, to induct a prescribed number of men into the army, train them quickly and efficiently and then release them to the reserve. Thus by 1812 there were over 250,000 trained men available for service without having increased the nominal size of the army. This reserve, known as the Landwehr, provided a trained and patriotic citizenry ready for the war to expel Bonaparte and his forces from German soil. The significant contribution of these troops[2] to the final victory caused the leadership to make the Landwehr system the basis of Prussian military organization for the next 45 years.

The conscription system established on 3 September 1814 required every able-bodied man to serve in the regular army from the beginning of his 20th year to his 23rd year and in the regular reserve from his 23rd to 25th year. He then served in the first levy of the Landwehr from the age of 25 to 32 and in the second levy from the age of 33 to 39. Finally, he passed into the Landsturm, a last-line reserve that included all men aged between 17 and 49 who were not currently serving in the regular army, its reserve or the Landwehr. As the weakest member of the Great Powers emerging from the Napoleonic Wars, this allowed Prussia, with a population of little more than ten million souls, to field a large army in time of war without having to maintain it in peace. Thus, on paper, the Prussian Army by 1830 stood as follows:

Regular army	120,000
Regular reserves	80,000
Landwehr, first levy	150,000
Landwehr, second levy	110,000
Landsturm	70,000
Total	530,000

In reality, the actual number of troops that could be embodied for combat in an emergency would number about 340,000. Extra numbers could be drawn from the second levy of the Landwehr and the Landsturm to form depot troops, and the garrisoning of fortresses and lines of communications. Later, the three-year term of service for the first-line troops was reduced to two, but restored to three again in 1852.

The Prussian Army was also established on a provincial basis with eight military districts. These were: East Prussia, Pomerania, Brandenburg, Magdeburg, West Prussia, Silesia, Westphalia, and Rhine. Each of these districts provided an army corps, which along with the Guard Corps, made nine. Each corps comprised two infantry divisions, each of two brigades, and a cavalry division of two brigades. An infantry brigade had two regiments, one regular and one Landwehr (first levy) plus depot troops and a cavalry brigade consisted of two regiments on the same basis. After 1815, infantry regiments had been increased from two battalions to three, in line with the practice of most European armies.

Regimental establishment, 1830–60

Infantry	
Guard infantry	4 regiments
Line infantry	40 regiments
Guard Jäger	2 battalions
Line Jäger	8 battalions
Guard Landwehr infantry	2 regiments
Landwehr infantry	40 regiments

Cavalry	
Guard cavalry	4 regiments (Gardes du Corps, Cuirassier, Dragoon and Hussar)
Line cavalry	32 regiments (8 Cuirassier, 4 Dragoon, 12 Hussar and 8 Uhlan)
Guard Landwehr cavalry	2 regiments (Uhlan)
Landwehr cavalry	30 regiments

Artillery and engineers	
Guard artillery	1 brigade
Line artillery (horse and foot)	8 brigades
Guard pioneers	1 battalion
Line pioneers	8 battalions
Military train (formed 1853)	1 Guard battalion, 8 provincial battalions

When the disturbances of 1848 finally erupted into street riots, the regular infantry of the Berlin garrison handled them ruthlessly and efficiently. The Landwehr however, called out for duty both at home and in the confrontation with Denmark, was found lacking. The patriotic fervour that had fuelled their enthusiasm for the Wars of Liberation had disappeared. For the officers of the Landwehr this was more marked. Extracting bourgeois businessmen and professionals from their work and families in a Prussian society that was growing more liberal and educated proved unpopular. Frederick William IV and his ministers, however had no stomach for confrontation with the rapidly evolving middle class and let things stand as they were. However, when his brother William became regent, his military sensibilities were appalled by state of the army. The Landwehr's performance during the mobilization of 1859 gave further cause for alarm. By this time, though, Prince William had already asked Lieutenant-General Albrecht von Roon, soon to be his new war minister, to prepare a report with recommendations for the reform of the army. This report and its results would have far-reaching consequences.

Roon's reforms

General of Infantry Albrecht Theodor Emil von Roon was born on 30 April 1803 near Colberg in Pomerania. His father, a Prussian officer, died when Albrecht was ten and he was raised by his grandmother. At the age of 13 he entered the Corps of Cadets and after military school in Berlin, was commissioned into the 14th (3rd Pomeranian) Infantry Regiment. His career immediately went in an academic direction and he studied at the war school in Berlin and later, in 1826, became an instructor of geography at the cadet school there. He developed his negative views of Prussian army efficiency when he rejoined his regiment in 1832 and served on General Karl von Müffling's staff. By 1835, when he was appointed to the General Staff, he was already an accomplished and well-known author on military and political geography. During this period he studied and wrote about army reform as well as making major and being appointed to the staff of VII Corps. He traveled extensively in Europe and was chief of staff of VIII Corps when the revolutions broke out in 1848. He distinguished himself serving under Prince William in the suppression of the Baden revolt and was awarded the Order of the Red Eagle (3rd Class) for his bravery. At the time of the Olmütz debacle in 1850 he was promoted to lieutenant-colonel and the following year to full colonel. Prince William, who had taken interest in Roon's ideas since 1848, appointed him to several important positions on the staff which, as a major-general from 1856, brought him into contact with Manteuffel and Moltke, who supported his theories. It was not surprising therefore, that when William became regent Roon would figure largely in his plans for army reform.

The War Ministry had not been altogether idle since Olmütz. For one thing, the population of Prussia had risen to eighteen million since 1815 and the annual intake of recruits had not changed from the 40,000 established at that time. This allowed for abuse of the system and exemption from national service became rife with the result that many men never served, while others stayed in the ranks

Albrecht von Roon (1803–79).

for years. Upon mobilization, the active army contained a disproportionate number of older soldiers. In other armies, such as the British Army, this provided seasoned professionals, but in Prussia it left the ranks full of men too used to civilian life. The ministry, now under Eduard von Bonin, considered all these factors and produced a report in February 1858, the recommendations of which were forwarded to William for consideration. The core of the ministry's proposals were that the active army and reserves should contain only men aged 20 to 26 with those over that age assigned to the Landwehr for the garrisoning of fortresses and rear areas. It also asserted that the active service term should be lowered again to two years; and to increase the number of recruits the physical standards should be somewhat lowered. Upon receiving the report, William decided that, before issuing his own judgement, he would pass it on to Roon for comment.

What was presented to the prince regent in April 1850 was much more than mere commentary on a ministerial report. It was a lengthy and precise document on Roon's military philosophy concerning the future of the Prussian Army and its personnel. In it he castigated the Landwehr system in its entirety, demonstrating its unsuitability in a Prussia geographically disadvantaged and sorely in need of armed forces that could react decisively in a crisis. Like Moltke, and other progressive officers in the army, he asserted that all the other powers on mainland Europe – such as Russia, Austria, and France – could, if attacked, withdraw on vast interior lines putting pressure on an enemy's supply lines. There was no such luxury for Prussia; surrounded as she was, such a war would be over in a matter of days. Therefore, an army with a strong offensive capability, able to act preemptively if necessary, was vital to the future security of the nation. With such imperatives in mind, Roon felt strongly that the Landwehr had no place in such an organization. The Landwehrman was by definition a citizen soldier and as such was a voter. His immediate world of family, property, and work dominated his perspective and the larger demands of the nation were not of much concern. Consequently, matters of military service had a low priority and his vote when asked for gave him a say in such matters, which Roon resented. He argued that the armed forces better served the nation when they were in the firm control of the state, which in fact meant the king. His proposals included a large increase in the conscription ratio, the permanent establishment of three years' service with the colours, and infantry battalions of eight companies each of 100 men. These battalions would be doubled on mobilization in regiments that would then form brigades. Roon's intellectual logic supposed that young men between the ages of 19 and 28 under effective discipline, leadership, and treatment would develop behaviours that would be easier to manipulate and respond to the wishes of the state as required. The Landwehr, on the other hand, made the army a political institution subject to the vagaries of liberal thinking and an officer corps in such an institution presented a systemic obstacle to sound leadership.

William's announcement that he preferred Roon's recommendations astounded the War Ministry. They complained that his proposals were prohibitively expensive and complicated, so they came up with a modification of their own presented in February 1859. The term of active service would be three years, with the three youngest classes of Landwehr becoming the active army reserve. Battalions would be of 800 men in four companies, half of active men and half of reservists; this was a compromise seen as more cost effective and flexible. William wasted no time acting on what he actually considered just a starting point and in August of that year, following the summer mobilization, he sent the Landwehr home. Then, over three months, he began a gradual series of furloughs for active men and the redistribution of new conscripts into Landwehr Cadre battalions. This was a popular move and by December, he had achieved the transformation of the army into the basis of its new structure without generating a single murmur of protest. To be sure the word "Landwehr" remained as part of its nomenclature and it appeared that political dissent would be muted.

However, William's assignment of Roon to the War Ministry in August 1859 prompted Bonin to take a period of leave. The minister then appeared at the Landtag and made his complaints public, and it was Manteuffel who intrigued behind his back to undermine him. Finally, on 27 November, Eduard von Bonin resigned under pressure and William, after a politically correct pause of thirty days, appointed Roon as war minister. Roon's first task of 1860 was to present the government's bill to the Landtag, which he did in February. In its essence, the bill called for the active army to be almost doubled in size by the addition of four Guard, thirty-six Line infantry and ten cavalry regiments. In addition, the annual intake of recruits would rise to 63,000 and the term of service would be three years with the active army, five in the reserve and eleven with the Landwehr. The Landwehr itself would be shorn of its second levy and the remainder reduced to 116 battalions, after its younger members had been placed in the reserve to be armed only in time of war. The cost of all this was to be nearly half the annual war ministry budget, some 9,500,000 thalers.

If there hadn't been a constitutional crisis before, there certainly was one now. The Landtag's response was predictable: they objected not only to the cost, which would add 25 per cent to the tax burden, but to the composition of the extra units which included more Guard regiments and the near-elimination of the Landwehr. The Liberal faction hated the idea of the Guard on principle as it symbolized detachment of the army from the people and vested control of the army in a royalist cabal. This is exactly what William, Roon and the army hierarchy wanted, and their insistence on the basic principles of the bill put both sides on a collision course. However, although the Landtag generally approved of the idea that the army should be reformed, the main sticking point became the term of service, which the lawmakers wanted retained at two years. This became a deal breaker for Roon and when it became obvious that the bill would not pass as written, he withdrew it. The government then proposed that a partial grant should be made to cover the next fourteen months, which would only be used to bolster already authorized units. In what would be generally recognised as a huge error, the Landtag agreed.

No sooner than the money was "in the bank", the government went back on its word. During the summer of 1860 it prepared its new formations for full entry into the line of battle amid the continuing heated exchanges between the government (mostly in the form of the military cabal led by Manteuffel) and parliament. On 2 January 1861, King Frederick William IV died and later that month, as king himself, William performed a ceremony that enraged his critics.

The four Guard and thirty-six infantry regiments presented their colours to him for dedication and consecration at the tomb of Frederick the Great in the Potsdam chapel. This act exposed the government's duplicity and convinced opponents that the army was to be separated from civilian control. Later, to further snub the Berlin establishment, William held his coronation at Königsberg in East Prussia, where his Junker base made him feel more comfortable.

Throughout 1861, the debate in parliament went to and fro, with Manteuffel leading the charge for the military camarilla.[3] Events grew so serious that during the summer, plans were drawn up for a government coup that William approved and troops were prepared to take over Berlin if barricades were erected. By March 1862, after the Landtag had submitted a bill supported largely by the new Progressive party (formed in June 1861) establishing the two-year term of service, William had had enough and dismissed the parliament. During the weeks before new elections, the nation teetered on the brink of a coup, or worse still, a civil war. When the new elections returned more Progressives and Liberals to the Landtag, leaving the conservatives with only ten seats, cooler heads began to emerge on both sides and they began to look for compromise. This was the moment that Manteuffel reached his peak and his visions of being "grand vizier" to the king passed into history. Roon had seen that there was a more moderate parliament in the offing and that Manteuffel's blustering was becoming an irritant that needed soothing. In the middle of 1862, the Landtag was stuck on the two-year service issue and events reached crisis pitch when William entered the fray and bluntly declared that the issue was so central to his conviction that if the Landtag prevailed, he would abdicate. As Manteuffel prepared to draw his sword in the king's cause, Roon went to his majesty and made the suggestion that he summon Otto von Bismarck, which he did on 22 September. The rest of the story is well known and its account appears previously in this volume.

Edwin Freiherr von Manteuffel (1809–85).

During the next four years, the results of the reforms would change the course of history and establish the structure of the Prussian, later Imperial German, Army until its demise in 1918. By August 1866, along with Bismarck and Moltke, Roon would be a national hero.

The General Staff

No history of the Prussian Army is complete without an account of the unique staff system that lay at the heart of its military system. The concept of creating a cadre of officers for the purposes of war planning and organization goes back to the beginnings of standing armies. Gustavus Adolphus had instituted such a council during the Thirty Years War and its elements were copied by the Elector of Brandenburg in the 1680s. With war strategy firmly in the hands of the monarch at this time, such a council would be little more than an advisory group, but Frederick the Great would give it more structure during the Seven Years War. The large area of operations encountered in this war caused Frederick to form his famous *Adjutantur*, attached to the quartermaster-general's staff whose responsibilities were much like that of a brigade-major in the later 19th century. The position of adjutant-general also increased in importance but there was no formal general staff at this time as Frederick, like his predecessors, was his own chief. It was after the 1806 catastrophe that a formal general staff system would emerge.

August von Gneisenau (1760–1831).

It was Scharnhorst who laid the foundation of the organization, making it Department II of the War Ministry and becoming the first chief of the General Staff. Gneisenau, who became chief after Scharnhorst's untimely death from wounds received at Groß-Görschen in 1813, further improved things until he resigned in 1816, bitter at the way Prussia was evolving. The great reformers of the Prussian Army, both before and after the Napoleonic Wars, including Gneisenau, his replacement Karl von Grolman and Hermann von Boyen, the war minister, had all been liberals at heart. After all, they had seen the decaying "old" order defeated at Jena and had created a citizens' army to win back their country. By 1819, however their views had collided with the absolutist nature of Frederick William III and in a crisis over the future of the Landwehr (a precursor of what was to come in 1862), they had been forced into retirement. The new army leaders were of the Junker breed that had regained its reputation after 1806 and would dominate the army for the remainder of its days. The General Staff, however, did survive and under Grolman's successor, General Müffling, it flourished. It was during his term of service that it became detached from the War Ministry and made a parallel organization with three main divisions; the first for personnel; the second for organization, training, manoeuvres, and mobilization; and the third for technical, engineering, and artillery matters. He also instituted staff rides[4] and the annual *Kriegspiel* (war game) that used models in sandboxes or on maps to simulate real war situations. At this time also, young officers who would figure large in the future of the Prussian army would join the General Staff, such as Roon, Moltke and Fransecky. More than anything else, however, it was the writings of Carl von Clausewitz, a staff officer who had served under both Scharnhorst and Gneisenau, that would influence and dominate Prusso-German military thought until 1945.

Born on 1 June 1770, Clausewitz was the son of an impoverished Junker infantry officer who was a veteran of the Seven Years War. He joined the army at the age of 12 and by 1807 he was a favourite protégé of Scharnhorst. He served with the army during the campaigns of 1813 to 1815 and in 1818 became director of the War Academy. When Gneisenau was brought back from retirement to command the forces on the Polish frontier during the crisis of 1830, he chose Clausewitz as his chief of staff. Tragically, both of them would succumb to the cholera epidemic that swept eastern Europe the following year. Before his death, however, Clausewitz had committed to paper his military and political philosophy; it was posthumously published by his wife in 1832 with the simple title *Vom Kriege* (*On War*). His beliefs are revealed clearly in the first chapter, which includes his most famous maxim – that war is policy by other means. This is not the place to discuss his work in detail, however, taken as a whole, the book is to war what Adam Smith's *Wealth of Nations* is to economics, and he examines the nature of conflict from every aspect including its moral, philosophical, political, and practical elements. It would be years before the book became the handbook for every officer in the German army and two world wars before it became required reading at every military academy in the world. It did, however, influence one man profoundly at the time and it was he who brought it to the attention of his peers largely by his adherence to its doctrines during the three conflicts that were to shape his own destiny. His name was Helmuth Karl von Moltke.

Carl Philipp Gottfried von Clausewitz (1780–1831).

Neither his appearance nor his demeanour would have suggested a military career to be Moltke's calling. Although he was tall, he had a delicate frame and his face presented a refined and scholarly ambience. Born in Mecklenburg on 26 October 1800, he was, like many of his contemporaries, the son of a poor noble who had served in both the Prussian and Danish armies. He himself joined the Danish service after being schooled at the Royal Cadet Corps in Copenhagen but at the age of 21, exchanged into the Prussian Army as a lieutenant in the *Leibgrenadier* Regiment. His early career was marked by sickness and penury, as without family funds, he struggled to maintain some semblance of self-respect among his brother officers. He wrote anonymously and did translations for extra cash but there was no indication of any political predilections or other distractions from the business of soldiering, a matter to which he attended with great diligence.[5] He attended the War Academy where Clausewitz, who was director of that institution at the time, made him a topographical specialist; he served in that department for some time.

Moltke joined the General Staff as a first lieutenant in 1833, and after barely two years was sent on an assignment that would significantly impress the young officer and shape his thinking in the future. The Sultan of Turkey, Mahmud II, conscious of the Prussian Army's reputation, had requested a team of military instructors to help modernize his army and Moltke's task was to report progress back to General Wilhelm von Krauseneck, who had replaced Müffling as chief of the General Staff. He later, along with some brother officers, formally joined the Turkish Service and became senior military advisor on the Sultan's staff. The first battle he ever witnessed was a fiasco. At Nisib on the Syrian border in 1839, he watched helplessly as the Turks, ignoring his advice, sent their troops into an Egyptian trap where they were destroyed.[6] Nevertheless, Moltke learned some valuable lessons and his writings on these experiences were bestsellers at home.

In 1842 he married an Englishwoman, Mary Burt;[7] and shortly afterward was sent to Rome for a few years as adjutant to Prince Henry of Prussia. At the time of the 1848 revolution, he was a staff officer with the VII Corps on the Rhine and his reaction to the riots in Berlin was significant. He wrote to his brother that if the army was unable to suppress the uprising and restore order in the city as well as the government's establishment of authority over the liberals, the country would collapse and he would then emigrate with him to Australia.

Following the 1848 revolution, Krauseneck was succeeded by Karl von Reyher who had been war minister during that period. The status of the General Staff under Krauseneck had declined largely due to the rise of the military cabinet favoured by Frederick William and when Reyher took over, the situation was worse. Over the next three years, six war ministers came and went and Manteuffel, as head of the military cabinet, nearly succeeded in taking over the General Staff and absorbing it into the cabinet, a move the king approved. However, Reyher prevailed in maintaining the staff's position despite the pre-eminence of Manteuffel's organization at this time. The army corps system, although successful on an organizational basis had, during the long years of peace, become somewhat of a private fiefdom for the individual commanders and many of them had acquired absolute authority over their districts. Successive ministries failed to gain complete control and many of the mobilization problems encountered during 1850 and 1859 were due to confusion, and a little obstinance, in the command system.

During this time, Moltke had observed and written much about Prussia's military position in Europe and his ideas, strongly influenced by Clausewitz, began to gain the attention of the hierarchy. His staunchly conservative views coupled with his assertion that the armed forces should be free from civilian control caused him, in 1855, to be appointed as Prince Frederick's adjutant. His travels around Europe, including several trips to Windsor,[8] further allowed him to observe the political and military situation in those countries. In 1857, Crown Prince William had him provisionally appointed chief of the General Staff, a position that was confirmed soon after William became regent, on 18 September 1858. This taciturn man arrived at this high position almost unnoticed. It certainly did not impress Manteuffel, who undoubtedly respected Moltke and his ideas, but felt him to be too scholarly to aggressively promote the position of the General Staff, which suited Manteuffel. It was, however, his very reserved and undemonstrative temperament that enabled him, over the next four years, to quietly and completely reform the organization and start it on the road to the ascendancy of the Prussian and German military systems.

From the beginning, Moltke perceived technology to be one of the principal elements in the transformation of the Prussian army into a superior fighting machine. The new bolt-action needle gun, the *Zündanelgewehr,* which had gradually been introduced into the Prussian army since 1848, required new tactics to make it a more efficient weapon in the hands of the ordinary soldier, and the arrival of steel breech-loaders and barrel rifling to the artillery needed expansion. But it would be the strategic importance of the railway and the telegraph that would dominate his attention in the early years of his long tenure. Moltke's strongly held belief, shared by Roon, was that, surrounded by powerful and potentially aggressive neighbours, Prussia's best defensive posture was one of rapid mobilization and concentration of troops at the critical point. To this end, railways and the telegraph were essential and it is unsurprising that Moltke was more familiar than most on the practical function of railways. He had been a director of the Berlin–Hamburg railway as early as 1841 and as chief of staff of VIII Corps on the Rhine he introduced the use of railways in the summer troop exercises of 1850. Just before his confirmation as chief in 1858, he had supervised manoeuvres in Silesia that emphasised the incorporation of railway tactics. In the early 1860s Moltke placed the railway and telegraph system under government supervision and had the rolling stock adapted for military use by making the interior furniture removable to convert to troop or cavalry horse transport.

When Moltke took over the General Staff, there were only 64 officers on the strength, and although he didn't increase that number immediately, he did reorganize the departments. The old 'divisions' were replaced by departments that concentrated on strategic theatres; the first handled Sweden, Russia, Turkey, and Austria; while the second handled Germany, Italy, Switzerland, and Denmark. The last dealt with France, Great Britain, Holland, Belgium, Spain, and the United States. He then designated six other departments including – naturally – a railway department, also planning, topography, personnel, finance, and history. He inculcated in his officers the concept of individuality and the responsibility to act independently within a larger scenario set by the General Staff Plan. This was also one of the defining contributions to the rise and eventual dominance of this remarkable organization. Moltke felt that the day of the great captain was gone. No more Napoleons, Marlboroughs or Wellingtons; just a faceless department of brilliant planners and staff officers who communicated advice and the larger picture of the battlefield to local commanders who would then make decisions accordingly. Needless to say, his position on the demise of great captains was premature, especially since he was to be known as one of the greatest in history. Nevertheless, his essential axiom was that with the coming of a new kind of warfare over vast areas, the isolated commander, brilliant or otherwise, would not be able to function without the support and guidance from those with a complete picture of the situation.

Moltke was able to keep himself and his staff out of the fray surrounding the constitutional crisis in the early 1860s. Along with Roon and Bismarck, he did communicate his views on Prussia's strategic situation and make plans with the full assurance that he was on the "same page" as his king and commanders. When the Danish War began in 1864, Moltke's position was purely as an advisor through the War Ministry, while direct command came via the king to the commander, Wrangel. The muddled beginning of the campaign and the stalemate after the Danish retreat to Düppel, provoked Roon to suggest Moltke's more active participation. It was only after the king's visit to the front and the removal of Falckenstein that Moltke was finally made (provisionally), Wrangel's chief of staff. His quiet but brilliant planning for the assault on Düppel and the successful waterborne landings at Alsen brought him to public attention and in a series of manoeuvres by Roon and a General von Tresckow, he was brought into the king's inner council.[9]

From now on, the strategy and planning for Prussia's future wars was firmly in the hands of the General Staff under Moltke. When the war with Austria became inevitable, he had already taken a firm grasp on the form his war plan would take. Even though his suggested deployment for the 1866 invasion of Austrian territory and destruction of Benedek's army was severely criticized, it was the plan that was adopted. However, uncertainty about Moltke, now 66 years old, was rife in the army right up to the time that he joined the king, Bismarck and Roon for the train ride to the front. Some, such as the king's ancient adjutant-general, Boyen were full of trepidation when he said to a friend: "The king in command, at the age of seventy, with the decrepit Moltke at his side! What will come of it all?"

NOTES

1. In addition to the battle of Jena, the battle of Auerstadt was also fought nearby, which compounded the Prussian defeat.
2. The volunteer troops (*Freiwilligejäger*) must also be included as many of their units were also absorbed into the Prussian army in 1814.
3. In a bizarre episode, Manteuffel provoked a duel with Karl von Twesten, a liberal politician who had published a paper claiming the army was acting in ways similar to 1806 and divide the army from the nation. After wounding Twesten, Manteuffel insisted on spending time in jail.
4. These General Staff rides, originally introduced by Scharnhorst, helped familiarize the officers with situations of terrain and route planning; concepts lacking in nearly all other European armies.
5. He is said to have translated the entire twelve volumes of Gibbon's *Decline and Fall of the Roman Empire* into German.
6. The Sultan and his Turkish commanders evidently placed more faith in their astrologers than they did in Moltke's advice.
7. She was the stepdaughter of his sister, who had married an English widower. Their long marriage was apparently very blissful although it produced no children.
8. Prince Frederick's future wife was to be Queen Victoria's eldest daughter Victoria Princess Royal, known as "Vicky".
9. This effort also saw the dismissal of von Manteuffel from the King's Council and the end of his bid to become the main advisor to William I.

CHAPTER EIGHT

The Prussian Soldier

Officers

When William I ascended the throne in 1861, the exalted position of the Prussian officer corps was firmly established in the army and society; a position it would retain not only until 1918, but in many minds, until 1945. Since the retreat of liberal influence in the army, which began after 1820, the social make-up of the officer corps had gradually reverted to the class that had traditionally filled its ranks for nearly two hundred years. A class whose loyalty to the crown was unquestioned and a class whose sons were bred for soldiering and most of all, for commanding soldiers: the Junkers.

Hermann von Boyen (1777–1848).

The harsh, sandy soil found east of the upper Elbe in the old marks of Pomerania, Brandenburg and East Prussia had produced a breed of hardy farmers, a landed gentry of Wendish or Polish-Prussian stock who, despite a certain poverty, aspired to a nobility they called Junkers. Following the Thirty Years War, the ruler of the Electorate of Brandenburg, Frederick William I (1640–88), later known as the "Great Elector", inherited a variety of lands and estates that he was able to weld into what was to become Prussia. From the beginning, the Junkers found a favoured place in eyes of the monarch and in exchange they provided him with officers for his army. This relationship at first was of a vassal nature, which, by placing their estates within the king's domain, produced some tension during his reign and that of subsequent rulers. It was Frederick the Great who released their lands back to them in return for an oath of "feudal loyalty" that enshrined their position in the leadership of the army. The exigencies of the Seven Years War brought many non-nobles to the officer corps and although the Junkers provided most of the officers to the cavalry, their percentage in the infantry was quite reduced. In peace however, Frederick despised these bourgeois officers and would work hard to rid his regiments of them.[1] Thus by the time of the French Revolution, the level of non-noble officers in the Prussian army had been reduced to less than 10 per cent. Subsequently, the quality of officers declined as their ranks became filled with men of limited intellectual abilities but unlimited arrogance, and the blame for the catastrophe of 1806 was clearly laid at their feet.

Scharnhorst, who had begun reforms before Jena, recognized that education and training were the basic elements of effective leadership and he reorganized the War School and cadet schools to provide them. In 1810, three new officer candidate schools were established, at Berlin, Breslau, and Königsberg. However, he and Gneisenau also favoured a Prussian army led by a meritocracy rather than a privileged class; the Wars of Liberation saw the creation of the Landwehr that also allowed officers of all classes into the ranks based on their ability. Following Waterloo, Gneisenau and War Minister Boyen tried to accelerate the process, but the Congress of Vienna had restored the position of the reactionary monarchies in Europe and one of the most conservative of these was Prussia. Over the next few years, the Junker nobility worked hard to reverse the liberalization of the army and Frederick William III, a king very conscious of the relationship between the crown and the officer corps, soon buckled to their will. By 1820, Gneisenau and Boyen had resigned and the number of middle-class officers in the army had been reduced dramatically, while the Landwehr had come under army, rather than civilian, control.

Despite the restoration of the old order in the Prussian Army, many of Scharnhorst's reforms remained intact. However the whole system of education and officer selection became subject to a continuous onslaught by reactionary officers who regarded schoolbook training as an insult to their noble birthright.[2] Despite this, Frederick William III and both of his sons who would succeed him, ensured that education played a part in officer selection by directives that strengthened the requirements in 1836 and 1844. The failure of the 1848 revolutions also put to rest any liberal influence after a brief attempt to regulate the schools by the Frankfurt parliament. However, when Frederick William IV passed into insanity in 1858, the educational levels of officer candidates had only risen marginally since the 1820s and his brother, William, as regent was more committed than ever to aristocratic control of the army. By 1860 the makeup of the officer corps was largely of noble origin, especially in the Guards, infantry and cavalry. In the Guards it was 95 per cent for infantry, 100 per cent for the cavalry and 67 per cent for the artillery. In the Line regiments it was 67 per cent for infantry and 95 per cent for cavalry, while the artillery and engineers only reached 16 per cent. The "technical" branches drew more commoners because they were less glamorous and more stringent educational qualifications were needed. As the Roon reforms took hold and the new regiments were embodied, the demand for officers increased dramatically and William, with his high command, strove to establish a selection process that would meet this challenge. It was among the first priorities that William would address when he came to the throne.

At the beginning of the 1860s, the process of military education and officer selection was much the same as it had been in 1815. The practical process of becoming an officer in the Prussian Army took three forms: entry through the cadet schools (*Kadettenschulen*); through the secondary education system or *Gymnasium*; or as a "One-Year Volunteer" (*Einejährig-freiwilliger*). There were five cadet schools in 1860: a senior school with a complement of four companies and four lower schools with two companies each. They were as follows:

SCHOOL	YEAR FOUNDED	APPROX NO. OF STUDENTS
Berlin	1717	400
Potsdam	1769	200
Culm	1776–1807/1816	200
Wahlstatt	1838	200
Bensberg	1840	200

These schools were considered the premier source for officer material and received preferential treatment along with their graduates. Boys entered the school between ten and twelve years of age after a rigorous inspection of their pedigree and physical suitability. During the next six or so years they would receive an academic education far less rigorous than that in civilian schools, but gain a proficiency in military studies second to none. Being under the purview of the inspector-general of military training and education, the schools and their pupils were subject to army regulations. Life was expected to be spartan and hard at these institutions. The future field marshal, Paul von Hindenburg, who was a student at Wahlstatt, remembered giving away all his toys and writing a will before he left home. Their days began with chapel after breakfast, then they were in the schoolroom at 8:00 a.m. for three hours of lessons. Afternoons were filled with drill, physical exercise, and the study of the military sciences. Unsurprisingly, there was much time spent on the building of character, patriotism and the martial attitude, appropriate ideals for those who would wear the "king's coat". While discipline was strict, some of the schoolmaster officers were known to be kind and would help those boys who needed extra tuition to keep up with their studies. There was little privacy and the young men were under scrutiny most of the time; although some of their spare time could be spent in the town during the evening, they had to be back early and after lights out at 10:00 p.m. they slept in large dormitories. Thus, by the time they were 17 or 18, they would have been transformed from the callow sons of noble families to future officers in the army, but there were two important steps to take before they took their place in front of squadron or company in a regiment. The first was the ensign's exam.

The ensign's exam was sat by those who had taken the route through the civilian school system. At the beginning of the 1860s, these young men were mostly of the privileged classes for whom a military career was secondary and an academic education had some importance. However, as the wars of unification took their toll of officers young and old, along with the great expansion of the armed forces, the need for more officers led to a large increase of bourgeois candidates. The Prussian and German secondary education system was far superior to any in Europe and the path beyond free elementary school system (*Volkschule*), which all children were expected to attend, was an onerous one. Only those whose fathers had the appropriate means, position, or influence, could even consider middle school (*Realschule*) which lasted six years, or the *Gymnasium*, which was nine years. In addition to academic training, the Prussian system was marked by its devotion to discipline; obedience was a primary requirement and boys exhibiting signs of insubordination were severely punished. Those completing their terms in either the *Realschule* or *Gymnasium* were eligible for the ensign's exam and by an army order of 1861, upon production of the *Prima*, *Oberprima* certificate or upon passing the exalted *Abitur* exam.[3] Eligibility, however also included an intense

Cadet Paul von Hindenburg at Wahlstatt in 1860.

screening for the class, breeding, and character attributes demanded by the selection committee. The acceptence procedure completed, the student would join the cadet school graduate as an equal before taking the exam.

As all young males were liable for military service, a peculiarly Prussian system was instituted in 1814 to allow for men for whom interruption of their academic studies would be harmful and make them eligible for a reserve commission. Known as the one-year volunteer (*Einejährig-freiwilliger*) certificate, this enabled the student to enter the ranks as a priviliged soldier. He had to provide his own uniform[4] and equipment (in the cavalry this included his horse and its furniture), which was often of better quality that that of the men. This, of course could be expensive but it did allow for him to complete his military obligation without harming his studies and give him a chance to become a reserve officer. Often these young men could reach the rank of lance sergeant-major (*vizefeldwebel*) during this year. Despite its obvious "win-win" advantages, the *Einejährig-freiwilliger* system was never quite accepted by the Prussian officer corps, especially at higher levels, largely because it created an "interim" class of officer who bypassed the mainstream and threatened their view of the professional officer. In any event, following unification, the system spread to the forces of all the other kingdoms and states and would survive until 1914.

Before taking the ensign's exam all students, regardless of class, educational qualifications or whether they were a cadet, had to go through a process which if they failed would disqualify them for a commission. Whichever regiment the boy chose, it was up to the colonel of that regiment to support him, and he with his father had to spend a day or so with the colonel and officers for evaluation. The boy not only had to demonstrate character, patriotism, and the desire to join the unit, but also that he had sufficient wealth to supplement his income, especially in cavalry regiments. Every part of the young man's background was examined and, not surprisingly, aristocratic youths were clearly preferred in the Guards regiments where the percentage of nobles neared 100 per cent. Jews were clearly discouraged from even applying, although during this time and the wars of unification, some did enter the technical and supply branches. From the 1880s, very few Jewish candidates were accepted.

Once the applicant had received a commitment from the commanding officer of his prospective regiment, he could then take the ensign's exam.[5] This was both a written and oral test, usually taken on a Sunday at one of the larger garrison headquarters. After 1880, this was taken in Berlin on a daily basis except for weekends. Upon passing the exam, the young man was formally accepted into his regiment as an officer-candidate or ensign (*Officiereaspirant, Avantageur* or *Fahnrich*) and had to serve in the ranks for a period of time which, before the 1880s, was usually six months, but declined to less than three by the turn of the century. The *Officiereaspirant* essentially served as a private soldier but wore non-commissioned-officer-quality uniform and a special sword knot which signified his appointment. Also, as time went on, he assumed the duties of a non-commissioned officer (NCO) and ate in their mess. Finally, before he went off to war school to finish his training and receive his commission, he would join the officers in their mess as *Fahnrich-portepee*.[6] As an officer candidate, he would receive better treatment than the men, not only because he was expected to exhibit the air of authority that would be essential to his career, but also because NCOs were hardly likely to abuse someone to whom they would later be subordinate. Finally it became time to face the final step in the making of an officer; the War School (*Kriegsschule*).

In 1854, General Eduard von Peucker became inspector-general of military training and education and immediately determined that, among other deficiencies, the system for training candidates before commissioning needed reorganization. The war schools introduced by Scharnhorst in 1810 had gradually been replaced by division schools, which by 1844 had reached 17 in number. Although reduced to nine later that year, the curricula were so diverse and erratic that the schools served little purpose beyond basic preparation for a commission. Peucker instituted four new establishments designated "War Schools": at Potsdam and Erfürt in 1859, Neisse in 1860, and Engers in 1863.[7] These schools were created exclusively for the purposes of advanced preparation for becoming an officer.

The War School at Engers, 1864.

The war schools became the equivalent of the military academy in other countries (other than the United States) where the subject matter was almost exclusively confined to military sciences. All prospective officers were expected to complete the course but there were exceptions, notably for those who passed the *Abitur* examination, though many of these students found it advantageous to attend. The other, more common exception was for cadet-school graduates who had passed the *Oberprima* and ensign's exam because much of their advanced curriculum paralleled the war schools but this practice too was phased out during the next twenty years. Life at the war schools was similar to that at the cadet schools but the hours were longer: students were busy from 8:00 a.m. until 10:00 p.m. with the usual mix of military studies, gymnastics, or sports and skill-at-arms. Spare time was limited mostly to weekends and discipline was tough with the ensigns' conduct and attitude closely watched, although punishments were not as severe as in cadet school and indiscretions such as insobriety were often lauded by their comrades.

The final exam, both written and oral, was taken in Berlin and in the 1860s most passed largely due to the expansion of the army to meet war commitments. Those who did not pass could retest at a later date and most did succeed in obtaining their commission, but there was one final hurdle to overcome before they took their place in a regiment, one which would remain the most controversial part of the selection procedure until 1914. This was the officers' vote.

After the commandant of the War School had received the results of the test, the ensigns were paraded before him. The only names read out were of those who had failed and the rest were given certificates of their success with those who had passed highest receiving King's Commendation. Upon return to their regiment, the graduates were liable for further probation, but this was rare and the colonel would then send to Berlin for the certificate that stated his "fitness for commission" (*Reifezeugnis zum Offizier*). Provided there was a vacancy and a favourable endorsement from the officer who "minded" the young man when he was an *aspirant,* the colonel would then invite the officers of the regiment to cast their vote. In the more fashionable regiments, such as the Guards or the cavalry, a young man's financial resources were of as much importance as his breeding. Although some regimental funds were available, they could not be counted on and it is certain that a young officer would not survive in such regiments on his own pay. However, this was all known to the colonel before the vote and rarely did any officer vote against his wishes. During the early 1860s, when the number of noble applicants outnumbered those of the middle class, election was virtually ensured and the growth of the army during the wars of unification did nothing to prevent the election of good bourgeois officers either. However, this process consecrated the feudal relationship between the crown and the officer corps. As the century progressed, the army grew larger while its combat commitment decreased and the discrimination, both class and religious, grew also.

Having been accepted into his regiment, the young officer settled into his routine. He still had some instructional classes to take, but his focus was on his duties, usually as one of three company sub-lieutenants (*seconde-lieutenants*). Commissioned artillery and engineer officers went for a year's course at the Combined Artillery and Engineer School in Berlin (also set up by Peucker) and were not fully placed on the strength of their units for a further twelve months. Unlike his British cousins who, even as subalterns, could secure extended leaves for big-game hunting or exploration if they had the necessary connections, the Prussian officer was restricted largely to garrison life. For those in Guards regiments stationed in and around the capital, life was more interesting with the Berlin theatre, opera and other social activities to enjoy but in the far provinces, the social environment was stifling. Even in Berlin however, without additional financial resources, life was dull. A particular Prussian pursuit that would become the ultimate personification of the Teutonic officer was the duel. An entire chapter could be written on the ethics and morality surrounding this practice, however suffice it to say that effrontery, real or imagined, could only be settled honourably by a duel with sword or pistol, and the resulting scar (at best) could be worn with distinction for the rest of one's life.

Hindenburg as a young Guards officer.

Promotion was slow; up to eight years to make first lieutenant, another six for captain and an additional eleven for major. To command a regiment as a lieutenant-colonel could take thirty to thirty-five years. Nevertheless, officers throughout the army were obsessed with promotion and in the absence of a regular system, vying for influence was a constant activity. Fortunately, for the officers who served in the period 1863 to 1871, active service was considerable and promotion was earned rapidly as casualties mounted and the army expanded.

The pinnacle of an officer's career was acceptance into the General Staff and during this period it was achieved as much by influence as merit, however education in this case was a definite requirement. In 1810 Scharnhorst had established the General War School (Allgemeine Kriegsschule) to train officers in advanced studies but it would be nearly fifty years until it had much influence on entry into the higher ranks.[8] In 1859, Peucker renamed it the War Academy (Kriegsacademie) and along with Moltke (a graduate) strived to mould it into the premier conduit for entry to the General Staff but it would be more than a decade before that was ever accomplished.

The victory at Königgrätz was gained by brilliant staff planning indeed, with much help from the needle gun and a great deal of luck. However, without the leadership of a professional officer corps, especially at company level, pressing home the attack and intelligently using their training to hold their ground and defeat their opponents, no amount of planning and weaponry would have prevailed. The wars of unification welded this unique corps into a body of men that became the envy of every army in the world. Its methods and practices became the source of study and imitation in military academies from St Petersburg to Osaka. In the four decades that followed the Franco-Prussian War, a culture of militarism was fostered throughout the expanding empire and under Kaiser Wilhelm II, heading a government unrestrained by civilian control, it dominated German life. Under these circumstances the officer corps, now completely Prussianized, thrived and it was the General Staff which drove the agenda that led to its Armageddon in the bloody fields of Flanders and Picardy in 1918. It can also be said that the true last stand of the Prussian officer corps took place not on the Western Front, but at places with names like El Alamein, Stalingrad, and the Ardennes.

Other ranks

In contrast to purely professional armies such as that of Great Britain, the rank and file of conscript armies tend to reflect the population as a whole. In Prussia's case this was certainly true, but after the 1860 reforms, the militaristic outlook of the officer corps had a marked effect on the men they commanded.

For most of the period from the end of the Napoleonic Wars, the Prussian soldier led a life that was less than challenging. Upon a designated day in the year that he reached twenty years of age, he would report to his local garrison headquarters for induction. After a cursory medical examination, having been pronounced healthy, he would join his fellow comrades into a brief orientation in barrack life, and discipline and given a uniform that probably didn't fit. For the next eighteen months to two years he was drilled mercilessly every day by harsh NCOs. Occasional field exercises and shooting practice would add a little variation to his daily life of drilling but it was drill, drill, drill that occupied his life until his actions upon the battlefield would be as consistent as those on the parade ground. Punishments for most indiscretions were severe beatings by the NCOs with canes and sticks with no officer supervision and some of these would place recruits in the infirmary. Formal punishments for crimes and other serious offences would lead to a public caning before the entire battalion with

Infantry NCO, grenadier, fusilier, jäger and musician, 1864.

long switches that would draw blood from the first blow. This was often followed by a period of days or weeks in the garrison lock-up. The barracks were sparse with few amenities and the soldier's spare time, with little money in his pocket, was spent in the regimental *kasinos* and in the town. After a period of about eighteen months to two years, he passed into the reserves and later into the Landwehr where the occasional annual drills failed to shorten the distance between civilian life and the army.

The first major mobilization since 1815 came in 1848, and startled Prussian officers found they had two completely different armies: the active army which put down the disturbances in Berlin and quelled the revolts in Saxony; and the Landwehr, whose attitudes to their service ranged from unwilling to hostile. Gone were the heady days of devotion and obligation. From this point onward the professional officer corps was determined to rid themselves of the Landwehr and transform the army to preserve Prussia's sovereignty in a world increasingly perceived to be antagonistic. The shambolic performance of the Landwehr in the mobilizations of 1850 and 1859 did nothing to change their minds, indeed by 1859 the changes were ready to be implemented.

The life of a soldier in the post-reform army was little different than that of his father or grandfather. However, the atmosphere was different and he was spending three years with the colours instead of two. His treatment by NCOs was still grim by any standards but punishments were delivered less harshly and with more senior supervision. His barracks were improved under a scheme by Peucker to provide more amenities for the men. Above all, his nutrition improved dramatically. Compared to his counterparts in most European armies, the Prussian soldier was a sturdier, better-fed and healthier individual. The combination of better German education and a thriving agriculture produced recruits who were fit for service far sooner than those in France or Russia. The Prussian obsession with precision drill had not changed and the concept that a man who could robotically obey orders on the parade ground would behave as expected on the battlefield was still strong among the military authorities. Again, however the introduction of the needle gun had changed battlefield tactics and the despite the parade-ground rigidity, a certain individuality was fostered in combat situations, especially amongst NCOs.

The Prussian NCO (*unteroffizier*) was a regular soldier in every sense of the word. If he passed through lance-corporal (*gefreiter*) and gained full corporal

(*corporal*) before his active service ended, he could qualify for *unteroffizier* in the regular army.[9] Upon acceptance he joined the ranks of the junior NCOs (*unteroffizier-ohne-portepee*). In 1859, two special schools were established for the training of NCOs at Potsdam and Jülich, which at this time were reserved for selected men qualified by their exceptional service for higher rank and were

NCOs and men of Uhlan and Dragoon regiments, 1864.

organized into two companies (of 200 men) at each school. The full benefit of the training in these schools however, was probably not felt until the time of the Franco-Prussian War. The average NCO was a hard taskmaster and often a bully. This type of man was regarded as a necessity in the Prussian army, a man whose sole task was to mould young men into efficient soldiers in the space of three years. The most senior rank was the sergeant-major on the regimental staff (*Stabsfeldwebel)* who was very much like his British equivalent – the regimental sergeant-major – and was affectionately (if that was possible) known as *Der Spiess* (loosely translatingas "daddy"). The prospect of an NCO becoming an officer, however, was almost impossible. Rarely were NCOs, even senior ones, commissioned from the ranks and, similar to the British Army, they were assigned to positions such as quartermaster or barracks inspectors. Even in the British Army there were several cases of rankers becoming senior officers[10] but this was practically unknown in the Prusso/German army before 1914. The Prussian NCO, as in any good army, was the very backbone of the system and the efficiency of the Prussian army owed as much to its *unteroffiziere* as it did to the General Staff.

The mobilizations for the Second Schleswig War in 1864 began nearly a decade of active service for most soldiers who had entered the system from 1860. By the time of the 1870 war, the Prussian army corps had developed a cohesiveness that was the envy of Europe. Although the provincial nature of the army corps reflected the regional diversity then in existence, the army of 1866 was one of the most homogenous on the continent; certainly in comparison to its Austrian nemesis. There were certainly differences between Pomeranians and Rhinelanders and although the army was largely protestant, the Polish Catholics of East Prussia were the only major minority group in the country. The soldiers who fought Bismarck's wars of unification would set a standard that won the admiration of the rest of the world and within a decade or less, the outward manifestation of everything military that was Prussian was copied all over the world.[11] The enormous expansion of the army after 1871 reinforced this impression and the military system in place ensured that the training and martial spirit fostered in recruits would never be compromised. Thus the ordinary German soldier, originating as he did from the Prussian prototype, would become the most formidable fighting man in the world during the first half of the twentieth century.

NOTES

1. It was said that toward the end of his reign, he would strike these middle-class officers with his crutch and have them removed from the ranks.
2. Old Field Marshal Wrangel is said to have forbidden his officers and adjutants to issue orders written by hand. Battles, he said, were won with "the sword and not the pen!"
3. Passing the Abitur exam was the ultimate recognition of German secondary education. One could not enter university without it and the path to senior government and diplomatic posts were ensured with it. Ironically, it would be later in the century that its importance would make an impression on the army; in the 1860s aristocratic credentials still counted for more.
4. His uniform bore specific insignia indicating his type of service. This was a black and white diagonally striped cord around the edge of his shoulder straps (See page 242).
5. Many commanding officers withheld their full endorsement of a candidate until they had passed the ensign's exam.
6. Literally "ensign with swordknot". The term "ensign" is used to describe the junior subaltern or the colour bearer in the British Army and is a naval rank in the US Navy.
7. Some of the division schools remained till after 1870, but were phased out by the addition of new war schools at Kassel in 1867 and Oranienstein in 1868.
8. Frederick the Great had attempted to establish an advanced war school in 1765 with the creation of the *Academie des Nobles*, but it never amounted to much as Frederick died before it gained acceptance.
9. Many conscript servicemen actually attained the rank of sergeant or higher, but elected not to enter the regular army and go in the reserves instead.
10. General Hector MacDonald rose from private to general before 1900 as did General "Wullie" Robertson, who eventually became chief of the General Staff (CIGS) during the First World War.
11. For example, by the 1880s the spiked helmet was copied in one form or another by the infantry in Great Britain, The United States, Portugal, Norway, Argentina, Chile, and Brazil; and the cuirassier spiked helmet was copied in many other countries.

CHAPTER NINE

Weapons, Strategy, and Tactics

THE END OF THE NAPOLEONIC WARS did not see the end of the Napoleonic doctrine of warfare. For the next half-century, the armies of the world went to war in the same old way: massed columns or lines of infantry advanced with the bayonet, stopping at intervals to load with the ramrod, and fire at the enemy, who awaited them in formation or behind redoubts. The artillery would occupy the centre and flanks, bombarding the defenders, while the cavalry were poised – en masse – to deliver the crushing blow. This method of warfare had been codified by one of Bonaparte's officers and admirer, Antoine-Henri, baron de Jomini, in his book *Précis de L'art de la Guerre*, published in 1838. Jomini's assertion that modern armies were only effective when moving on interior lines, with the freedom to bring massive force to bear at the point of choice, remained the axiom of the times. From the wars of South American liberation to the 1848 insurrections, the Crimea, and the Italian Wars of Independence, campaigns were conducted, knowingly or unknowingly, on Jominian principles. The influence of Clausewitz, whose book had been published six years before that of Jomini, was yet to be felt in wider military circles, though it did affect important members of the Prussian General Staff, including Moltke, who saw a profound shift in the way wars would be fought in the future.

Antoine-Henri, baron de Jomini (1779–1869).

Leading the way in this shift was the enormous impact of technology. Between 1815 and 1860, the Industrial Revolution began to transform European society. The advance of the steam engine had led to the invention of the steamboat, the railway, and the improved processing of metals, such as iron and steel. By 1855 Sir Henry Bessemer, an Englishman, had developed a way to make steel harder and more flexible, and his converter was quickly adopted. Clothing and equipment were now manufactured using automated processes, and as industrialization took a hold on the developed world, its benefits were quickly adapted for military use.

Railways and the telegraph

No sooner had the historic 1825 train journey from Stockton to Darlington been completed than the military advantages of a railway system were grasped at the highest levels. In Germany, where the first steam locomotive had appeared as early as 1815, railway networks with defensive possibilities had been proposed, while the first commercial routes were being planned. The first route was from Minden to Cologne, and the entrepreneurs of that enterprise, along with advocates of national unity such as Ludolf Camphausen and Freidrich List,[1] eagerly lobbied for a network designed, not only for the military protection of Prussia, but for the unification of Germany itself. List himself was particularly strident that an efficient railway network would insulate Prussia and later, a unified Germany, from surprise attack and envelopment from an aggressive France or Russia.

The army establishment in Prussia, while recognizing the military uses of steam and railways, were not as convinced that such a vast strategic potential existed. As a transporter of heavy stores and troops over the long term, they had no doubt of the railway's strength, but initial studies had shown that troops and artillery on the march took less time, or only a fraction longer, to get to their destinations than existing track, locomotives and rolling stock allowed. The advocates also had little success with the Prussian bureaucracy, mostly in the persons of Karl von Nagler, the postmaster-general, and *Seehandlung* director, Christian von Rother.[2] In the early 1830s, neither man saw any real advantage to railways and allowed little governmental support for such projects. However, the sheer commercial opportunities offered by the building of railways prevented bureaucratic and military indifference from hindering entrepreneurial progress, and the cities of Germany gradually became linked. There was some military interest however, as the convenience of railway travel became clearer. In 1839, the Potsdam to Berlin line carried 8,000 members of the Prussian Guard to annual exercises, and within a few years, Saxon and Bavarian troops would also experience rail travel. Although these efforts were largely symbolic, the mere fact that they had taken place furthered the likelihood of more military acceptance by the Prussian High Command.

For one person, however, the advent and growth of the German railway system was a matter of some significance. In 1841, Helmuth von Moltke was approached by the Berlin–Hamburg Railway to join their board of directors. This offer was made principally because of his links to states such as Denmark and Mecklenburg, through which the line would be run, as well as his being on the Prussian General Staff. As previously mentioned, he had been on loan to the Ottoman Army for several years, in regions where the concept of a railway was a long way off. Despite this, Moltke had been on the staff for some twelve years, and he quickly grasped the strategic and political benefits of a strong and secure network of railways. Like List before him, he soon became an advocate, and wrote various essays and articles in prestigious newspapers, supporting railway expansion. Before long, he had developed a mindset that would later serve him well, including the concept of strong government control over private enterprise, to ensure a militarily efficient rail network. After only four years with the Berlin–Hamburg line, Moltke had to leave the board to take up staff duties in Coblenz. Despite his continuing work, and that of others, the Prussian military and bureaucratic establishment remained sceptical of the value of railways.

The electric telegraph, however, was an idea that was quickly accepted, and adapted both commercially and militarily from the start. Speedier communications over long distances had been the objective of many an ambitious inventor for centuries, but despite many recent improvements, results were always limited by visual restrictions. In 1825, British inventor William Sturgeon invented and demonstrated an electromagnet, which was later perfected by American John Henry in 1830, and Germany's Baron Schilling in 1832, to become an electric telegraph. In Germany, telegraph pioneer Wilhelm Weber had a working system in Göttingen by 1833, and could send a message over two miles. Commercial adaptation of the device followed when Sir Charles Wheatstone set up a telegraph for the Great Western Railway in 1837, and in the USA, Samuel B. Morse had demonstrated his code, and established a commercial telegraph operation by 1844. Within a decade, the telegraph had become an integral part of communication systems all over the world.

The revolutions of 1848 would quickly concentrate the minds of the establishment when it came to the military use of both the railway and the telegraph. There is no doubt that the quick suppression of the uprisings, especially in Germany, owed much to both technologies. The railway, especially, came into its own by allowing the speedy transfer of troops to the trouble spots. In both Saxony and Baden, Prussian soldiers were able to disembark from trains at railheads held by government forces, and deploy where needed before revolts could become more organized. It must also be said that the revolutionaries themselves quickly realized the value of seizing locomotives and rolling stock, for their own purposes as well as to evade advancing forces, and in some cases tracks were destroyed. The point, however, was well taken, and in military circles the concept of moving troops by rail was now established within the doctrine of military planning.

The next major event involving military rail use in Prussia came in 1850, and this time the exercise concentrated the mind in a very different way. The first major showdown with Austria over the hegemony of Germany prompted the mobilization of Prussian forces, and the debacle that followed on the railways played no small part in the Olmütz humiliation. The chief of the General Staff, Carl von Reyher, appointed in 1848, had realized the importance of rail and tried to form a group of officers to oversee its coordination in time of war. The chaotic mobilization of 1850 proved that there was much work to be done. Cavalry horses on some trains were separated from their riders heading in other directions, stores were sent to distant railheads, far from their assigned destination. Whole battalions disappeared altogether, as empty trains showed up at depots where staff officers waited to disembark them. The disaster was further compounded when Austrian mobilizations in the Olmütz area proceeded flawlessly.

Fortunately for Prussia, lessons were learned, and Moltke's observations and recommendations became increasingly influential. The Prussian commerce minister at this time was August von der Heydt and he put a great deal of energy into improving the railway infrastructure in Prussia, including an increasing share of state-owned track and equipment. When Moltke was appointed to the post of chief of staff in 1858, the railway system came into its own as a strategic asset. He worked tirelessly with Heydt to improve every detail of the network. Although a "railway corps" was still an idea of the future, certain NCOs in infantry and Jäger battalions were detailed to liaise with staff at railway depots. The ability to change usage from civilian to military was incorporated into the design of all rolling stock, with moveable seating and collapsible horse stalls.

Above all, coordination between railway staff and military planners was improved dramatically. No amount of structural and physical plant improvements could compensate for the need to organize timetables, and train movements, down to the last detail.

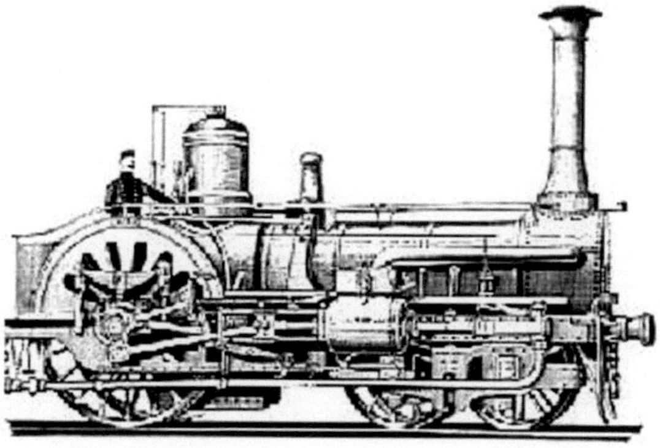

German locomotive, 1854.

The war between Austria and France over Italian independence provided another opportunity to test the effectiveness of the railway network. It was well noted how quickly and efficiently the French were able to concentrate their armies in Lombardy. Moltke, in anticipation of war with France, pressed the government to ready troops to proceed by railway to defend the Rhine. However, despite an assurance to Austria that Prussia would mobilize, the government dithered and Moltke was somewhat put in his place by Heydt. Finally, Prussia decided to mobilize six corps, and was in the process of doing so when Austria was crushingly defeated at Solferino, and sued for peace. Thus, the mobilization of 1859 was almost stillborn, and although more lessons were learned, Moltke was totally unsatisfied with the effort. Prussian hesitancy had halted the mobilization process at the beginning, and when it was restarted, rolling stock had already been moved to other parts of the network.

Amidst the reorganization of the army in the early 1860s, Moltke never lost sight of the importance of the railways to the defence of Prussia. His approach to such a defence was not so much in bricks and mortar, but in mobility. It was essential to be able to move troops around Germany fast enough to respond to any threat before it could materialize. In a few short years, Moltke, now joined by a growing number of proponents, had influenced not only the Prussian government, but the entire German Confederation, to view the railway as a principal component of a common defence. By 1860, there were more than 10,000 miles of railway lines, with sufficient numbers of locomotives and rolling stock to transport six army corps, their horses, stores, and equipment, all in a single day. In 1861, a commission was set up to review the military capabilities of the railway network. Members were drawn from Austria, Prussia, Bavaria, and Hanover, and it was auspicious that the Prussian representative was a certain Captain Wartensleben.[3] After three months of inspections, the commission recommended sweeping changes to the railway networks in Germany. These included greater co-operation between the commercial and military establishments, to standardize equipment, coordinate timetables, locate major junctions and marshalling yards in strategic positions, and a proposal to double track thousands of miles of lines, to allow an unhindered flow of traffic both ways. As the strategic structure of the railway systems now began to evolve, Moltke began to conceive the master plan that would take the Prussian Army to Bohemia in six years, and Paris in ten.

Denomination of the Troops conveyed.	Strength.						Points of Departure on first getting into the Train.	Departure from the Hamburg Station at Berlin.						Refreshments.						Arrival in Hamburg.		
				Carriages.											For Hot Meals.			For Coffee.				
															Time.			Time.				
	Officers.	Men.	Horses.	2-wheel.	4-wheel.	Railway.		Date.	Hour.	Minute.	Date.	Hour.	Minute.	Place.	From	To	Place.	From	To	Date.	Hour.	Minute.
Brigade Staff and 6th Brandenburg Infantry Regiment, No. 52, Staff and 2nd Battalion	30	820	30	1	5	76	Frankfort-on-O.	7	9	3	8	2	—	—	—	—	Witten-burg.	7.37	8.37	8	3	10
One Ammunition Train of Reserve Park	1	17	6	—	31	66	Magdeburg	8	8	20	—	—	—	—	—	—	"	2.44	3.44	9	9	55
One 6-pr. Battery of Brandenburg Field Artillery, Regiment No. 3	4	151	120	—	16	80	Wittenburg	8	6	30	8	11	45	—	—	—	"	5.42	6.42	9	12	55
One 12-pr. Battery	4	151	120	—	16	80	Wittenburg	8	2	45	9	3	—	—	—	—	"	7.37	8.37	9	3	10
Fusilier Battalion of Infantry, Regiment No. 52	25	802	13	5	2	70	Sorau	8	10	14	9	7	45	Witten-burg.	1'20	3	Berlin	5.55	7.45	9	9	33
Infantry Regiment No. 18, Staff and 1st Battalion	28	815	24	1	4	72	Guben	9	3	18	9	10	—	"	3'30	5	"	8.40	10.	9	11	13
One Ammunition Train of Reserve Park	1	17	6	—	31	66	Magdeburg	9	3	40	—	—	—	—	—	—	Witten-burg.	6.55	10.55	10	4	26
One 4-pr. Battery of Brandenburg Field Artillery, Regiment No. 3	4	155	120	—	16	80	Wittenburg	9	1	15	9	6	30	—	—	—	"	11.55	1.55	10	7	41
One Ammunition Train of Reserve Park	1	17	6	—	31	66	Magdeburg	9	4	20	—	—	—	—	—	—	"	2.44	3.44	10	9	55
Divisional Staff and one 12-pr. Battery, Regiment No. 3	6	156	128	—	17	86	Wittenburg	9	6	30	9	11	45	—	—	—	"	5.42	6.42	10	12	55
6th Brandenburg Infantry Regiment No. 52, 1st Battalion	25	802	13	1	3	68	Frankfort-on-O.	10	4	6	10	8	45	—	—	—	"	2.44	3.44	11	9	55
Infantry Regiment No. 18, Fusilier Battalion	25	802	13	5	2	70	Guben	10	3	48	10	11	45	—	—	—	"	5.42	6.42	11	12	55
Brandenburg Yäger Battalion No. 3	25	802	21	9	1	74	Luckenwalde	11	3	30	11	8	45	—	—	—	"	2.44	3.44	12	9	55
Infantry Regiment No. 18, 2nd Battalion	25	802	13	1	3	68	Guben	11	3	48	11	11	45	—	—	—	"	5.42	6.42	12	12	55
Total	204	6,285	653	23	179	1,022																

NOTE.—The numbers in *italics* denote the night, or between the hours of 6 p.m. and 6 a.m. The troops had their breakfast in quarters, previous to getting into the trains.

Contemporary table showing how the 10th Prussian Brigade was moved to Hamburg by rail in 1864.

The tensions that finally arose over the fate of the Danish duchies had been well anticipated by Moltke. Although he had not reached a position where he could dictate strategy, he would strongly urge the government to heed his advice over any conflict that came about. Foreign intervention was a real possibility, so a quick campaign should be planned, to achieve the war aims before such an intervention. Central to this planning was the railway system, so that troops could be in the war theatre within a day or two of mobilization. Indeed, when the order of federal execution was announced, 6,000 Saxon troops were sent to Holstein by train from Leipzig, starting on 22 December 1863, and joined their Hanoverian comrades there on Christmas Day. The Austrian and Prussian troops who replaced them in January were also shipped in by train, and were ready to cross the frontier by 1 February 1864. Because the Danish railway system was not nearly as advanced as the Prussian, neither system had much impact on the general conduct of the war, but officials did have their work cut out for them dealing with freezing track, and snowbound rolling stock. After Moltke had been sent to take command of operations, towards the end of the war, and had organized the difficult landings at Alsen, he was able to issue the welcome order that the troops should be transported home by train, instead of marching, which had been the original plan.

By 1865, Moltke had full control over the operations of the Prussian Army, and was able to plan his campaign for the inevitable clash with Austria. As previously discussed, the key to his plan was rapid mobilization, and the ability to

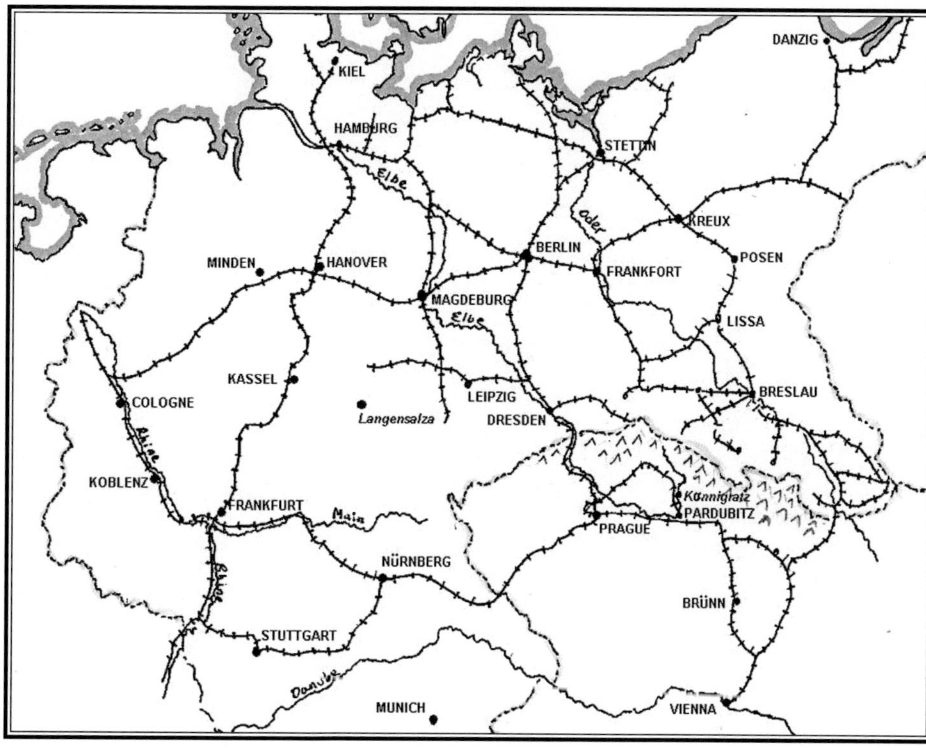

The German railway system in 1866.

concentrate his armies in the area of operations earlier than the enemy. His deliberations were unique, as he had no precedent to work with. He well understood the impact that the railway had made on the outcome of the American Civil War, and had studied it with care. However, railways never formed part of strategic planning in that conflict, neither for Union nor Confederate, and although troops and stores were often moved quickly to war zones, it was done in reaction to events on the ground, so that tracks, junctions, and telegraph lines became targets for both sides. In all of his planning, Moltke's biggest fear was that political issues would cause delays that could be fatal to his designs, and he was right. Time after time, Moltke had stressed that Prussia should mobilize before the Austrians. He knew that Prussia could bring its forces together far faster than Austria, which would be constrained by the limited railway assets in Bohemia. If the Austrians were to fully mobilize first, it could be a disaster for Prussia. William I, however remained hesitant, and put up continuous objections to early mobilization. These delays alarmed Moltke. His plan had to be modified daily, and when the order came at last, his final plan was as risky as it was bold. The start point for the right wing of the Second Army Corps, was at Neisse in Silesia, more than a hundred kilometres from that of the First Army Corps, in the centre. This "stretching out" of Prussia's forces worried many, and predictions of failure were rampant. Moltke, however, was sure that the railway network that he had so assiduously nurtured for the past twenty years would perform as required and that the risks were worth the gamble.

In the final analysis, Moltke's gamble paid off, but as usual, the success was tempered with reality. Although the railways delivered the troops to their start points as planned, their ability to supply the army during and after the campaign left much to be desired. Overconfidence by officials led to perishable stores being loaded fresh at one end of Germany, only to be rotten when they finally arrived, many, many days later, at their destinations. No plans had really been made to control or unload stores at depots, so wagons often arrived unheralded at junctions and stations, and were left there forgotten. Others were shunted off onto branch lines, and "lost", or re-routed back to where they came from. Because of this breakdown, many Prussian soldiers fought the battle of Königgrätz on empty stomachs.

The lesson was, nevertheless, well learned. European war strategy began to centre on mobilization, and any doubts about its importance were eliminated by the results of the Franco-Prussian War. It would be forty-five years until the next major European conflict, and Europeans, especially the Germans, had honed the efficiency of the railways to an art form. Mobilization depended on the railway, and the railway, to a degree, became ever more dependent on the military timetable. The results proved catastrophic. As the mobilizations of 1914 got under way, no political or diplomatic initiative could stop them. The trains were moving, and carrying millions of young men toward the tragic consequences that would ensue.

Zündnadelgewehr: infantry weapons and tactics

The Story of the Needle Gun

From the very first encounters in Bohemia, at Hühnerwasser and Podol, the Austrian soldiers, decimated in their columns by the Prussian needle gun, knew that a different kind of war was confronting them. Combined with appalling generalship, this weapon clearly sealed the fate of the Austrians and their allies in the Seven Weeks War. It had the same effect as the machine gun would have on the Western Front half a century later and, like the machine gun, it was not a secret weapon suddenly sprung upon the world – it had been a known entity for nearly thirty years.

The journey from muzzle-loading musket to breech-loading rifle was not the result of a sudden invention. The concept had been the quest of many a gunsmith since the dawn of firearms and especially since the mid-18th century. The problems nearly always lay in the difficulty of creating a gas-tight breech combined with a safe igniting system for the cartridge. The need for something other than the ramrod was exacerbated by the introduction of rifling. The greater accuracy and range of these weapons were somewhat offset by the aggravation of ramming the bullet and charge down the grooved barrel.

Johann Nikolaus Dreyse in later years.

Toward the end of the Napoleonic Wars, the flintlock musket was beginning to be replaced by the percussion musket, especially among sportsmen. This system replaced the flint with a small explosive cap that ignited the charge when struck by the hammer. Early examples were unreliable and somewhat dangerous and it was the search for a more reliable cap that eventually led to the needle gun. In 1812, a Swiss gunsmith working in Paris, named Samuel Pauly, patented a self-contained cartridge with a detonating cap at its base. However, his and other designs produced into the 1820s continued to experience safety problems. Ironically, it was one of Samuel Pauly's erstwhile employees who found a solution.

Johann Nikolaus Dreyse was born in Sömmerda, Thuringia, on 20 November 1787. His father was a locksmith and it was as a locksmith that Dreyse worked for Pauly during his youth, while drifting in Europe. When his father died in 1814, he returned to Sömmerda and in due course, began to approach the problem of reliable percussion caps. His early attempts were little better than those already on the market, but while he was working on that solution, he tried to improve on Pauly's effort to produce a more efficient cartridge. He found that a small amount of fulminate at the base of the bullet could be detonated by driving a needle through the powder in the cartridge paper. As the company he had founded in 1824 continued to produce percussion caps, Dreyse himself began experiments with smooth-bore muskets, connecting the cocking mechanism to a needle located in the chamber that would pierce the cartridge when the trigger was pulled.

The trials were relatively successful but without some financing, he could not progress far. His early attempts at securing backers was not successful and he was rebuffed by both the Prussian and Austrian war ministries. He therefore turned to producing sporting guns with a revised method of cartridge ignition and a certain Captain Priem of the Prussian Army began to take an interest in the project.

In 1830, Priem took Dreyse back to the Prussian War Ministry and he was given a project to convert some old flintlocks to his system but the results were unsatisfactory as they were prone to premature discharge. However, as Priem had persuaded Prince William and the crown prince to use the sporting guns, the concept was kept alive. Dreyse improved the locking system and later won a contract to produce 1,100 muzzle-loading smooth-bores for the Prussian Army. In 1835 these were delivered to the fusilier battalions of the 4th and 11th Infantry regiments. No sooner had they been placed in the hands of these soldiers than the project was declared a failure as they remained dangerous to use and no one, including Dreyse, foresaw any possible future for a muzzle-loading smooth-bore needle gun.

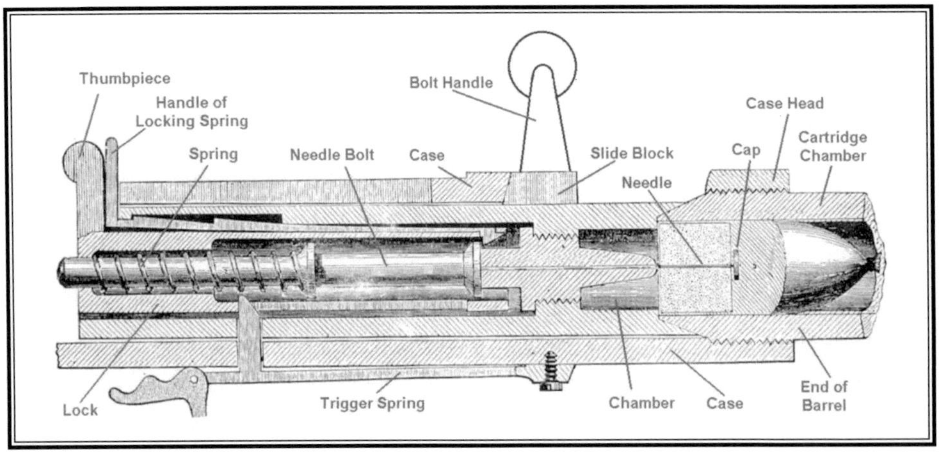

The breech mechanism in the needle gun.

Dreyse, however was not easily discouraged. He immediately went back to work, and the same year came up with the solution in the form of a breech mechanism that used a bolt, like a common door bolt, that was hollowed out. The needle was now attached inside the bolt with a spring and in order to cock the weapon, the bolt was pushed forward and turned down. When the trigger was pulled, the needle pierced the cartridge paper and powder, striking the fulminating cap to ignite. Despite a host of problems including inaccuracy, overheating, gas leakages in the breech and jamming, one aspect of this weapon impressed observers most of all; it fired twice as fast as any other gun, either smooth-bore or rifle. By 1838, Dreyse had refined the weapon enough for it to be tested in field trials and in a personal demonstration, fired 100 rounds without any serious deterioration of the breech or barrel, astounding the trial committee.

Despite misgivings, work on the needle gun continued and Dreyse profited from his relationship with Captain Priem (who became major in 1837) and his ongoing influence over the royal princes. Priem's enthusiasm for the needle gun was such that he boasted to the crown prince that Prussia's borders would be limitless with sixty thousand well-led soldiers armed with such weapons. It was with much satisfaction, therefore, that on 4 December 1840 Dreyse was informed of an order from Frederick William authorizing the purchase of 60,000 needle guns. The purchase was conditional that the weapons would not be issued immediately, but kept in storage for use in a national emergency. It was treated as a secret weapon even though there was common knowledge of its existence and in spite of its obvious advantages it was not necessarily seen as the most effective military firearm in existence at the time.

Several gunmakers and inventors in Europe had worked to improve the rifled musket, to allow the infantryman to fire more rapidly without compromising accuracy. A certain French officer, Colonel Thouvenin, had devised a solution whereby a thin steel post was inserted into the base of the breech block. A conical bullet was then rammed home over the post (after the gunpowder) and when fired, the bullet expanded into the groove of the rifling as it travelled through the barrel. Tests proved that the rifle was accurate over 700 paces, much better than the needle gun and the bullet could be rammed home as fast as a smooth-bore. To be sure, the Thouvenin system had its problems, such as damage to the bullet when rammed, and a breech that was easily fouled, but it proved to be an effective weapon for the French army in North Africa.

Such was the success of the Thouvenin system, that it was adopted by the Prussian jäger and their M1835 Jägerbüchse was converted. By 1847, debate about the merits of the Dornbüchse (as the jäger weapon was called) and the needlegun was raging. The Guard Reserve Regiment was chosen by a royal commission to compare the weapons, and the needle gun was declared the winner. Despite this, the jäger tenaciously hung on to their preferred weapon until the mid-1850s. All debates aside, Dreyse's weapon was about to put to its first test in combat.

A month after the 1848 revolutions broke out, the king directed that all of the fusilier battalions of the Guard and regular regiments be issued with the needle gun, a task that was completed in late 1849. Apart from training to use the weapon, there had been no consideration given to the tactical implications of a rapid-firing breech-loader on the battlefield. Nevertheless, soldiers learn quickly under fire and as the Prussian forces were dispersed around Germany to put down insurrections, the advantages of the new weapon became plain to see. In Saxony, the four-day battle during May 1849 to suppress the revolutionaries in Dresden was won in large part by the fusiliers of the Garde Grenadier Regiment Kaiser Alexander and the 24th Infantry Regiment profiting from the quick-firing ability of their rifles to keep the heads of enemy marksmen down while their comrades outflanked the barricades. Dissidents had seized a number of the needle guns when they stormed the Berlin arsenal the previous year and Prussian forces experienced a few cases of the rifles being used against them in some of the street fighting. The weapon was to prove successful in the Schleswig-Holstein campaign of 1849 and when used by the forces under Prince William during the expedition to Baden. His report produced upon his return to Berlin praised the needle gun and declared it satisfactory, especially in defensive situations and – despite criticisms from various sources including the influential General K. W. von Willisen who argued that entrusting such weapons to ordinary soldiers was too costly – advocated its distribution throughout the army.

When the king, accepting his brother's advice, ordered a major increase in the supply of breech-loaders to the army it required a major reassessment of the

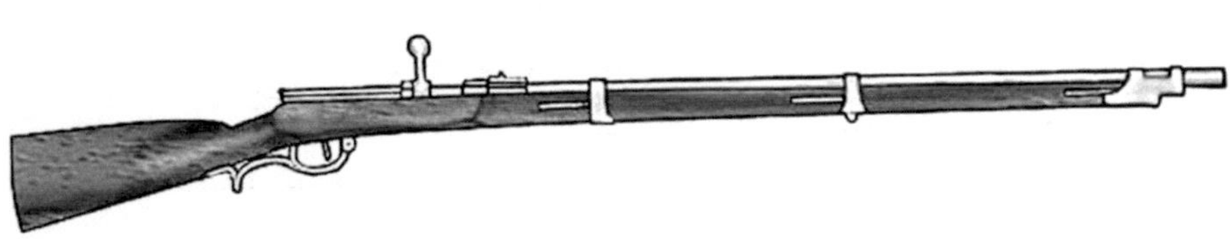

Prussian needle gun, 1862.

Prussian arms-manufacturing capabilities. By this time, fewer than 60,000 rifles had been issued, but with production at only 15,000 a year, it would take many years to fulfil a requirement that would be nearly 300,000 for the entire army including reserves. Creating a new factory was not a simple proposition. Dreyse's factory in Sömmerda was custom-built to produce the needle gun, followed by another private operation in Suhl. The tooling and machinery were very specialized as the construction of the breech-loader and its mechanism were necessarily more precise than for the smooth-bore musket and it was considerably more expensive. By 1851, production at these two plants had reached 22,000 units a year; and as the government acquired more arms factories at Spandau and Potsdam, the jäger and sharpshooters of the Guard were issued with their weapons. Although the production situation seemed to be in hand, the discussion continued unabated about how the rifle would be most effective. Tactical issues stayed far behind the practical concerns about ammunition expenditure and individual soldier loads, but soon the officials considering these matters were confronted by new realities brought home by conflicts abroad. They were also faced with a challenge from a different kind of weapon to the needle gun, battle-tested in major conflicts and used with tactics that left the victors with an enviable impression of its value.

The first major European conflict since the Napoleonic Wars erupted in the Crimea in 1854 when Britain and France sided with Turkey against an expansionist Russia. The Prussians were well out of it, but their military observers at the seat of the war sent back enthusiastic reports on the part played by the Minié rifle in the fierce battles that were being fought. The entire British army and all French light troops and Chasseurs had been re-equipped with the Minié before the war started and had been well trained in their use. They were very effectively used against the Russians, mostly armed with old smooth-bores, who were felled by the thousands at ranges to which they could not respond. What was it about this rifle that merited such attention? With the needle gun practically considered as the Prussian infantry weapon for decades to come, why was this thinking suddenly brought up short?

It was, in reality, merely a bullet. Since the 1840s a French army captain, Claude-Étienne Minié had addressed the issue of the rapid reloading of a rifled musket. In 1849, he produced and patented a bullet that was shaped in the form of a cylinder with a conical top. There were three grooves on the barrel of the cylinder and in the base there was a small round hollow in the centre into which a small zinc plug was inserted. The ignition of the cartridge would force the plug into the body of the bullet, expanding it into the rifling as it sped through the barrel. The enthusiasm for the Minié system was due to its infinite superiority over the smooth-bore, being twice as accurate at 750 paces and ten times as accurate at 400 paces. Its accuracy over 1000 paces for marksmen made every rifled musket obsolete. In addition, troops needed no particular training to use it, as its function was the same as the old weapons with lock and hammer action and requiring the ramrod. What made it instantly successful was a simple fact: every musket, either rifled or smooth-bore, could be converted to accept the new ammunition. Smooth-bore muskets, of course needed rifled barrels but the conversion was quick and efficient and armies could be re-equipped relatively quickly.

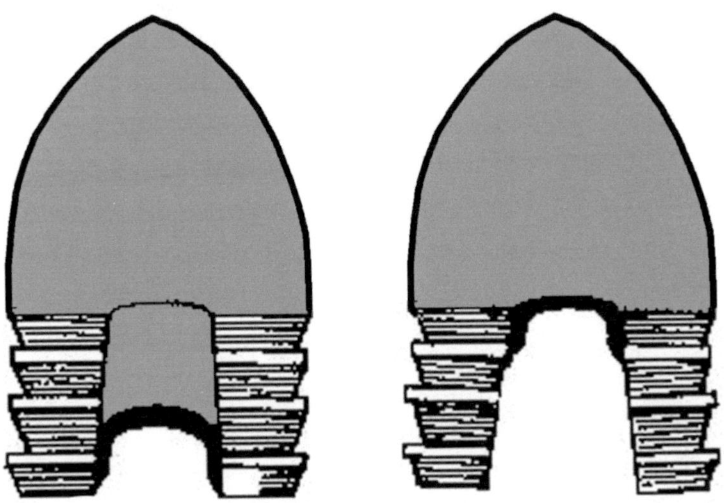

Before *After*

A Minié ball before and after firing.

In Prussia, all bets were suddenly off. The detractors of the needle gun had found a *cause célèbre* with which to argue their case. Every aspect of the Minié rifle met the needs of the army in matters of cost, speed of re-supply, and training. To the modern observer, the advantages of a breech-loader would be self-evident, but in the 1850s the system seemed more of a novelty, and an inconvenient one at that. Not only was the tooling more extensive, but problems had emerged in practical use such as the needle proving fragile and breaking regularly, and the bolt jamming. For five years, the debate swayed back and forth with committees being formed and disbanded. King Frederick William IV was probably not the most decisive monarch, and he developed a confusing approach to the issue. His brother William, however, remained a constant champion of Dreyse's rifle throughout the debate. A committee of 1855 declared their preference for the Minié system by ten to eight, mostly as a response to the king's exasperation and within a year, 300,000 weapons had been converted. The king, however remained obdurate and constantly changed his mind, even when General Willisen, a Minié supporter, suggested some uniformity by issuing needle guns to Landwehr units where the parent corps already had them. Finally, in 1858 the king had a stroke, followed soon by others that incapacitated him completely. Upon ascending to the regency, Prince William ordered the rest of the army, including the Landwehr, to be issued with the needle gun. The decision was final and the discussion was over. The *Zundnagelgewehr* was the rifle of the Prussian Army.

Infantry tactics 1850–66

It was not the prospect of the breech-loading needle gun that caused European military leaders to review infantry tactics, it was the Minié. For the first time since Napoleonic times, large European armies had clashed in the Crimea. Little had changed in principle, but the Minié's extended range allowed the British and French to deliver fatal volleys to the Russians before they were in range themselves. For the first time, firepower was a major consideration on the battlefield and the concern was not only for those on the delivering side, but how those on the receiving end would handle it. The longer range affected every aspect of the battlefield; Not only infantry, but cavalry and artillery gun crews, rear-echelon troops, and staff were now all vulnerable to rifle fire. Moving the artillery out of range only reduced their contribution to the battle and cavalry charges could be easily broken up before they were even close to their objective. The challenge facing general staffs throughout Europe was to develop tactics to enable the infantryman to do what he was supposed to do in order to win battles; go through the enemy and overwhelm them.

For many, the answer lay in altering skirmishing tactics so that *chasseurs* and sharpshooters with Miniés could keep the enemy's heads down and prevent advances, while themselves offering widely spaced targets difficult to drop. To this end the French expanded their regiments of *Chasseurs à Pied* dramatically between the Crimea and the Franco-Austrian War of 1859. However, many also saw that the only way to counter the long-range rifle was fight defensive battles, forming trench lines and other static fortifications and wearing the attacker down until offensive action could be successful.

From 1854 onwards, the armies of Europe re-armed themselves with Miniés. In addition to the French and British armies, those of Austria and Germany introduced versions of the system, each with their own modifications. For the Austrians, it was the Lorenz M1854, completely issued to their infantry battalions by 1858 and for the Bavarians it was the Podewils. Other German states such as Baden, Württemberg and Hessen-Darmstadt adopted the Wild rifle. The rest of the principalities and duchies with troops in VII and VIII Bundeskorps would purchase rifled muskets from them or Prussia with varying degrees of political expediency. The most obvious advantage was that, for the first time the Bundesarmée was equipped with a standard ammunition calibre.

Statue of Dreyse at the memorial to the 71st Infantry Regiment at Sommerda.

In 1859, France went to war with Austria to aid Italy in her penultimate step to unification. The battles of Montebello, Magenta, and Solferino succeeded in achieving their aims, but in doing so raised the debate over infantry tactics a few notches further. The Austrians, newly equipped with their Lorenz rifled muskets were judged to be the better armed, however the French were able to overwhelm them, not with their own Miniés, but with the bayonet. For Napoleon III this was the culmination of a military philosophy he had been promoting since his reign began. At last the French had proved that élan and courage could overcome technology and provide a reinforcement of morale to troops intimidated by that technology. The fact that the Austrians were badly led and poorly trained, not only in their field manoeuvres, but in the use of their own weapons, was not immediately apparent. For the French, it was a conviction that would survive through 1870 until 1914, with disastrous consequences. In any event, the doctrine spread and even the defeated Austrians revised their infantry tactics to make the bayonet-tipped infantry charge the centrepiece of their battle plan, with calamitous repercussions in 1866.

Prussia was probably the only state where the decisions were unique. Although the polemic was similar to that in the rest of Europe, the ingredients were substantially different. Until 1858 the army had possessed two kinds of infantry firearm, the Dreyse breech-loader and the Minié rifle. Prince William put a close to the debate when he became regent and from 1859 the needle gun was gradually issued to all branches of the service with most units fully equipped from 1861.[4]

With regards to infantry tactics, the initial discourse was centred on the use of ammunition. It was widely asserted that the average infantryman, armed with a rapid-firing breech-loader, would most likely waste ammunition: why fire one round when you can fire three? This inclination was deemed to be difficult to overcome on the battlefield, and again stood in the way of the inevitable: coming to grips with the enemy. As early as 1853, Prince William directed that the skirmishing lines of infantry battalions armed with the needle gun now form themselves into smaller units or *Gruppen* led by an *Unteroffizier*, thus raising the NCO from a parade-ground martinet to a true squad leader on the battlefield. When extended to all infantry battalions in the army in 1854, the system became enshrined into Prussian battle tactics. Although this seemed a revolutionary approach in the mid-1850s, it was actually a limited one. The concept of the infantry column advancing in tight formations and closing with the enemy continued to be the principal doctrine on the battlefield while skirmishing remained the preliminary action before the general advance.

The conclusions drawn from the French victories in 1859 were actually greeted with relief by many in the Prussian army. It was as if the vast changes on the battlefield projected by those champions of the breech-loaders and other long-range rifles were come to naught. The infantry charge was safe and the old adage of the Russian army that "the bullet is stupid but the bayonet is smart" remained true. Despite this thinking, Prussian tactics were about to evolve, largely based on the thoughts of the most important man on the Prussian General Staff.

Initially, Moltke's thinking had revolved around the defensive battle to counter long-range rifles forcing the enemy to either attack or retreat. He perceived battles of manoeuvre, of flanking operations, and envelopment. Extensive reports on the Franco-Austrian War convinced him that the Austrian defeats were largely because of poor leadership and the inert character of the Austrian soldier, not French élan. He dismissed the tactics of the skirmishing line, describing it as ineffective and prone to causing unnecessary casualties. With the rapid fire and 600-yard range capability of the needle gun, defenders could use terrain, vegetation, and buildings for cover and pick the enemy off at will. The charge, when it came, would be against an enemy severely weakened by losses they were unable to sustain. It was the strategy of the offensive and the tactics of the defensive that would win the future war.

Prussian regulations of 1861 however clearly emphasised the tactical offensive. The objective of these tactics was to force the enemy into the open, cut off his reserves, and defeat him piecemeal. The tactical formation was the company, which was nimble enough to adapt to the situation and form its own battle group when the objective was clear. The problem, however, was that despite these regulations, the average battalion commander's thinking was a decade behind and this was proved in the summer manoeuvres of 1861, in which the battalion still remained the formation of choice for the commanders and to foreign observers it appeared that despite revolutionary weaponry, the attacking forces "came on in the same old way".

The main campaign of the 1864 war against Denmark did little to convince the same observers that much had changed. While the Austrians distinguished themselves at Ober-Selk and Oeversee with bayonet charges, the Prussians avoided battle at Missunde by taking the roundabout road to Düppel. It was only in the final stages of the war in a minor engagement at Lundby, when a company of Danish infantry surprised a Prussian force encamped near the town, that the merits of the needle-gun became clear. The Prussians, briefly forewarned of the attack, quickly deployed before the Danes could outflank them and in the twenty-minute firefight that ensued, dropped 88 of the 180 men in the Danish company, of which 22 were killed. The Prussians suffered three men wounded.

So it was that in late June 1866, the Prussians went to war in a world convinced of an Austrian victory. Although much was said about the indifferent generalship of Benedek and his commanders, more was said of the terrifying needle gun. It was considered a war-winner and within five years, the muzzle-loading rifle had been consigned to antiquity. The armies of the world rapidly re-equipped with breech-loading rifles and within twenty years the preferred breech-loader was a bolt-action rifle. Nearly 100 years later, the final versions of Dreyse's conception were finally being replaced worldwide by modern assault rifles.

The guns: steel rifles and breech-loaders

When Crown Prince Frederick William ordered Colonel Prince Kraft zu Hohenlohe-Ingelfingen, the commander of the Guard reserve artillery, to blast away at the Austrian right flank at Königgrätz, the experienced gunner knew that his moment had come. The order was given to alert the crown prince's cousin, Frederick Charles, that the Second Army had arrived on the battlefield. For the next few hours the colonel would move his guns forward with the advanced guard of the crown prince's army, engaging the Austrian batteries above the village of Jericek and beyond. He would order his batteries to limber up again and again, switching positions and breaking the rules, such as positioning his guns at the base of a hill and firing upwards. His batteries would be reinforced as the Second Army's onslaught continued. Together, outnumbering the Austrian gunners, they would support the infantry at Chlum and Sweti until the end of the battle. Had Hohenlohe-Ingelfingen obeyed his original instructions, he and his artillery would have remained behind with the main body and their contribution to the battle would have been peripheral. Determined man that he was, he reinterpreted his orders, and decided to be up front where the action was taking place. So, he pushed his mounted gunners around the slower-moving infantrymen, splashing them with mud and ripping through the fields of high-standing barley, until he was at the forefront of the drama.

Sadly, Hohenlohe's handling of his batteries was the only bright spot in the performance of the Prussian artillery during the campaign. In both Frederick Charles' First Army and the Army of the Elbe, the artillery had allowed itself to be little more than a bit player in the great enterprise. Even as they advanced to battle, it seemed as if they were in the way of the infantry, when their limbers and caissons were ordered aside to let the marching troops pass. As the battle started, the mixture of smooth-bore and rifled guns was not effectively used. At the Bistritz crossings, the infantry were pummelled by the well-placed Austrian artillery on the heights, and when the Prussian gunners came up their reply was lamentable. At first, they could not get the range with the smooth-bores. However, even when the longer-range rifles were brought up, their flat trajectory prevented them from delivering the kind of 'plunging' fire needed. Even in the Swiepwald, where the Austrians had difficulties finding Prussian targets without hitting their own men, there were only four batteries, and their response was equally ineffective. As the Austrians and Saxons retreated from the Army of the Elbe, instead of hammering them as they fled, the Prussian gunners were able to do little more than keep their heads down. If the course of the battle of Königgrätz had depended on artillery, then the Austrian army would have prevailed. However, despite the gallantry of the Hapsburg gunners, it was the Prussian infantry with their Zündnadelgewehr that defeated them. Although the dogged brown-coated artillerymen fought their guns to the muzzle, they were unable to prevent the tidal wave that overwhelmed them. At the end of the day, Benedek's wish that the retreat should be covered by his artillery, to the last man if necessary, was carried out with courageous dedication. It was their action that probably influenced Moltke not to pursue the vanquished army beyond the Elbe that day.

How was it that the Prussian artillery's performance during the campaign was so lacklustre? This branch of the army was meant to be superior in skill and training to the infantry. Historians have generally laid the blame on a mindset where losing guns in battle was so unacceptable that artillery commanders adopted an attitude of undue caution. Whatever the cause, it was a surprising result, because the preceding years had seen the Prussian army at the forefront of the technological advances which were being made in ordnance. In fact, it was the efforts of a determined metal salesman from the Ruhr region of Germany who changed the course of artillery design, and whose last name became the byword for the military industrial relationship in Europe for the next seventy years. That name was Krupp. However, before his story is told, it is necessary to trace the progress of the artillery branch in Prussia from the end of the Napoleonic Wars.

Prussian artillery after 1815

In his book *Railroads and Rifles*, Dennis Showalter suggests that if the Prussian artillery had been compared to a step-child before 1806, it was more like an illegitimate half-brother after 1815. There is much truth to this, mostly because, following twenty-three years of almost continuous warfare, governments all over Europe had little inclination to spend monies on expensive military technology.

Infantrymen with muskets and bayonets were considerably cheaper than gunners and cannon. The calamity of 1806 left the Prussian artillery so short of equipment that when the War of Liberation began in 1813, they had to beg, borrow, and steal cannon from wherever they could. By 1815, the army possessed a mishmash of pieces from all over Europe, varying so much in calibre, weight, and condition that few artillery brigades possessed batteries with the same type of cannon. Shortly before his death, Scharnhorst (himself a gunner) had instituted a body of men charged with overseeing the artillery arm, with the specific aim of improving the quality of their equipment. This body was known as the Artillerie-Prüfungs-Kommission (APK). This was an unsurprising move, given his dedication to this branch, and his treatise *Handbuch der Artillerie*, which became the primer for Prussian artillerymen for years to come. Scharnhorst also appointed its chief, Prince August of Prussia, who would head the commission until his death in 1843.

Prussian 9-pounder.

In 1816, the APK oversaw the replacement of the disparate artillery inventory, with standard patterns of both cannon and associated equipment. This was known as the System c/16, and consisted of 6- and 12-pounder field cannon, along with 7- and 10-pounder howitzers. Unfortunately, this system was designed in haste, and produced pieces that were too heavy and slow to fire. In addition, they were, despite an improved laying system, wildly inaccurate. Nevertheless, the army was satisfied with the standardization that the system c/16 brought and this, to the Prussian mind, was as important as anything else. For the next thirty years or more, the APK would preside over the numerous technical and organizational issues affecting the ordnance of the Prussian army. Considerable attention was given to shrapnel, the destructive shell that sprayed lead shot in all directions when it exploded, and was particularly murderous to infantry. Named after the British artillery lieutenant who invented it in 1784, the shell was widely used during the Napoleonic Wars. However, it was an unreliable weapon to say the least, as it rarely burst where it was supposed to, therefore negating much of its effectiveness. Developing a reliable fuse to control that burst consumed the APK for much of the period, but without much success. By 1866, it had even been withdrawn from service. There was also debate about the use of artillery in general, with advocates of both the horse and foot branches vying for ascendancy. The quest for more mobility tilted the argument in favour of the horse artillery, and while tight budgets dramatically restricted training and equipment for the foot batteries, in the 1820s and 1830s, the mounted branch was left untouched. This policy inevitably produced an imbalance between the two branches as the emphasis was placed on the cavalry style of the horse gunners. Less attention was paid to the effectiveness of the equipment they towed, than the dash and élan exhibited before they had dismounted, and were ready to serve their guns.

The discussion over the respective merits of horse and foot batteries could not escape the notice of the APK, and inevitably led to other issues involved in improving mobility. Of these issues, weight was the most challenging. Since the beginning of the century, bronze had largely replaced iron as a material for cannon barrels. It was a superior metal for two reasons; it was lighter than cast iron, and more durable, meaning that it was less likely to burst when fired. Of course, bronze was considerably more expensive than iron, and it is not surprising that the War Ministry pushed for a return to cast iron. After all, they argued, improvements in metallurgy and manufacturing would probably produce a more viable product. There was little enthusiasm for such a prospect within the ranks of the artillery or the APK. In the late 1830s, work began on a new range of artillery equipment with an eye to mobility, and in the year for which it was named, the System c/42 was introduced. The guns were essentially the same as the c/16s, except that the carriages were lighter, and the limbers and caissons were designed to allow the crew to ride on them. Eliminated from the inventory were the unwieldy heavy howitzers. The adherents of mobility had prevailed. Even so, there were detractors who argued that the new designs had been made without regard to what they considered to be the essence of artillery: fire power. They argued that the new 6-pounders were too light, and should be replaced by at least 9-pounders. This once again brought the argument back to materials. Events would soon intervene, however, to put discussions on hold. The revolutions of 1848 involved Prussian troops in combat for the first time since 1815. The artillery was used in Baden and Schleswig-Holstein, but their performance was not good. Insurgents were often armed with rifles, which had enough range to hit the gunners while they were serving their pieces. This forced the artillery to limber up and retreat. When they did bring their guns to bear, they were less than effective. In summation, it appears that the guns and equipment performed as required, and it was tactics that fell short. Ironically, a vast improvement in cannon technology had been lying in a Berlin warehouse for nearly two years. The item was not so much overlooked, as not requiring urgent attention. It was a cast-steel cannon barrel shipped for testing from the metal works of a certain Alfred Krupp.

Alfred Krupp, rifled-steel cannon and breech-loaders

Born on 26 April 1812, Krupp was the scion of a merchant family from Essen, where the family's earliest appearance in the town records go back to the late 16th century. His father, Freidrich, had started a foundry in 1811 to duplicate English cast steel. His efforts were unsuccessful, and when he died in 1826, he left his company and family almost in ruins. Alfred was the second child of four but was the eldest son, and so at fourteen years old, he took over the reins of the family business. He was a skinny and angular youth, and his character immediately embedded itself in the firm and its methods. In his book *The Arms of Krupp,* William Manchester describes him as, "Restless, brilliant, imaginative, tormented, farsighted and . . . supremely practical." His journey to the doors of the Prussian War Ministry and the APK was complicated and eventful, and, indeed, the story is worth a book of its own. His goal was the same as his father's – to duplicate the quality of English steel so that he could compete for government contracts. He had set himself an almost impossible task, as the English manufacturers had dominated the European market for five decades. However, by the early 1830s, he was producing a good enough product to sell to small users like watchmakers and goldsmiths. The Prussian government was not impressed enough to either provide contracts or loans, so the company surfed on the wave of bankruptcy for a decade or more.

Alfred Krupp (1812–87).

Krupp's energy was almost a form of perpetual motion. He slept badly. He ate little. He was always on the move. Soon, instead of steel ingots, he was producing small rollers for spoons and forks, and as these improved, he secured better and bigger contracts. He travelled extensively, and in 1838, he toured Europe on what can only be described as a spying mission. He visited France and Britain, where he spent five months,[5] and although it is not clear what exactly he achieved, he was deeply impressed by the latter country, even anglicizing his first name when he returned. Disaster befell the company in 1840, when Krupp obtained his largest contract to date. The Viennese government ordered a rolling mill for the imperial mint, which Krupp delivered accordingly. Unfortunately, the Austrian government found excuse after excuse for not paying him (citing matters of quality), and it took a year's worth of superhuman efforts on his part to finally receive a modest payment. It was only enough to prevent total insolvency. Slowly, the firm recovered, as it continued to produce marketable products. The spoon and fork rollers were patented in Britain, and a prize was won by his brother for a set of chimes at the Berlin Industrial Exhibition of 1844. Things were going well enough at this time for Krupp to turn his attention to something entirely different.

The quest for more lucrative products was never far from the mind of this restless entrepreneur. He was testing locomotive wheels and springs, with an eye to the almost guaranteed expansion of the railways, and new types of machine tools were already on his drawing boards. He had also experimented with something that appeared to be a hobby, but turned out to be something more. Krupp had, over about seven years, developed a method to produce hollow-forged steel musket barrels, and he appeared pleased enough with the results that he had ridden over to the nearby Saarn Arsenal to see what the officers there thought of them. They were duly impressed, but also convinced that his invention would come to nothing because of the cost. In addition, they pointed out that there was nothing wrong with the barrels they were already using.[6] They did, however, agree to keep the barrels and test them at some point. He had then taken samples to the Berlin exhibition, along with his brother's chimes, but they attracted no attention. He remained convinced that his product was a viable alternative to iron barrels, but his fast-moving mind had seen an even better use – cannon barrels. He then contacted the War Ministry itself, this time armed with some flattering complements on his product from the French War Ministry. The reply was the same as before – thanks, but no thanks. The issue was always the same – cost.

There was however this time a caveat from the War Ministry. They would look at the issue of cast-steel cannon barrels some time in the future. As Krupp went to and fro, with the various government entities, there was another awkward interlude, in which a chance to manufacture cuirasses for the heavy cavalry regiments seemed within grasp. Unfortunately, this was then snatched away by a competitor (the original manufacturer) because of connections within the regiments themselves. In late 1844, he made another proposal to the ministry: to produce a thin-walled, cast-steel 3-pounder cannon barrel for testing. This time he received an immediate and surprisingly positive reply.[7] It took three years for him to actually cast and ship it, but when he finally did, in September 1847, it was left at the Spandau Arsenal, uncovered and ignored for another two years. In frustration, Krupp decided to take on the APK itself, and relentlessly pushed the commission to test the barrel, which they finally did, on 2 June 1849. The results were astounding. Attempt after attempt was made to burst the barrel, using heavier and heavier charges, without result. It was only after a massive (and unlikely) charge was placed that they succeeded, not in bursting the barrel, but blowing it to bits! Celebration, however, was premature. There was much more work to be done.

The APK was not prone to making hasty decisions. It was a ponderous and cautious body. Krupp, however, was at this time happy to let them ponder. His interest in producing axles, wheels, and springs for railway carriages had finally paid dividends. Krupp's steel seamless tyres were in demand all over Europe, and his patents were recognized everywhere.[8] At last, the company was on a firm financial standing, owing to its principal's boundless energy and skill as a salesman. Even so, steel cannon barrels never strayed far from his mind. In 1851, along with ingots, cuirasses, and railway wheels, he showed his cannon, mounted on a glistening carriage, at the Great Exhibition in London. It was an astonishing success, and won the firm another gold medal. Even so, despite all this attention, there were still no orders. Meanwhile, the APK had turned its attention to a number of technical issues that were confronting most European armies. The increased range of rifled firearms had put the gunners in a quandary. If batteries could no longer deploy safely close to the enemy, how would *their* range be increased. Was the answer rifled cannon barrels? Tests were made using bronze barrels, and the range was indeed increased. Rifled muzzle-loading (RML) guns, though, were slow to load, and could not be fired fast enough to halt rapidly advancing infantry. Thus began the debate about breech loading. The transition from spherical shot to shells restarted the discourse on shrapnel. Never before had artillerymen encountered such a bewildering array of technology.

A Krupp heavy gun.

Krupp was never far from the discussions, and he constantly probed for access to the decision-makers. Soon after the Great Exhibition, he presented King Frederick William IV with one of his cannon, which was duly displayed at the Potsdam Palace. There, it took the fancy of Tsar Nicholas when visiting in 1852. Nicholas was more impressed with Krupp's cannon than Dreyse's rifle but not enough, it seems, to generate any orders. Even when Krupp made the Russian army a gift of a cast-steel cannon, it came to nothing. After firing the weapon thousands of times without any damage, the Russians declared themselves extremely impressed, and promptly placed it in a museum. (Within five years, the Russians were ordering guns from Krupp regularly.) Meanwhile, Krupp took a trip around the German federal states such as Brunswick, Württemberg, and Hanover. Again, this yielded interest but little in the way of sales. He then made a connection with someone who would eventually lead him and his products into the innermost circles of influence. This was what he had always sought.

Prince William of Prussia was the consummate military man; brave, disciplined, and dedicated to his trade. As his brother, the king, descended into mental incompetence, William was gaining ascendancy in the affairs of state, most especially in matters military. He was no technician, but he was quick to recognize the importance of innovation, when it was related to the army. Having seen the cannon at Potsdam, he wanted to see the foundry from whence it came. In the summer of 1853 Krupp, now a married man, was happy to host His Royal Highness, and show him round the establishment.[9] The visit was a great success, and from that moment, the prince would take a keen interest in the firm of Friedrich Krupp. The APK also had a new chairman in 1854; Lieutenant-General August Enke, a strong proponent of rifled cannon, who arrived fully prepared to shake up this august body. Unfortunately, he had an opponent in the form of the inspector general of artillery, General Hahn, who supported the use of shell-firing smooth-bores. The next fifteen years saw a continuous battle between the two men over each system. In retrospect, this rivalry would have ironic implications as the artillery's performance in the wars of 1864 and 1866 would show.

For more than a decade Krupp would leave the APK somewhat to its own devices. He could do this with confidence, partly because he now had a royal patron, but also because his foundry was busy filling orders for steel railway tyres, axles, and springs on a regular basis. Also, the concept of rifled steel cannon was gaining ground throughout the military establishment, and in 1856, Enke ordered two 6-pounder barrels from Krupp which were tested the following January. The general consensus was that an army equipped with such artillery might well rule the battlefield. However, the technical aspects of such thinking put any such decisions far into the future. Also, the stiff opposition of General Hahn to steel rifles further complicated the issue. The question of an effective breech dogged the experts for some time. Bronze breechblocks wore out too fast, and even steel blocks needed to be expertly designed to prevent leakage. In 1859, the APK was convinced it had an airtight design. In the same year, the field artillery was reorganized with each brigade now having three foot battalions, one of 7-pounder howitzers, and two of 12-pounder guns. The mounted battalion retained the 6-pounders. Why any reorganization was deemed necessary for the artillery at that time is baffling, since there was yet to be a decision on when and how they would be equipped with new shell and rifled guns. Krupp was particularly upset, because there was still little prospect of any forthcoming orders, despite the fact that he had been providing the government with samples for nearly ten years. William of Prussia, prince regent since 1858, increasingly became more important to Krupp's fortunes. Enke had invited the prince to witness a test firing of a 6-pounder cast-steel breech-loading rifle from the Krupp works. Noting William's satisfaction with the results, Enke and his staff recommended a purchase of one hundred of the rifles from the Krupp firm. At the suggestion of General Constantin von Voights-Rhetz, the prince regent surprised them all by insisting on an order for three hundred, to be manufactured and delivered with all dispatch.

Politics and warfare

Krupp personally went to pick up the order in Berlin. Now, at last, he could move freely amongst the most powerful. Bismarck, newly appointed as minister-president by William, was sent down to Essen to visit him. They got on famously, especially when it came to the appreciation of horses. Krupp would correspond regularly with the likes of Bonin and Roon. Of course, Krupp had an agenda. As he was now a major supplier to the Prussian government, he wanted to lock in his position and secure himself a monopoly. This was not only for his cannon, but also (and particularly perhaps) for his railway products. The last thing the APK wanted was a supplier with a monopoly, a view shared by August von der Heydt, the commerce minister. One issue that confirmed this attitude was that, after extensive testing, the Krupp breech-block design was now found wanting. The APK also turned their attention to foreign manufacturers. The performance of the French artillery, especially their light 4-pounders, in the recent war with Austria had been impressive enough for them to examine cannon from the French manufacturer Schneider. Krupp was naturally furious, but he was somewhat hoist with his own petard as he was, like any good entrepreneur, selling his products all over the world. In fact, Russia was probably his biggest customer. Eventually, however, his influence at court paid off when the prince regent, over the strongest objections of Heydt, ordered that Krupp's patents associated with the state railways be extended another seven years. Then, however, Krupp went too far. He offered his breech-block patent to the War Ministry, on condition that he could secure a fifteen-year contract. He fully expected William's support, but even the prince (who would become king in a few months) balked at this suggestion, and Roon considered it outrageous, especially when the Krupp design wasn't even considered acceptable. Krupp was abruptly informed that he could bid on cannon contracts like everyone else, but would receive no monopoly.

Alfred Krupp and his difficulties were far from the thoughts of the APK and the Prussian artillery arm at this time. What was concentrating their minds was somewhat more fundamental. How would they use the vast new array of technology now available? What, exactly, would be the role of the artillery in future battles? The polemics remained the same as before – mobility versus firepower, and rifles versus smooth-bores. Added to this heady mixture was the ingredient of muzzle- versus breech-loading. A special commission had been established by William to make recommendations on the organization and armament of the artillery. The commission judged that batteries of eight guns were too unwieldy, and should be reduced to six, which of course, meant yet another reorganization of the artillery. The mobility proponents in the commission also latched on to the 4-pounder rifles that had been the stars of the Franco-Austrian war of 1859, and their recommendations included suggestions that four batteries of each regiment should be so equipped. At every turn, the commission's recommendations added more confusion to an already complicated situation. The 4-pounder rifle ended up as the only solid decision made, and the Krupp company was asked to supply samples for testing. The guns sent by the firm were mounted on carriages, and had breeches of Krupp design and manufacture. The breech-blocks did not fare well in the tests, and later evaluation by the APK, towards the end of 1862, damned the gun with faint praise, citing only the advantages made to mobility by the carriage and the lighter ammunition. This controversy also delighted Hahn, who held fast to his doctrine of firepower. In any case, the debate was soon to be truncated by international affairs. The Schleswig-Holstein situation had now evolved into war.

The Prussian expeditionary force[10] under Field Marshal Wrangel and Prince Frederick Charles crossed the border into Schleswig on 1 February 1864, with close to 40,000 men. It comprised elements of the Westphalian and Brandenburg army corps with a combined Guards division.[11] Included also was a strong artillery contingent consisting of 110 guns, of which 38 were rifled. At first they met little resistance, except for the slushy roads, but they found their first obstacle at the town of Missunde where they intended to cross the river Schlei. It seemed a job for the artillery, and a bombardment began on 2 February. Sixty-four Prussian guns poured fire into and around Missunde for the entire day almost without effect. The 28 guns of the Danish defenders continued to fire the whole time and by the next morning it was clear the Prussians would have to do something else. Having failed to force the Danish defences, Frederick Charles decided that a crossing further east was in order, and this took place the following day. The Danes' elation was short-lived, as Austrian successes in the centre had forced a retreat from the fortifications known as the Dannewerke. By 8 February, the Prussians had advanced as far as the fortified town of Düppel, and rather than making an immediate assault supported by field artillery, Frederick Charles decided on a siege. By 21 February, he had decided the twelve rifled 24-pounders he had were inadequate, so he asked Berlin for an additional eight or twelve. Towards the end of the month, 24 of them were on their way. It took until 27 March to totally invest the town, and the first siege parallel was in place by 29 March. There were 13 batteries[12] in place by 1 April (the first five had been in position since mid-March), bringing about 58 guns to bear upon Düppel. It turned out that the smooth-bores were ineffective at this range so, on 7 April, a half-parallel with two extra batteries was started, 800 feet nearer which, when finished, did not prove much better. However, it became apparent that the siting of the rifled guns further back had turned out to be much more effective. In fact, the destructive power of the rifled guns astonished both attacker and defender alike, as breastworks, redoubts, and buildings crumbled under their onslaught. A change of command of the artillery also took place at the same time, when General Gustav Hindersin arrived and took over the operations, which had been criticized for the slow going. This rough-tongued martinet was able to shake things up, and in ten days the final assault would take place. Before that happened, a second parallel with four batteries (Nos 18–21) was established on 9 April, and at the particular request of the king, a third parallel with eight batteries, on 12 April. By the time the infantry stormed the redoubts on 18 April, there were 28 batteries totalling 112 guns (of which 74 were rifled and only 14 smooth-bore, with the rest howitzers and mortars), firing over 4,700 shells on the last day of the siege. The surrender of Düppel was the decisive event of the war. There would be an armistice and a conference in London followed by a brief resumption of the war, resulting in the invasion of Alsen Island. A second armistice on 12 July effectively ended the conflict.

Krupp 6-pounder breech-loader.

The experience of the Second Schleswig War gave proponents of rifled artillery a huge boost, but as long as General Hahn was on the scene, they would not gain sway. However, Hindersin was now inspector general, and even before the Danish War was over, he was pressuring the War Ministry for more rifled cannon. The Landtag had refused more funds for the military budget, but in the political atmosphere prevailing in Prussia, this meant little. The weapon on the mind of Hindersin and his staff was the 4-pounder rifled breech-loader manufactured by

Krupp. The argument was made that despite the leaky breech mechanism, it was the most effective weapon that the artillery could have. One of his main allies was Prince Hohenlohe-Ingelfingen, who was himself becoming a prominent artilleryman, but was also an adjutant and favourite of the king. Hohenlohe-Ingelfingen's access paid off.[13] After being invited to demonstrations and test firings, the king resolved to re-equip the artillery with the Krupp guns. As all this was going on, Alfred Krupp himself, well aware of the goings-on in Berlin, and in his usual manner, had inserted himself in a way that probably made the government uncomfortable; he told Roon that he would offer credit of two million thalers for four hundred cannon. Unfortunately for Krupp, Roon did not take the bait, and instead gave the impression that Krupp's guns were overpriced, despite the high quality of the steel. In the end Krupp had to settle for half a loaf, as in late 1864, he was presented with an order for 300 cast-steel rifled barrels only, along with a price so low that it seemed hardly worth it. He accepted the order anyway, and although the manufacture began immediately, it was nearly a year before he began delivery.

Conclusions

General Hahn retired in 1864 and died the following year, taking his opposition to rifled ordnance to his grave.[14] Hindersin, nevertheless, proceeded with the rearming of the artillery. His own preference would have been to withdraw all smooth-bores from the inventory. However, the delivery schedule of the Krupp cannon barrels, along with mounting them on the proper carriages, was such that all smooth-bores had not been replaced when war loomed in 1866. In any event, the artillery had again been reorganized in January 1865, to cater for the new equipment. One horse battery per regiment would be refitted with the new guns, and by June of that year, the three howitzer batteries of field artillery regiments were converted into four batteries, armed with six 4-pounders each. There was hardly any time for practical training, let alone a rethinking of doctrine. Hindersin did instruct artillery officers to abandon parade drills, and pay more attention to field exercises, but the last fifteen years had been spent focusing on technology, rather than developing a philosophy on how to use it.

The artillery went off to war in 1866 with only two of each army corps' four 12-pounder batteries re-equipped with 4-pounder rifles. Few would consider this lack of re-armament as a cause for the Prussian artillery failure at Königgrätz, although lack of sufficient training with the new weapons surely contributed. Fortunately for Prussia, and shortly Germany, the army took its lessons seriously. In the four years intervening before 1870, the artillery developed a doctrine and training system that would prove to be effective and decisive in the war with France.

For Alfred Krupp, the news from Bohemia in 1866 was very satisfactory until he was informed that about eight of his guns had exploded in the breech and killed several crews. He was devastated and wrote a grief-laden letter to Roon asking for forgiveness. However, for the firm of Friedrich Krupp, the future was secure. The Franco-Prussian War would lead to more lucrative orders, not only from Prussia, but the south German states as well. Soon he was supplying much of the world with guns and steel products. Alfred Krupp died in 1887 at the age of 75, leaving a company that would grow into a behemoth. The rest of the story has become a lesson of history. The company became more and more intertwined with the progression of German militarism. It built the guns that pounded the lives out of millions of young men in Flanders and elsewhere in the Great War, and it built the tanks that swept across Europe, the Russian steppes and the Libyan desert from 1939 to 1945. It built the submarines (U-boats) that sent tons of ships and their crews to watery graves in both world wars. The name of Krupp would be inexorably linked to both the Kaiser and Führer, attracting revulsion and bringing a scion of the family into the dock at Nürnburg. Old Alfred Krupp fortunately was long dead by then. He had died with his reputation secure, and he was to take comfort, and certainly pride, by the sobriquet that appeared in a Berlin newspaper article in 1864 describing him as "der kanonenkönig"... "The Cannon King".

The Cavalry Battle on the Plain of Stretesitz by Václav Sochor.

Sabre and lance: cavalry weapons and tactics

It is a magnificent panorama capturing the moment that all mid-19th century commanders dreamt of; the final cavalry clash. The opposing squadrons, massed in thousands, are shown just before the moment of impact. A three-meter gap separates the two forces as their horses, nostrils flaring, hurtle towards each other with their riders' swords thrust forwards and the collision only seconds away.

Václav Sochor's great painting portrays the cavalry battle on the plains of Stresetitz, which was later claimed to have been one of the greatest cavalry encounters ever witnessed. For Frederick Charles it was meant to have been the decisive engagement of the battle, sweeping the Austrians from the field. For

Benedek it was designed to stop the Prussians in their tracks and allow his army to consolidate and stem the tide that was overwhelming him. Neither commander's aim was achieved. Like their brothers in the artillery, the contribution of the Prussian cavalry to the victory at Königgrätz was not significant but for very different reasons.

Of the three main branches of the 19th-century army, it was the cavalry that received the least attention, especially in Europe and particularly in Prussia.

While the infantry and artillery were focused on new and groundbreaking technologies, the cavalry remained principally armed with weapons that had been in use since the dawn of warfare – the sword and lance. The 18th century had seen cavalry used again and again with great success as shock troops; battle winners able to overcome infantry struggling to reload their weapons after discharge. This concept had probably reached its zenith in the Napoleonic Wars, especially in the hands of Bonaparte himself. But the massed cavalry charge was already in trouble when disciplined infantry had learned to form squares specifically to repel mounted attacks. In fact, the two great cavalry charges at Waterloo, that of the British Union Brigade, and Kellerman's massive attack later in the battle, were largely ineffective; the latter especially because of the British squares. By the time of the Crimean War, the tactics had not changed and the results were more disastrous. At Balaclava, the charge of the Heavy Brigade was declared a success, but only in chasing the Russian cavalry off after a line of Highlanders, exposed and alone on the plain had stopped the Russians with their Minié rifles. There then followed the most famous cavalry charge in history, that of the Light Brigade, a woefully ill-conceived event heroically undertaken by six hundred men against artillery in prepared positions. The results were evident to all who watched, but the lessons, such as they were, were not learned. In the Franco-Austrian War of 1859, the French cavalry proved superior to the Austrian, and the French infantry squares at Solferino held fast against the Hapsburg hussars and uhlans. However, the Austrian cavalry were used more effectively in the reconnaissance role.

It was a conflict far away, across the Atlantic, that would re-define the role of mounted warfare until the arrival of the tank. The American Civil War was fought on a vast scale that dwarfed European geography. From the beginning, the war would develop in locations that were great distances apart and the railway and telegraph would play an important part in Union and Confederate strategies. In the light of this new mobility, cavalry quickly developed as long-range reconnaissance and raiding troops. Instead of being held back as battle reserves, they would often be ahead of main bodies, engaging the enemy first. In battle there were few massed cavalry charges, and instead the cavalry would be split into small detachments that would dash and try to break up infantry formations. They became masters at long-distance raiding, breaking up railway tracks, and cutting telegraph lines. They would appear far behind the lines often disrupting supplies and keeping civilian populations nervous. Great cavalry commanders would emerge such as Jeb Stuart for the South, along with comrades Nathan Bedford Forrest, Wade Hampton, William Quantrill, and John Hunt Morgan with many more. For the North were Elon Farnsworth, Benjamin Grierson, Armstrong Custer, and Philip Sheridan. The greatest cavalry clash of the war was at Brandy Station, but Farnsworth's disruption of Stuart's foray at Gettysburg on the third day was notable. Although the war began with only five US regiments – two dragoon, two cavalry and one of mounted rifles – they soon were converted to cavalry. Even before the war began the US Army had eschewed the nomenclatures of European armies. There were no hussars or cuirassiers, dragoons had only a brief existence and the single unit of lancers (Rush's) did not survive as such for long. The Confederates had no time for such distinctions either. Further south, in Latin America, a similar type of warfare had evolved with an emphasis on irregular cavalry units. The devastating Wars of Triple Alliance and the Pacific War would see the same sort of cavalry tactics as the American Civil War.

By the time of the Seven Weeks War, there may not have been enough time to absorb the lessons of the American Civil War, although Moltke had keenly digested information he gained from his own observers. He made masterful use of the telegraph and particularly the railway, which was decisive in his mobilization and envelopment plans in June 1866. The use of cavalry however was, like the artillery, left in the hands of the army commanders. In the Schleswig campaign of 1864 the Prussian cavalry played a very small part. At the crossing of the Schlei they were set to pursue the retreating Danes, but the weather proved impossible, with horses and riders slipping on the ice, so the action was abandoned. From then on, their duties seem to have been administrative, especially when static warfare set in. Again, partly because their campaign was more mobile, the Austrians made better use of their light cavalry in the reconnaissance role.

From the beginning of the 1866 campaign, the intention was to keep the bulk of the cavalry in reserve, to use it as the decisive force to finish off the enemy and pursue it from the field. Cavalry regiments assigned to infantry divisions were supposed to be used as reconnaissance troops to scout ahead and provide intelligence on the enemy. In the end they were to perform neither function well. Commanders were so eager to get the infantry into the battle, to use their superior firepower to overwhelm the Austrians, that, like the artillery, the cavalry were kept far to the rear of the advancing troops. When it came to scouting, it was most often Esterhazy's Austrian cavalry that found their enemy first and although the infantry would make the decisions in the ensuing clashes, the Prussian cavalry was of little help. As they advanced into Bohemia, Frederick Charles had expected major Austrian resistance at Reichenberg, but lack of a cavalry screen prevented him from knowing the town was free of enemy troops. The same thing happened again when they reached the Iser river – prepared for Austrian concentrations of up to 140,000 at Jung-Bunzlau, and they found less than half of that when they arrived. As the advance continued there were cavalry clashes to be sure, and in many cases the Prussians prevailed, but the main decisions at all the preliminary battles for all three armies were made by the infantry.

In the introduction to his wonderful book on the battle, Gordon Craig paints the image of the Prussian uhlans advancing to the Bistritz River early on the morning of 3 July 1866.[15] Alas it would be much later in the battle before the Prussian cavalry was heard of again. With the First Army struggling to maintain its position in the centre, Bonin and his Army of the Elbe appeared to have a chance to outflank the Austro-Saxons on their left. The order to do so was brought by Colonel Doering from the king's Headquarters and it required the Canstein Division to advance with Goltz's cavalry brigade. Bonin was reluctant to do so without additional cavalry, which was when he somehow managed to get Alvensleben's Cavalry Division (from First Army) to be transferred to the Army of the Elbe.[16] His failure to then use the additional cavalry contributed to his failure to force the decision in his sector. More failures would come on other fronts including the so-called disappearance of Second Army's Cavalry Division until 4:00 p.m.

Prussian Hussars 1864.

So now we come to the clash at Stresetitz. The engagement between nearly 40 Austrian squadrons, and 31 Prussian squadrons, was actually not a single clash but several, at least two main fights. In each case the Austrians marginally bettered their enemies, inflicting heavy casualties on at least two regiments. They would have achieved Benedek's desire to stop all the Prussians in their tracks, however, the more they prevailed, the more they came under fire from Prussian infantry and artillery advancing from the north. Eventually it broke them and the proud Austrian troopers galloped back toward the Elbe. The Prussian cavalry had been somewhat scattered and were in no shape to pursue.

It is entirely possible that the Prussian commanders' faith in their infantry armed with the needle gun was so overwhelming that the use of cavalry never really figured clearly in their plans. There is no doubt that the infantry achieved what the Prussian cavalry could not, and the Austrians could not prevent them. The lessons from the Americas may have become better understood during the 1870 war with France, as the Prussian cavalry contribution was far more effective in that conflict. There were some classic charges such as that at Mars-la-Tour, but the cavalry's role as scouts and raiders became much more prominent. In fact it was in the Franco-Prussian War that the uhlans earned their reputation and the very utterance of the word "Uhlans!" would spread fear, until the advent of trench warfare in late 1914 heralded the decline of the cavalry.

Cavalry Weapons

Given the lack of clarity when it came to the cavalry role in future wars, it is not surprising that the technological revolution in armaments that benefited the infantry and artillery left the mounted troops with much the same weaponry they had carried for centuries. The sword, lance, pistol, and carbine were the weapons carried by the Prussian cavalry in 1866. The needle-carbine (*Zündnadelkarabiner*) was basically the same as the infantry rifle, but with the shorter barrel. The first

Prussian 1850 model percussion pistol.

prototypes appeared in 1853 and carbines were issued to all squadrons of the Guard Dragoon Regiment in February 1857. This was known as the M/57 model and was issued to all regiments of hussars and dragoons beginning in April the same year. Cuirassiers and uhlans did not carry the carbine during the 1866 war, but it did finally become standard for all cavalry in 1870. From a tactical point of view the use of the carbine for cavalry had changed very little. It was supposed to be used in dismounted engagements, especially in the scouting mode or to harry the enemy's forward scouting units.

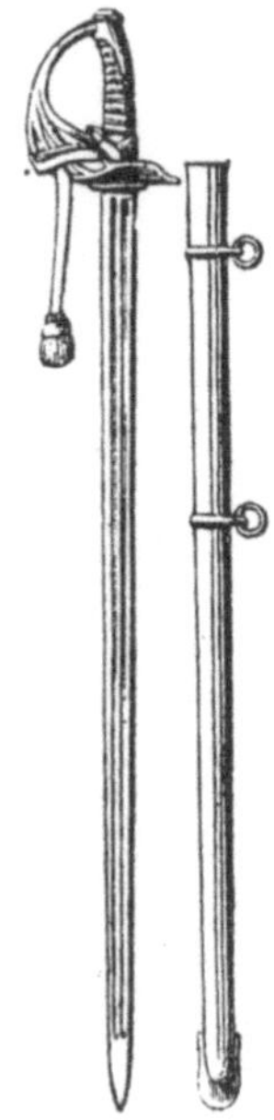

In the absence of carbines, cuirassiers and uhlans carried the 1850 model (M/50) percussion pistol which apparently was found very useful during the cavalry battle on the plains of Stresetitz (as many officers had purchased revolvers privately there could be some confusion as to which handgun was in fact more useful).

All mounted soldiers carried swords. From January 1857, dragoons, hussars and uhlans carried the 1852 (M/52) model cavalry sabre. This was basically a curved slashing weapon for use in horse-to-horse combat. The cuirassiers carried a heavy straight sword known as a *Pallasch*, which in one form or another had been carried by this cavalry branch since the time of Frederick the Great.

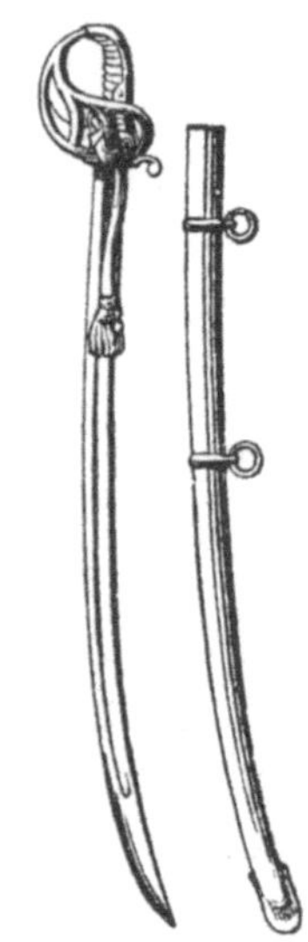

Cavalry swords. Top, cuirassier sword (pallasch) and scabbard; bottom 1852 pattern sabre and scabbard carried by other mounted troops.

The lance carried by the uhlans was the 1852 pattern. It was made of untreated wood (usually ash) and had a triangular fluted spear point above a metal tube that fitted over the shaft and was secured by a flange with two screws. There was a pointed metal "boot" attached to the bottom. Metal eyelets (at first three, but later six) were screwed in below the spear-point to which the white over black lance pennant was attached. At this time, NCOs did not carry the lance.

The basic armaments of cavalry never did change before the advent of mechanization. The use of the lance was expanded to all the German cavalry (and to the cavalry of other countries including Britain) in the 1890s. In some cases only the front ranks or certain squadrons used it, but apart from parades it had little effect on tactics for cavalry. The arrival of quick-firing, long-range infantry and artillery weapons, not to mention the machine gun, doomed the horse-mounted soldier rapidly. Fortunately for those accustomed to riding into battle, the tank would prove to be a very suitable replacement mount in the 20th century.

NOTES

1. Exiled to America in 1825 for political agitation, List returned triumphantly to Germany eight years later having made a financial success of his sojourn in the USA.
2. See chapter 10.
3. Wartensleben would become Moltke's principal railway expert, and would head up the first Railway department in the Prussian General Staff.
4. The M1857 cavalry carbine was not fully issued until 1863 and most of the pioneer battalions did not receive their rifles until after the Danish War.
5. His experience in England reads like a comic novel. He apparently wore disguises and used intrigues to infiltrate English factories that were entirely unnecessary. Little that he was seeking was secret – his hosts would have gladly shown him anything he wanted to see!
6. At the time of Alfred's visit, the Saarn Arsenal was already in the process of manufacturing Dreyse's needle gun.
7. Which at a later date was deemed to have been some sort of mistake!
8. Krupp's steel tyre manufacturing continued for many years and was such an important component of the firm's output that the trademark Alfred designed in 1875 consisted of three interlocking wheels. The logo would last as long as the company was in existence.
9. Alfred married Bertha Eichhoff on 19 May 1853. Their granddaughter Bertha, who took over the business when she came of age, gave her name to the giant mortars (Big Berthas) that bombarded the Belgian fortresses in 1914.
10. It was a joint Austro/Prussian Army – the Austrian contingent having about 23,000 men giving a total of 61,600 men. The Austrians advanced up the west and central part of Schleswig leaving the Prussians to move up the eastern shore.
11. For the complete Prussian order of battle see Appendix A.
12. A battery in this context consisted usually of four to six guns.
13. He was rewarded with the command of the Guard Artillery Brigade.
14. He ordered that no rifled cannon be part of his funeral cortège nor that they be used to fire any salutes.
15. "On the morning of 3 July, 1866, as Prussian Uhlans cantered toward the Bistritz River and were challenged by the Austrian batteries on the heights of Lipa, Austria was still regarded as the strongest power in central Europe and was generally accorded the right to speak in international affairs for the German states as a whole. By nightfall, as the broken Austrian columns struggled back across the River Elbe, that proud position was irrevocably destroyed . . ." Gordon Craig, *Koniggrätz*, Introduction.
16. See Chapter 5.

CHAPTER TEN

The Royal Prussian Navy

FOR CENTURIES, THE BALTIC SEA had been the province of Norse, later Scandinavian, seafarers. The late Middle Ages saw the rise of the Hanseatic League; the cities of this economic alliance protected their trade with armed merchantmen operating in both the Baltic and North seas. By the early 17th century, the Dutch were dominant in the region, although Denmark and Sweden would control most of the Baltic coast at the end of the Thirty Years War. It was the Electorate of Brandenburg under Frederick William I (The Great Elector) that made the first German attempt at creating a navy. The founding of an East India Company in 1657 and an African Company in 1682, prompted Frederick William to establish a small naval force, manned largely by Dutchmen, which operated out of Emden on the North Sea. However, soon after Frederick William's death the companies were dissolved and the assets sold. Neither Frederick I (r. 1688–1713), who founded the Kingdom of Prussia, or his successor, Frederick William I (r. 1713–40) had any interest in maritime affairs or a navy. By the reign of Frederick II (The Great), Britain was master of most European waters and the growing fleet of Russia controlled much of the Baltic Sea. Britain, however, was also Prussia's ally during most of the conflicts disturbing the peace of Europe between 1740 and 1763,[1] so Frederick had little need of a navy, preferring to concentrate his attention on his renowned army. The only waterborne activity of a military nature undertaken by Prussia was to place a small protective flotilla at the mouth of the Oder in 1760, but it was soon sent to the bottom by the Swedes. In matters of maritime trade, Frederick was more sanguine and he sanctioned a small Asiatic Company early in his reign but it soon foundered. Later he established an organization which survives to this day, the Seehandlung,[2] a trading entity which would have a great influence on the formation of the Prussian Navy. Although he stipulated that the acquisitions of the Polish port city of Danzig, along with the province of West Prussia, would make a Prussian navy feasible, he never acted on this condition when they were annexed in 1772. One surviving symbol of Frederick's reign was the first Prussian naval flag or jack, which was designed for the short-lived Asiatic venture. It showed a black Prussian eagle on a white field. With minor modifications it would remain in use until 1870.

The French Revolution and Napoleonic Wars did little to advance the prospects of a Prussian navy for several reasons. Firstly the Prussians stayed out of the fighting between 1795 and 1806, while Prussian seaborne commercial trade did well, largely because it sailed under the protection of most of the combatants. However, Prussia's disastrous foreign policy misjudgements in 1806 led to a French invasion and the catastrophic defeats at Jena and Auerstadt. Recovery and revenge followed with every effort put into rebuilding the land forces and ejecting Napoleon and his armies from German soil.

A difficult birth

By the end of 1815, Prussia's Baltic coast had expanded considerably and although a North Sea outlet was denied by the Congress of Vienna (the port of Emden was awarded to Hanover), Prussia still had access to the world's waterways. However, despite the efforts of many individuals and organizations, there was very little progress over the next thirty years towards the creation and expansion of a Prussian navy. This was for two reasons: first, the end of the Napoleonic Wars offered a European period of peace that had not been seen for generations, making military expenditure politically difficult to secure; and second, Prussia, along with other German states, and with the help of the Seehandlung, put the bulk of available resources into the development of a merchant fleet. This period did see the first appearance of personalities, organizations, and vessels that would provide the foundation for the continuation and development of Prussian, later German naval forces.

The first man to be commissioned into the Prussian Navy was Diederick Johan Longé, a Finn who had been in Swedish and British service. He had commanded six gunboats of the Swedish Navy, each armed with two cannon, all of which were transferred to Prussian service in August 1815 along with the port at Stralsund. His commission (and that of his fellow officer, Heinrich Murck) was confirmed by the king in 1816.[3] At the same time the construction of a schooner, designed by Longé, was proposed. Completed as the *Stralsund* in 1817, Longé sailed it on its maiden voyage to Memel the same year. It flew the new naval flag of a black eagle on a white field with an iron cross in the upper hoist. Apart from the six gunboats and the schooner, a small postal yacht was armed and named *König Friedrich Wilhelm*. Despite the establishment of a navigation school in Danzig by the king himself, little of a positive nature advanced the cause of the Prussian Navy after the voyage of the *Stralsund*.[4] While the vessels remained inactive in Stralsund, the War Ministry decided to transfer Longé and Murck to Danzig in 1822. They took the *Stralsund* along with them (the six gunboats had been sold in 1820), and Longé soon set to work on the construction of three small river gunboats. To man these boats, the War Ministry assigned a small detachment of the Guard Pioneers, which later became known as the Garde-Mariniers. A coastal gunboat called the *Danzig*, designed by Longé, was completed in 1825, which he and Murck sailed back to Stralsund, along with the *Stralsund*, in 1827. It was their last voyage. As money dried up, the *Stralsund* was sold in 1827 and the *Danzig* a decade later. The two lieutenants and the small cadre of Garde-Mariniers had little to do but watch merchant vessels come in and out of the port as the three gunboats idled. For the next twenty years, Longé, now a captain, offered plans to various naval commissions but all were ignored or deferred. He and Murck remained the only commissioned officers until 1845 when Longé retired as a colonel. (Murck died two years later, still a lieutenant).

Despite Longé's frustrations there were some other significant events and personalities that would keep the hopes and dreams of a Prussian navy alive, albeit barely. Between 1822 and 1848 Prussia operated twelve armed merchant vessels under the control of Christian Rother and the Seehandlung. Despite flying the flag and doing business all over the world, the operation was never profitable. However, the merchant marine did allow the Navigation School to use their vessels for training occasionally with the obvious benefit of employing the graduates.

Frederick William III continued to champion the formation of a navy and to that end in 1829 he ordered a vessel – a corvette – to be built as soon as possible. However, it would be thirteen years before his order bore fruit and when it was finally laid down in 1842, foreign, mostly British, shipwrights had to be employed to finish the construction. When launched, the *Amazone* boasted twelve cannon (imported from Sweden) and was set to fly the Prussian naval flag at all times. A Danish naval captain, Baron Dirckink-Holmfeld, was engaged to command it as a training vessel for the Navigation School. He was never commissioned and remained employed by the Finance Ministry as a civilian. However, Dirckink-Holmfeld was able to persuade Boyen (war minister again after Rauch's death) to allow him to train the cadets as future naval officers rather than merchant marine officers.[5] When the *Amazone* set sail on its first cruise in 1844, it was manned by some of these cadets along with merchant seamen and three additional officers formally from the Danish Navy. It visited many ports in the Eastern Mediterranean including Constantinople. The *Amazone* would be the most significant Prussian vessel to exist for the next twenty years.

Various committees and commissions examined the formation of a navy between 1820 and 1848 without accomplishing much. In 1823 War Minister Rauch had wanted a 1,200-man navy with two schooners and 24 gunboats. In 1836 General August von Reiche headed a commission that recommended a schooner, a corvette, and 60 gunboats be built as well as six steamships, reflecting the new technology then emerging. In 1840, under the direction of the Prussian Army's artillery staff two gunboats were launched in Danzig of both Danish and Swedish design, known as *Kanonenjolle 1* and *2*. For five years the artillery tested the boats (manned by the Garde-Mariniers) without impressing anyone. While this was going on, the 1836 plan was revived in 1844 without the 60 gunboats but

The Amazone.

with 16 steamships. Every single initiative came to nothing despite powerful proponents.

Prince Adalbert of Prussia (1811–73).

In 1846 Boyen proposed the hiring of a Dutch naval officer, Captain-Lieutenant Jan Schröder, to replace Dirckink-Holmfeld. He would also be a Finance Ministry employee, but would hold the rank of captain in the event of hostilities. King Frederick William IV agreed to these conditions and Schröder was appointed in July 1846. One of his first tasks was to tighten the conditions for entry to the Navigation School, with an emphasis on a more military atmosphere. The students would henceforth be paying for their tuition rather than be on scholarship and would be selected from families with social standing. Schröder took the *Amazone* on two cruises that year, the first to the Mediterranean again and the second to the North Atlantic, this last one with three freshly minted second lieutenants from the Navigation School – Eduard Jachmann, Arthur Schirmacher and Robert Herrman.[6] Despite a minor collision with a Hanoverian merchantman off Newfoundland, and some desertions in New York, they were successful cruises.

This long period of such little achievement was about to come to an end but two people need mention whose influence and attention toward the end of this time would have great impact on the years to come. One was Prince Adalbert of Prussia, the other was the economist Freidrich List.

Prince Adalbert was a nephew of King Frederick William III, and as a young Guards officer he had made sea voyages to Britain and Russia. In the mid-1830s he had presented to the king a plan – to build three armed paddle steamers in a British shipyard – that was quickly rejected based on cost. After other voyages, including one in the Black Sea on an Austrian vessel, he was made commander of the Guard Artillery in 1839. His naval interests grew over the coming years and his expertise in artillery was matched by his grasp of emerging naval technology. He became inspector general of artillery in 1842 following a cruise to Brazil and by the late 1840s he was Prussia's leading naval exponent and would be destined to take a major role in the crisis looming on the continent.

As much as patriotic sentiment was a factor in the desire for a Prussian navy, the need for economic progress figured just as large. Freidrich List was a

German nationalist, born in Württemberg, with strong liberal leanings in his early years, which caused him to leave the country. After seven years in the USA he returned to Germany in 1832 and settled in Leipzig. At this time his economic theories were centred on the expansion of the Zollverein (customs union), in which a national railway system and merchant fleet played a central part. Naturally, he argued, a navy would be required to protect a merchant fleet, declaring that no other nation that had a coast-line was without a naval force of some kind. He acknowledged the fledgling Prussian fleet (in the form of the *Amazone*) and the growing Austrian Navy and was passionate that there should be a national German fleet with a national flag flying on every vessel. He became the leading economist in Germany, despite the fact that his protectionist views were largely ignored, but his writings would influence the minds of naval proponents at a crucial time.[7]

The 1848 revolution and the First Schleswig War

The revolutionary tide that swept across Europe from February 1848 was preceded a month earlier by a proclamation by the king of Denmark, Frederick VII, that the duchies of Schleswig and Holstein would be united with his kingdom. The largely German-speaking populations of these duchies immediately rose in revolt.[8] With substantial moral support and volunteers from all over Germany, the rebels organized and were routed by the Danes at the battle of Bov (Bau) on 9 April 1848. Within two weeks a combined German force, including a large Prussian contingent, crossed the Eider River beginning the First Schleswig War between Denmark and the German Confederation. The Danish Navy immediately began blockading the German coast and seizing Confederation vessels. Suddenly, the failure of Prussian (and German) naval policies in the preceding thirty years had come home to roost.

The north German states along the North Sea and Baltic coasts scrambled to respond to the Danes by arming merchantmen, paddle steamers, and other vessels. Naval committees were formed and individuals appointed. In Prussia, Prince Adalbert was charged with organizing coastal defences. In May the German Confederation's assembly convened in Frankfurt and the focus immediately shifted from locally raised naval forces to a national German navy. A committee was formed and jointly headed by a Prussian general and an Austrian diplomat,[9] and from this moment the direction of the conflict became a political debate and the harbinger of a wider confrontation that would arise between Prussia and Austria.

The first proposal was to build two frigates, four corvettes, some armoured steamships, and 200 small gunboats. The funding required for this proposal became immediately divisive with Austria and the south German states refusing to pay. Austria argued that Trieste, her only major port, was just as important as the north German ports and should be equally protected.[10] Despite these objections, the assembly approved the funding and ironically, it was upon Austrian vessels that the first black/red/gold German flag was flown. Amidst the proceedings in the assembly, sentiment for a national fleet had grown rapidly across the populations of the German states and talk of unity was widespread.

Despite initial victories at Schleswig, Missunde, and Oeversee in April, the Prussians made few gains against the Danes and a Danish rout of Saxon forces at Düppel in June forced the conflict into a stalemate. By this time, European powers, especially Britain and Russia, were pushing for a resolution of the crisis and the arrival of a Swedish expeditionary force in Denmark brought the parties to the negotiating table. A cease-fire was agreed and signed on 25 August, which called for a seven-month truce to arrive at a settlement.

A month or so later the Technical Naval Commission was created, taking the place of the previous committee under Radowitz and Bruck. Leading this commission was Prince Adalbert of Prussia who arrived to take up his position in November. Radowitz remained on the commission, which also included Jan Schröder, Otto Donner of the Schleswig-Holstein Navy, and Karl Rudolf Brommy of Saxony. By this time, some of the vessels belonging to the Baltic German states had been transferred to the German fleet. These included the Hanseatic ships *Hamburg, Bremen* and *Lübeck*, and later about 27 small gunboats that were under construction at the Elbe shipyards of Ems and Weser. The commission's deliberations over the winter of 1848–49 centred on the type of fleet required, whether it should be of a defensive nature to address the current crisis only, or a full sea-going fleet that would have prospects of becoming a naval power.[11] In the end the commission compromised and approached the assembly with a plan requiring 15 frigates, five steam frigates, 20 corvettes and 80 coastal tugboats (to be towed by 10 steamers). The issue of personnel also taxed their minds as, with the best will in the world, there were few available men in Germany to officer the ships. Foreign naval officers and men were considered and approached. A serious discussion took place between the commission and representatives of the United States.[12] A US frigate, the *St Lawrence*, had paid a visit to Bremerhaven and its captain, Hiram Paulding visited Berlin and Frankfurt, but the precarious condition of the German fleet during the armistice gave him pause. He and Commodore Parker, the US representative (and would-be commander of the fleet) recommended no involvement by the US in any German navy. After offering command of the fleet to several other candidates, the commission finally settled on Captain Brommy. As a veteran of the Greek War of Independence, where he had commanded the Greek navy against the Turks, Brommy had valid credentials but he still faced the problem of finding officers and by the time the cease-fire ended he had assembled a motley collection of officers from various countries to work with him. His personnel of junior officers, NCOs, cadets and crew left even more to be desired and was made up of German volunteers and foreign (mostly British) seamen. The state of his personnel prevented Brommy from taking any kind of offensive action until they had been trained.

The truce came to an end in the latter part of March 1849, and for the short time that hostilities continued, there was only one naval action involving the German fleet. When the war resumed, Brommy's fleet was standing at Bremerhaven. It consisted of eight paddle steamers, three from the Hamburg flotilla (*Hamburg, Bremen* and *Lübeck*) and the rest purchased from various British shipyards and passenger lines. They were the *Grossherzog von Oldenburg*, *Frankfurt*, *Ernst August*, *Erzherzog Johann*, and the *Barbarossa.* All were armed with British guns from Woolwich. The German fleet was not the only naval force operating against the Danes. The rebel Schleswig-Holstein government also had a small navy, which from 1848 to 1850 engaged the Danish Navy on a regular basis until its demise after the Battle of Friedrichstadt (4 October 1850). Its most significant action (as far as the German Navy was concerned) was on 5 April 1849, when Eckenförde, a Schleswig port, was attacked by the Danes. The Danes came off worst as its larger ship, the *Christian VIII*, ran aground and caught fire while the *Gefion* was captured by the rebels and presented to the Frankfurt Parliament. Hastily renamed *Eckenförde*, the ship nevertheless could not be manned and remained idle in Bremerhaven.

On 4 June, Brommy, in his flagship *Barbarossa*, accompanied by the *Hamburg* and *Lübeck*, decided to take on the Danish ships blockading the mouth of the river Weser. They soon caught up with the *Valkrien*, a corvette lagging behind the fleeing vessels, but before they could engage her, she slipped into the British waters of Heligoland. Reluctant to create an incident, the flotilla broke off the engagement and returned to Bremerhaven. Thus ended the German fleet's only naval encounter of the war. On land the Danes had succeeded in defeating Confederation forces at Düppel and Kolding in April as well as stopping a Prussian cavalry advance at Vejlby on 31 May. A successful Danish sortie from Frederica on 6 July convinced the Germans, and particularly the Prussians, that the war needed to come to an end, so another cease-fire was agreed on 10 July.

By this time, the infrastructure of the German Confederation was beginning to fragment and the Frankfurt parliament would soon collapse. The consequences of the 1848 revolutions and the growing antagonism between Austria and Prussia had come to a head with Prussia's humiliation at Olmütz as the result (see chapter 2).

A Prussian navy takes shape (1850–62)

The ships

Prince Adalbert and Schröder, now a commodore, returned to Berlin in February 1849, when the Technical Naval Commission had completed their recommendations. Despite the formation of a "German" fleet, Prussia still reserved

Prussian naval ensign from 1816.

the right to defend its own coast-line. The development of a Prussian navy had not yet been trumped by Brommy's fleet at Bremerhaven. At the onset of the war, the only Prussian sea-going ship was the *Amazone* and there were barely enough experienced men to crew her.[13] On the advice of Adalbert and the War Ministry, Frederick William IV ordered the construction of 36 40-ton gunboats, and six 21-ton gunboats. Various shipyards were employed to do the work and the first of the gunboats, named the *Strelasund*,[14] was launched in August 1848, just after the first cease-fire with Denmark. After Adalbert's return to the Prussian capital more vessels were obtained. The postal ship *Preußische Adler*, and *Köningin Elizabeth* (an old wooden hulled vessel), were armed and added to the fleet during the armistice as well as the paddle steamer *Danzig*. After the resumption of the war, the activities of this small flotilla were more embarrassing than effective. The *Köningin Elizabeth* and *Danzig* both ran aground during exercises and in late June the *Preußische Adler* enjoyed a brief and indecisive cannon exchange with a Danish vessel in the Baltic near the mouth of the Niemen River. By the end of the war the Prussian Navy consisted of these vessels and the 42 completed gunboats. It wasn't much, and could barely be described as a flotilla, let alone a navy, but it was a more positive state of affairs than two years earlier.

Although hostilities between the German Confederation and Denmark had come to an end in July 1849, it would be a nearly a year before the war was officially concluded by the Treaty of Berlin on 2 July 1850. All the while, the question of a German navy remained somewhat alive. Although Brommy and his fleet remained idle in Bremerhaven, they became the object of various tugs-of-war between pro- and anti-navy forces in Germany and Austria. One of the reasons was that the Danes still remained at war with the rebels in Schleswig and Holstein. After defeat at the Battle of Idstedt on 25 July 1850, the rebels attempted to storm Friedrichstadt in October but were bloodily repulsed, ending the fighting. After much contentious debate, Danish rule was restored to the duchies by January 1852. Throughout 1850 and 1851, efforts were made to come to a decision on the German fleet. Austria and Prussia nearly came to an agreement on its continuation, and the newly reconvened Diet proposed funding, but Bismarck, now envoy to the Diet, was against such a fleet and its future died before it began. Despite appeals by Hanover to retain a fleet to protect the Zollverein, it was decided to sell off the ships and disband it. Although the Austrians provided funding for Brommy's squadron to remain in Bremerhaven through the spring of 1852, it was virtually over and the ships began to be sold off. Prussia acquired the *Barbarossa* and *Eckenförde* for a song.[15] The rest of the ships were sold back to British firms or commercial entities in Bremen. Brommy handed over the last ships in March 1853 and struck the flag of the German Navy.[16]

From 1850, Prussia began the process of ship procurement and building in a serious manner. The pace of the programme was not as fast as Prince Adalbert and his small coterie of officers would have liked. However, a navy was not a navy without ships. In late 1850 the 660-ton *Mercur* was purchased from the Seehandlung and rated a corvette, but this only replaced the *Danzig*, recently handed back to its civilian owners. The first ship to be built in the royal dockyard at Danzig was the unsurprisingly named steamship *Danzig*, of 1,450 tons, designed by the British naval architect, Scott Russell. Problems with construction of the shipyard itself delayed the launching for many months. In the meantime two smaller iron-hulled steamships, the *Salamander* and *Nix*, were built for the Prussian Navy at Russell's shipyard in England. These 330-ton ships were launched in late 1850 and early 1851 and the *Danzig* finally went down the slipway in April of that year.

With solid conservative leadership in Prussia and an acquiescent Landtag that would approve funding, naval expenditures were granted to allow a period of modest growth for the Prussian Navy. In 1853 Prussia purchased some land from Oldenburg on the estuary of the Jade River. This transaction would give Prussia a naval base on the North Sea. Despite ambitious plans for the base, they were in no hurry to proceed with them, which was fortunate, as access to the base by land was restricted without a railway.[17] The onset of the Crimean War in 1854 caused Prussia to be cautious while maintaining strict neutrality. Although the French and British navies sent vessels into the Baltic, there was little action. A transaction in 1854 took place between Britain and Prussia which saw the *Nix* and *Salamander* (which had experienced constant technical problems) exchanged for the sailing frigate *Thetis*. In March of that year the 350-ton schooner *Hela* joined the fleet and her sister ship *Frauenlob* would enter service in the spring of 1856. There was a two-year hiatus until the 350-ton yacht *Grille* was launched in April 1858 followed by the screw corvette *Arcona* in May. A year later, the navy's last paddle steamer was completed, the *Loreley* (430 tons), the first Prussian vessel equipped with German engines. In December 1859 the *Gazelle*, sister ship to *Arcona*, was launched. Prussia mobilized during the 1859 war between Austria and France with

The Grille *in 1864.*

her Italian allies. The mobilization included the navy and Adalbert even ordered the old gunboats of the First Schleswig War era to be made ready, an order he soon rescinded because of their decrepit condition and the lack of crews to man them.

The outcome of the Franco-Austrian War brought the issue of a German navy back to life. The smaller German states realized that an expansion of that war could have allowed a foreign fleet or fleets to blockade German shores with ease. Prussia, whose fleet, though growing steadily, was still too small to address such a blockade, had a mixed reaction. They were in the middle of a constitutional crisis which would see Crown Prince William become regent and Bismarck became minister-president. They were very much focused on enlarging the army, and despite support for a navy, William, Bismarck and the War Ministry were reluctant to take funds away from that programme for naval expansion. Adalbert and the pro-navy faction saw a Prussian-led German fleet, and the smaller states were enthusiastic about the proposal, offering to provide financial support. It was Austro-Prussian tension that got in the way as Austria – whose fleet and its capabilities were greater than that of Prussia – saw a German navy under their leadership. Negotiations did take place and some agreement was seen over a three-squadron proposal revived by Austria with a Prussian-led element taking care of the Baltic and North seas, while the Austrians operated in the Adriatic and Mediterranean. However Austria was, by the early 1860s, involved in a naval race with the new Kingdom of Italy and the German Navy question was again shelved as attentions of the principal parties began to focus elsewhere.

As part of Prussia's aspirations to assume leadership of a German navy, Adalbert had proceeded with the construction of eight 350-ton gunboats during this period (*Basilisk*, *Blitz*, *Camäleon*, *Comet*, *Cyclop*, *Delphin*, *Drache*, and *Meteor*), all launched between 1859 and 1862 along with 15 240-ton un-named gunboats launched in 1860. These were specifically designated for coastal defence, a posture which by 1862 had assumed more importance with the naval expansion of Denmark. By now, Adalbert's 1855 fleet plan was a distant dream and the prospects of a navy on a par with other European nations far out of reach. There were some hasty purchases. The 740-ton clipper ship *Elbe* was purchased from a Hamburg firm in 1859, and in 1862 three ships, the frigate *Niobe* (1,300 tons) and the brigs *Musquito* and *Rover* (both 510 tons) were bought from Britain. More frustrating than anything was that Prussia could not keep up with revolutionary new technologies that were now appearing at an astonishing pace. The *Gloire*, the first armour-plated frigate, was launched by France in 1859. This was followed by the Royal Navy's iron-hulled HMS *Warrior* in 1860 and soon similar vessels were appearing in Austria, Italy, and Russia. The first naval engagement between the iron-turreted USS *Monitor* and the CSS *Virginia*[18] in the American Civil War set the seal on the age of wooden fighting ships. In Prussia the news was greeted with enthusiasm and monitors were hailed as being cheaper and more effective that larger-iron hulled ships like the *Warrior*. But by this time it was almost too late as any naval expenditure was secondary to the needs of the army. It was ironically Denmark that purchased Europe's first monitor, the *Rolfe Krake*, which within two years would become the scourge of the Danish coast.

The armament of the Prussian Navy's ships was no less important than the vessels themselves. It is hardly surprising that most of the initial artillery for the fleet came from Great Britain. During the 1850s, ships purchased from other countries routinely stopped in England to be fitted out with cannon. The *Danzig*, the first Prussian ship to built in the Royal dockyard, had purchased its 12 heavy guns from the firm of Thomas & Charles Hood of London and manufactured at Woolwich. Towards the end of the 1860s, Prussia increasingly turned to Sweden. The *Thetis*, *Frauenlob*, *Hela*, *Gefion*, and *Gazelle* all received their guns (over 150 of them) from Swedish firms. It is remarkable to reflect that before 1867, no naval artillery was purchased or considered from Alfred Krupp, who was by then supplying numerous foreign navies with cannon as well as supplying the Prussian Army and other armies.

Organization and manpower

During the war with Denmark, the king of Prussia formalized the command structure of the naval forces. The High Command (*Oberkommando*) was formed, with Adalbert at its head and Schröder operational commander, although it remained part of the War Ministry as the Naval Section (Marine-Abteilung). Despite the issue of a German navy still hanging over them, Adalbert and Schröder proceeded with the organization and training of the Prussian Navy. In late 1849 a regular *Marine* section of two companies was established in Stettin where Schröder had his headquarters. The next year the unit was divided; one company becoming a corps of seaman (*matrosenkorps*) and the other formed into a battalion of naval infantry (*seebataillon*). The latter were trained by army personnel, wore army uniforms,[19] and were recruited from the normal influx of conscripts. The former remained, for the most part, volunteers who came from the merchant marine. As the Schleswig War wound down, many recruits would be found in Brommy's fleet in Bremerhaven. In addition to these two formations a naval construction, or shipyard company (*Werftkorps*) was also created.

Attention was also paid to the command structure, and the development of the officer corps. In 1850 there were only ten regular and 30 reserve officers in the entire force. Despite the availability of many foreign officers after the Schleswig War, Adalbert was particularly anxious to recruit native Prussian candidates but it was not immediately possible. The first few applicants accepted into the navy were German although not Prussian.[20] In 1852 the old Navigation School was replaced by the Sea Cadet Institute (Seekadettan-institut) and moved to Stettin. Among the educational and training systems copied were those of the US Naval Academy in Annapolis, Maryland. The two-year (later four-year) curriculum included seamanship, navigation, gunnery and other naval sciences. After the third year cadets could qualify for a training cruise. The entrance exam was hard and modelled on the *Arbitur* secondary civilian schools. This made the acceptance and retention of cadets difficult as did the acts of moving the institute back to Danzig in 1854, and then a year later to Berlin. A Guard artillery officer, Haller von Hallerstein, was appointed director of the Seekadettan-institut in 1855 and would serve 11 years. In 1854 the entire establishment of sea officers (including sea cadets) had risen to about 35 and would only grow to 64 by 1862. To allow more officers to serve aboard ship, army officers were seconded to the navy as administrative (*beamte*) and medical officers. The *seebataillon* was in better shape, and had a complete officer corps. An artillery section was created in 1858 to man pieces aboard ship and to perform some coastal duties.

The mid-1850s saw the navy's position strengthened within the Prussian ministerial establishment as the Marine-Abteilung was formally separated from the army and given the status of an admiralty. Adalbert became supreme commander of the navy while the minister-president headed the political element of the Admiralty. At the same time Adalbert resigned as general inspector of artillery and was appointed "admiral of the Prussian coasts", which was not a very satisfactory title.[21] He also started to wear the naval uniform of his rank, and rarely wore his army uniform again. One of his first acts was to move the Naval Headquarters from Stettin to Danzig, and Schröder, now a rear admiral (*Contre-Admiral*) was put in command. Soon after William became prince regent in late 1858, there were more changes. The minister-president, now a Hohenzollern prince, no longer headed the political side of the Admiralty and Schröder was appointed to head a newly created Navy Administration (Marineverwaltung) with ministerial power. Adalbert retained overall operational command at the Oberkommando der Marine.[22]

Despite the efforts of Adalbert and other officers like Schröder and Jachman, the navy could hardly be described as an efficient fighting force by 1864. Not only did it lack ships, but above all it lacked competent deck officers (*deckoffizieren*) and seamen (*matrosen*). This situation did not arise through the negligence of sea training as, from 1850 onwards, Prussian sailors had learnt much afloat.

The only vessel capable of an ocean cruise in 1849 was the *Amazone*, which even Schröder thought was not large enough for proper sea-going training. The larger corvette *Mercur*, purchased in 1850, was seen as a more appropriate vessel and chosen to accompany *Amazone* on a training cruise the same year. Unfortunately the *Amazone* was involved in a collision and the *Mercur* had to proceed alone that November on a South Atlantic voyage that took them to Rio de Janiero, returning to Stettin in mid-June the following year. The years 1851 and 1852 saw mostly Baltic cruises and involved the steamships *Barbarossa, Nix*, and *Salamander*, the latter two escorting Frederick William IV on his annual August trips to and from Rügen. A major cruise was organized for late 1852 and after extensive repairs carried out during the previous eighteen months, the *Amazone, Gefion*, and *Mercur* were dispatched to the South Atlantic. The squadron was commanded by Schröder, who took the *Gefion* as flagship. They stopped at Monrovia, Liberia on the way south, reaching Montevideo in March 1853 after calling at Rio de Janiero and Buenos Aries.[23] On the return trip they made ports of call in the Caribbean and Norfolk, Virginia and arrived in Portsmouth in July. Schröder was feted at Osborne House after the two ships were inspected by Queen Victoria and Prince Albert.

The Crimean War put a halt to most major cruises in 1854 but, despite Prussia's desire for strict neutrality, Adalbert could not resist sending warships close to the seat of the war. The *Danzig* was dispatched to the Mediterranean in June 1853, followed by the *Gefion* and *Mercur* after their return from Britain. They based themselves at Smyrna along with Austrian ships and those of other neutrals without entering the Black Sea. They returned via Alexandria, Egypt in February 1854. Apart from placing a few cadets with the Royal Navy during Baltic operations in 1854 and 1855, Adalbert kept Prussian ships and personnel away from the conflict.

After resuming blue-water cruises in late 1855, the next four years saw Prussian ships visiting ports in South America, West Africa, and the Mediterranean. A squadron led by Adalbert, consisting of the *Thetis, Frauenlob, Amazone, Danzig*, and *Mercur*,[24] visited the channel ports of Cherbourg and Plymouth before the *Thetis* and *Frauenlob* left for the South Atlantic and the *Danzig* went into the Mediterranean. It was on the North African coast that men of the *matrosenkorps* and *seebataillon* experienced their first combat landing. In a punitive expedition of August 1856, to deal with pirates who had threatened Prussian (and German) merchant ships, the *Danzig*, with Prince Adalbert aboard, landed on the Moroccan coast, near Melilla. Adalbert led a landing party ashore and in the ensuing skirmish, seven men were killed and many, including Adalbert himself, were wounded. The results were not immediately clear but Prussia had joined a long list of nations attempting to eradicate North African piracy including Great Britain, the United States, France, and more recently Austria and Sardinia. Following intervention by Spain in the region during the 1850s and 1860s, much of Morocco fell under Spanish rule and the problem was solved. There were cruises in the North Sea and Baltic in 1857 for the *Amazone*, and in the Mediterranean for *Thetis* (which lasted through much of 1858), and the *Gefion* took a trip to the Caribbean in 1858. It returned to Danzig in October, having stopped in Norfolk, Virginia where a number of cadets deserted.

Jachmann.

As *Gefion* made its way home, the Franco-Austrian War broke out in Italy and forced it to take a safer route home north of Scotland and down the North Sea. While the crisis was on, Adalbert made sure that his ships remained in service[25] and participated in artillery exercises in the Baltic. In the autumn of 1859, preparations began for Prussia's most enterprising cruise ever. Unlike many of the others, this was not a training cruise, but a scientific, commercial, and diplomatic expedition with an ambitious agenda. The Victorian age had become a period of expansion and Prussia was determined not to be left out. The objective was East Asia and the officers and crew, along with scientists and a high-ranking diplomat (Count Eulenburg, who joined the squadron in Singapore) were tasked with making trade treaties, scientific discovery, and otherwise showing the flag. Not least among their objectives was the prospect of colonial acquisition. The squadron was initially made up of the *Arcona*, *Thetis*, and *Frauenlob* and, as both the *Amazone* and *Mercur* were deemed unfit for such a journey, so the clipper ship *Elbe* was purchased to replace them. The commander of the squadron was Captain Sundewall, a Swede who was aboard the *Arcona*. The cruise was certainly successful as far as trade was concerned as treaties were signed with the Japanese, Chinese, and Siamese but they failed to gain any colonies. A plan was proposed to annex Formosa,[26] but it was soon abandoned because Sundewall felt his resources were woefully inadequate for such an enterprise and Eulenburg feared Chinese reaction would harm their recent treaty. The expedition was not without tragedy as in September 1860, the *Frauenlob* was sunk in a storm off Tokyo Bay and the entire crew of 44 was lost. The remainder of the ships returned to Danzig during 1862, the *Elbe* in May and the *Arcona* and *Thetis* in December.

The toll taken on both ships and men after so many years of continuous cruising was severe. With such a small fleet, Prussia felt it had little choice but to take risks if it were to ever rank with the world's great navies. Apart from the loss of the *Frauenlob*, the East Asia squadron had been bedevilled by accidents and breakdowns that had begun before they had even left European waters. The *Arcona* was forced into Southampton by a storm early in the cruise causing the squadron to winter there and the *Elbe*, which left for Singapore on its own, was severely damaged off the South African coast. On the return journey, the *Thetis* had to stop for repairs in Brazil. By 1861 the *Danzig* had become a rotting hulk and the *Mercur* and *Gefion* were in little better condition. Worse, the venerable *Amazone* was on its last legs, which led to perhaps the worst tragedy suffered by the Prussian Navy so far. She was on her way to join the *Hela* in Spanish waters when on 14 November she went down in a massive storm in the North Sea off the Dutch coast with over a hundred dead. The losses of the *Amazone* and *Frauenlob* had a dramatic effect on recruiting. The intakes of 1862 and 1863 were so small that Adalbert considered closing down the Seekadettan-institut. In addition to recruiting problems, the training cruises had affected existing personnel. Desertion was rampant, especially in the Americas. The great migration to the United States by Germans had begun after 1848 and young German seamen in the Prussian Navy were not immune to the lure of the vast open spaces in America. Seamen routinely jumped ship in Norfolk, Virginia and in South American ports. Desertion was so high on the South American leg of the 1853 cruise that Schröder had to prohibit shore leave, and the *Gefion* had similar problems in Norfolk during its 1858 cruise. Sickness and accidents accounted for even further losses. All navies had to deal with sick and injured sailors but Prussia seemed to suffer more than average. On the Far East cruise, the 44 lost on the *Frauenlob* accounted for fewer than half of the 102 fatalities on the voyage.

As the new decade began, cracks appeared in the leadership of the Prussian Navy which, while not affecting the command and control of its operations, led to the break-up of the most enduring friendship in the service. By the summer of 1860, the relationship between Prince Adalbert and Vice-Admiral Schröder had already become frayed by their opposing views on Prussian colonial policy. Now differences over the use of the decrepit *Danzig* and the recently launched *Gazelle* led to a complete break, especially when Schröder defied the authority of both the prince and William, the prince regent, to use the *Danzig* in gunnery exercises. Schröder's retirement before the end of the year was accelerated by his actions. The political and international climate was now, however, beginning to change. With the accession of William to the throne, Bismarck as minister-president and Roon as war minister, Prussia had put Europe on notice. The expansion of its army to nearly double its size was seen, especially by Austria, as an aggressive sign of its aspirations. The Prussian Navy had not shared in the army's growth, which disappointed navalists in the kingdom a great deal, not least Prince Adalbert. Now they found themselves on the verge of two conflicts, neither of which they were capable of confronting. Consequently the navy played a small part in the first and almost no part in the second.

The Prussian navy bows out – 1864–66

When federal troops from Hanover and Saxony marched into Holstein in mid-December 1863, the only Prussian vessel far away was the *Gazelle*, which was in the East Indies while the *Preußische Adler*, along with the gunboats *Basilisk* and *Blitz*, were cruising in the Mediterranean off the Levantine coast. The ancient

Action at Swinemunde.

Gefion, which had accompanied the *Gazelle* as far as Plymouth, had just returned home. Bismarck had already advised Adalbert to bring all ships home as soon as possible and on his own initiative cancelled cruises scheduled for the *Niobe* (the new cadet ship), *Rover* and *Musquito* to the West Indies.

The state of personnel, both officers and men, was lamentable. There had been no recovery from the drop in recruiting of the previous two years and the administration was forced to offer commissions to officers in the merchant marine. Cadets with only two years in the Seekadettan-institut were also commissioned and some recent graduates found themselves in command of vessels. Although conscription ensured that enough men were drafted into the *seewehr*, there was a huge shortage of seagoing NCOs and trained men, so many spent the war at naval bases being drilled by army NCOs.

The Danes had succeeded in blockading all the major Baltic ports, including Stettin and Danzig. As the campaign progressed on land, the navy's most senior captain, Eduard Jachmann, led a squadron out of Swinemünde on a mission to break out. The flotilla consisted of the *Arcona*, his flagship, the *Loreley*, the *Nymph*, and six small gunboats. As he passed the island of Rügen near Jasmund they met the approaching Danish vessels, consisting of six ships including two frigates and three steamships. It was an unequal match. A short exchange of gunfire ensued before Jachmann decided to return to Swinemünde. The Danes pursued them although the Prussians returned fire continually as they retreated. They reached port safely with a badly damaged *Nymph* (with 13 casualties) but all ships still afloat. Jachmann was rewarded with a promotion to admiral for this action. Apart from two minor sorties from Danzig (one of which was commanded by Adalbert himself) there were no more actions in the Baltic during the war. The major naval action took place off Heligoland on 9 May, involving the Austrian flotilla under Admiral Tegetthoff and the three Prussian ships returning from the Mediterranean (see chapter 3). Although they took only a small part in the battle, the three Prussian ships were able to return to Cuxhaven where they remained for the rest of the war.

Although the Prussian fleet in the Baltic remained bottled up until the allied victory in June, it did not stop Adalbert and the navy administration from addressing the need for new ships. One ship, the *Veneta*, a corvette was nearing completion when the war broke out.[27] In one of the more interesting deals, Prussia negotiated a transfer of three vessels, built in France and intended for the Confederate navy. The

United States was able to intervene and redirect the transaction. Correspondence between H. Kreisman of the United States Legation in Berlin and the US Secretary of State William H. Seward on this matter is instructive:

> Of the three vessels that was building at Bordeaux for the rebels, and which, with the consent of the French government, have been acquired by Prussia, one has already arrived at Bremerhafen [sic]. Her name was changed from *Yedo* to *Augusta*, and she is now duly commissioned and armed and equipped as one of his Prussian Majesty's steam corvettes. This is the same vessel that, when the ship left Bordeaux, was believed to be destined, under the pirate Semmes, to become *Alabama No. 2*. Now that the truth of her destination has become known, French and English sympathizers with rebel piracy are greatly chagrined. The two remaining vessels are to be delivered to Prussia so soon as completed. Besides these purchases, there is reason to believe the Prussian government has attempted to effect others in the United States, through Dr. Schleiden, the minister of the Hanseatic towns, in Washington. If any vessels have been bought in America for Bremen and Hamburg, the real party in the bargain are not they, but Prussia.[28]

On 22 August 1864, Kriesman replied to Seward:

> I have the honour to acknowledge the receipt of your despatch No. 11, dated July 28, 1864.
>
> Another of the three vessels built at Bordeaux for the insurgents, but now transferred to Prussia, the *Victoria*, a steam corvette, the mate to the *Augusta*, late *Yedo*, has been completed, and her speedy arrival at Cuxhafen, Hamburg, where she is to receive her armament and crew, is looked for by the Prussian authorities. The third, a steam frigate of powerful dimensions, I am informed, will likewise soon be completed, and will constitute the pride of the Prussian navy. I will duly advise you when she shall have been delivered, by Mr. Armami, the builder, to the Prussian government.

That vessel was the *Cheops*, quickly renamed *Prince Adalbert*, which joined the corvettes *Victoria* and *Augusta* in May of 1865. The *Prince Adalbert* turned out not to be the pride of the fleet as its short career was continuously problematic. Another vessel, the *Arminius*, a twin-turreted monitor, was purchased from Samuda Brothers of Great Britain and also delivered in May. It was the first armoured warship in the Prussian navy. Two more ships, this time built in Danzig, were under construction between the two wars; the *Hertha* and *Medusa* (sister ships of the *Nymph* and *Veneta*).

In 1864, King William I, on the advice of Adalbert, ordered that the curriculum at the Seekadettan-institut be modified to include more training at sea and courses in class directed more to naval matters. A new institution, the Navy School (Marineschule) was created to accept graduates from the Seekadettan-institut. The Marineschule was to be established in Kiel, where Prussia planned to build a major naval base and begin construction of the canal across the Holstein isthmus. Roon's announcement of Prussian intentions astonished the *Landtag* and created controversy at the ensuing Gastein Convention. However, the die was cast and by late 1865 Jachmann had moved much of the fleet to Kiel and the base was already under construction.

There was little need for Adalbert to make naval preparations in advance of the war with Austria as Moltke's war plan for a massive campaign in Bohemia precluded any. In fact, Prussia's alliance with Italy in April 1866 ensured that Hapsburg naval attentions would be focused on the Adriatic rather than the North Sea or Baltic. Consequently, Adalbert joined the king's headquarters suite with the army in Bohemia while the navy remained largely in port. It did assist the army in its Hanoverian campaign and was vital to secure the ports of Emden and Stade. The *Arminius* was the most active Prussian vessel during these operations. Apart from the regular mobilization of *seewehr* personnel, the navy did not see fit to bring back all the officers who had served in the Danish War. The training of cadets did continue apace and the class of 1865–66 that sailed on the *Niobe* included a young man by the name of Alfred Tirpitz.[29] The war ended seven weeks after it began and the navy quickly began to establish itself at the newly annexed Hanoverian ports. Within a year, the North German Confederation had been formed and almost immediately it took control of naval affairs. Administratively speaking there was little change, but Adalbert now had the luxury of recruiting from a larger pool of manpower and, given the geography, manpower with a maritime heritage.

A new chapter had begun in the maritime history of Germany. The Royal Prussian Navy was no more and for a short time it became the Bundesmarine, which, during the Franco-Prussian War, found not much more to do than it had in 1866. Its transformation after that was into the Imperial German Navy, which became a pillar in the acquisition and maintenance of German colonies and in the Wilhelmine era engaged in a destructive naval race with Great Britain. The consequences of that race would end at Scapa Flow in 1919 when the remnants of a proud fleet scuttled itself rather than be handed over to new masters.

NOTES

1. The War of Austrian Succession (1740–48) and the Seven Years War (1756–63).
2. The original name was the Societé de Commerce Maritime and later Preußische Seehandlung which translates as "Prussian Maritime Enterprise".
3. The Prussian war minister, von Boyen, tried to have the commission stopped and any naval establishment terminated.
4. None of the first cadets at the Navigation School were ever commissioned.
5. One of the students was Eduard Jachmann who would become an admiral in the Prussian Navy.
6. Schröder returned from the Mediterranean trip with the body of Prince Henry of Prussia who had died suddenly in Rome. The Prince's adjutant, Helmuth von Moltke, also made part of the journey and was impressed by Schröder's professionalism.
7. Freidrich List committed suicide in 1846.
8. Holstein was a member state of the German Confederation.
9. General von Radowitz of Prussia and Carl Ludwig Bruck of Austria.
10. Trieste was blockaded by various hostile Italian states (such as Naples) after the bombardment of Vienna and Austria's campaign to thwart the Italian independence movement.
11. Prince Adalbert had already produced a paper, *Denkschrift über die Bildung einer Deutschen Kriegsflotte*, which looked at each scenario – defensive, intermediate, and sea-going, naturally favouring the latter.
12. The United States was one of the only two countries (Belgium was the other) that recognized the Frankfurt Diet.
13. They were in need of 60 men to complete the crew.
14. This boat was funded by the naval committee (*flottenverein*) chaired by the now-retired Longé.

15. *Eckenförde* was almost immediately renamed *Gefion*, its original Danish name.
16. Brommy became an admiral in the Austrian Navy and died in 1860. His coffin was draped in the black/red/gold flag of the German Navy.
17. The railway had to cross Mecklenburg and Hanover and tensions with the latter from the late 1850s delayed the project. The problem was solved by 1867 and the area eventually became the massive naval base known as Wilhelmshaven.
18. The battle was fought at Hampton Roads on 8 and 9 March 1862.
19. The blue uniform had white piping instead of the poppy red worn by the army.
20. It is ironic that most of the German officers who found employment after 1850 did so in the Austrian service.
21. One account, almost certainly apocryphal, states that the king refused him the title of "admiral of the fleet" because Prussia did not possess a fleet!
22. Adalbert's rank no longer included the reference to "Prussian coasts" while Schröder was promoted to vice admiral (Vize-Admiral).
23. The *Mercur* acted as supply ship, meeting up with the other two at Montevideo and returning home thereafter.
24. This was the largest Prussian squadron assembled in modern times. The event was somewhat marred when the *Danzig* collided with the *Mercur*. The latter had to return to Danzig for repair.
25. With the exception of the *Arcona* which remained in Danzig.
26. Napoleon III had assured Count Eulenburg of France's approval for such an annexation.
27. The *Veneta* led one of the unsuccessful sorties to break out of Danzig in April.
28. Seward to Kreisman 13 July 1864.
29. It was not a particularly brilliant class. Only 11 out of the 26 boys (including Tirpitz) passed the entrance exam to the Marineschule in Kiel. The Seekadettan-institut in Berlin had been closed in 1865.

CHAPTER ELEVEN

Organization and War Strength

Of ALL THE ARMIES IN the world, none was more clinically structured than that of Prussia. Since the Napoleonic Wars, the focus of Prussian strategic thinking had been defensive, not only in a reactive posture but, preferably for them, in a pre-emptive mode. With no colonial or other distractions, and the likelihood of attack coming from the countries which bordered Prussia – Russia, France, or Austria – any conflict was certain to be on a large scale. Therefore, the direction and control of large formations such as army corps was central to military planning, and it was decided early on to make this element the primary structure into which all other units would be inserted. This was quite a departure from the thinking of other European armies. At the opposite end of the scale there was Great Britain, which had no larger permanent formation than the regiment, with brigades and divisions being formed on an ad hoc basis. In the rest of Europe, such as France, Italy and Austria, permanent brigades of two or three regiments had appeared in the middle of the century, and in Russia, infantry divisions had been established with brigades as sub-units. For the most part, however, the all-arms division and the army corps were formations created in wartime and were structured to fit the conditions at hand.

In 1836, the Prussian Army possessed nine army corps, one Guard and eight provincial corps. With the exception of the Guard Corps, which had a few additional units, each corps was identically organized, with the same number of infantry and cavalry regiments, divided into brigades and divisions, with an attendant artillery brigade and an engineer battalion. An army corps had two infantry divisions of two brigades, each brigade consisting of two three-battalion regiments. There were two cavalry brigades of two regiments; two heavy cavalry regiments (one each of cuirassiers and dragoons) and two of light cavalry (hussars or lancers), with an artillery brigade and a pioneer battalion. A supply train battalion (formed in 1850) was later added to each corps.

The Roon reforms of 1859 (see Chapter 7) put an end to the balance between the active army and the Landwehr, doubling the size of the former and converting the latter to a separate trained reserve. The basic structure of the nine provincial army corps remained the same, and their permanent establishment now stood as follows:

Permanent establishment of the post-Roon reform provincial army corps

Army Corps	Infantry regiments	Jäger	Cavalry	Arty.Eng.Trn.
Guard	1G. 2G. 3G. 4G. GF. 1GG. 2GG. 3GG. 4GG.	GJ. GS	GDC. GC. 1GD. 2GD. GH. 1GU. 2GU. 3GU.	1GBde. 1GBn. 1GBn.
I (E. Prussian)	1. 3. 4. 5. 33. 41. 43. 44. 45.	1J.Bn	3C. 1D. 1LH. 2LH. 8U.	1 Bde. 1Bn. 1Bn.
II (Pomeranian)	2. 9. 14. 21. 34. 42. 49. 54. 61.	2J.Bn	2C. 3D. 5H. 11H. 4U.	2 Bde. 2Bn. 2Bn.
III (Brandenburg)	8. 18. 20. 24. 35. 48. 52. 60. 64.	3J.Bn	6C. 2D. 3H. 9H. 3U.	3 Bde. 3Bn. 3Bn.
IV (Magdeburg)	26. 27. 31. 32. 36. 66. 67. 71. 72.	4J.Bn	7C. 6D. 10H. 12H. 6U.	4 Bde. 4Bn. 4Bn.
V (W. Prussian)	6. 7. 12. 19. 37. 46. 47. 58. 59.	5J.Bn	5C. 4D. 4H. 1U. 12U.	5 Bde. 5Bn. 5Bn.
VI (Silesian)	10. 11. 22. 23. 38. 50. 51. 62. 63.	6J.Bn	1C. 8D. 6H. 2U. 11U.	6 Bde. 6Bn. 6Bn.
VII (Westphalian)	13. 15. 16. 17. 39. 53. 55. 56. 57.	7J.Bn	4C. 7D. 8H. 5U. 10U.	7 Bde. 7Bn. 7Bn.
VIII (Rhenish)	25. 28. 29. 30. 40. 65. 68. 69. 70.	8J.Bn	8C. 5D. 7H. 7U. 9U.	8 Bde. 8Bn. 8Bn.

Although the two-division/two-brigade infantry formation was maintained, there was an additional infantry and cavalry regiment in each corps. This allowed for a reserve regiment for each arm, but during wartime, these were distributed among extra divisions or brigades. The Guard Corps also had an extra light battalion (*Guard Schützen*) and three extra cavalry regiments.

The strength of each battalion, squadron, or battery was firmly established, and upon mobilization these establishments were to be quickly made up by bringing in the first-line reservists and other auxiliary personnel to put the unit on a war footing. The various branches were organized as described below.

Infantry and Jäger

There were nine Guards regiments, 72 Line regiments, and 10 Jäger battalions. Every infantry regiment, regardless of status, had an official complement of three battalions, each of 1,002 men, exclusive of officers and staff. Each battalion contained four companies. The companies were numbered consecutively from the 1st company of the 1st battalion to the 12th company of the 3rd battalion. The third battalions of all Guard, Grenadier and Musketeer regiments (9th–12th companies) were designated fusiliers (distinguished by black leather equipment). All battalions of the Fusilier Guards and regiments 33 to 40 were fusiliers. Jägers had just a single battalion with four companies.

Regimental staff: The commanding officer (a colonel or lieutenant colonel), a major, the adjutant (often a 1st or 2nd lieutenant) The regimental sergeant-major, drum-major and quartermaster (usually an ex-senior NCO).

Battalion staff: A field officer (usually a major), a surgeon, an assistant surgeon, a paymaster, a quartermaster, battalion sergeant-major, drum-major and two clerks.

Company establishment: A captain, one 1st lieutenant, three 2nd lieutenants, one officer candidate, one sergeant-major, four sergeants, 19 corporals, ten lance-corporals, two drummers, two buglers, one medical orderly and 204 men.

There were, of course anomalies to this, especially at mobilization. At the start of the Second Schleswig War in 1864, the infantry regiments formed in the Brandenburg and Westphalian Corps that were used in the campaign were considerably under paper strength. A typical battalion consisted of 22 officers, 56 NCOs, 17 musicians and 729 other ranks. This was mostly due to fewer than needed men having passed through the system since the 1859 reforms. There was however a benefit, as fewer men were easier to control especially for the young officers. In 1866, things were better, but even then, strengths were not always met. The regimental history of the 2nd Foot Guards notes the following distribution of company officers on mobilization in 1866:

Distribution of company officers, 2nd Foot Guards, 1866

Company	Captain	1st lieutenant	2nd lieutenant	Officer candidate	Other
1	1	3	1		
2			1	2 (1 Reserve)	1
3		1		2 (1 Reserve)	
4		1		3 (1 Reserve)	
5		1		3 (1 Reserve)	1
6		1		3 (1 Reserve)	
7		1		3 (1 Reserve)	
8			1	3 (1 Reserve)	
9			1	3 (1 Reserve)	1
10		1		3 (1 Reserve)	
11		1		3	1 (deputy sgt major)
12		1		3 (1 Reserve)	1
(1 Reserve in parenthesis means one of the 2nd lieutenants was from the reserve.)					

The sergeant-major ran the company books and appointed other sergeants to important positions such as company quartermaster, armourer, tailor etc. The official complement of men was augmented by transport drivers and officers' servants, who also looked after the officers' horses. The commanding officer had three mounts; the major and adjutant on the regimental staff, the battalion commander, and the company commander all had two mounts each; and the surgeon was sometimes mounted.

Battalion transport consisted of the ammunition wagon, drawn by six horses and driven by two drivers; the supply (*montierung*) wagon which carried sundry items such as the money chest, paymaster's books, and supplies for the repair of equipment and clothing, which was drawn by two horses with one driver; the officers' baggage wagon, with four horses and one driver, and finally, the hospital cart which had two horses and one driver. Each company had one pack animal, which carried officers' rations, greatcoats, blankets, and the company paychest, along with the books. The Fusilier Guards, fusilier regiments, and the fusilier companies of the regular regiments had a two-horse cart carrying the same as the pack horse, plus the repair items usually carried in the battalion wagon by the musketeer companies. At regimental level, there was a two-horse baggage cart for officers and staff, driven by one of the officers' servants.

At the moment of mobilization, a depot battalion was formed, with a small cadre of officers and NCOs to process incoming recruits. When formed, it consisted of 18 officers and 1,002 men, much as the regular battalion. Jäger battalions maintained depot companies of four officers and 201 men. Under perfect conditions, these depot battalions would march out of barracks thirty days after the regiment had left for the seat of the war, to replace losses at the front. Obviously, conditions were seldom perfect, and replacement troops did not fill the gaps when battle casualties were severe, or sickness widespread. In the case of the 1866 war, most of the depot battalions never reached the front, having instead replaced garrison troops on the line of march. On paper, the complete infantry mobilization in 1866 stood as follows:

Complete infantry mobilization in 1866

	Regiments	Battalions	Companies	Personnel
Foot Guards:	4	12		12,024
Guard Grenadiers	4	12		12,024
Fusilier Guards	1	3		3,006
Guard Jägers		1		1,002
Guard Sharpshooters		1		1,002
Line Grenadiers	12	36		36,072
Regiments of the Line	52	156		156,312
Fusiliers	8	24		24,048
Line Jägers		8		8,016
		253		253,506
Depot battalions of Guard and Line		81		81,162
Depot companies of Jägers/Rifles			10	2,500
				83,662
Officers				7,074
Surgeons, paymasters, quartermasters				1,012
Staff NCOs				1,348
Musicians, clerks, drivers, orderlies and non-combatants				8,528
				17,962
Total of all infantry, officers and men				355,130
Total vehicles (wagons, carts etc)				1,945
Approximate total horses				9,910

Cavalry

The cavalry consisted of ten Cuirassier regiments (two Guard, eight Line); ten Dragoon regiments (two Guard, eight Line); 13 Hussar regiments (one Guard, 12 Line) and 15 Uhlan (lancer) regiments (three Guard, 12 Line). All cavalry regiments consisted of a staff and four squadrons, except the 1st, 2nd, 3rd and 4th Line Dragoons, along with the 7th, 8th, 9th and 11th Line Hussars all of which consisted of five squadrons. The Gardes du Corps divided its squadrons into two companies, which in that regiment became the primary administrative unit. Each squadron contained approximately four officers and 150 other ranks.

Regimental staff: The commanding officer (colonel or lieutenant-colonel), a major, the adjutant (lieutenant or 2nd lieutenant), trumpet-major, and a standard-bearer (a sergeant-major or sergeant). In addition, there were a senior and two junior surgeons, two or three veterinary officers, and a paymaster. Fifteen men acted as drivers, medical orderlies, farriers, officers' servants, and clerks. Some of these men performed two or more of these tasks as required.

Squadron establishment: A commander (usually a captain), two or three lieutenants (1st or 2nd), a squadron sergeant-major, four sergeants, nine corporals, 20 lance-corporals, three trumpeters and 110 troopers. In addition, there would be a small complement of volunteers and officer candidates on the strength.

Regimental transport consisted of one medicine cart with two horses, a field forge with two horses, and an officers' baggage wagon with four horses. Each squadron had a wagon drawn by two horses. The total number of horses per regiment was about 90 officers' chargers, 620 troopers' horses, and 18–20 draught horses. In addition, there were four to seven carriages for officers.

As with the infantry, regiments leaving for the front in 1866 had differing establishments. The Gardes du Corps was probably typical: 29 officers, seven sergeant-majors, one ensign, 58 NCOs, 18 trumpeters, and 553 troopers. There was also one staff surgeon, one assistant surgeon, a paymaster, and some 44 drivers, a saddler, and an armourer. There was no mention of a veterinary officer.

The depot squadron consisted of four officers, and 200 NCOs and troopers. Because the training of cavalry soldiers was more extensive than that for infantry, the reserves available were more numerous, and replacement squadrons were ready to march sooner than they were in the infantry.

Cavalry mobilization in 1866

	Regiments	Squadrons	Personnel
Guard Cuirassiers	2	8	1,200
Guard Dragoons	2	8	1,200
Guard Hussars	1		4 600
Guard Uhlans	3	12	1,800
Line Cuirassiers	8	32	4,800
Line Dragoons	8	36	5,400
Line Hussars	12	52	7,800
Line Uhlans	12	48	7,200
		200	30,000
Depot squadrons		48	7,200
Officers			1,136
Surgeons, paymasters, quartermasters			240
Staff NCOs			130
Musicians, clerks, drivers, orderlies and non-combatants			1,924
			3,430
Total cavalry officers and men			40,630
Total wehicles (wagons, carts, carriages)			1,744
Total horses			42,624

Artillery

In 1864, the fortress and field artillery elements were separated into their own regiments within the corps district. This allowed for one Guard and eight Line field artillery regiments, and a Guard and eight Line fortress artillery regiments to be formed. Prior to this, the batteries were mixed and the horse sections consisted of three batteries. From late 1864, the mounted artillery had four batteries.

Field Artillery Regiment Structure (Guard and Line)

Horse Section	
Mounted Battery No. 1	4 12-pounder guns
Mounted Battery No. 2	4 12-pounder guns
Mounted Battery No. 3	4 12-pounder guns
Mounted Battery No. 4	4 12-pounder guns
Mounted Battery No. 5	4 12-pounder guns
Mounted Battery No. 6	4 12-pounder guns
1st Foot Section	
12-pounder Foot Battery No. 1	6 12-pounder guns
4-pounder Foot Battery No. 1	6 4-pounder guns
6-pounder Foot Battery No. 1	6 6-pounder guns
12-pounder Foot Battery No. 4	6 12-pounder guns
2nd Foot Section	
12-pounder Foot Battery No. 2	6 12-pounder guns
6-pounder Foot Battery No. 2	6 6-pounder guns
4-pounder Foot Battery No. 2	6 4-pounder guns
6-pounder Foot Battery No. 4	6 6-pounder guns
3rd Foot Section	
12-pounder Foot Battery No. 3	6 12-pounder guns
6-pounder Foot Battery No. 3	6 6-pounder guns
4-pounder Foot Battery No. 3	6 4-pounder guns
4-pounder Foot Battery No. 4	6 4-pounder guns
Total batteries	18
Total 12-pounders	24 mounted, 24 foot
Total 6-pounders	24 foot
Total 4-pounders	24 foot
	96 guns

Not every battery rolled out on mobilization with a full complement of serviceable guns, and in both 1864 and 1866, the gun types were mixed. In the Second Schleswig War, the Brandenburg and Westphalian Artillery brigades (the Prussian artillery component) were armed with 24 7-pounder howitzers, 36 12-pounder smooth-bores, 16 6-pounder smooth-bores, and 28 6-pounder rifled cannon. The perceived success of rifled cannon required further equipment changes, and by 1866, 54 of the 144 batteries had been equipped with rifled cannon. Since these were new guns, it is not surprising that the deficiencies in total gun complements were in the smooth-bore batteries. (See Chapter 9 for more on the subject of Prussian artillery.)

Regimental staff of a field artillery regiment: The commanding officer (colonel or lieutenant-colonel), the adjutant (lieutenant or 2nd lieutenant), a trumpet-major, five surgeons, 16 assistant surgeons, two or three veterinary officers, and a paymaster. In addition there were two corporal clerks, an artificer, two farriers and 28 drivers. (There were two trumpet-majors in the Guard artillery.)

12-pounder mounted battery establishment. A captain, a 1st lieutenant, two 2nd lieutenants, two sergeant-majors, six sergeants, six corporals, 12 lance-corporals plus 124 gunners/drivers. There were also two trumpeters, a medical assistant, a saddler and six drivers/officers' servants.

12-pounder foot battery establishment. A captain, a 1st lieutenant, two 2nd lieutenants, two sergeant-majors, four sergeants, eight corporals, 12 lance-corporals, plus 116 gunners/drivers. There were also two trumpeters, a medical assistant, a saddler, and eight drivers/officers' servants.

4-pounder foot battery establishment. A captain, a 1st lieutenant, two 2nd lieutenants, four sergeant-majors, four sergeants, eight corporals, eight senior lance-corporals, nine lance-corporals, plus 108 gunners/drivers. There were also two trumpeters, a medical assistant, a saddler and four drivers/officers' servants.

6-pounder foot battery establishment. A captain, a 1st lieutenant, two 2nd lieutenants, four sergeant-majors, four sergeants, eight corporals, ten senior lance-corporals, eight lance-corporals plus 114 gunners/drivers. There were also two trumpeters, a medical assistant, a saddler and four drivers/officers' servants.

Regimental transport and horses: One officers' baggage wagon drawn by four horses, 54 officers' (including surgeons, paymasters etc) horses, and 38 men's horses (39 in the Guards, including one for extra trumpet-major).

Horse battery transport and horses: The gun and limber team was drawn by six horses, as were the four caissons, two provision wagons, and the field forge. The medical cart was drawn by two horses, and there was a provision pack horse attached to each battery. There were a total of six officers' and 118 men's mounts.

Foot battery transport and horses: The gun and limber team was drawn by four horses, and the six caissons, two provision wagons, and the field forge were all drawn by six horses. The medical cart was drawn by two horses, and there was a provision pack horse attached to each battery. There were a total of six officers' and 126 men's mounts.

Ammunition columns

On mobilization, each field artillery regiment formed nine ammunition columns. These columns carried the ammunition for the artillery, infantry, and all other units issued with firearms. They were divided into two divisions, one of five columns, the other of four. The five-column division consisted of 25 wagons, with two officers, 175 men, and 174 horses. The four-column division consisted of 24 wagons with two officers, 173 men, and 170 horses. In this way wagons could be replenished more effectively at the ammunition depot, and allowed for columns to be attached to infantry divisions when they became divided.

Ammunition reserve park

This was also divided into two divisions, each of eight columns of 33 wagons. This park was the central ammunition depot and was placed strategically, usually near a railhead, to allow vehicles to collect replenishments quickly to return to the battlefield. Each division had 264 carriages and was manned by nine officers.

Fortress regiments

Fortress regiments were only mobilized in wartime. As in the field artillery, there were one Guard and eight provincial regiments. These consisted of a staff and two sections, each section consisting of four companies. These troops were sent to garrison important fortresses in Prussia.

Fortress regiment staff: commander (field officer), one to three supervising officers (usually majors), an adjutant (1st or 2nd lieutenant), a pyrotechnic officer (1st or 2nd lieutenant), four extra officers (2nd lieutenants), a paymaster, 13 sergeant-majors, 27 sergeants, and a corporal clerk.

Section staff: Commanding officer (field officer), a captain, an adjutant (lieutenant), a corporal clerk and surgeon.

Company establishment: A captain, one 1st lieutenant, two 2nd lieutenants, four sergeants, two trumpeters, 12 corporals, a surgeon, a medical orderly, three artificers, and 188 men.

On mobilization, a depot artillery division was formed, which consisted of a horse battery, and three foot batteries, each of four guns with 14 officers and 556 men, plus 189 horses.

Artillery mobilization in 1866

	Batteries	Columns	Divisions	Guns	Personnel
Horse Artillery	54			216	8,424
Foot Artillery	108			648	16,416
Total	162			864	24,840
Ammunition columns		64			3,132
Ammunition park					390
Total					3,522
Fortress artillery					3,600
Depot divisions			9		5,004
Officers					1,024
Surgeons, paymasters, quartermasters					178
Staff NCOs					116
Musicians, clerks, drivers, orderlies and non-combatants					2,314
					3,632
Total artillery personnel					40,598
Total guns					864
Total vehicles (wagons, carts etc – exclusive of guns)					2,163
Approximate total horses (including gun teams)					12,300

Prussian Guards marching out of depot in Berlin, June 1866.

Engineers and pioneers

There were two components of this branch in the army organization. The Engineer Corps consisted largely of officers who had technical specialities in fortifications, entrenchments, bridge building, and other construction projects. The majority of these officers were professionals who, in time of war, were on the headquarters staff of the army or army corps to which they were attached. They would plan and supervise the projects required by the army to keep it moving, or protect it when it was static. The pioneer element provided the troops who accompanied the army on the march. Their role was similar to that of the combat engineers in a modern army. The Guard, and each provincial army corps, had one battalion of pioneers, each one consisting of four companies. Pioneer troops also manned the pontoon, bridging, and telegraph trains that accompanied each army corps.

Pioneer battalion staff: The commanding officer (a colonel or lieutenant-colonel), a major, the adjutant (1st or 2nd lieutenant) sergeant-major, paymaster, surgeon, quartermaster, staff-bugler, two clerks, and 22 drivers.

Company establishment: A captain, one 1st lieutenant, three 2nd lieutenants, one sergeant-major, four sergeants, 23 corporals, 12 lance-corporals, one drummer, one bugler, two medical orderlies, and 200 men. In addition there were six drivers for company transport.

Battalion and company transport: Battalion transport consisted of an officers' baggage wagon, three equipment wagons, and a field forge, each with four horses and two drivers, along with an ammunition cart, with two horses. There were also six carriages. Each company had a repair wagon drawn by four horses, and a hospital cart with two horses. The company had one pack animal, which carried sundry items required by the company on the march.

Pontoon train: The train, which accompanied each army corps, consisted of 48 individual pontoon wagons, and 28 plank wagons, each drawn by four horses. The complement was two officers, four sergeants, and 174 men.

Heavy bridging train: The number of vehicles in this train varied depending on the type of equipment and material available or required by a particular army corps. It is likely that it consisted of at least 30 wagons, drawn by four horses each. It was manned by two officers and 56 other ranks.

Field telegraph division: These were attached to the Royal Army Headquarters, and the headquarters of each field army. Thus, there were five divisions mobilized in 1866, for all theatres. Each consisted of three officers, 137 other ranks, and ten wagons with 73 horses.

On mobilization a depot pioneer company was formed in each district, which consisted of four officers and 250 men.

Pioneer Corps mobilization in 1866

	Battalions	Companies	Personnel
Guard Pioneers	1		1,002
Line Pioneers	8		8,016
			9,018
Depot companies		9	2,250
Officers (Pioneer Corps only)			207
Surgeons, paymasters, quartermasters			36
Staff NCOs			12
Train soldiers			2,502
Musicians, clerks, orderlies and non-combatants			312
			3,069
Total of all Pioneer troops, officers and men			14,337
Total of all vehicles (wagons, carts etc)			1,229
Approximate total of all horses			4,300

Military train

The military train was added to the provincial army corps roster in 1850. In modern parlance, their function was to provide the logistics for an army in the field. They supplied the transport and personnel for the commissariat, field bakeries, and field hospitals. The train battalion of each army corps consisted of two companies.

Train battalion staff: The commanding officer (a colonel or lieutenant-colonel), a major, the adjutant (1st or 2nd lieutenant) sergeant-major, paymaster, surgeon, veterinary officer, quartermaster, staff-bugler, and eight clerks.

Company establishment: A captain, two 1st lieutenants, four 2nd lieutenants, one sergeant-major, four sergeants, 12 corporals, 32 lance-corporals, two drummers, one bugler, two medical orderlies, and 600 transport soldiers.

The military train was responsible for the following:

Commissariat train: 160 wagons drawn by four horses each, with 490 train soldiers from the 1st Company.

Field bakery: Five wagons drawn by four horses each, and manned by 118 personnel from the 2nd Company.

Heavy hospital train: Three trains each of 11 wagons.

Light divisional hospital trains: Twelve trains each of 11 wagons and ambulances. On mobilization a depot train company was formed in each district, which consisted of two officers and 300 men.

Military train mobilization in 1866

	Battalions	Companies	Personnel
Guard Train	1		1,226
Line Train	8		9,808
			11,034
Depot companies		9	2,700
Officers			153
Surgeons, paymasters, quartermasters			36
Staff NCOs			27
Musicians, clerks, orderlies and non-combatants			405
			621
Total of all military train troops, officers and men			14,355
Total of all vehicles (wagons, carts etc)			2,970
Approximate total of all horses			13,365

Medical troops

On mobilization, surgeons and medical officers were attached to the various army and army corps headquarters. They were then assigned to the hospital trains that were then forming. It is interesting to note that surgeons down to the most junior had only recently attained military status. The ordinary medical officer was still rated as a civil appointment. Also assigned to the field hospitals were hospital assistants (*Lazarettenhilfe*) who, although wearing a specific uniform, were raised on an ad hoc basis as the army mobilized. The stretcher-bearer corps (*Krankentrager*) was established on a corps basis, at three detachments per army corps.

Medical troops mobilization in 1866

	Detachments	Personnel
Army surgeons and medical officers (estimate)		780
Hospital assistants (estimate)		1,520
Guard stretcher-bearer detachments	3	180
Line stretcher-bearer detachments	24	1,440
		3,920

Landwehr

The first levy of the Landwehr was embodied to form the garrison and line of communications troops. This consisted of men between 28 and 32 years old. It was constituted as follows:

Landwehr first levy

	Regiments	Battalions	Personnel
Infantry			
Guard	4	12	12,300
Line	32	96	98,400
Independent battalions		8	8,200
Total		116	118,900
	Regiments	**Squadrons**	**Personnel**
Cavalry			
Heavy cavalry	1	4	600
Uhlans	5	20	3,000
Dragoons	1	4	600
Hussars	5	20	3,000
Total		48	7,200

Despite these theoretical numbers, almost none of the Landwehr infantry battalions reached anything like full strength, with most mustering around 500 men per battalion, although some reached 800 or so. The most likely figure of embodied Landwehr is around 75,000–80,000, where there was a partial embodiment of the second levy. The Landwehr cavalry were more successful, and manage to muster nearly six thousand. As the war progressed, a further seven Landwehr cavalry regiments were raised, adding an additional 4,200 men, but the war ended before they were available in the field.

Summary of the troops mobilized in 1866

Active Army

	Units	Men	Officers/Aux	Vehicles	Horses
Infantry	253 bns	253,506	17,962	1,945	9,910
Cavalry	200 sqns	30,000	3,430	1,744	42,624
Artillery	864 guns	31,962	3,632	2,163	12,300
Pioneers	9 bns	9,018	3,069	1,229	4,300
Military Train	9 bns	11,034	621	2,970	13,365
		335,920	28,714	10,051	82,499

Depot troops

	Units	Personnel
Infantry	83 bns	83,362
Cavalry	48 sqns	7,200
Artillery	9 divs	5,004
Pioneers	9 coys	2,250
Military Train	9 coys	2,700
		100,516

Landwehr

	Units	Personnel
Infantry	116 bns	118,900
Cavalry	76 sqns	11,400
		130,300

Total number of all ranks mobilized: 595,450

Part Four
Uniforms of the Prussian Army 1860–67

CHAPTER TWELVE

General Uniform Notes

FOR ALMOST THIRTY YEARS after the end of the Napoleonic Wars, the development of Prussian army uniforms followed the general European trend in style and cut. The infantry wore the bell-topped shako along with tight blue coatees and long grey or white trousers. As the post-Napoleonic flamboyance ebbed throughout Europe, the uniforms lost their more expensive elements of lace and adornment. The shako eventually lost its loops and tassels and the coatee became somewhat looser. The other branches of the army, such as artillery and engineers, were dressed similarly while the cavalry, consisting of cuirassiers, dragoons, hussars and uhlans (lancers) wore their respective, and generally conventional, uniforms. Cuirassiers wore breastplates over white coatees, with a Romanesque helmet. The cornflower-blue coated dragoons and the hussars with their variously coloured dolmans and pelisses wore the infantry shako. Uhlans were dressed in dark-blue coatees and regimentally coloured plastrons with the Polish czapka.

In the early 1840s the tide of austerity, combined with a growing nationalism, saw a more radical change, and uniforms began to follow a more practical style. Tunics appeared, at first with long skirts, soon shortened for comfort. In 1842, along with tunics, the Prussians introduced the *Pickelhaube* or spiked helmet, as other European nations, led by France, began to wear shakos that were shorter and more conical, soon evolving into the kepi.

The Pickelhaube

The helm, nicknamed the pickelhaube, was the uniform item that defined the appearance of the Prussian and German armies for the next seventy-five years. Introduced by Royal Cabinet Order (*Allerhöchste Kabinettsorder* – AKO) of 23 October 1842, this headdress would soon come to define the image of all German soldiery for the next seventy-five years. The legend is that the Prussian king, Frederick William IV, was visiting Tsar Nicholas in St Petersburg when he saw a black spiked helmet, a prototype for the Russian Army, on a table in his study. He asked if Nicholas would mind if he showed it to his own senior army officers. The Tsar apparently assented. The Prussians made modifications and it appeared two years earlier than the Russian model, generally recognized by its use in the Crimean War. This dramatic and distinctive headdress was nearly 38 cm (15 inches) high overall. Made of boiled and lacquered leather, the body, rounded at the top and about eight inches high was surmounted by a brass spike of almost 13 cm (5 inches) mounted on a quatrefoil base attached by four brass studs. The spike itself was hollow brass, slanting outwards down to a waist and then a short inwards slanting neck with two ventilation holes above a ring of small domes known as the "Ring of Pearls" (*Perlring*) at the base of the spike. In the artillery, the spike above the waist was replaced by a ball – which represented a cannon ball, but was also essential for the safety of horses and crew when men were working around the gun teams.

Prussian helm, introduced in 1842.

The front peak of 6.5 cm (2½ inches) was squared and bound by a brass edge secured by a stud at each side where the peak was attached to the body. The rear peak was unbound, flared and rounded. A brass spine ran down the back of the helmet from the rear arm of the quatrefoil to the lower edge of the rear peak, fitted by two brass studs; one in the middle of the body, the other in the middle of the rear peak. Both peaks were stitched to the body. Convex brass chin-scales were secured to either side of the helmet by decorative bolts with brass heads, and the Prussian leather cockade of black/white/black was attached to both bolts, underneath the chin-scales. The brass helmet plate was the Prussian eagle, plain with ball and sceptre in its claws, and wings upward. The plate was attached by two bolts passing through the front of the plate, changed within a year to two studs soldered to the rear. Guards and grenadiers wore their own variations. Also, regiments with silver lace generally replaced the brass fittings with white metal.

There was little difference in appearance between the helmets of officers and other ranks. The helmet plate, spike, chin-scales, and bindings were of gilt or silver and the studs on the quatrefoil were in the shape of eight-pointed stars. The quatrefoil itself was often bevelled around the edges. The leatherwork was of a finer material and the stitching and workmanship were superior. The cockades were made of cloth with the white circle of gold lace. As in most armies of the time (and later) many officers chose to purchase their helmets privately and within certain limitations, some latitude was allowed on appearance and much was allowed on workmanship and materials.

All Guards, Grenadier regiments, musicians, and some other regiments with certain traditions and dress distinctions, wore plumes in either black or white, or in the case of musicians, red. Those regiments or individuals entitled to wear a plume (*Haarbusche*) had a removable spike that unscrewed from the waist.

In 1856, flat brass chin-scales replaced the convex type in the infantry, but not in the cavalry or artillery and the cockade was changed from leather to tin. Experience in the field had shown that the helmet could be unwieldy and that it tended to fall off easily, and an AKO of 24 December 1857 determined the 1842 model too heavy, therefore it was to be reduced slightly in size and many were cut and re-sewn for the sake of economy. On 10 May 1860, another AKO was issued that further reduced the height of the helmet, this time by about approximately 3 cm (1½ inches). A large number were again cut down and re-sewn. At the same time, the front plate needed a reduction in size to fit the new height. This new plate was adorned with a scroll (bandeau) with the motto "MIT GOTT FÜR KOENIG UND VATERLAND" (With God for King and Fatherland). Economies prompted the use of older plates with the bandeau soldered on. This was the helmet that was worn during the wars of 1864 to 1866.

Uniforms

General

Tunic

The tunic (*Waffenrock*) was the same cut and style for the following units and corps in both the Guard and Line:

Corps/unit	Basic colour
Infantry	Dark blue
Jägers	Holly green
Sharpshooters	Holly green
Dragoons	Cornflower blue
Artillery	Dark blue
Pioneers	Dark blue
Train	Dark blue
Hospital Corps	Dark blue
Staff Corps	Holly green

The tunic and collar were of the basic colour of the unit. On the collar were patches, extending to about 1.25 cm (½ inch) to the rear of the shoulder strap button. The tunic was piped down the front edge and on the three-pointed flaps on each side of the skirt at the rear. The collar patch and piping were in unit colours. There were eight buttons down the front and at each point on the skirt flaps at the rear. The

Front view of tunic with Brandenburg cuffs, and rear view with Swedish cuffs.

cuffs were either of Brandenburg or Swedish style depending on the unit. Brandenburg cuffs were round with a rectangular flap with three buttons arranged vertically. Swedish cuffs were round with two buttons arranged horizontally at the top. Guard units had litzen attached to both cuffs and collar. The shoulder straps were rectangular, narrowing to a point above the button. They were coloured according to unit and bore regimental numbers and other distinctions.

The general staff (below the rank of general) and all military officials wore the officers' version of the infantry tunic. The uniforms of cuirassiers, hussars, uhlans, and other special units are described completely under their own sections.

Trousers

For everyday and field wear, foot troops wore trousers of dark-grey cloth with a red welt down the sides. They had a front flap that fastened each side with leather buttons. There were no pockets. For parades in summer, white linen trousers with the same attributes as the grey ones were worn.

For mounted troops, the trousers were of the same cloth and general style as those for the foot troops, with the addition of black leather reinforcement on the seat, inner leg and around the trouser bottoms of about three inches. The red welt ran all the way to the bottom of the leg. For dismounted parades and walking out, the trousers were the same as those worn by the foot troops but of a somewhat tighter fit.

Footwear

Ankle-length leather shoes with leather loops in front and back were worn. Reinforced eyelets either side of the front loop allowed a leather thong to pass through and tighten the shoe. In this period there were no such things as "right" and "left" shoes, the form was universal, and wear by the soldier formed the fit. The experiences of the war in Denmark prompted the introduction of the leather jackboot, which was first used during the 1866 war. This would become another enduring and recognizable feature of the German soldier's appearance for years to come.

Forage caps

The only undress head covering worn in the entire Prussian army was the universal woollen cap or "*Mutze*". For other ranks, this was a peakless cap of tunic colour with band and piping in unit colours. The front was decorated with a small Prussian cockade. For senior NCOs the cap had a leather peak (*Schirmutze*) like that worn by officers.

Drill uniform

This was made of coarse un-dyed cloth that had a distinctly off-white appearance. It was not worn by cavalry. It was also not authorized for use on campaign. The trousers were often worn with the tunic and equipment for local exercises or shooting practice.

Greatcoat

The greatcoat worn by all dismounted troops in cold weather was of coarse dark-grey cloth. It had a large stand collar on which there was a patch of the same colour as that on the tunic. The shoulder straps were the same colour as the tunic, piped with the colour of the shoulder straps worn on the tunic. The regimental number was worn on the shoulder straps where applicable. The coat was fastened by six buttons of the same metal as those on the tunic. A hood could be attached in extreme cold weather, which fitted under the helmet and allowed the chin-scales to pass through. Mounted troops wore the same coat, but it was longer and had a large slit at the rear to fit over the saddle. When not mounted, the slit was closed with leather buttons.

Equipment

The Prussian infantryman was one of the better-equipped soldiers in Europe in this period as much thought had been given to how to make him more efficient.

Gürtelrüstung equipment.

The *Gürtelrüstung* (literally "belt equipment") was designed to support his valise and pouches from the waist.

Side-arms carried by dismounted troops. From left: artillery sidearm; infantry M52 sidearm; infantry fascine knife; jäger/Schützen sidearm; fusilier sidearm; pioneer fascine knife.

Belt and side-arm

The belt was of black or white leather, and secured by a hook to a universal brass plate which bore the royal Prussian crown surrounded by a ring with the legend "GOTT MIT UNS" in white-metal. The belt supported a frog on the left side that held the side-arm – a short sword with a straight blade in a black scabbard. Attached to the hilt was a strap with a decorative knot called a *Säbeltroddel* that will be discussed later. There was no bayonet scabbard.

Cartridge pouch (Patronen tache) for the 1850 model load-carrying system. Each pouch held 20 rounds fitted into a wooden block.

Ammunition pouch

Black leather ammunition pouches were introduced with the new equipment. At first there was only one pouch, which was attached by two straps to the front of the belt, hanging below the waist plate. By 1860, two pouches were being worn, one on either side of the belt to balance the load, attached where the valise straps hooked. The single pouch in front was then worn only for parades. Each pouch held 30 cartridges.

Valise

The valise was of black canvas over a cane frame to maintain the shape. The whole was covered in un-tanned cowhide for durability. On each side there was a small pocket with a flap and button. The valise was carried by straps, in white or black leather, that passed over the shoulder and hooked under the belt by means of a flat brass hook. The face of the hook was an oval topped triangle that was the width of the belt. In the Guard infantry and artillery, the hook was in the form of a grenade. To steady the valise, a black strap either side of the bottom hooked up to each front chest strap on a flat ring at the back of the strap.

Mess kit and haversack

The mess kit and water bottle, nesting into the form of an unpainted tin cylinder, could be fitted to the top or the back of the valise. During the 1866 campaign a new water bottle that slung over the right shoulder was authorized. The white canvas haversack (or bread bag) was worn over the left shoulder under the belt and valise straps to hang on the right side.

Equipment for mounted troops

For mounted troops, the equipment varied slightly between the various branches. Most mounted other ranks wore a white shoulder belt with a large black leather pouch attached. The belt had a carbine loop and swivel that slung under the pouch. Sword belts and slings were worn over the tunic by cuirassiers and dragoons and under the tunic by hussars and lancers. The sword belt itself was of plain white leather secured by a square open brass buckle at the waist. Other equipment, including horse furniture, varied by cavalry arm and will be discussed under each section.

Uniforms for officers

As in many European armies, most Prussian officers purchased their uniforms privately. However, the officer class consisted mostly of sons from Junker families, who for the large part were not rich, and to whom expensive tailors' bills were not welcome. This explains the relative austerity of Prussian officer uniforms compared to their European cousins, with the exception of Guards regiments.

Although conforming closely in style and cut to the other ranks' uniforms, there were differences. In the infantry, and all other units except cuirassiers, hussars and uhlans, the tunic was surprisingly devoid of gold lace, for reasons already stated; nevertheless it was more elegant and of finer quality materials. The collar was cut higher, and owing to the sword belt being worn under the tunic, there was a tailored slit where the sword hilt emerged to allow the scabbard to pass through to the frog. For mounted units, there was no slit as sword slings were worn instead of a frog. The cuffs were plain, like the men's and all the buttons were gilt or silver according to regiment. In the Guards regiments, there was much gold and silver lace, which will be discussed in the appropriate sections.

With the exception of hussars, all officers wore laced epaulette straps with gilt or silver crescents at the shoulder. Bullion fringes were worn by ranks above major. Rank was indicated by silver or gilt diamond-shaped stars on the epaulette field. They were attached to cloth loops on the shoulders and a button at the top. The cloth underlay colour for the epaulette without fringe was red, except for cuirassiers and uhlans for whom it was the colour of the collar patch, and those units wearing light-blue facings.

Rank as shown on epaulettes

Rank	Bullion fringe	Stars
Second lieutenant (seconde-lieutenant)	No fringe	None
Lieutenant (premier-lieutenant)	No fringe	One
Captain (hauptleute, rittmeister)	No fringe	Two
Major	Bullion cloth fringe	None
Lieutenant-colonel (oberst-lieutenant)	Bullion cloth fringe	One
Colonel (oberst)	Bullion cloth fringe	Two
Major-general (general-major)	Heavy bullion wire fringe	None
Lieutenant-general (general-lieutenant)	Heavy bullion wire fringe	One
General (der infanterie, cavallerie, etc)	Heavy bullion wire fringe	Two
Colonel-general* (general-oberst)	Heavy bullion wire fringe	Three
General-oberst with the rank of field marshal (general-feldmarschall)	Heavy bullion wire fringe	Three stars/crossed batons
Honorary general-feldmarschall	Heavy bullion wire fringe	Two stars/crossed batons
General-feldmarschall	Heavy bullion wire fringe	Crossed batons

** No equivalent rank in the British or US armies*

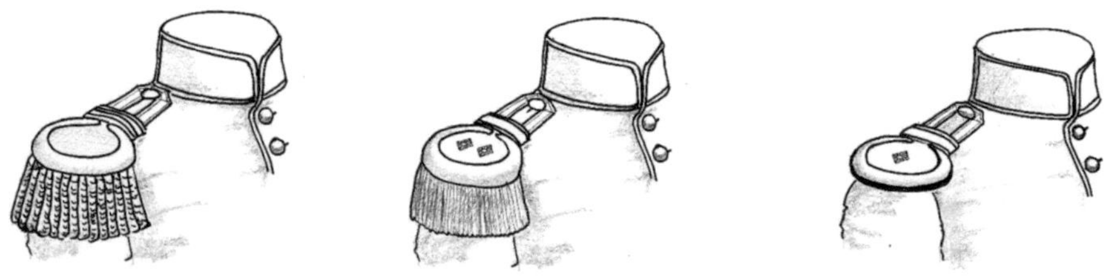

Officers' epaulettes.

Just prior to the 1866 campaign, twisted silver and black cord shoulder straps were introduced as being more practical in the field. These will be described later.

Again, excepting the hussars, all officers wore a sash around the waist. This was of silver cloth, about 6.5 cm (2½ inch) wide with two black stripes, 1 cm (½ inch) from the top and bottom edge. The sash was tied in a stylized knot on the left hip with the two ends hanging down with two large silver tassels with 30-cm (12-inch) fringes of mixed silver and black. The whole finished level with the knee and for fashion's sake the rear tassel was often a little higher than the front. Adjutants, including hussars, wore a slightly wider sash over the right shoulder (secured under the epaulette by a loop) and had a simpler knot just above the hip with the same hanging tassels and fringe.

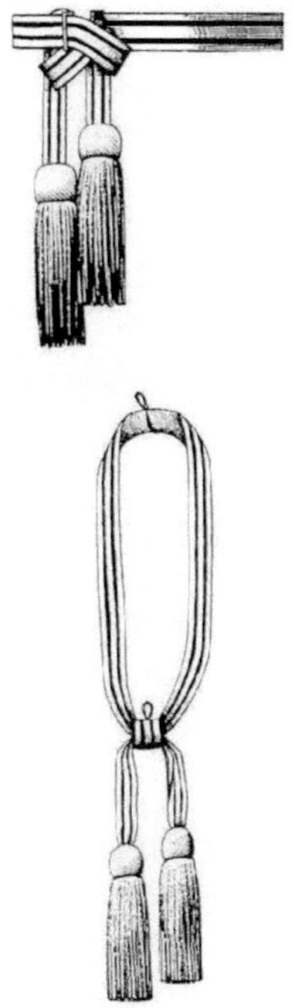

Sashes: left, officers; and right, adjutants.

Undress

The most common form of undress was the frock *Überrock*, which was worn by all officers except hussars. This could be worn in most undress situations and was generally worn by most officers when parade dress, gala dress or court dress were not required. It was double-breasted and fastened down the right side, six buttons on each side. The collar was high and squared in front and the skirt reached to just above the knees. There were two buttons at the waist in the rear. Officers wore this with the peaked cap or with the helmet for certain occasions.

For infantry, foot artillery, engineers, pioneers and military officials, the coat was black. For cuirassiers, uhlans, horse artillery and train it was dark blue and for dragoons it was cornflower blue. The collar was entirely in unit colour with piping as prescribed and the deep cuffs were also piped around the tops. Epaulettes as described above were worn on the shoulders. When the undress shoulder cords were introduced in 1866, these became the normal wear with this garment.

Greatcoats

The officers' greatcoat (*Paletot*) was of fine quality dark-blue-grey cloth and double-breasted with six gilt or silver buttons down each side. It had a stand and fall collar which, when folded down was the colour of the tunic, and when turned up was in the tunic patch colour. When turned up in bitter weather, the collar could be fastened across the front by a cloth strap attached to two buttons on each side. Two buttons secured a short cloth belt at the top of the rear skirt and there were two vertical pockets on the side. The deep turn-back cuffs were often used to store important dispatches or papers.

In addition to the paletot, a *Mantel* could be worn, especially when mounted. This was a long single-breasted coat coming to just above the ankles with a much wider and deeper collar than the paletot, but in the same colours. There was a long slit at the back to facilitate riding, which fastened half way down by a strap and button when the wearer was not mounted.

Officer's überrock.

Trousers

The grey-black trousers for officers were of finer cloth than the men's, with a red stripe down the side. They could be secured under the instep by a leather or cloth strap. When mounted, officers of foot troops had the seat reinforced with leather, which were worn on all occasions when on horseback. In summer white linen trousers with instep straps, but without stripes, were worn, unless on duty with troops wearing grey trousers. For levées or gala occasions white cassimere trousers with instep straps and without stripes were worn. The leg wear for cavalry officers varied considerably and will be dealt with in the appropriate sections.

Officers' equipment

The officers' sword belt was of plain black leather as it was worn under the tunic. In the infantry, the sword and scabbard fitted into a frog at the waist. On campaign and on exercise this was worn over the tunic, but under the sash. The sword straps and knots were of silver and black lace. For some parades, officers wore the valise with white or black straps conventionally over the shoulders and attached to the bottom of the valise behind. When it came to campaigning, most officers purchased equipment such as mess kit, pistol holsters, and pouches privately and considerable freedom was taken in how they wore them.

Sword knots, from left, infantry officers and senior NCOs; cavalry officers and senior NCOs; and officer candidates.

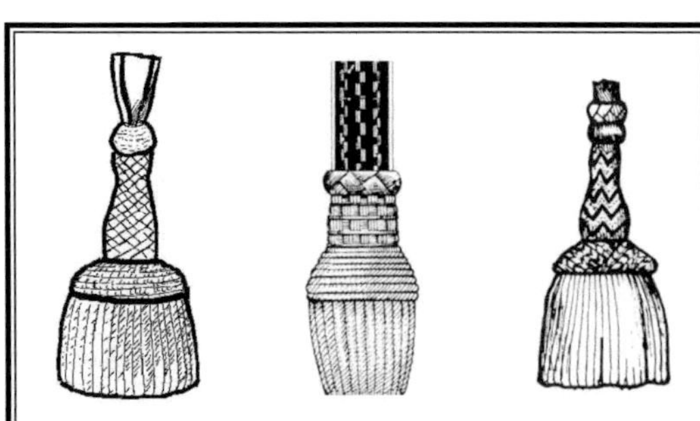

Rank distinctions of NCOs *(Unteroffiziere)*

The system of non-commissioned officer ranks was peculiarly German in both nomenclature and distinction. There were basically three classes: *Unteroffiziere Mit Portepee* (senior NCOs – literally "with officer sword knot"), *Unteroffiziere Ohne Portepee* (junior NCOs – *without* sword knot), and *Mannschaftsdienstgrade* (soldiers' ranks). The knots were in black and silver lace.

NCOs and rank distinctions

Rank group	Translation	Distinctions
Unteroffiziere Mit Portepee		
Feldwebel, *Wachtmeister*, *Oberfeuerwerker*, *Obermeister*, *Vize-Feldwebel* (Landwehr only) etc.	Regimental-sergeants major (all branches), staff sergeants, quartermaster sergeants, conductors of train, artillery etc	Officers' sword and knot. Officers' helmet and furniture. Officers' peaked cap (*Schirmütze*). Gold or silver lace edge to collar and cuffs. Large heraldic button on collar.
Unteroffiziere Ohne Portepee		
Sergeant, *Fähnrich*, *Offiziers-Antwärter*, *Kapitulanten*	Sergeants, company quartermasters, acting officers, ensigns, officer candidates	NCOs' side-arm knot, (*Fähnrich* wore officers' cockade, and sword knot). Officers' peaked cap. Gold or silver lace edge to collar and cuffs.
Mannschaftsdienstgrade		
Ober Gefreiter, *Hautboisten*	Corporal, bandsmen	Large heraldic button on collar.
Gefreiter, *Einjährig-Freiwilligen*	Lance-corporal, one-year volunteer	Gold or silver lace edge to collar and cuffs. Small heraldic button on collar.

NCO collars, from left Feldwebel; sergeant; gefreiter. NCO cuffs: Swedish; Brandeburg. NCO lace: top plain, bottom Guard. Heraldic buttons.

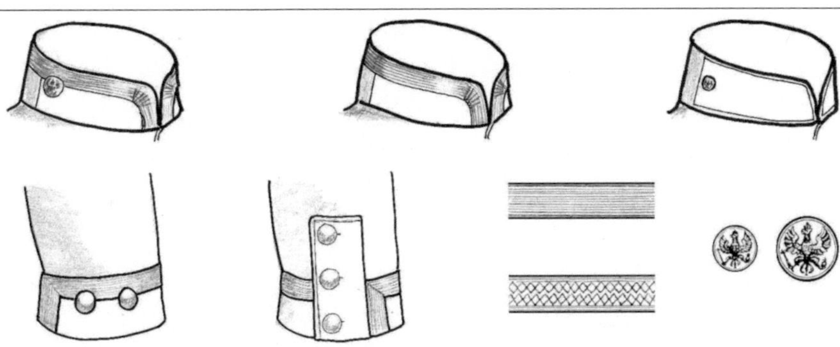

The senior feldwebel usually wore the waffenrock of finer material than the men's with the addition of gold lace on collar and cuff as described. The lace was of plain, ribbed form for all branches except for the Guards and Hussars, who wore a cross-stitched bullion type.

Skill at arms and other distinctions

Certain distinctions were displayed on the shoulder straps. The one-year volunteer (*Einjährig-Freiwilligen*) had a twisted black and white woollen cord stitched to the edge of the strap (except at the shoulder). Soldiers re-enlisting wore a cloth strip of white wool with a black thread at the base of the strap. NCOs who had passed through riding school wore a strip that was red for uhlans and horse artillery (or yellow for red straps), button colour for dragoons, collar colour for cuirassiers, and for hussars a loop of twisted yellow cord mixed with jacket colour. NCOs passing the instruction schools in gymnastics, signalling and bayonet as assistant instructors wore two strips of white cloth above the button on the shoulder strap.

From left to right: re-enlisted private; riding school NCO; one-year volunteer; signalling volunteer.

Marksmanship badges were awarded in three classes, from best shot in company up to best at regimental level. The awards consisted of a white woollen strip with a black line worn on both sleeves above the Swedish cuffs or from the button to the edge of the patch on the Brandenburg cuffs. The initial class was worn nearest to the top of the Swedish and the lower edge of the Brandenburg.

The best shot in the Musketry School course was awarded a special distinction of a lace strip in button colour with two black stripes. In addition, the buttons on either the Swedish or Brandenburg cuff were decorated with the heraldic eagle.

At this time, there were no special awards for swordsmanship or other skill-at-arms proficiency.

Marksmanship badges. From left: 2nd class; 1st class; musketry school best shot.

Musicians

Musicians in the Prussian Army were designated as follows: bandsmen (*Hautboisten*), trumpeters (*Trompeter*), buglers (*Hornister*), fifers (*Pfeifer*), and drummers (*Tamboure* or *Trommler*).

All bandsmen, cavalry trumpeters, buglers of the Guard-Sharpshooters (*Garde-Schutzen*) and the Jäger battalions wore the NCO uniform with bandsman's wings (*Schwalbennester* – literally "swallow's nests"). These were of collar-patch colour with the NCO lace in button colour (in the case of Guards, the decorative lace). For cuirassiers and dragoons they were of the facing colour and for hussars, they were of the Attila colour. Cuirassier trumpeters did not wear the cuirass. All these musicians wore the NCOs' sword-knot.

Bandsmen in the Guard infantry (except Grenadier regiments), trumpeters of Guard field artillery and buglers of *Garde-Schutzen* and Garde-Jäger had a short 3-cm (1¼-inch) fringe in silver or gold under the *schwalbennester*. Staff musicians (i.e. band-sergeants, sergeant-trumpeters, or buglers) in Line regiments had a longer 7-cm (2¾-inch) fringe and those that were Feldwebels or *Wachtmeisters* (trumpet-majors) carried the officer sword and sword knot. The drum-major (*Regiments-Tamboure*) wore the same distinctions as the staff bandsmen. Prussian drum-majors never wore the decorative baldric so often worn by their counterparts in most other countries and other German states.

The drummers, fifers, and buglers of Line infantry and train regiments were dressed as ordinary privates and wore plain white lace on the *schwalbennester*. In the Guard infantry they wore white lace with the 3-cm (1¼-

Musicians' collars. From left: line infantry drummer; staff musician; cavalry trumpeter.

inch) fringe. Drums throughout the army were of the shallow brass shell type with white hoops decorated with red triangles in a vandyke pattern. The skins were tightened by the post and screw method rather than the ropes. The drums were attached directly to the belt by a large brass eagle clasp on a short leather adjustable strap. White drum aprons were worn. All musicians wore a red plume in their full dress headdress.

Horse furniture

Bridles and saddlery

Bridles were of polished brown leather including the brow-band, cheek and nose straps. The buckles, rings, and tongues were all in brass for officers and polished steel for the men. The men's horse's steel bridoon was omitted on officers' chargers. The leather wallets were quite large and often, a leather horseshoe case was strapped to one. The high, arched saddle had wide flaps lined with numnah. The girth was of heavy woven material and a surcingle was used.

Shabracque

The shabracque used by officers of all units except general officers and cavalry was of tunic cloth, rounded on both ends and worn over the wallets. It was edged with a gold or silver lace band 4 cm (1½ inch) wide with a 1-cm (½-inch) wide band inside. For *Flügeladjutants* and officers of Guard infantry there was a Guard star in proper colours on the rear corners. For general staff, War Ministry, adjutants, Line infantry and Landwehr infantry the rear corners were decorated with the royal cipher surmounted by a crown.

Colours and standards

The field of the Guard standards was white, edged with a silver/black fringe. In the centre was a black heraldic eagle on an orange field within a silver wreath surmounted by a large crown. In each corner were crowned ciphers within silver wreaths. The remaining regiments had the same standards with a large black cross in Maltese form behind the central device and reaching to the outer edges. The swallow-tailed standards were longer top and bottom with the swallow coming out of the fly. Standard-bearers wore wide leather belts faced and fringed in button colour with a 1-cm (½-inch) stripe of facing colour.

From top left, Guard infantry colour; Line infantry colour; Landwehr infantry colour; Guard cavalry standard; Line cavalry standard.

There were three campaign streamers available by 1866: the 1813–15 streamer was orange with a thin white and black stripe on either side. The 1848–49 streamer was black with a white stripe on either side and awarded with or without swords. The 1864 streamer was black with an orange stripe on one edge and a white one on the other. It was also awarded with or without swords. Streamers of particular regiments will be described later.

CHAPTER THIRTEEN

General Officers, Staff and War Ministry

Parade and gala dress

Headdress

The helmet for gala and parade dress was that prescribed for all officers of the army. All the mountings were of gilt or gilding metal. The plate was the Guard eagle with star and the cockade was black and gilt metal. For parade and state occasions a black and white feather plume was worn, the black feathers lying under the white.

General's waffenrock with aiguillettes.

Tunic

The waffenrock was of fine dark blue Melton cloth. The high red collar was cut at an angle in front and the Swedish cuffs were also in red. Both collar and cuffs were edged with serrated gold lace and decorated with a gold oak-leaf pattern as were the blue three-pointed skirt flaps, which were edged with two stripes of gold lace, the inner one serrated, the outer plain and piped red. Each cuff had two buttons on the top, the skirt flaps had no buttons. The front of the tunic was piped red and fitted with twelve gilt buttons all the way down the front including the skirt. The eight down to the waist were fastened and the four below the waist were left undone. The shoulders were decorated with

Rear skirts on a general's tunic.

gold shoulder knots, the right one with interwoven gold aiguillettes, which hung across the right chest and hooked to the button at the top of the tunic.

Sash and side-arm

The silver sash with black stripes was worn on all formal occasions. The side-arm was either the officer's dress sword (*Degen*) or the prescribed side-arm for branch of service the general represented; infantry, artillery or cavalry.

Trousers and footwear

For levées and gala occasions white kersey trousers were worn. For parades and state occasions, dark blue-grey trousers were worn. These were piped red down the outside seam with two 4-cm (1½-inch) wide red stripes either side, which became known as "triple stripes". The short riding boots for mounted duties were worn with spurs, as were the dress shoes worn for dismounted occasions.

Undress

Undress cap

The undress cap (*Mütze*) was of blue cloth with a black patent leather peak. The band and piping were red.

Tunic

The tunic worn for everyday dress and on service was the same cut and style as the gala tunic, including the row of twelve buttons down the front. The red collar was square cut in front and plain, as were the red Swedish cuffs with two gilt buttons. The rear skirts had two three-button flaps, which were piped red. For normal wear the bullion epaulettes were worn with this garment, including the aiguillettes. From 1865, on service, gold shoulder cords with a red underlay were taken into use. Rank devices were worn on these.

Undress frock

The double-breasted überrock was of dark-blue cloth with red collar and piping. The collar itself was piped blue. The inside lining of the breast flap was also red, which showed when left open. Bullion epaulettes, later gold shoulder cords, were worn on most occasions. The helmet (without plume) or the *Mütze* could be worn in this order of dress.

Greatcoat

The dark grey greatcoat, paletot, and the mantel had a red collar piped blue on the outside and blue piped red on the inside. The inside breast linings were also red. In the field, first in 1864 and extensively in 1866, riding breeches were taken into use. These had triple stripes like the long trousers and were tucked into either knee-high boots or the high Brandenburg boots, similar to the Cuirassiers.

Horse furniture

The bridle was of dark brown polished leather with the brow-band, cheek- and upper nose-straps in black patent leather. The brow-band was decorated with gold lace and a short blue fringe hung down from it. The buckles, rings, and tongues were all in brass and the bridoon and bit were of polished steel. All other leatherwork, including wallets and saddlery, was of dark brown leather. The shabracque was dark blue cloth rounded in front and pointed in the rear. It was edged with a gold lace band 4 cm (1½ inch) wide with a 1-cm (½-inch) wide band either side. In the rear corners was a Guard Star surmounted by a crown, all in proper colours. The wallets were also covered in blue cloth edged with 2-cm (¾-inch) wide gold lace and a smaller crown over a star. On service there was a plain blue shabracque with a single 4-cm (1½-inch) band of gold lace around the edge. The wallet covers were similarly covered and the gold lace was 2 cm (¾ inch) wide.

Adjutant-generals

Except for the tunic, the uniform worn by the adjutant-general was similar to that of the general officer. In this case the tunic had eight buttons and was blue with red collar and Swedish cuffs. The collar and cuffs were decorated with two gold lace bars with the red light, each cuff with two buttons. The rear skirt had three button flaps all piped red. The silver bullion epaulettes with aiguillettes were normally worn and the half-moons were in gilt. By a royal order of 1 January 1861, the monogram of Wilhelm I, surmounted by a crown, was worn on the silver field of the epaulette. Horse furniture and shabracque were the same as for the general officer.

Generals á la suite

The undress uniform for generals á la suite were as for the adjutant-general but with all buttons, lace, helmet plate and fittings in silver. Horse furniture and gold-laced shabracque were the same as for the general officer with silver lace replacing the gold.

Flügeladjutants

The undress uniform for flügeladjutants was as for generals á la suite, except for the substitution of a horsehair plume for the feather one on the helmet, silver half-moons on the epaulettes and the royal monogram surmounted by a crown on the field. The greatcoat did not have the red lining on the inside breast.

According to a series of royal orders from 1861 to 1863, all general officers were to wear the monogram of the king surmounted by a crown on the epaulettes, and would also wear the aiguillettes in gold or silver on the right shoulder when wearing the uniform of their rank with the sash. The horse furniture was regulation and the shabracque was the Guard version with silver lace.

General officers in regimental uniforms

Many generals were honorary colonels (chefs) of Guard and Line regiments and often wore their regimental uniforms. When wearing these uniforms, the black and white feather plume in the helmet and the aiguillettes in gold or silver were the only distinguishing marks of their rank apart from the bullion epaulettes carrying the rank stars and batons. General officers of hussars wore the shoulder cords of their

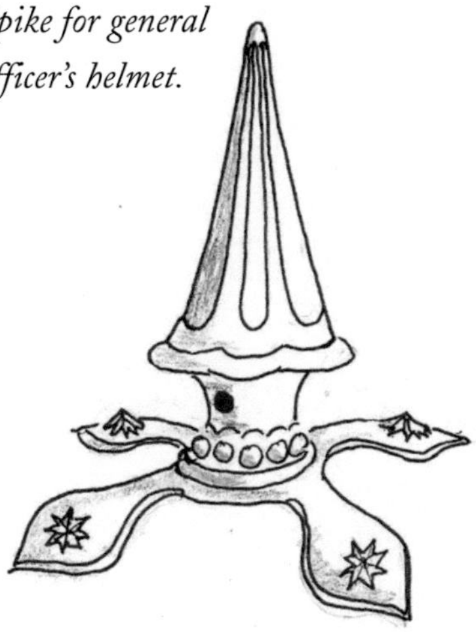

Spike for general officer's helmet.

Helmet eagle for general officers and staff.

rank and cuirassier generals wore the black and white feather plume in their helmet, except those of the Gardes du Corps and the Guard Cuirassiers who wore the eagle in gilt. All carried the sword appropriate for their arm of service.

Guard star worn by officers on headdresses, pouchbelts and other appointments.

Colonels on the staff of a general officer

Regimental uniforms were worn. The headdress, be it pickelhaube, cuirassier helmet, hussar cap or uhlan cap bore the same eagle and star plate as a general, in the appropriate metal, and for parades a white horsehair plume, or the case of hussars a plume of white osprey feathers. The aiguillettes were worn on the right shoulder in silver or gold along with the adjutant's sash. Staff-colonels of cavalry regiments did not wear the pouch belt.

The General Staff

Officers of the General Staff wore the same uniform as the flügeladjutant, with a white horsehair plume worn in the helmet for parades. The facing colour was crimson (*Karmesinrot*) instead of red and all lace was silver. The tunic had a blue collar with crimson patch and the epaulettes had silver half-moons with a crimson field, underlay and strap. The triple stripes on the trousers were also crimson. Aiguillettes were not worn but the adjutant's sash was worn by all officers except the chief of the General Staff. The undress cap had a crimson stripe and piping and the überrock and greatcoat were likewise piped with the collar and breast opening in crimson. The sword carried was the officers' degen with sword-knot. The shabracque was the Line version with silver lace.

The War Ministry

The uniform was identical in every way to that of the General Staff except that all the lace and metalwork was in gilt or gilding metal. The waist sash was worn but not the aiguillettes or adjutant's sash.

Personnel adjutant to a royal prince

This attractive and unique uniform was worn by the special aides-de-camp to the princes of the royal household serving in the army. The helmet had silver fittings and Guard eagle plate and brass chin-scales. The tunic was single breasted, with eight silver buttons down the front. The square-cut collar was red as were the pointed cuffs (called "Polish" cuffs). The silver lace on collar and cuffs consisted of two 1/2-cm (1/4-inch) stripes all round the collar and the top of the cuffs were edged inside by a thinner stripe with four loops above and below on the collar and forming a small Austrian knot below on the cuffs, with two loops either side. Silver aiguillettes were worn and the epaulettes had a red field and silver half moons. Trousers were dark grey with a single 4-cm (1½-inch) stripe running down each outside seam. The überrock, greatcoat, mantel and undress cap were as for the infantry. The side-arm, carried on slings under the tunic, was the cavalry sabre. The shabracque was the Guard version with silver lace.

Leib-Gendarmerie

The helmet was that of the cuirassiers in polished steel with brass fittings. The plate was a Guard star in silver. It was worn with a white horsehair plume for parades.

The tunic was in holly green faced with cornflower blue and fastened by eight brass buttons down the front, and which was piped red along with the collar and cuffs. The collar was square cut and the cuffs were pointed in Polish form. There were two gold Guard lace bars on the collar and one on the cuff with a brass button at the top. As all ranks were NCOs, there was a band of gold NCO lace around the top and front of the collar and the top and back edge of the cuffs. The epaulettes were in uhlan form with brass scales on the edge of the red straps. The field was red decorated with the Guard star in gold and the half-moons were in brass.

The trousers were dark grey piped red on the outside seams. There was a 4-cm (1½-inch) wide cornflower-blue cloth stripe on either side of each seam.

A white pouch belt was worn over the left shoulder with a black leather pouch decorated with the Guard star. The cavalry sabre was suspended from straps on a white belt worn around the waist over the tunic. It had a plain brass open buckle.

The greatcoat (mantel) was dark grey with a green collar, cornflower-blue patch piped red, and red shoulder straps. The holly-green undress peaked caps had a cornflower-blue band and the piping was red.

On 11 June 1860, the position of commander of the Leib-Gendarmerie was created. The uniform authorized was the same as the men's with the exception of officers' lace on the collar and cuffs only (no NCO lace), and a gold laced leather pouch belt with green lining and a silver Guard star on the pouch.

The shabracque was the Line version, but green edged with three 4-cm (1½-inch) stripes in cornflower blue, red, and cornflower blue, with red piping on the outside and inside edges.

Mounted Feld-Jäger Corps

This corps was formed by Frederick the Great in the 1740s as a military courier service. The helmet was the same that of as the Guard dragoons including the plate and fittings and was worn with a white horsehair plume for parades. The tunic was the same as for jägers, in holly green with red collar patches and Swedish cuffs. In 1847, officers of the corps were authorized to wear gold Guard lace on the collar and cuffs, which the men wore in yellow silk with a gold stripe in the middle. The epaulettes had a dark-green field with gilt half moons. The lace on officers' straps were silver and gold on the men's. No sash or pouch belt was worn and the leather-reinforced trousers had a red stripe down the outside seams. The sword belt was worn under the tunic and the side-arm was the Löwenkopf sabre.

In undress, the überrock was dark green with red collar and piping and the greatcoat collar was dark green on the inside and red with green piping on the outside. The dark-green peaked cap had a red band and piping.

The shabracque was the dragoon version in dark green with red piping and stripe and a Guard star on the rear corner.

Staff corps

Organized as both an infantry and a mounted corps, this unit acted as the military field police and line of communications security for the high command. Operating as corps-level units their dress distinctions varied, based on whether they were attached to the Guard corps or to the provincial corps.

Infantry staff corps

The helmet was the infantry-style pickelhaube with the Guard eagle and star for the Guard-attached units and the regular eagle with bandeau for the provincial units. The tunic was holly green with cornflower-blue collar patch and Brandenburg cuffs, including the cuff patch. The tunic front, top of collar cuffs, and patches were all piped red. The collar of units attached to the Guard had two yellow lace bars with red centres on the patches, none on the cuffs. Those of the provincial corps units had but one bar on the collar. The shoulder straps were red with the corps number in Arabic yellow numerals for the provincial corps, plain for the Guard. NCOs wore the same distinctions as for infantry with the normal differences between Guard and Line NCO lace. Trousers were dark grey with red stripes down the outside seams flanked by 4-cm (1½-inch) cornflower-blue stripes either side. The greatcoat was the infantry pattern with cornflower-blue patches and the same shoulder straps as the tunic. The undress cap was green with cornflower-blue band and red piping, with a peak for NCOs only. In 1861 the leather equipment was white as for infantry, but changed to black as for fusiliers in 1865. The side-arm knot was white.

The cavalry corps was dressed the same as the Leib-Gendarmerie in the Guard except that the Polish cuffs were devoid of lace. The cuirassier helmet also had the Guard star on front but no plume was worn. The epaulette field and underlay for the brass half-moons were red with no device and the leatherwork was white. The provincial mounted corps had the same uniform, save for the brass Line eagle worn on the helmet, one bar of lace on the collar and the yellow army corps number worn on the epaulette field. The trousers were the same as for the infantry corps except for the leather reinforcement. The greatcoat and undress cap were also the same. The shabracque was the same as that of the Leib-Gendarmerie.

CHAPTER FOURTEEN

Infantry

Foot Guards

There were four regiments of foot guards and a Guard fusilier regiment at this time. Two of the foot Guard regiments were raised in 1860.

The blue tunic had a red collar, Swedish cuffs and piping. The buttons on the shoulder straps bore the company number. Two litzen were worn on each side of the collar and the cuffs and the lace, shoulder straps, and buttons were as follows:

Dress distinctions of the Foot Guards regiments

Regiment	Lace	Buttons	Shoulder straps
1 Garde-Regiment zu Fuß	White	White	White
2 Garde-Regiment zu Fuß	White	Brass	Red
3 Garde-Regiment zu Fuß	White	Brass	Yellow
4 Garde-Regiment zu Fuß	White	Brass	Light blue
Garde-Fusilier-Regiment	White	White	Yellow

Officers wore silver or gold litzen on collar and cuffs. The epaulette half-moons were also of button metal and the field was in shoulder-strap colour with red underlay except for the 1st and 3rd regiments in which case the field was silver.

In undress the officers' überrock was as described in general notes, as was the blue mütze with red band and piping. Officers and senior NCOs wore peaks.

Headdress

The regular headdress was the pickelhaube with the Guard eagle and star on the front plate. For the 1st Regiment and the Guard Fusilier Regiment, the plate and fittings were in white metal and for the remaining three, they were in brass. All regiments had brass bosses and chin-scales. The full-dress plumes were white horsehair for the foot guards and black for the Guard Fusiliers. Drummers and musicians for all the regiments wore red plumes. For officers of the 1st and 3rd Foot Guards and the Guard Fusiliers the plate and fittings were silver. For the 2nd and 4th regiments they were of gilt. The Guard star had an orange enamel centre with black eagle and the bosses and chin-scales for all were gilt.

For parades and gala occasions – and only when white trousers were worn – the 1st Foot Guards wore a special headdress. The 1st and 2nd battalions wore a mitre cap in "Old Prussian" style. It was fitted with a brass front plate, pointed at the top and about 25 cm (12½ inches) high. The plate was adorned with a large Guard star surmounted by a crown in brass. The top of the plate was fitted with a woollen pompom with a black centre. Around the head was a white 10-cm (4-inch) band rising to a slight point on the sides and back from which rose a red pointed "bag" which was fixed to the back of the brass plate at the top and down the sides. The bag was piped on the sides and back down to the points on the headband. The chin-scale bosses were brass grenades and a similar grenade was on the back of the headband. The 3rd, or Fusilier, Battalion had a similar cap, only about 7.5 cm (3 inches) shorter and with brass eagles instead of grenades and the bag only fixed to the top point of the brass front plate. For officers the front plate was gold-plated silver and the Guard star with orange centre and black eagle and the crown were also of silver and the fittings of gilt. The pompom was silver and black.

Other ranks helmet eagle and star.

Mitre caps for Foot Guards, on left Fusilier Battalion, on right G grenadier battalions (officers).

Greatcoat, trousers, and equipment

The dark-grey greatcoat had red collar patches and the same shoulder straps as the tunic. Dark grey trousers with red stripes were worn in winter and for daily duties and white ones for parades. In summer off-white duck fatigue trousers could be worn in hot weather.

Equipment was white for the 1st and 2nd battalions of the four Foot Guard regiments and black leather for the 3rd battalions. The Guard Fusilier regiment wore black for all battalions. The belt clasp for the valise straps was in the form of a brass grenade and worn by all guard regiments. The side-arm was the infantry or fusilier sword for the men and officers wore the sword of their rank. The shabracque for mounted officers was the Guard pattern. The side-arm tassels for the NCOs were white with a black zigzag pattern for knot and slide with a tassel in white. The men's side-arm knots (*Troddel*) were different for every company and followed a pattern set out in the table below which was common to all infantry regiments except where noted. All troddel straps were white, as were the tassel fringes. (The top of the tassel was known as the crown and the stem was the "acorn".)

Troddel colours by company

Battalion	I				II				III (Fusilier)			
Company	1	2	3	4	5	6	7	8	9	10	11	12
Slide	White	Red	Yellow	Blue	White	Red	Yellow	Blue	White	Red	Yellow	Blue
Stem	White	White	White	White	Red	Red	Red	Red	Yellow	Yellow	Yellow	Yellow
Crown	White	Red	Yellow	Blue	White	Red	Yellow	Blue	White	Red	Yellow	Blue

Guard Grenadier regiments

There were four Guard Grenadier regiments, the last two of which were raised in 1860.

Helmet

This was the same as for the Foot Guards except that the helmet plate was the Grenadier eagle, which did not have the Guard star but did have the "Vaterland" bandeau. This was in brass for the men and gilt for officers. All the fittings were brass or gilt and the horsehair plume for parades was white.

Tunic

The same as for the Foot Guards except that the cuffs were of the Brandenburg style with blue cuff patches and no litzen. For officers, the two gold litzen on each side of the collar were in the form of leaves with tassels reminiscent of the Guard lace worn by Frederick the Great's army. The main distinctions of the Guard Grenadiers' uniforms were as follows:

Dress distinctions of the Guard Grenadiers

Regiment	Men's lace	Buttons	Men's shoulder straps
Kaiser-Alexander-Garde-Grenadier-Regiment No. 1	White	Brass	White with red crown above monogram "A" over "I"
Kaiser-Franz-Garde-Grenadier-Regiment No. 2	White	Brass	Red with yellow crown above monogram "F"
3 Garde-Grenadier-Regiment Königin Elizabeth	White	Brass	Yellow with red crown above monogram "E"
3 Garde-Grenadier-Regiment Königin	White	Brass	Light blue with red crown above monogram "A"

On the officers' epaulettes the monograms were in gilt on a field the same colour as the men's shoulder straps. The half-moons were gilt and the underlay was red.

All other elements of dress were the same as for the Foot Guards except that the mounted officers' shabracque had a gold lace grenade on the rear corners instead of the Guard star.

Infantry of the Line

The 72 regiments of infantry were equally distributed in eight permanent Provincial Army Corps and 36 brigades. The first twelve regiments were grenadiers and regiments 33 to 40 were designated fusiliers. Regiments 41 to 72 were all raised in 1860.

Helmet

The pickelhaube was fitted with the Line eagle plate with bandeau in brass. For grenadier regiments 1–12 the breast shield on the eagle bore the monogram "FWR". For the remaining regiments, the breast shield bore the monogram "FR". Regiments 1–12 also wore a black horsehair plume for parades. The following regiments had particular elements of the helmet plate that were unique:

The 1st East Prussian Grenadier Regiment No. 1 bore a scroll bearing the date "1619" above the head of the eagle and between the wings.

The 2nd Pomeranian Infantry Regiment No. 9 bore a scroll below the breast shield with the legend "COLBERG 1807"

Foot Guards collars and cuffs: from left, officer's collar; other ranks' collar; other ranks' cuff.

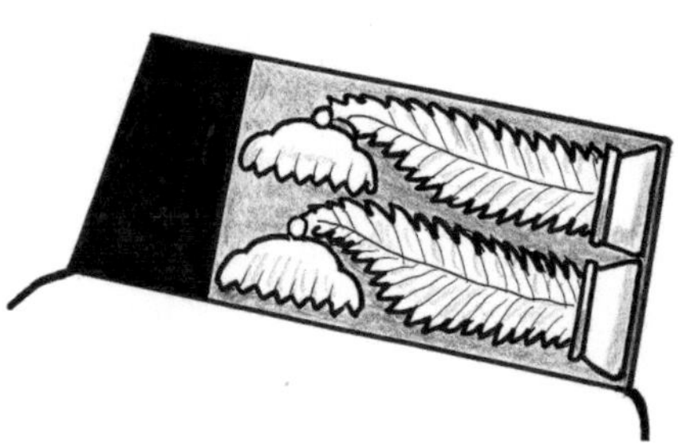

Guard Grenadier regiments officer's collar.

The Pomeranian Fusilier Regiment No. 34 bore a scroll below the breast shield with the legend in two lines "Fur Auszeichnung d. vormalig Königl. Schwedischen Leib-Regt. Königin".

Tunic

The blue tunic had red collar and Brandenburg cuffs and the regiments were distinguished from each other by the number on the shoulder straps. The army corps to which they belonged was indicated by the shoulder-strap colours and the white piping or lack of it on the three sides of the cuff patch. The numbers on the shoulder straps were yellow on the red straps and red on the white, yellow and blue straps.

Dress distinctions of the Prussian Line Infantry, 1860–66

Army corps	Regiments in corps	Shoulder straps	Cuff patch piping
I	1, 3, 4, 5, 33, 41, 43, 44, 45	White	White
II	2, 9, 14, 21, 34, 42, 49, 54, 61	White	-
III	8, 18, 20, 24, 35, 48, 52, 60, 64	Red	White
IV	26, 27, 31, 32, 36, 66, 67, 71, 72	Red	-
V	6, 7, 12, 19, 37, 46, 47, 58, 59	Yellow	White
VI	10, 11, 22, 23, 38, 50, 51, 62, 63	Yellow	-
VII	13, 15, 16, 17, 39, 53, 55, 56, 57	Light blue	White
VIII	25, 28, 29, 30, 40, 65, 68, 69, 70	Light blue	-

Guard Grenadier regiments helmet eagle.

Shoulder strap monograms. From left, 1st Guard Grenadiers; 2nd Guard Grenadiers; 3rd Guard Grenadiers; 4th Guard Grenadiers.

Instead of a number, the following regiments had monograms on the shoulder straps:
Grenadier-Regiment No. 2 – crown over FWR over IV in red
Grenadier-Regiment No. 7 – crown over WR in red
Grenadier-Regiment No. 8 – crown over FWR over III in yellow
Fusilier-Regiment No. 40 had white-metal (silver for officers) buttons on the tunic.

All other items including helmet, and the half moons on officers' epaulettes, remained as per regulation.

Greatcoat, trousers, and equipment

The dark grey greatcoat had red collar patches and dark blue shoulder straps piped in the army corps colour with the numbers or monograms the same colour as those on the tunic straps. The trousers and remainder of the equipment was the same as for the Guards except that the valise strap hook on the waistbelt was of plain triangle-shaped brass.

For officers, all items were the same as the men's with the usual distinctions of gilt for brass etc. The epaulettes bore the same devices as the men's in gilt on the same colour fields. Half-moons were gilt and underlay red. The shabracque for mounted officers was the Line pattern.

Jägers and Schutzen

There was one Guard Jäger battalion, one Guard Schutzen (sharpshooter) battalion and eight provincial Jäger battalions, all raised before 1816.

Shako

The jäger wore the infantry pickelhaube until 1854, when it was replaced by the shako. At first the shako was a conical leather cylinder with the wider part attached to a fore- and back-peak like the spiked helmet.

The fore-peak was bound in brass and it was worn with brass chin-scales. In 1860 it was modified to take on the form it was to keep – with minor changes

– until the end of the German Empire. Indeed it was even worn in cloth form by German police until the mid-1950s. Made of boiled leather, it was about 14 cm (5½ inches) high in the front and back. The front was upright and the back sloped and quite rounded with a 1¾-cm (2/3-inch) band of leather round the bottom and a one-piece top leather "lid" with a 1-cm (½-inch) rim. The front and back peak were made of a composition material, the front peak bound in leather. The chin-scales were done away with for the men and replaced with a leather chinstrap

Infantry helmet and shako devices. Top row from left: Line infantry; Grenadier Regiment No. 9. Middle row: Jäger shako Battalion No. 1, 2, 5 & 6 (pre-1862), Grenadier Regiment No. 1, Jäger shako Battalion No. 3, 4, 7 & 8 (pre-1862). Bottom row: Fusilier Regimen No. 34; all other Grenadier regiments.

Grenadier shoulder strap monograms. Left, Grenadier Regiment No. 2; Middle, Grenadier Regiment No. 7; and right, Grenadier Regiment No. 8.

attached to brass side posts in the body. The oval white/black/white wooden cockade or "Feldzeichen" was attached to the top rim and a black horsehair plume issuing from behind it was worn for parades. Officers and senior NCOs still retained the brass chin-scales.

Garde-Jäger and Garde-Schutzen

Shako

The shako badge for both units was the Guard star in white metal for the men and silver with enamel centre for the officers and senior NCOs.

Tunic

The eight-button tunic was a dark shade of green known as holly green and it was piped down the front and on the rear skirts in red. For the Garde-Jäger, the

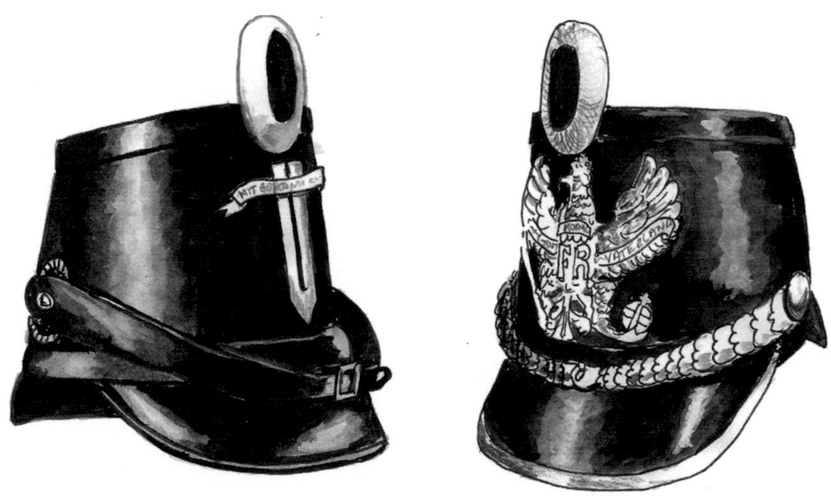

Jäger shakos. Left: Shako c.1861 worn by battalions 3, 4, 7 and 8; right: shako c.1865 worn by all battalions from that time. (officer's version shown).

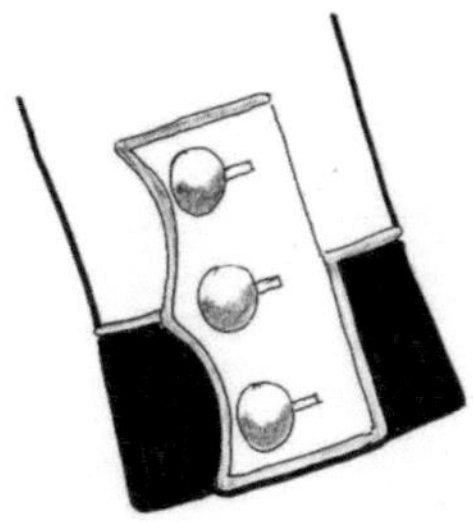

Garde-Schutzen cuff detail.

red collar patch and Swedish cuffs were decorated each with two litzen in gold lace for officers and yellow camel hair for other ranks. The Garde-Schutzen battalion had black collar patches and French cuffs (velvet for officers and senior NCOs). There was a three-pointed green patch on each cuff. The collar, cuffs, and cuff patches were all piped red and the collar only was decorated with litzen in gold lace and yellow camel hair. The shoulder straps were red as was the field of the officers' epaulettes with gilt half moons. For musicians, the swallow's nests were red with yellow or gold lace in the Garde-Jäger and black in the Garde-Schutzen.

Undress

The feldmütze was green with red band and piping for the Garde-Jäger and with black band and red piping for the Schutzen. Officers and senior NCOs had peaks. The officers' überrock was black with red collar piped green for Garde-Jäger and black velvet collar piped red for Schutzen.

Greatcoat, trousers, and equipment

The greatcoat and trousers were the same as for the infantry, the greatcoat with red shoulder straps and collar patch. The officers' greatcoats for the Garde-Jäger had green velvet collars on the inside (when folded down) or red patches with green piping outside. For Garde-Schutzen officers, the collars were green cloth on the inside and black piped red on the outside.

All equipment was black leather as for the infantry, and the valise had the peculiar adornment of the pelt of a badger's head forming the flap. The soldiers wore the standard infantry sabre with green strap and troddels for men and white slide, black/white acorn, green crown for officer candidates. These troddels were attached to the sabre's frog on the belt not to the hilt itself.

Shako star for Garde-Jäger and Garde-Schutzen.

Line Jäger battalions

The 1860 shako was fitted with a smaller eagle plate than that on the pickelhaube. Battalions 1, 2, 5, and 6 had the "Grenadier version" with the FWR monogram in the breast shield; battalions 3, 4, 7, and 8 had the FR monogram. All shields carried the "Vaterland" bandeau. The order for the adoption of eagle plate came some months after the regiments had been issued with the new shakos, to which had been fitted the old shako devices. For battalions 1, 2, 5, and 6 this had been the FWR monogram in brass with the Vaterland bandeau on a small scroll below. For the remaining four battalions it had been a vertical brass button lace (point down) with the Vaterland bandeau on a scroll above. It seems that as late as 1864, some units had still not replaced these devices.

The dress of the Line Jäger battalions was the same in all respects as that of the Garde-Jäger Battalion with the following exceptions: the green tunic with Swedish cuffs had no litzen on collar and cuffs and the red shoulder straps had the battalion number in yellow (for officers the number was gilt on the epaulette field). The greatcoat had green shoulder straps piped red with yellow battalion numbers. Musicians and buglers had red swallow's nests with yellow or gold lace and fringes where appropriate. The equipment was all the same.

CHAPTER FIFTEEN

Cavalry

Cuirassiers

There were ten regiments of cuirassiers, two of which were in the Guard. These were the Gardes du Corps, the premier regiment of Prussian cavalry and ceremonial bodyguard to the king, and the Garde Cuirassier Regiment. All the regiments were raised before 1816.

Cuirassier helmet.

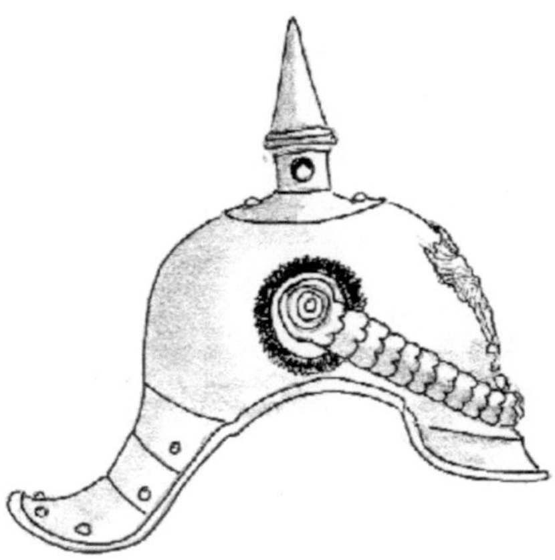

Helmet

The helmet, first introduced in 1842 and modified in 1862, was reminiscent of the heavy cavalry helmets worn in the middle and latter part of the 17th century. It was made of polished steel for all regiments except the Gardes du Corps, Garde Cuirassiers and Regiment No. 6, for whom it was made of tombak (alloy of copper and zinc). The front visor was stepped or ridged, and the deep rear neck guard was made of separate plates, riveted on the sides, like a lobster-tail ending in an upward curve at the bottom. The collar of the spike was attached to an oval base fixed to the helmet top by two rivets in front and two behind. There was a vent hole either side of the collar. The collar and base, the edging of the visor and neck guard, the rivet heads and the actual spike were in tombak for steel helmets, and German silver for tombak helmets. The chin-scales and side posts were in brass for all helmets. The visor was painted black underneath. The plume was not worn by cuirassiers except musicians, all of whom wore a red one. The Line helmet eagle in brass was worn by all Line regiments except No. 6, which wore it in white metal. The two Guard regiments wore the Guard star with Vaterland inscription in the circle.

For officers the helmet had finer fittings of gilt or silver. The spike column was fitted into a cruciform base to the helmet and the vent holes were four small triangles in the form of a cross on either side. The spike was fluted and the front visor was lined underneath with green baize.

Koller

Cuirassiers did not wear the tunic, instead wearing a buttonless coat called a *Koller*, which was fastened down the front with 14 hooks and eyes. It was made of an off-white, somewhat coarse kersey material, and had a rounded collar and Swedish cuffs. The collar patches and cuffs were faced in regimental colour, as was the piping on the rear seams of the sleeves, the back and around the armholes and on the edge of the three-pointed skirt flaps. The tunic front was trimmed around the collar with regimental lace. This continued down the front of each side of the koller to the skirts. This lace, known as *kollerborte*, was of white linen about 2 cm (3/4 inch) wide with two 0.5-cm (1/4-inch) wide stripes of facing coloured braid at each edge showing 0.5 cm (1/4 inch) white between. The top and rear of the cuffs were edged with the same lace, and the buttons were of silver or tombak according to regiment. The shoulder straps were white edged in the facing colour. NCO lace for cuirassiers was thinner than for other regiments and was placed over the central white strip of lace on the collar and cuffs.

Officers wore the same tunic as the men, but made in fine white Melton cloth. The collar and cuffs were in facing colour, and the kollerborte was of silver or gold lace, depending on the regiment. The lace was approximately 3 cm

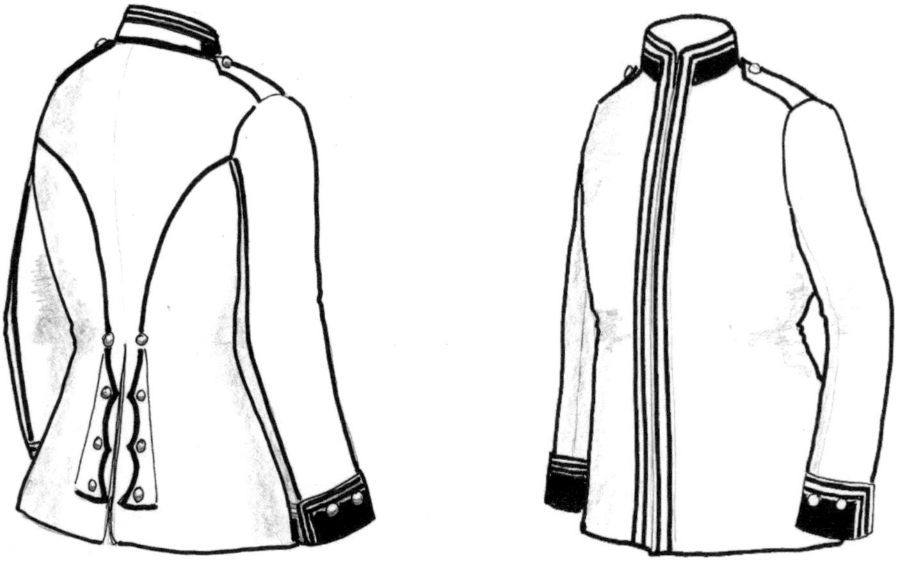

Cuirassiers' koller, other ranks.

(1¼ inch) wide leaving 1 cm (½ inch) of silver or gold lace showing between the facing coloured braid. Buttons and appointments were in lace colour. Epaulette fields were white, and the underlay of the crescents were in facing colour.

Trumpeters and musicians wore the swallow's nest wings with angled stripes in facing and button colour with the usual fringes to distinguish staff trumpeters and musicians.

Cuirass

The cuirass consisted of a breast- and back-plate of either polished steel or tombak, depending on the regiment. Both plates had a 2-cm (¾-inch) steel rim (on both steel and tombak) with 36 brass studs equally spaced all round. When worn, the plates were connected by metal hinge straps, of scalloped brass plates backed by leather and secured to the back plate at the shoulders by hinges. The straps had a brass flange which hooked onto studs on the breast plate about two-thirds way down its length. A thin leather belt was attached by studs at the lower sides of the back plate. This was brought around the waist, and fastened with a small buckle. The plates were lined with quilted natural linen and the neck and armholes had a black coarse cloth ruffling edged white all round. The cuirass was not worn by trumpeters or musicians.

The officers' cuirasses were of better quality than the men's. The fastening straps over the shoulder had lion's head motifs at the ends on the back plates and an oak-leaf pattern where they attached to the breast studs.

Tunic

NCOs and men wore a blue undress tunic for garrison duties. It was fastened down the front with eight buttons and had two buttons at the rear. The collar patch was in facing colour. The tunic worn by the two Guard regiments differed (see later section). The officers' tunic was of blue cloth and had a round collar and Swedish cuffs of facing colour decorated with kollerborte of silver or gold lace. There were

Cuirass for other ranks.

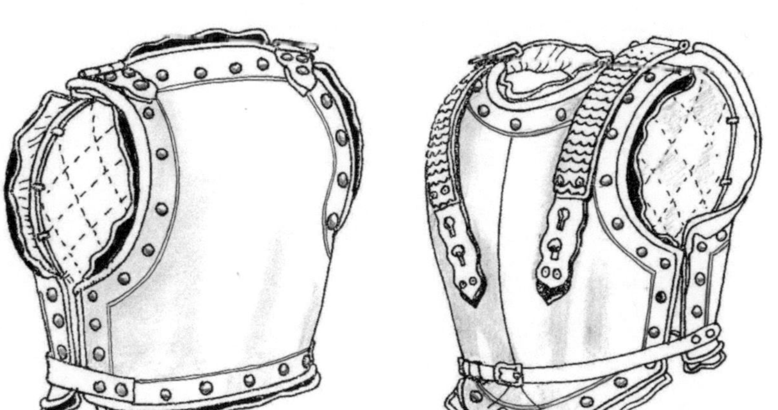

eight gold or silver buttons down the front, which was piped in facing colour, as were the rear three-pointed skirt flaps with two buttons. The epaulettes with white field were worn with the tunic, until they were replaced with shoulder cords in 1866.

The men's garrison jacket soon evolved into the tunic like the officers but with the other ranks' kollerborte instead of the officers' lace. Several regiments were wearing this garment for garrison duties by 1866 but it did not become official wear until 1874.

Undress, trousers, and greatcoat

The mütze was white with band and piping in facing colour. Senior NCOs wore peaks. The trousers were the leather-reinforced dark grey overalls with red piping. The Guard regiments had already adopted the white kersey breeches with high leather boots, which were being gradually introduced into the Line Cuirassier regiments. Some were wearing them in the 1866 campaign, but they were not official until 1868. Greatcoats had white shoulder straps without piping and the collar patch was in facing colour.

For officers the überrock was blue with facings and piping according to regimental custom (see chart on p.271); the peaked mütze was normally worn with this item although it was worn on campaign by officers with the helmet and cuirass, the skirts being hooked back to facilitate riding. The officers' greatcoat had a blue collar (except where noted) when folded down and facing colour (see chart on p.271) when turned up. Some were piped similarly to the überrock.

The grey trousers with red stripe were worn for dismounted duties. By 1866 most officers were wearing them on campaign. For special gala occasions, white kersey or Melton trousers could be worn. These had a stripe of officers' kollerborte lace down the outside seams.

Equipment and saddlery

A white pouch belt was worn over the left shoulder with a large black leather pouch that rested just above the right hip when worn. The flap of the pouch was decorated with a large round plate upon which the Line eagle was embossed. The white sword belt was worn over the koller by the men and the side-arm was the cuirassier pallasch. The sword knots were standard for all cavalry regiments (Except Gardes du Corps) and were as follows:

Cavalry sword knots

Squadron	1	2	3	4
Crown	White	Red	Yellow	Light blue
Tassel	White	White	White	White

Note: Officer candidates had a reddish strap with the addition of an acorn (stem) in tassel colour.

White leather gauntlets were authorized for officers and men of the two Guard regiments, the personnel of the Line regiments were allowed to buy them at their own or regimental expense. The 1850 cavalry pistol (see later section) was carried either attached to the pouch belt or in the off-side saddle wallet. On exercise and campaign, the greatcoat was rolled and carried on the saddle at the rear. From photographs and contemporary illustrations, it seems that no other personal equipment – such as a bread bag – was carried by the rider, it was all distributed on the horse furniture.

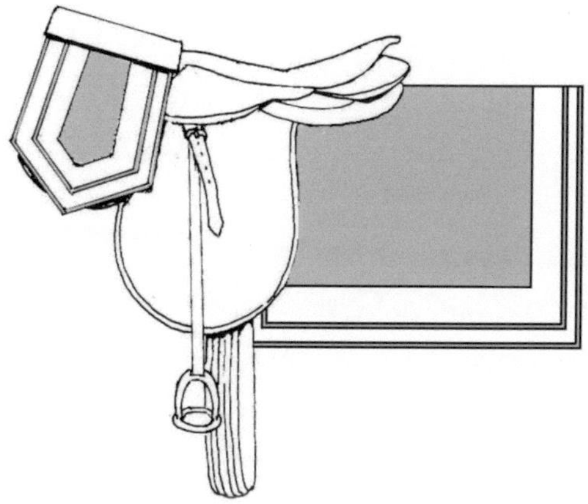

Cuirassiers' saddle and shabracque for other ranks.

Officers wore a pouch belt of silver-laced leather edged with facing colour. The pouch belt was smaller than the men's, and had the royal cipher with crown in gilt on the flap. For normal duty the waist sash was worn over the koller (the tassels only protruded from under the cuirass). The adjutants' sash was not worn when wearing the cuirass. The officers' sword belt was worn under the koller and the slings were of button colour edged with facing colour and the officer's pattern pallasch was carried.

Horses and horse furniture

From 1857, all cuirassier and heavy cavalry horses had to be at least 15 hands high. The regulations only excluded piebalds, duns and similar horses but the regiments seem to have favoured darker brown horses or black. Only trumpeters were allowed to ride greys and from 1864 were required to do so. The cuirassier saddle and bridle was the standard heavy-cavalry type as described in the general section. The large leather wallets carried all the soldiers' personal effects in the field (including the pistol) with the nearside (left) one containing pistol ammunition and a leather shoecase. The mess tin was carried in a leather case to the right of the rolled greatcoat behind the rider. A tubular canvas feedbag was strapped over the greatcoat with a short length of rope with a metal ring hanging to the left side. These ropes, joined together from several troopers made a long picketing rope in bivouac.

The shabracque was unique to the cuirassiers. The rear part under the saddle was rectangular of facing colour (except where noted) and edged from the inside with a 4-cm (1½-inch) wide and a 2-cm (¾-inch) wide strip of button lace separated with a "light" of the facing colour. The wallets were covered with facing-colour cloth, which were straight on three sides and pointed at the bottom with lace stripes only 3 cm (1¼ inch) and 2 cm (¾ inch) wide. Officers' shabracques were the same, only with gold or silver lace.

Standards and kettledrums

Standards were square for the two Guard regiments and regiments 1, 6, and 7 and swallow-tailed for regiments 2, 3, 4, 5, and 8.

All regiments had kettledrums. The kettledrum banners were made in seven panels in regimental colour, either oval or square with pointed ends, each edged with lace and tassels. Each panel was alternatively decorated with devices of ciphers, heraldic eagles, monograms or crowns.

Facings and distinctions of Cuirassier regiments

Regiment	Koller		Tunic	Officers' überrock	Greatcoat		Shabracque
	Facing colour	Lace and button colour	Collar, cuffs, and tunic piping	Collar and piping	Officers' collar (turned up) and piping	Men's collar patch	
Gardes du Corps	Red	Silver	Red	Red	Red	Red	Red
Garde Cuirassiers	Cornflower blue	Silver	Cornflower blue/ red	Cornflower blue/ red	Cornflower blue/ red	Cornflower blue	Cornflower blue
Silesian Cuirassier Regiment No. 1	Black	Gold	Black/ white	Black/ white	Black/ white	Black	Black
Queen's (Pommeranian) Cuirassier Regiment No. 2	Crimson	Silver	Crimson	Crimson	Crimson	Crimson	Crimson
East-Prussian Cuirassier Regiment No. 3	Light blue	Silver	Light blue	Light blue	Light blue	Light blue	Light blue
Westphalian Cuirassier Regiment No. 4	Orange	Silver	Orange	Orange	Orange	Orange	Orange
West Prussian Cuirassier Regiment No. 5	Rose red	Silver	Rose red	Rose red	Rose red	Rose red	Rose red
Brandenburg Cuirassier Regiment Tsar of Russia No. 6	Russian blue	Gold	Russian blue	Red	Russian blue	Russian blue	Red
Magdeburg Cuirassier Regiment No. 7	Lemon yellow	Silver	Lemon yellow	Lemon yellow	Lemon yellow	Lemon yellow	Lemon yellow
Rhenish Cuirassier Regiment No. 8	Light green	Gold	Light green /white	Light green /white	Light green /white	Light green	Light green

Individual Regimental Distinctions

Gardes du Corps

Helmet

Cuirassier helmet made of tombak and fitted with the Guard star. For parades and gala occasions, the spike was replaced by a large German silver eagle with spread wings which was plain for the men but with gilded crown for officers.

Koller

Same as for other regiments with the addition of one white litzen either side of the collar and two on each cuff. The litzen for officers was of silver lace.

Cuirass

Officers and men wore cuirasses of tombak with steel edging. For very special occasions (originally for New Year parades only) a black iron cuirass, presented by the tsar of Russia in 1814, was worn. It was trimmed round the arm, neck and waist with red woollen cord. The hinges were the same as for the regular cuirass and there were no studs round the edges.

From 1841, a special supraveste was worn over the koller for special guard duty at royal palaces and residences. This item mimicked a cuirass but was made of red cloth with white edging round the shoulders, neck and waist. The front and back were decorated with a large Guard star in white with an orange centre on which was the black eagle. For officers the star was in silver as was the edging to the supraveste. The shoulder belt, pouch and sword belt were the same as for normal parade wear at this time. The helmet was always adorned with the eagle for this duty.

Tunic

The waffenrock was dark blue, as described above, with red collar patches and cuffs decorated with litzen as on the koller. The front and rear skirts had red piping. Officers' tunics were the same with silver lace and the addition of epaulettes as for the koller. For NCOs and other ranks the litzen were white and all rank lace, swallow's nests and other distinctions were as worn on the koller.

Gala tunic

In 1856 the officers of the Gardes du Corps were authorized to wear a red tunic for court levées and gala occasions. The tunic had a red collar and Swedish cuffs, with two silver litzen on each collar and on each cuff. It was piped on the front and rear skirts in blue. Epaulettes were worn as on the koller.

Greatcoat, trousers, and leg wear

The greatcoat had a red collar when turned down. The Gardes du Corps had been ordered to wear the white kersey breeches since December 1861. The breeches were worn tucked into high-jacked leather boots. The grey overalls were reserved for dismounted duties. For exercise and on campaign, a softer leather boot called "Old Brandenburg", that covered the thighs to just below the tunic or koller, was worn. Officers at court levées and gala occasions could wear the high boots, or white trousers with one strip of kollerborten down each leg.

Equipment.

The organization of the Gardes du Corps was different to that of the rest of the cavalry in that it had eight companies rather than four squadrons. The sword knot colours for these companies were as follows:

Sword knot colours for the companies of the Gardes du Corps

Company	**1**	**2**	**3**	**4**	**5**	**6**	**7**	**8**
Acorn	White	Black	Red	Red	Yellow	Yellow	Lt blue	Lt blue
Tassel	White	White	Red	White	Yellow	White	Lt blue	White

Note: Officer candidates wore a round button over the acorn in tassel colour and for the 2, 4, 6, and 8 companies the acorn had a white vandyked line.

Officers wore a waist-belt with the red or blue tunic, which was silver with two black stripes and red edging. The shoulder-belt pouch was decorated with the Guard star.

Shabracque

The shabracque was the regular pattern of red cloth with white edging, but the corners were decorated with the Guard star surmounted by a crown. The red wallet housings were similarly decorated.

Standards and kettledrums

The Gardes du Corps carried a standard presented in 1798, and the streamer for 1813–15. The kettledrums were presented to them in 1810 to replace those lost at Jena. These were the drums of the former Cuirassier Regiment No. 12. Banners were often awarded and varied greatly. They were certain to have been of red and silver panels with devices that would have included the Guard star, the cipher of Wilhelm 1 and a black heraldic eagle.

Garde Cuirassier Regiment

Helmet, koller, and cuirass

The helmet was the same as that worn by the Gardes du Corps, including the eagle for parade dress. The koller was laced with light blue and white regimental kollerborte, and the litzen were worn on the collar and cuffs. The cuirass was also of tombak for all ranks. Officers' distinctions were the same as that of the Gardes du Corps.

Tunics

The blue tunic was the same as for the Gardes du Corps, with light-blue collar and cuffs with litzen piped red. The tunic front and rear skirts were also piped red. Officers of the Garde Cuirassiers were awarded the honour of wearing the red gala tunic in February 1862. It differed from that of its senior regiment by having light-blue collar and cuffs piped white. The tunic front and skirt flaps were also piped white. The litzen on the collars and cuffs were silver.

Überrock, greatcoat and leg wear

The collar of the überrock was light blue piped red and the cuff piping was red. Like the Gardes du Corps, the collars of the greatcoat and paletot were red when turned down. When turned up, the patches were light blue piped red. Unlike the Gardes du Corps, the Garde Cuirassiers wore the dark grey leather-reinforced cavalry overalls with a red stripe. The white kersey breeches and long boots were not taken into wear until after 1866.

Shabracque, standard and kettledrums

The light-blue shabracque and wallet housings displayed the Guard star with crown and were piped red instead of light blue between the two stripes of white or silver on the edges.

The square standard carried at this time had the 1813–15 streamer. The kettledrums were of silver and had been presented in 1822.

Cuirassier Regiment No. 1

The black collars and cuffs, bands, and piping on all the caps and garments worn by officers were of velvet. The turned-down collar on the greatcoat was black velvet instead of blue. The front and rear skirt flaps of the blue tunic were piped white as were the collar and cuffs of the überrock.

The square standard bore the 1813–15 streamer. The silver kettledrums carried by this regiment were the oldest in the Prussian army, having been awarded in 1718.

Cuirassier Regiment No. 2

The helmet eagle bore a scroll with the legend "Hohenfriedburg 4.Juni 1745". The NCOs of this regiment wore a tombak cuirass and in addition to the eagle device on the flap of the black leather pouch, all ranks had a brass grenade either side with bombs in the corner and flames angled toward the round plate.

The swallow-tailed standard (commemorating the regiment's origin as dragoons) with streamers for 1813–15 and 1848–49 with swords was carried at this time. The silver kettledrums were presented in 1820.

eagle and pouch flap for 2nd Pomeranian Cuirassier Regiment.

Cuirassier Regiment No. 3

The swallow-tailed standard had streamers for 1813–15.The silver kettledrums were won in 1758, taken from the Russians at the battle of Zorndorf.

Cuirassier Regiment No. 4

The regiment carried the swallow-tailed standard (commemorating its origin as Dragoon Regiment No. 2) with streamers for 1813–15 and 1848–49 with swords. The kettledrums, awarded in 1822, were silver.

Cuirassier Regiment No. 5

The dragoon-pattern swallow-tailed standard (they were converted from 4th Dragoons in 1819) with streamers for 1813–15 was carried. The silver kettledrums also came from their former regiment.

Cuirassier Regiment No. 6

All ranks of this regiment wore helmets of tombak. The NCOs and unterofficiers also wore the cuirass in tombak. The shoulder straps of the koller and tunic bore the monogram of Tsar Alexander I of Russia.

The collar, cuffs and piping of the blue tunic, the überrock and the greatcoat patch were red. The shabracque and wallet housings were also red with yellow edging.

The regiment carried the square standard with streamers for 1813–15 and 1864 with swords. It also bore a special parade streamer presented on 11 June 1823 by the Grand Duchess Alexandra Feodorovna of Russia. The kettledrums, awarded in 1810, were silver and belonged to the pre-1806 10th Cuirassier Regiment (The Regiment Gendarmes).

Shoulder strap device for 6th Cuirassiers.

Cuirassier Regiment No. 7

The regiment, converted in 1819 from the 4th Cuirassiers, carried the square standard with streamer for 1813–15 and silver kettledrums, awarded in 1818, of the former Leib Regiment No. 2.

Cuirassier Regiment No. 8

The front and rear skirt flaps of the blue tunic were piped white as were the collar and cuffs of the überrock and the outside collar patch of the greatcoat.

This was the only regiment other than the Gardes du Corps to retain its pre-1819 number. Despite this, it carried the dragoon-style swallow-tailed standard with streamers for 1813–15 and 1848–49 with swords.

The kettledrums were of silver and were presented in 1827. The regiment also possessed a pair of copper kettledrums.

Dragoons

There were ten regiments of dragoons at this time. Two were Guard regiments, the junior of which was raised in 1860. Of the Line regiments, four were raised in 1860. In January 1862 the 7th (Westphalian) and 8th (2nd Silesian) regiments swapped their numbers in the line including their dress distinctions.

eagle plate for Dragoon regiments.

Helmet

Dragoons wore the pickelhaube with brass or white metal fittings according to regiment. Fittings were silver or gilt for officers. The Guard regiments wore the Guard eagle and star and for the Line regiments, the plate was the "Dragoon" eagle, which had the sceptre in its left claw and a sword in the right. The wings were somewhat more spread. Regiment No. 1 wore the Grenadier eagle. The Guard regiments wore white horsehair plumes and the Line regiments white. Musicians had red plumes.

Tunic

The eight-button cornflower-blue tunic had rounded collar and Swedish cuffs. For the two Guards regiments the collar patches and cuffs were red, for the Line regiments the collar patches were in facing colour and the cuffs were in tunic colour. The tunic was piped down the front and the rear skirt flaps in facing colour as were the top and rear of the cuffs in the Line regiments. The Guard regiments wore two bars of litzen on collar and cuffs in the button colour. The shoulder straps were also in regimental colour. For officers the fields on the epaulettes were in facing colour, the crescents in button colour and the underlay for those without fringes was red except in regiments 3 and 7 in which they were rose (or pink). Trumpeters and musicians wore swallow's nests, striped at an angle in facing and button colour.

Undress, greatcoat, and leg wear

The mütze was cornflower blue, with band and piping in facing colour. From 1861, Regiment No. 2 wore a small brass eagle above the cockade on the crown of the cap. The leather-reinforced cavalry overalls were worn by all regiments. The outer seam piping was red except for regiments 3 and 7, which had rose outer-seam piping. The shoulder straps on the greatcoat were cornflower blue with piping in facing colour and the collar patches were also in facing colour.

The facings and piping of the officers from regiments 2 and 6 on all items were black velvet. The überrock was cornflower blue with collar, breast flaps and cuff piping in the colour of the facings, the collar was piped cornflower blue. The turn-down collars of the officers' greatcoats and mantels were in tunic colour and all other items were the same as for the men. For court levées and gala occasions officers wore cornflower-blue trousers with triple stripes of facing colour. Gloves were white.

Pouch for Line cavalry.

Dress distinctions of Prussian Dragoons (from February 1862)

Regiment	Lace	Collar patch	Cuffs	Cuff Piping	Grey Trouser Piping
1st Guard Dragoon Regiment	Silver	Red	Red	_	Red
2nd Guard Dragoon Regiment	Gold	Red	Red	_	Red
Lithuanian Dragoon Regiment No. 1	Gold	Red	Cornflower blue	Red	Red
Brandenburg Dragoon Regiment No. 2	Gold	Black	Cornflower blue	Black	Red
Neumärk Dragoon Regiment No. 3	Silver	Rose	Cornflower blue	Rose	Rose
1st Silesian Dragoon Regiment No. 4	Silver	Light yellow	Cornflower blue	Light yellow	Red
Rhenish Dragoon Regiment No. 5	Silver	Red	Cornflower blue	Red	Red
Magdeburg Dragoon Regiment No. 6	Silver	Black	Cornflower blue	Black	Red
Westphalian Dragoon Regiment No. 7	Gold	Rose	Cornflower blue	Rose	Rose
2nd Silesian Dragoon Regiment No. 8	Gold	Lemon yellow	Cornflower blue	Lemon yellow	Red

Equipment and horse furniture

The men wore a white waist belt with open brass buckle and a white shoulder belt with carbine swivel and black pouch. The pouch flap bore the Guard Star for the two guard regiments and the Line eagle on brass disc for other regiments. Officers wore the silver pouch belt with facing colour underlay and the silver Guard Star, or for the Line regiments the crowned FWR monogram in gilt, on the black patent-leather pouch flap. Sword belt and slings were worn under the tunic.

The men carried the 1852 cavalry sabre (those of Regiment No. 2 had brass guards), and the 1857 carbine. The officers and senior NCOs carried the same pattern with a fish-skin grip instead of leather-bound wood. From February 1861, officers and senior NCOs of Regiment No. 1 were permitted a small silver eagle on the sword guard. Officers wore the lion's head sword in undress. Officers generally purchased pistols privately for use on campaign.

Dragoon mounts fell under the same regulations (or lack of them) for cuirassiers, except that their horses were of a lighter colour, but not pale. The saddles and bridles were standard cavalry issue and the shabracque was cornflower blue with standard facing-colour edging. The Guard star decorated the front and rear corners for the guard regiments.

Dragoons carried their greatcoat and equipment distributed on their saddles much the same as the cuirassiers. The carbine was carried in a peculiar fashion. It was slotted upside down, barrel first, through a hole in the front shabracque, behind the off-side (right) wallet into a special housing. A strap went around the small of the stock, looped through the swivel ring and then around the top of the saddle on the right. The trooper had to fit his thigh between the upturned butt and the saddle when mounting.

Standards and kettledrums

The Guard and regiments 5, 6, 7, and 8 had square standards and regiments 1 to 4 were swallow-tailed. All were regulation at this time. The 1st Guard and regiments 1 to 4 had 1813/1814 streamers and Regiment 7 had the 1864 streamer. Kettledrums were only carried by two regiments. Those of Regiment No. 1 had been taken from the Saxon Guard Carabiniers at Kesseldorf in 1758 and Regiment No. 2 carried ones captured from The Bavarian King's Dragoons in 1810.

Hussars

Only five regiments claimed ancestry to the famous hussar regiments of Frederick the Great's cavalry, four of which survived the catastrophe of Jena. One of them was divided to form the two Leib regiments. The remainder were formed from volunteer and National Guard regiments raised between 1808 and 1815. In 1862 there were 13 regiments including the Guard Hussars.

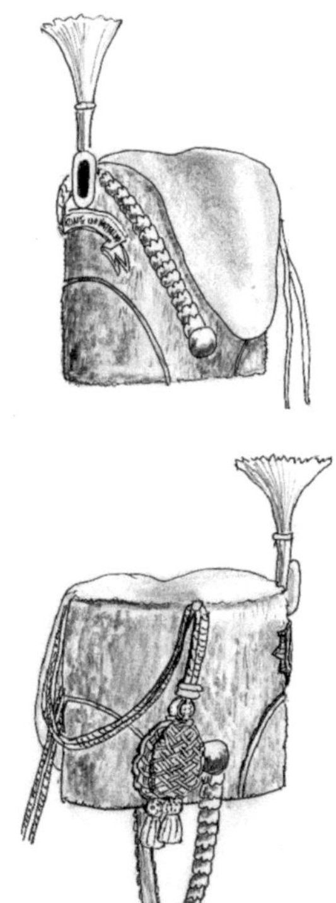

Hussar caps. Above: Line regiment, front. Below: Guard Hussar Regiment, rear.

Headdress

All hussar regiments wore the hussar cap (*Husar-Mütze* or *Pelz-Mütze* – *Colback* in France and Busby in Britain). This was of black sealskin for men, and was some 20 cm (just under 8 inches) high at both the front and back. There was a turned-up peak at front and back, edged with a very thin black leather band. Over the left side hung the cloth busby bag (*Kolpak*) in regimental colour under which were attached the cap lines at the top of the cap, in white for the men, and mixed black and white for NCOs. The cap lines were secured around the neck with no tassels or decorations. For the Guard Hussars the cap lines looped from behind the kolpak to the right side where it hung down with two tassels just behind the chinstrap boss.

At the top centre of the busby was an oval cockade, white with black centre, under which was the cap device in button colour. For the Guard Hussars it was the Guard star with Vaterland bandeau in brass, for the Leib regiments 1 and

Hussar regiments Vaterland bandeau.

2 it was the Vaterland bandeau with Death's Head below, all in whitemetal, and for Regiment No. 7 it was the FWR monogram above the Vaterland bandeau. For all other regiments it was simply the Vaterland bandeau in the form of a scroll. The chin-scales, attached to bosses either side of the cap, were brass for all regiments. For parades, a white horsehair brush plume was worn attached behind the cockade with a brass ring around it about 4 cm (1½ inches) from the base. NCOs wore a white plume mixed with black, and red plumes were worn by trumpeters and musicians.

Officers wore a cap made of otter fur in dark brown, which also had a front and rear peak. The cap lines were in silver except for the Guard Hussars, who wore gold. The plumes for officers were much taller than the men's, emanating from a short black horsehair brush in a gilt tulip base. They were heron feathers for the Guard Hussars and regiments No. 1, 2, 3, and 7. For the remaining regiments they were vulture feathers. Officers of all regiments wore the same devices as the men in gilt or silver and the star for those of the Guard Hussars had an enamel centre.

Above: Headdress monogram for 7th Regiment, and below, 'Totenkopf' badge for Lieb Hussar regiments 1 and 2.

Hussar jacket (Attila)

The hussar jacket, modelled on the Austrian pattern, was introduced in 1853 and replaced the dolman (waist-length jacket) and pelisse which had been in fashion for over 60 years. It was called an *Attila* by the Germans, a name derived perhaps from the original hussars' origins in Hungary where the legendary conqueror and his people finally settled. This garment was somewhat shorter than the tunic or waffenröcke and was edged all round the top and bottom of the collar, the front and around the skirts with lace, in white or yellow according to button colour. Across the front were five rows of lace frogging, terminating on each side in a button on a loop and fastening down the front with toggles. The back and rear skirts were also decorated in lace with one on each side seam terminating in a trefoil below the shoulder and three loops on either side of the skirts, also ending in trefoils. There were two olives or buttons at the rear waist and Austrian knots adorned each pointed cuff.

Hussars wore single-loop shoulder cords in button colour instead of shoulder straps. One-year volunteers had a black and white woollen strip around the outside of the cord and officer candidates had a black and white woollen loop at the shoulder end of the cord. NCOs' rank lace was worn beneath the Austrian

Hussar Attila with sash.

knots on the cuffs and around the top of the collars. The swallow's nests for musicians and trumpeters were of Attila colour with diagonal lace strips in button colour. The Attila was of finer cloth for officers and the frogging was in gold or silver lace. The front shirts of officers' Attilas had an angled false pocket in lace with trefoils on either side. The collar and cuff lace varied depending on rank. On the collar the top band of lace was 3.5 cm ($1\frac{1}{3}$ inch) for colonels, 3 cm ($1\frac{1}{4}$ inch) for lieutenant colonels, 2.5 cm (1 inch) for majors and 1.3 cm ($\frac{1}{2}$ inch) for captains and below. The lower lace on the collar was 1.3 cm ($\frac{1}{2}$ inch). The cuffs had a 1.5-cm ($\frac{1}{2}$-inch) band surmounted by a 0.75-cm ($\frac{1}{4}$-inch) Austrian knot. Instead of epaulettes, hussar officers wore shoulder cords. These cords, which eventually developed into the undress shoulder boards of the entire army, were of black silk and silver mixed lace. Colonels wore wide intertwined double looped cord, field officers wore intertwined single looped cord and captains and below wore two straight strips of flat double cord. All carried the stars according to their rank with lieutenants, no stars.

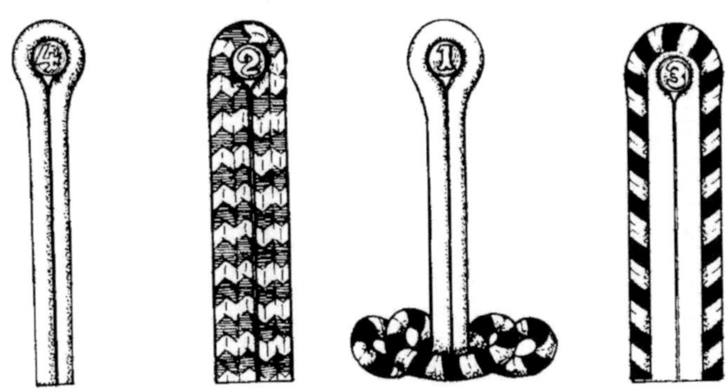

Hussar other ranks' shoulder cords. From left: men and NCOs; graduate of military riding school; kapitulant (re-enlistee); one-year volunteer.

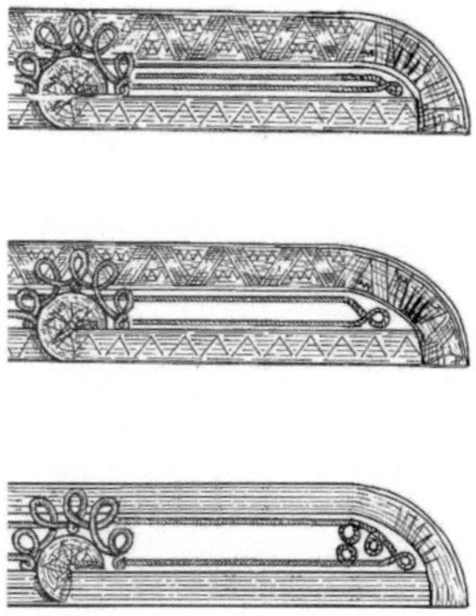

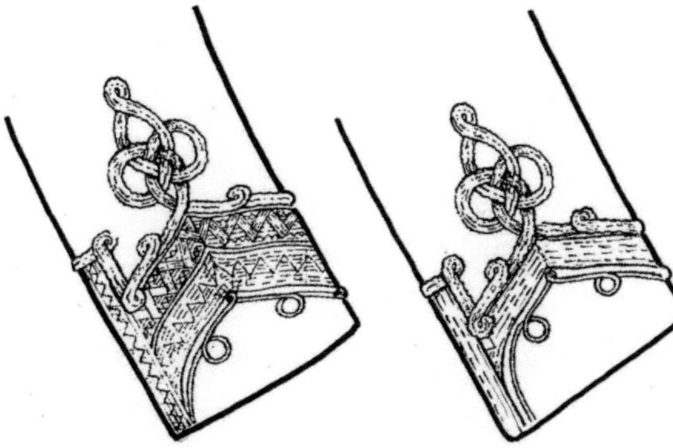

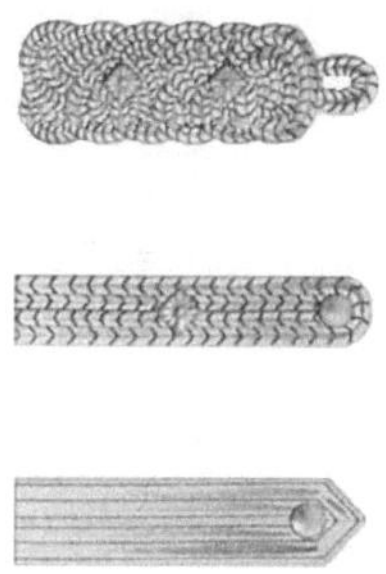

Left, collars for officers of Line Hussar regiments: colonel of regiment; field officers, captains and lieutenants. Centre, Hussar officers' cuffs: left field officers; right captains and lieutenants. Right, shoulder cords for Hussar officers: colonel of regiment; field officers; captains and lieutenants.

The *Wachtmeister* (regimental sergeant-major) of the Leib-Hussar Regt. No. 2 wore the same looping on the Attila as the officers.

From February 1861, the officers of the 5th Regiment were allowed to wear an Attila on which the buttons on the ends of the loops were connected by a silver 3-cm (1¼-inch) fringe down each side.

In 1865 the Guard Hussars were permitted to wear a pelisse, which had been abolished for all regiments in 1853. It was dark blue, lined and edged with white fox fur. It was decorated with yellow frogging as on the Attila and slung from the left shoulder secured by a chain around the neck. It was to be worn for parades only. Since 1857 chefs (colonels) of Hussar regiments had worn a pelisse trimmed as the officers' Attila and edged with Kamchatka beaver fur.

A barrelled sash was worn with the Attila. There were four barrels or loops of regimental-coloured cloth with three sections (worn in front) of white or yellow cord. The sash was secured to a toggle on the cloth at the rear by the cord, which looped back around the hips and attached to the sash in front. For officers the cords were of gold or silver lace.

Officer's interim Attila.

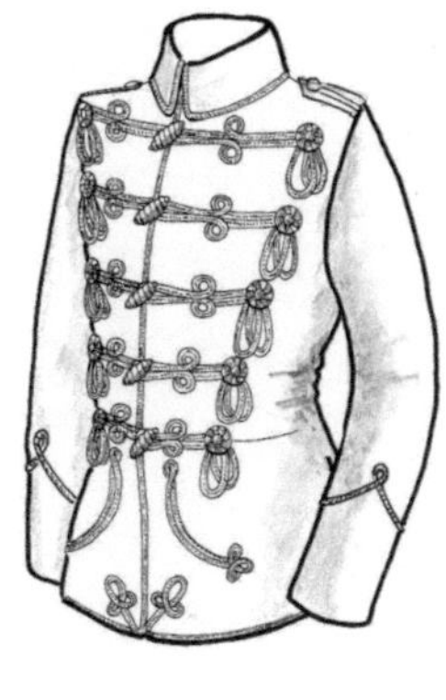

Leg wear, undress, and greatcoat

The men wore the standard leather-reinforced cavalry trousers with piping down the outer seams in red for all regiments except the 5th, which had crab-red stripes, and the 10th, which had pompadour red (a deep pink). The mütze was in tunic colour for all except the Guard Hussars, for which it was blue. The band was of regimental colour and the piping on the crown and above and below the band was in button colour. Personnel of regiments 1 and 2 wore a small silver death's head on the crown above the cockade. When wearing the mütze with the Attila, the barrelled sash was not worn. The shoulder straps of the greatcoat were in Attila colour and the patches in regimental colour.

Officers' leg wear was the same as the men's. A finer pair of trousers (un-reinforced) was worn for walking out and other dismounted occasions. The mütze was fitted with a peak. The greatcoat collar was the same colour on the outside as the men's greatcoat collar patches. On the inside (folded down) they were the same as the men's shoulder straps with piping in button colour. Officers of Regiment No. 1 had black velvet on the inside collar and Regiment No. 2 on the outside collar.

For gala wear officers were permitted to wear tight riding breeches of Melton cloth in special colours (see chart). They were decorated on the front of each thigh with an elaborate Austrian knot, point downward in button colour, with eyehole lace all round. With these breeches, they also wore soft patent-leather hussar boots which came to just below the knee, and which had 2-cm (3/4-inch) button colour lace around the tops with a tassel in front. Spurs were also worn.

Instead of the überrock, Hussar officers wore a garment known as an "Interims Attila." This item was cut in the same manner as the Attila, and of the same colour except in the Guard Hussars and Regiment No. 3 for which it was blue. The lace was of white or yellow and black camel hair. It was thinner than the lace on the dress Attila and was looped across the front as on the dress garment. The stand and fall collar was laced on the front and lower edges only and the cuffs were deep with a single band of lace looped just once. The shoulder straps were similar to that worn on the dress uniform, but of plain black and white camel hair. For the Guard Hussars, the lace was silver and black. The barrelled sash was not worn with this garment.

Decoration on officer's gala breeches.

Dress distinctions of the Prussian Hussars (1)

Regiment	Attila colour	Attila lace and piping	Kolpak	Mütze colour	Mütze band	Greatcoat	Greatcoat shoulder strap
Guard-Hussar Regt.	Red	Yellow	Red	Blue	Red	Red	Red
Leib-Hussar Regt. No. 1	Black	White	Red	Black	Red	Red	Black
Leib-Hussar Regt. No. 2	Black	White	White	Black	Black	Black	Black
Brandenburg Hussar Regt. No. 3	Red	White	Red	Red	Blue	Blue	Blue
1st Silesian Hussar Regt. No. 4	Brown	Yellow	Yellow	Brown	Brown	Brown	Brown
Pomeranian Hussar Regt. No. 5 (Blücher Hussars)	Crab red	White	Crab red	Crab red	Black	Crab red	Crab red
2nd Silesian Hussar Regt. No. 6	Dark green	Yellow	Red	Dark green	Red	Red	Dark green
King's Hussar Regt. No. 7 (1st Rhenish)	Russian blue	Yellow	Red	Russian blue	Red	Red	Russian blue
1st Westphalian Hussar Regt. No. 8	Dark blue	White	Light blue	Dark blue	Light blue	Light blue	Dark blue
2nd Rhenish Hussar Regt. No. 9	Cornflower blue	Yellow	Cornflower blue	Cornflower blue	Cornflower blue	Cornflower blue	Cornflower blue
Magdeburg Hussar Regt. No. 10	Dark green	Yellow	Pompadour red	Dark green	Pompadour red	Pompadour red	Dark green
2nd Westphalian Hussar Regt. No. 11	Dark green	White	Red	Dark green	Red	Red	Dark green
Thüringian Hussar Regt. No. 12	Cornflower blue	White	White	Cornflower blue	Cornflower blue	Cornflower blue	Cornflower blue

Dress distinctions of the Prussian Hussars (2)

Regiment	Lace	Barrelled sash colour	Interim Attila	Gala breeches	Sabretache colour	Shabracque	Shabracque border
Guard-Hussars	Gold	Red	Blue	Blue	Red	Blue	Red
Regiment No. 1	Silver	Red	Black	Black	Red	Black	Red
Regiment No. 2	Silver	White	Black	Black	Black	Black	Black
Regiment No. 3	Silver	Red	Blue	Blue	Red	Blue	Red
Regiment No. 4	Gold	Yellow	Brown	Cornflower blue	Brown	Brown	Yellow
Regiment No. 5	Silver	Crab red	Crab red	Black	Black	Crab red	Black
Regiment No. 6	Gold	Red	Dark green	Red	Red	Dark green	Red
Regiment No. 7	Gold	Red	Russian blue	Red	Red	Russian blue	Red
Regiment No. 8	Silver	Light blue	Dark blue	Dark blue	Dark blue	Dark blue	Light blue
Regiment No. 9	Gold	Cornflower blue	Cornflower blue	Cornflower blue	Cornflower blue	Cornflower blue	Cornflower blue
Regiment No. 10	Gold	Pompadour red	Dark green	Pompadour red	Light blue	Dark green	Pompadour red
Regiment No. 11	Silver	Red	Dark green	Red	Dark green	Dark green	Red
Regiment No. 12	Silver	White	Cornflower blue	Cornflower blue	Cornflower blue	Cornflower blue	Cornflower blue

Equipment

All ranks wore the sword belt under the Attila. The sword was the 1852 pattern sabre with black leather sword straps on which the knots were the same colour scheme as for all cavalry. A black leather sabretache was worn by all other ranks, which was suspended from the sword belt by three leather straps. It was positioned so that the top of the sabretache came to just behind the knee. The flap was decorated with a brass FWR monogram below a crown. The Guard Hussars'

Hussar sabretaches. From left, officers; other ranks.

Guard cavalry pouch.

sabretache flap was covered in red cloth with a yellow border, with the crowned FWR monogram in yellow in the centre. Hussars wore the standard cavalry pouch belt in white leather with the carbine swivel. The flap of the black leather pouch had no decoration except for that of the Guard Regiment and the two Leib regiments who had the Guard star. Troopers carried the 1857 cavalry carbine.

Officers' sword slings and sabretache slings were of silver lace edged in Attila colour. The dress sabretaches were of red leather faced with regimental colour (see chart on pp.285–6) with a 2-cm (3/4-inch) border in button colour, plus an additional thin line of piping on the outside. Filling the flap was a large royal monogram below a crown, also in regimental lace colour. The top border of the sabretache, where the three rings attached, was of red leather. The red leather also formed a thin border around the flap. On service and campaign, the officers wore a black leather sabretache with the royal monogram in gilt or silver. The pouch belts were also of silver lace edged in Attila colour and the black leather pouch had the gilt FWR monogram, except for the Guard who wore the star in gilt and regiments 1 and 2 who wore the monogram in silver.

Officers carried the M1852 cavalry sabre, which in the Guard and Leib regiments had the star on the hilt (also carried by NCOs). Officers tended to purchase their own pistols for campaign.

Horse furniture and saddlery

There were no regulations or orders covering the colour of hussar horses. The selection of lighter-coloured mounts was encouraged and horses of the same colour in each squadron tended to be the regimental rule. For the men, the bridles and saddles were the same as for cavalry generally, as was the personal equipment and its distribution. The carbine was carried in the same way as described for dragoons.

The shabracque was swallow-tailed at the rear and rounded in front. There was a vandyked edge of regimental colour all round and the outer edge was

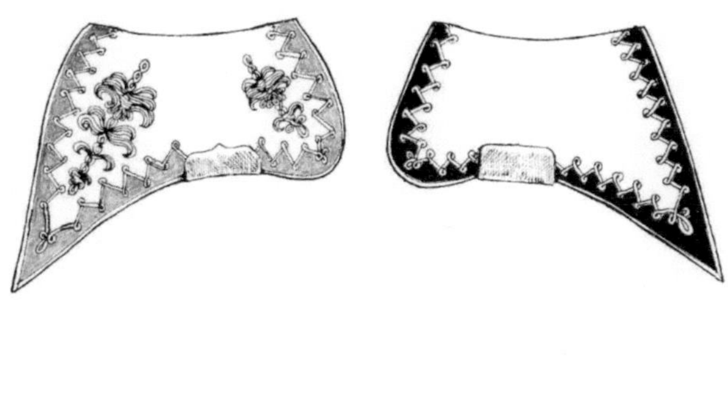

Hussar shabracques, for officers and for other ranks.

piped in button colour, as was the vandyked edge the piping of which formed a small loop or eyehole at the top and bottom of each point. The star was placed in the rear corner for the Guard Hussars.

The bridles of the officers were unique to hussars, and of regimental pattern. The two Leib regiments had black leather harnesses, while the other regiments had light brown. All had crossed leather face straps with a brass plate on the martingale. The Guard Hussars and regiments 5, 9, 10, 11, and 12 had throat plumes attached to gilt or silver crescents on straps hanging from the bridle. The plumes of the Guard, 9, 10, and 11 were black and those of 5 and 12 were white. Regiments 4, 6, and 7 had crescents only, while the two Leib regiments, the 3rd and the 8th, had decorative stars. At this time Regiment No. 3 had the entire harness decorated with cowry shells, a practice that was adopted by the Guard in 1867 and other regiments in later years.

The shabracque for officers was the same as that for men except for gold or silver lace edging and an elaborate floral leaf decoration in the rear corner. For officers of the Guard Hussars, the outer edge of the shabracque was of 3-cm (1¼-inch) lace and the star decorated the front and rear corners over the floral pattern.

Standards and kettledrums

In 1861 all hussar regiments had square 1814-pattern standards of regulation patterns, white field for the Guard and black for the remainder. In 1860, regiments 4, 5, 9, and 10 repaired and modified their standards by adding white corner wedges because they had been otherwise worn out. All regiments carried the 1813–15 streamer, and regiments 3, 8, 11, and 12 carried the 1849 streamer, all with swords. The 1864 streamer was carried by The Guard (with swords), regiment No. 3 (with the Alsen Cross) and Regiment No. 8 (with swords).

Kettledrums were carried by regiments 1, 2, and 3. The 1st Leib Regiment's silver drums had been taken from the von Reusch Hussars at Katholisch-Hennersdorf in 1758. The 2nd Leib Regiment was awarded drums in 1858, similar to those the 1st Regiment but of copper. The 3rd Regiment's drums were presented in 1857 (also taken at the battle of Katholisch-Hennersdorf).

Uhlans

Descended from the Bosniaks of Frederick the Great's army and the Towarczys of the French revolutionary wars, the Uhlan (or Lancer) arm had by 1861 become the largest of the Prussian Army. Of the 15 regiments, one Guard and four Line regiments were raised in 1860.

Uhlan cap-line flounders. From left: officers; NCOs; other ranks.

Lancer cap

Originally introduced in 1815, the *Tschapka* worn at this time was the 1843 model. It had seen a few modifications but was basically the same headdress. The skull was made of boiled and black-lacquered leather and was fitted with a round leather peak at the front. Fixed on top of the skull was a round leather stem atop which was a flat leather mortarboard with the points fore and aft. On the four sides of the mortarboard, narrowing down to the top of the skull, were panels of ribbed cloth in regimental colour. The leather edge of the mortarboard showed above the panels. An oval black/white cockade was attached to the top left side front edge, behind which a white hanging plume in a brass stem was fitted. The cap lines, which were white for all regiments, went once around the stem where it met the skull and from behind the front plate looped up and attached to a ring on the right point of the mortarboard. The cap lines then went round the neck, ending in flounders dropping from the left shoulder in front. Chin-scales were brass for all. For NCOs the hanging plume was black over white, the peak was bound in brass and the cap lines and flounders were of mixed black and white wool. Since 1822 the *Wachtmeisters* of the Guard regiments had had the cap lines and flounders in silver thread and black wool. For trumpeters and musicians the cap was the same as for NCOs except for a hanging red plume.

Uhlan tschapkas. From left, officer, 3rd Regiment; other ranks.

The cap plates were attached to the top panels with the base resting on the top of the skull. For 1 and 3 Guard regiments the Guard eagle and star were in German silver, while for 2 Guard Regiment the eagle was in brass and the star in silver. Regiments 1, 2, and 3 had a brass Line eagle with Vaterland bandeau and FWR breast shield. Regiments 4, 9, 10, 11, and 12 had a brass Line eagle with Vaterland bandeau and FR monogram. Regiments 5, 6, 7, and 8 had a white-metal Line eagle with Vaterland bandeau and FR monogram. For officers the cap was the same as for the men, only of better materials. There was a false leather round peak or flap on the back of the skull with the peak reaching above the stem. The top edge of the mortarboard, the edges of the panels, and the cap lines and flounders (which for officers were more like large tassels) were of silver and black lace and the cockade was of silver with a black centre. The chin-scales were gilt for all as was the edging to the front peak. The front eagle plates were of gilt or silver with Guard stars in silver with enamel centres.

In 1862 the officers of Regiment No. 3 were awarded the honour of a gold lace 4-cm (1½-inch) band around the top of the skull and the rear peak was edged with a thin band of gold lace.

For both officers and men in the field, the tschapka plume was removed and the cap was fitted with a black oilskin cover which was laced through eyelets at the back like a boot. Openings allowed the cockade and the cap line ring to be exposed. Officers of some regiments privately purchased light plain black leather tschapkas for campaign.

Lancer jacket

When the Hussars adopted the Attila in 1853, the Uhlans were ordered to wear the double-breasted *Ulanka*, also copied from the Austrians. This garment replaced the *Kollet* worn since Napoleonic times. This dark-blue jacket was double-breasted with seven buttons down each side, one at the top below the middle of the shoulder and six from mid-chest down. The jacket was piped all round the plastron front (forming a "scallop" at each shoulder where the top button was placed), on the front skirt, on the back seams and the edge of the skirt flaps in facing colour. From an army order of February 1854, the ulanka was fitted with a detachable plastron (*paraderbatten*) for use in parades and gala occasions. The plastron, collar, and Polish cuffs with buttons were all in regimental facing colour. Instead of shoulder straps the jacket was fitted with

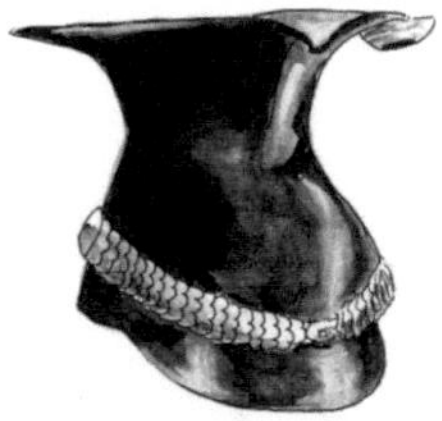

Officers' undress leather tschapka.

detachable epaulettes in similar form to those of officers of other branches except that there were brass scales on the front and back edges of the epaulette straps. The field was in regimental colour and the crescents and scales were brass for all regiments except Guard regiments 1 and 3 for which they were white metal. Regiment No. 3 had the monogram of Tsar Alexander II in the field in brass. The crescent underlay was red for all regiments. The ulanka was always worn with a girdle (*Päßgürtel*), which was blue edged in facing colour with a vertical loop the same width and colours of the girdle where the buckle would have been. Two litzen were worn on the collars and one on the each cuff by the Guard regiments, white for the 1st and 3rd, yellow for the 2nd. NCOs wore collar and cuff lacing in the normal fashion and trumpeters and musicians wore swallow's nests under the epaulettes (which looked rather odd).

For officers the tunic was remarkably similar to the men's, except for the quality. The epaulette crescents and scales were of gilt (or silver in the 1 and 3 Guards) and instead of the Päßgürtel, the silver officers' sash with black stripes was worn.

Uhlan tunic, the Ulanka.

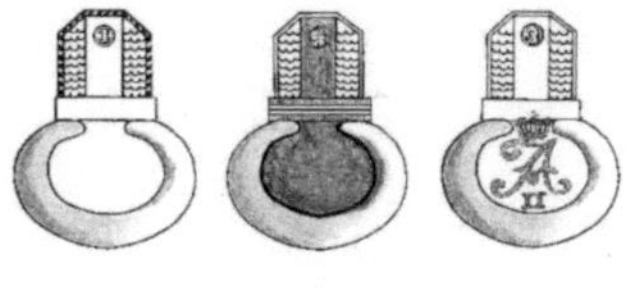

Uhlan epaulettes, from left: One-year volunteer; kapitulant; Regiment No. 3.

Dress distinctions of the Uhlan regiments

Regiment	Lace/buttons	Collar, cuffs, piping, greatcoat collar patch	Plastron (paraderbatten)	Epaulette field, tschapka panels, greatcoat shoulder-strap piping
1st Guard-Uhlan Regiment	Silver	Red	White (piped red)	White*
2nd Guard Uhlan Regiment	Gold	Red	Red	Red*
3rd Guard Uhlan Regiment	Silver	Yellow	Yellow	Yellow*
West Prussian Uhlan Regiment No. 1	Gold	Red	Red	White
Silesian Uhlan Regiment No. 2	Gold	Red	Red	Red
1st Brandenburg Uhlan Regiment No. 3	Gold	Red	Red	Yellow
1st Pomeranian Uhlan Regiment No. 4	Gold	Red	Red	Light blue
Westphalian Uhlan Regiment No. 5	Silver	Red	Red	White
Thüringian Uhlan Regiment No. 6	Silver	Red	Red	Red
Rhenish Uhlan Regiment No. 7	Silver	Red	Red	Yellow
East Prussian Uhlan Regiment No. 8	Silver	Red	Red	Light blue
2nd Pomeranian Uhlan Regiment No. 9	Gold	White	White	White
Posen Uhlan Regiment No. 10	Gold	Crimson	Crimson	Crimson
2nd Brandenburg Uhlan Regiment No. 11	Gold	Yellow	Yellow	Yellow
Lithuanian Uhlan Regiment No. 12	Gold	Light blue	Light blue	Light blue

* Greatcoat shoulder straps for Guards regiments were not piped.

Undress, greatcoat and leg wear

The mütze was dark blue with band and piping in facing colour. The leather-lined cavalry overalls were worn by all regiments. The outer-seam piping was red except for the 10th Regiment, for which it was crimson. The shoulder straps on the greatcoat were blue piped in epaulette colour (see chart opposite) except in the Guards where they were in epaulette colour with no piping.

The officers' überrock was dark blue with collar, breast flaps and cuff piping in the colour of the facings, the collar was piped dark blue. The turn-down collars of the officers' greatcoats and mantels were in tunic colour and when turned up, the same as for the überrock. For court levées and gala occasions, officers wore dark blue trousers with triple stripes of facing colour. For the 1st Guard Uhlan Regiment, the stripes were white either side of the red seam. Gloves were white.

Equipment and horse furniture

The men wore a white shoulder belt with black pouch and carbine swivel. The pouch flap bore the Guard star for the three guard regiments and no decoration for other regiments. Sword belt and slings worn under the ulanka were white. Sword straps were white with knot colours as for all cavalry. Officers wore a silver or gold pouch belt with blue cloth underlay and the black patent-leather pouch with silver Guard star, or for officers of Line regiments, the crowned FWR monogram in gilt. Sword belt and slings were worn under the tunic.

The men carried the 1828-pattern ash lance with black hand-strap and steel tip. The pennant was of white canvas over black Merino wool and swallow-tailed. Until 1865, NCOs did not carry the lance but from that time all ranks, sergeant and below were ordered to do so. The pennant for NCOs was white canvas with a black Prussian eagle stitched either side.

The side-arm was the 1852 cavalry sabre. A cabinet order of 1 March 1860 allowed the Wachtmeister of Uhlan Regiment No. 1 to carry the French-pattern sabre. The M1851 cavalry pistol was carried instead of the carbine.

Like dragoons, the officers and senior NCOs carried the 1852-pattern sword with a fish-skin grip instead of leather-bound wood. Officers wore the lion's head sword in undress. On campaign, like all cavalry officers, they generally used privately purchased pistols.

Uhlan horses were generally selected along the same guidelines as those of the dragoons. Trumpeters rode grey or white mounts in many regiments. The saddles and bridles were standard cavalry issue and the shabracque was dark blue with standard facing-colour edging. The Guard star decorated the front and rear corners for the Guard regiments. Greatcoat and equipment was distributed on the saddles in the same way as it was in the dragoons.

Standards and kettledrums

Standards were square for the three Guard regiments and Nos. 1, 3, 9, 10, 11, and 12. Regiments 2 and 4–8 were swallow-tailed. Regiments 1 to 8 had the 1813–15 streamer. Regiments 6, 7, and 8 had the 1849 streamer with swords. In addition, Regiment no. 3 had a special streamer presented by Empress Maria of Russia in 1857. At this time kettledrums were only carried by Regiment No. 7. They were silver drums presented by the Grand Duke Karl of Saxe-Weimar-Eisenach on 26 May 1827.

CHAPTER SIXTEEN

Supporting Corps

Artillery

The artillery was organized into brigades rather than regiments. A brigade consisted of three field divisions, each of four foot batteries and two fortress detachments and a horse artillery division of six batteries. In 1861 the artillery comprised a Guards brigade and eight provincial brigades. These were as follows:

East Prussian Artillery Brigade No. 1
Brandenburg Artillery Brigade No. 3
Lower Silesian Artillery Brigade No. 5
Westphalian Artillery Brigade No. 7
Pomeranian Artillery Brigade No. 2
Magdeburg Artillery Brigade No. 4
Silesian Artillery Brigade No. 6
Rhenish Artillery Brigade No. 8

Helmet

The M1860 helmet was fitted with a ball instead of a spike, but was in all other respects the same as the infantry pattern. The Guard units had tombak fittings with Guard eagle and white-metal star. The 4th Company of the Guard Fortress detachment had the "COLBERG 1807" inscription on a scroll below the star from 1861. The Guard Artillery Brigade wore white plumes in their helmets for parades and the trumpeters red plumes.

Line artillery helmet and Guard artillery eagle.

The Line brigades had fittings and Line eagle in brass. In 1, 3 and 6 Brigade the eagle bore the breast shield with the FWR monogram, the remainder having the standard FR on the breast. In the Pomeranian Artillery Brigade No. 2, the "COLBERG 1807" honour scroll was worn by foot batteries 2 and 4, No. 3 Fortress Company and horse batteries 1 and 2. In Brandenburg Artillery Brigade No. 3 it was worn by Foot Battery No. 1. Officers' helmets were the same as for men, with the usual differences of quality.

Tunic

The waffenrock was the infantry pattern with black collar patches and cuffs. The tunic front, rear skirts, collar patch and cuffs were piped red. The Guard batteries and all horse artillery batteries had Swedish cuffs. In the Guard, the collar patches and cuffs bore the Guard litzen in yellow camel hair. The foot batteries of the Line brigades wore Brandenburg cuffs with the cuff patch in blue. Shoulder straps were red for all with the Guard having plain and the Line bearing the brigade number in yellow. Attached to all brigades was a *Feuerwerksabteilung* (ordnance section) and personnel of this section wore an "F" on the shoulder straps. Trumpeters and musicians of the Guard had black swallow's nests with yellow lace. Foot and fortress units had white lace (gold for staff musicians) and all horse artillery trumpeters wore gold lace (with fringes for staff trumpeters).

Artillery feuerwerker shoulder strap.

For officers, the black collar and cuffs were of velvet. The epaulettes had red fields and underlay with gilt crescents and the brigade numbers on those of the Line artillery were in gilt.

Undress, leg wear and greatcoats

The mütze for the men was blue with a black band piped red either side. There was also red piping around the crown. For officers the band was in velvet and a peak was added. The trousers were the infantry pattern for foot and fortress units and cavalry pattern for the horse artillery. Greatcoat collar patches were black. Shoulder straps were red for the Guard and blue piped red with the brigade numbers in yellow for the Line. Mounted units wore the cavalry pattern greatcoat.

The überrock for officers of foot and fortress units was black with black velvet collar piped red. The breast opening and cuff piping was also red. For horse artillery officers the überrock was blue but the distinctions were the same. The trousers were as for the men and for gala occasions the trousers were of white kersey in the dismounted branches. For the horse artillery the gala trousers were blue with two black velvet stripes 4-cm ($1\frac{1}{2}$-inch) wide with a red stripe in the middle and red piping on either side. Greatcoat collars were black velvet piped red when turned down and blue when turned up.

Equipment

Foot and fortress artillery were equipped the same as for infantry with white leatherwork, the valise straps being attached to the belt by grenade-shaped hooks as in the Guard infantry. The belt supported the M1849 Infantry fascine knife (short sword).

Sword knots for foot artillery troops

Foot artillery division*	Acorn	Battery	Slide and crown
1st Division	White	1 Heavy Foot Battery	White
		2 Field Battery	Red
		3 Howitzer Battery	Yellow
2nd Division	Red	1 Heavy Foot Battery	White
		2 Field Battery	Red
		3 Howitzer Battery	Yellow
3rd Division	Yellow	1 Heavy Foot Battery	White
		2 Field Battery	Red
		3 Howitzer Battery	Yellow

*Some brigades had a 4th division, which would have had a light blue acorn.

For Fortress Artillery the 1st Battalion had a light blue acorn and the 2nd a light green one. Each of the four companies within the battalion had white/red/yellow/light blue slides and crowns respectively. No firearm was carried by the foot artillery.

Horse artillery personnel wore a white pouch belt with a black leather pouch upon which was a brass three-flamed grenade with the FWR monogram on the bombe. They wore the same belt as the foot artillery with slings for attaching the 1852 artillery stirrup hilted sabre. They also carried the M1850 cavalry pistol.

Horse artillery sword knots

Battery	1	2	3	4	5	6
Crown	White	Red	Yellow	Light blue	Light green	White
Tassel	White	White	White	White	White	Red

Officers, both foot and mounted, wore a blue, gold-laced pouch belt with a black patent-leather pouch which was adorned with a Guard star in silver for the Guard Artillery Brigade and the crowned FWR monogram in gilt for the Line artillery. The 1852 pattern cavalry sabre was worn on gold-laced blue slings attached to a belt under the tunic.

Horse artillery pouch device.

Horse Furniture

The horse artillery shabracques were of regulation pattern, rounded on both front and back corners with a black stripe edged red all round and a thin red stripe on the edge of the shabracque. It was the same for officers except that the stripes were specified as 1.5 cm (1/2 inch) for the red and 4 cm (1 1/4 inch) for the black. The Guard star decorated the rear corners of the shabracque in the Guard Artillery Brigade.

Colours

Colours were the same as the infantry pattern and were carried by each division. All batteries of the Guard, 1st and 2nd brigades carried the 1813–15 streamers. The 1849 streamer with swords was carried by the 2nd Division of the 4th Brigade, and the 1864 streamers were carried by the 2nd Division of the Guard, the 3rd Division of the 3rd Brigade (with swords), the 1st Division of the 7th Brigade (with swords) and the Horse Artillery division of the 8th Brigade.

Ordnance Corps (Zeugspersonal)

The ordnance personnel were attached to the army corps headquarters and wore the same uniforms as the Line artillery with Swedish cuffs. The officers' epaulettes had a black velvet field and they carried an infantry officer's sword. The ordnance feldwebel and the ordnance sergeant bore gold lace on collar and cuffs, the feldwebel with officer's sword and the sergeant with the infantry side-arm and a plain white woollen troddel.

Pioneers and engineers

The pioneers or sappers had a long ancestry going back to the miners and sappers of Frederick the Great's day. In 1861 they were organized into single battalions distributed into the Guard and provincial army corps on the same basis as the artillery. Hence battalion 1 was East Prussia, 2 was Pomerania, 3 Brandenburg and so on. There were four companies in each battalion. The Engineer Corps consisted entirely of officers and were attached to army corps headquarters. The uniform was also the same as the artillery in most respects except for the differences set out below:

Helmet

This had a spike attached rather than a ball, and the fittings were all in white-metal except the chin-scales which were tombak for the Guard and brass for the Line. The helmet eagle for the Guard was decorated with a silver Guard star and the Line had the regulation eagle with the FWR monogram on the breast shield for battalions 1 and 3 and the FR for the remainder.

The Guard wore black plumes on parade and buglers and musicians of all battalions wore red plumes. For officers all fittings were silver and the chin-scales were gilt.

Tunic

This was of infantry style with black collar and Swedish cuffs with red piping as in the artillery. The Guard wore white litzen on collar and cuffs and all buttons were tin. Red shoulder straps with yellow battalion numbers (plain for the Guards) were worn. All NCO lace was silver and the black swallow's nests for musicians bore white lace for the Line and silver lace and fringes for the Guard and staff musicians of the Line.

All pioneer and engineer officers had black facings of velvet and both Guard and Line had two silver litzen on collars and cuffs with officers of the Line having staff-pattern litzen. The crescents on the epaulettes were silver with the battalion numbers in gilt. The field and underlay were red.

Other items of dress

The mütze, trousers and greatcoat were the same as for foot artillery, the latter with tin buttons. For officers, the überrock, trousers, white parade trousers and gala trousers were all the same as worn by foot artillery with silver instead of gold lace and buttons. Officers of the Engineer Corps wore the dark blue gala trousers of the horse artillery, with their black and red stripes down the seams.

Equipment and horse furniture.

All equipment was the same as for foot artillery except that the leatherwork was black. The valise hooks on the belt were brass and of Line infantry pattern except in the Guard Battalion in which the brass grenade pattern was used. The side-arm was the pioneer fascine knife (or sword) with serrated edge. The other ranks' troddel colours were as for the first battalions of the infantry.

Engineer Corps other ranks troddel colours

Company	1	2	3	4
Slide	White	Red	Yellow	Blue
Stem	White	White	White	White
Crown	White	Red	Yellow	Blue

NCO side-arms and sword knots/troddels were as for infantry. The pioneer troops carried the 1849 Minié rifled carbine; although the M1854 Jäger rifle was authorized in 1865, not many units were carrying it during the 1866 campaign. Officers were armed similarly to infantry officers and the shabracque for mounted officers was the same as for the artillery, the Guard with the star on the rear corners.

Colours

The pioneers carried the same style of colours as the artillery. The awards were largely the same for the pioneer battalions attached to the artillery brigades.

Military train

The train battalions came into existence in 1853 and were assigned to the provincial army corps on the same basis as the artillery and pioneers. Each train battalion consisted of two companies.

Headdress

The jäger shako was worn by the NCOs and other ranks. It bore the Line eagle

Guard Train Battalion shako.

with the FR monogram on the breast in brass and in other respects was the same as for the jäger. The Guard had the star on the front the same as the Guard Jäger. The Guard wore a white plume for parades while musicians wore a red plume.

Officers of the military train did not wear the shako but instead wore the spiked helmet of infantry pattern with a spike. In the Line battalions, the eagle and fittings were in gilt with FR on the breast and those in the Guard had the spread eagle in gilt with the star in German silver.

Tunic

The eight-button dark-blue tunic had rounded collar and Swedish cuffs. For the Guard battalion the collar patches and cuffs were light blue, for the Line battalions the collar patches were light blue and the cuffs were in tunic colour. The tunic was piped down the front and around the rear skirt flaps in light blue, as were the top and rear of the cuffs in the Line regiments. The Guard wore two white litzen on collar and cuffs. Buttons were tombak for the guard and brass for the Line. On the shoulder straps of the Line battalions was the army corps number in red. NCOs had distinctions in gold lace. The drummers wore light-blue swallow's nests with white lace (with fringe for the Guard). Mounted staff trumpeters wore light-blue swallow's nests with gold lace.

Officers wore infantry-pattern tunics with all distinctions the same as for the men except for the quality. Guard train officers had two gold litzen on collar and cuffs and the underlay of the epaulettes was light blue for all. The silver and black sash was worn by all officers.

Other items of dress

The mütze and greatcoat were the same as for infantry except for the light-blue facings. The latter had dark-blue shoulder straps with light-blue piping and red army corps numbers. Trousers for foot troops were the same as infantry with the red stripe, mounted troops wore the same as cavalry. For officers, the überrock was dark blue with light-blue collar patches. Trousers and white parade trousers were all the same as infantry. The greatcoat had a dark-blue turn-down collar, which was light blue when turned up.

Equipment for dismounted troops (such as the field bakery and stores personnel) was as for infantry. The waist belt had a brass open buckle. They carried the infantry side-arm with the same troddel company colours as pioneers.

Mounted soldiers (column drivers and all NCOs) wore a white pouch belt with black leather pouch, undecorated for the Line but with a star for the Guard. They carried the stirrup-hilted sabre with black leather straps for the sword knots, the company colours of which were described as "the same as for Hussars".

Officers wore a blue gold-laced pouch belt with the crowned FWR monogram in gilt on the pouch flap (silver star for the Guard). Shabracques were the same as for all mounted officers with rounded ends and the stripe and piping in light blue. The Guard had the star on the rear corners.

The Landwehr

Landwehr Infantry

After the reorganization of 1859, the Landwehr was much reduced. In the infantry there were four Guard Landwehr regiments (two Foot Guard and two Guard Grenadier) with 32 linked and eight independent Line infantry regiments.

Uniform

The main difference between the regular and Landwehr infantry was the headdress. The Landwehr wore the jäger shako decorated with a black metal oval disc with a white border. For the Guard Landwehr, the centre of the disc was fitted with a Guard star with the Landwehr cross superimposed on the centre in silver with the Vaterland motto inscribed. For the Line regiments a large Landwehr cross with Vaterland motto alone was worn. Some battalions did not even have the shako but instead wore the mütze with a peak and the Landwehr cross on the crown.

The Landwehr cross.

The rest of the uniform matched the parent regiments, which in the Line were the first four regiments of each army corps. (i.e. Landwehr Regiment No. 15 = Inf. Regt. No 15 of Army Corps VII with light-blue shoulder straps, red number and white piping on cuff patches). The company number on the shoulder-strap buttons were in Roman numerals for the Landwehr instead of Arabic. Troddels were the same as for the infantry. Equipment was the same except that many battalions still carried the old large cross-belt cartridge pouch fixed to the back of the belt under the valise instead of the pouches on the front of the belt. The greatcoat and mütze were the same, the latter with a Landwehr cross on the crown and sometimes a peak.

Landwehr infantry shako and Guard Landwehr shako plate.

Landwehr cavalry

The cavalry of the Landwehr was drastically reorganized and most of the units were disbanded. The units remaining were the 7th Heavy Cavalry Regiment (Cuirassier), 2nd Dragoon Regiment, 1, 2, 5, 6, and 10 Hussar regiments and 1, 2, 3, 4, and 8 Uhlan regiments. Although seven more units were raised for service in 1866, the entire Landwehr cavalry was disbanded after the war.

Except for the headdresses, the cavalry wore the uniforms of their opposite numbers in the regular cavalry. The 7th Heavy Cavalry wore the Cuirassier helmet with Landwehr cross on the brass eagle breast, but no cuirass. The Hussars wore the old *Mirleton* with the "wing" in regimental colour (same as the busby bag on the regulars) with a Landwehr cross on the right side and the regiment number on the front. The chin-scales were brass. For officers the "wing" was of silver lace material.

The Uhlans wore the infantry or dragoon helmet with the eagle in brass and the Landwehr cross on its breast. They were ordered to wear the uhlan tschapka in 1861, but few regiments, if any, adopted it before the war.

Landwehr Hussars Mirleton cap and Landwehr heavy cavalry helmet eagle.

Departments of the army

The non-combatant departments (*Beamte*) of the Prussian Army were generally deemed to be more or less civil organizations. The officers (or correctly "officials") were thus divided into two categories. The first were the "*Obere Militärbeamte*" (high military officials) where the officers' appointments or positions were given a comparative military rank. There were then the *Zivilbeamte der Militär-Verwaltung* (civil officials of military departments) who were accorded no rank status. Within organizations such as the medical services, there were officials of both levels, which can cause confusion. The uniform descriptions below have thus been organized by branch, department, or service rather than rank status in the army.

Medical Services

*Surgeons (*Ärzte*)*

By an army order of 25 July 1865, surgeons of the Medical Department below the surgeon general were awarded comparative military rank one level higher than that established in 1859. In 1866 the rank status was as follows:

Surgeon general of the army (*Generalstabsärzte de Armee*) ranked as a colonel.

Chief surgeon of an army corps (*Corps-General-Ärzte*) ranked as a lieutenant-colonel.
Senior staff surgeons (*Oberstabsärzte*) ranked as majors.
Staff surgeons (*Stabsärzte*) ranked as captains.
Surgeons (*Oberärzte*) and assistant surgeons ranked as first and second lieutenants.
Medical officer (*Unterärzte*) was a civil position.

Uniform

The helmet was of infantry pattern with gilt fittings and the Line eagle with FR on the breast. The tunic was also of infantry pattern with blue Swedish cuffs all piped red and all buttons were gilt. The epaulettes had a blue field with red underlay and the stars of comparative military rank were worn on the field. Gold litzen were worn on the collar and cuffs according to rank.

Rank dress distinctions of the medical services

Rank	Collar litzen	Cuff litzen	Epaulettes
Surgeon general of the army	Two	Two	Gold fringe/two stars
Chief surgeon of an army corps	Two	Two	Gold fringe/one star
Senior staff surgeon	Two	Two	Gold fringe/no star
Staff surgeon	One	None	Two stars
Surgeon	One	None	No star
Assistant surgeon	None	None	No star

The collar and cuffs of the surgeon general of the army were also of velvet. The medical staff did not wear the silver/black sash. The junior medical officers (*Unterärzte*) ranked as NCOs and wore the assistant surgeons' uniform with plain-blue shoulder straps with gold piping.

The mütze with peak was blue, piped on the band and crown in red. A small gold eagle was worn on the crown above the cockade. The black überrock had a blue collar with red piping which was also on the cuffs. Trousers and other items of dress were as for infantry. The infantry sword or degen was worn on a belt under the tunic. If and when mounted, staff surgeons and above used the infantry-pattern shabracque.

From 1 May 1866, a red cross on a white armband was worn on the left sleeve by all medical personnel while in the field.

*Apothecaries (*Militär-Pharmacie*)*

This was a civil department and senior staff apothecary and pharmacists all wore the infantry-pattern helmet with gilt fittings and tunic with blue collar and Swedish cuffs piped cornflower-blue around the collar, cuffs, tunic front and rear skirt flaps. There were two gold litzen on collar and cuffs. The buttons were gilt and carried the heraldic shield of Prussia. The epaulette field was cornflower blue, the underlay was dark blue and the shoulder loops were gold with two blue stripes. The mütze with peak was blue piped on the band and around crown in cornflower blue with the gold eagle on the crown and the überrock was the same as the Medical Department, with cornflower-blue piping. All other items were the same as for medical officers. Despite their civil status, they did carry swords.

*Army hospital staff (*Lazarett-Ökonomie-Stab*)*

This department was responsible for the management and financial administration of garrison hospitals. The uniform was identical to the Apothecary staff. However, here only the chief hospital inspector on the medical staff of the army wore two gold litzen on the collar and cuffs. The hospital inspector and his assistant had plain collar and cuffs.

*Field hospital orderlies (*Lazarettgehilfen*)*

These were trained medical personnel who tended to the wounded in field hospitals. Although there were NCOs, the officers were from the medical staff.

Uniform

Orderlies wore the infantry helmet with eagle plate and FR monogram. They wore the blue infantry tunic with blue collar and Swedish cuffs all piped red. Buttons were of tombak and there were no shoulder straps. The peakless mütze was blue with red piping, and the greatcoat had dark-blue collar patch and no shoulder straps. (Plain blue shoulder straps for the tunic and plain grey ones for the greatcoat were authorized in 1866, but were not adopted until after the war.) Infantry trousers were worn except for mounted orderlies who wore cavalry type. NCOs wore gold lace.

On the march, the infantry valise with black leather straps was worn and instead of the ammunition pouches on the black belt, black leather pouches (somewhat larger than the ammunition pouches) containing bandages and ointment were carried. For orderlies accompanying mounted troops, a black leather bag was worn over the shoulder. The red cross on a white armband was worn in the field.

*Stretcher-bearers (*Krankenträger*)*

Mobilized in time of war and drawn from the Landwehr, the stretcher-bearers were formed into companies and attached to the army corps.

Uniform

Instead of the helmet, a mütze with peak and black leather chin-strap was worn. The band and piping were crimson. In the units attached to the Line, the crown of the mütze above the cockade bore the Landwehr cross with the Vaterland inscription. The Guard wore just the cockade. The dark-blue tunic had crimson collar and crimson piping on the front, rear skirt and top edge of the Swedish cuffs. All buttons were made of tin. The Guard units had crimson collar and cuffs, both decorated with Guard litzen. Shoulder straps were crimson with the army corps number in yellow for the Line, plain in the Guard. The trousers were the same as for infantry except that the stripe was crimson and the greatcoat had crimson collar patches and blue shoulder straps piped crimson with the yellow army corps number for the Line and plain crimson shoulder straps for the Guard. NCOs lace was silver.

Equipment was as for infantry in black leather, usually with one ammunition pouch. Stretcher-bearers were authorized to carry the M1851 cavalry pistol in a black leather holster on the right side, but later were issued with the Minié carbine, which was carried on a brown leather sling. The infantry side-arm was worn, probably with the same troddel colours as for the 1st Battalion in line with other support corps, but there is little definite information. As with other medical troops, the red cross on a white armband was worn on the left upper arm in the field.

*Veterinary officers (*Roßärzte*)*

The veterinary requirements of the Prussian Army were, before 1862 handled regimentally by the farriers and shoesmiths. In that year a corps of NCOs was formed from the regimental farriers, which was expanded the following year.

The first uniform consisted of an infantry-pattern helmet with brass FR eagle and fittings and a blue überrock with black collar piped red along with the deep turned-back cuffs. The blue peaked mütze had a black band and piping. There was no eagle on the crown. In 1865, as this department expanded it was placed under the War Ministry and a new uniform was authorized. This was ordered to be of artillery pattern, including the helmet with ball. The NCO status of the *Stabs-Roßärzte* and *Roßärzte* remained the same so the shoulder straps continued to be black with gold braid on the edges. The officers' sword and knot was carried. The other items are presumed to have remained the same and there is no clear information on any distinction between Stabs-, Ober- or regular Roßärzte on the shoulder straps.

There was a re-organization of the corps in 1872 when a veterinary staff was assigned to each army corps. It is interesting to note that although Roßärzte were raised to officer status in 1882 there were no officers commissioned as veterinarians in the German army until 1910.

Administration departments and services

As stated before, the various civil departments were divided into those with and those without comparative military rank. The uniforms were basically the same for all departments and is described as follows:

Helmet

The helmet was of infantry pattern with gilt or silver fittings. The chin-scales were gilt or silver depending on button colour.

Uniform

The dark-blue tunic had eight buttons down the front, a dark-blue rounded collar and Swedish cuffs. The tunic front, top and front of collar, top and back edge of cuffs and skirt flaps were all piped in departmental colour. The epaulette fields, underlay and straps were also of piping colour and the fields bore the heraldic arms of black eagle on a white shield surmounted by a crown. Instead of the rank stars, gilt or silver rosettes were worn either side of the shield. The buttons, the collar litzen, the epaulette crescents, the epaulette lace, and retaining loops were all in gold or silver. The epaulette crescents were of lace formed over pressed, ribbed felt. Apprentices and junior clerks in these departments had no epaulettes but wore shoulder straps of piping colour with a 1.5-cm (1/2-inch) gold or silver edging all round.

The überrock was black with blue collar and departmental piping on that and the cuffs. Blue peaked mütze with piping on band and crown with gilt eagle on crown above the cockade. Greatcoat with dark-blue collar on the inside and outside, the colour and material (i.e. velvet) of the tunic collar plus the piping. Infantry officers' degen and sword knot on a belt were worn under the tunic. No sash was worn. All other items were the same as for infantry. Below are the various departments listed with the appointments and uniform distinction where different from above.

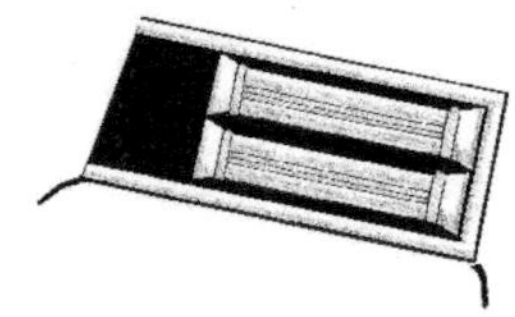

Senior military official's collar; and military official's epaulette.

Departments with comparative military ranks

Administration (*Intendatur*)

Uniform distinctions – Blue velvet collar and cuffs for all grades; crimson piping including the outside seam on the trousers; silver lace and buttons.

Senior military administrators (*Intendanten als Kreigsräte*): Silver border to collar, two litzen on collar and cuffs, epaulettes with silver fringe, one gold rosette.

Administrators (*Intendanten)*: Two litzen on collar and cuffs, epaulettes with silver fringe, one gold rosette.

Administrators grade II (*Intendanten-Räte)*: As above, but no rosette.

Assessors (*Assessoren*): Two litzen on collar and cuffs, one gold rosette.

Administration secretary: one gold rosette.

Secretarial assistants and apprentices: no rosette.

Military official's peaked cap.

Military justice department (*Militär-Justiz*)

Uniform distinctions – Red piping; silver lace/buttons

Inspector-general (*General-Auditeur*): Blue velvet collar with silver border all round, two litzen on collar and cuffs, epaulettes with silver fringe, two silver rosettes.

Deputy-inspector-general (*Ober-Auditeur Den Gen. Auditoriats)*: Two litzen on collar and cuffs, epaulettes with silver fringe, one silver rosette.

Deputy-inspector-general on army corps staff *(Korps-Auditeur)*: Two litzen on collar and cuffs, two silver rosettes.

Official on inspector-general's staff (*Auditeur)*: Two litzen on collar and cuffs, one silver rosette.

Military court clerk (*Militär Gerichts Aktuarian*): No litzen, no rosette.

(The word *Auditeur* does not translate as Auditor in the English sense of the term. "Inspector" is the most descriptive translation.)

Paymasters department (*Zahlmeister*)

Uniform distinctions – White piping; silver lace/buttons; dark blue underlay on epaulettes.

Paymaster class 1 (*Zahlmeister 1 Klasse*): One gold rosette.

Paymaster class 2 (*Zahlmeister 2 Klasse*): No rosette.

Fortifications department (*Fortifikations-Beamte*)

Uniform distinctions – Red piping; silver lace/buttons.

Department-secretary (*Fortifikations-Secretäre)*: Black velvet collar and cuffs, no rosette.

Civil officials of military departments

All buttons bore the heraldic shield with crown, the underlay of the epaulettes was blue for all and the epaulette loops were gold with two thin blue stripes.

Field paymaster personnel War Chest (*Feld Kriegkassen*)

Uniform distinctions – White piping; gold lace/buttons.

Field paymaster (*Kriegs-Zahlmeister*): One gold rosette.

Cashier and book-keeper (*Kassiere-Buchhalter*): No rosette.

Clothing department (*Bekleidungs-Depot*)

Uniform distinctions – Red piping; gold lace/buttons.

Supervisor (*Rendant*): One silver rosette.

Controller (*Kontrolleur*): No rosette.

Quartermaster department (*Magazin-Personnel*)

Uniform distinctions – Yellow piping; gold lace/buttons.

Quartermaster (*Proviantmeister/Magazin-Rendant*): One silver rosette.

Controller (*Kontrolleur*): No rosette.

Garrison administration (*Garnison-Personnel*)

Uniform distinctions – Light blue piping; gold lace/buttons.

Director and chief inspector (*Direktor* and *Ober-Inspektor*): One silver rosette.

Inspector (*Inspektor*): No rosette.

Controller and assistant (*Kontrolleur*): No rosette.

Armourer's department and arsenal staff (*Zeughaus-Büchsenmeister*)

For the armourer (*Büchsenmeister*), a grey peaked mütze was worn, with red piping on the upper and lower band and crown. The überrock, with two rows of brass buttons, was also grey with red piping along the top of the collar, the top of the cuffs and the rear three-pointed skirt flaps. The grey trousers had red piping. There were no shoulder straps. A Fusilier side-arm was worn, the belt and frog worn under the coat with a slit for the sabre hilt to be revealed. The troddel was gold lace. For mounted personnel the cavalry sabre was worn with black leather strap and gold lace knot.

Ancillary units and organizations

Palace Guard Company (Schloß-Garde-Kompanie)

The Palace Guard Company (Schloß-Garde-Kompanie) was raised in 1829 as the Guard-NCO-Company (Garde-unterofficier-companie) to provide ceremonial guards for the royal palaces and castles. It consisted of retired NCOs of good character and long service. It was renamed Schloß-Garde-Kompanie in 1861 with an establishment of one senior NCO ranking as *Feldwebel-Lieutenant*, two ranking as *Feldwebel-sergeant* and five as *Feldwebel-unteroffizier*, with 62 NCOs.

Uniform

For full dress and gala occasions, the company wore the Grenadier version of the 1st Foot Guards mitre cap, but with all brass items – including the grenades and chin-scales – in silver. The tunic they wore was introduced in 1861, replacing the Napoleonic coatee that had been worn since the unit's creation. It was longer in the skirt than the contemporary infantry tunic, more like the 1843 version. It had a full red collar and cuffs with red piping on the rear skirt flaps and no piping on the front. Instead, there were 14 bands of white woollen lace across the front, approximately 3-cm (1¼-inch) wide and equally spaced, running down the chest from the neck to the lower edge of the skirt. The length of the lace shortened slightly as it approached the waist and lengthened again to the bottom of the skirt.

Shoulder strap for Palace Guard Company.

The tunic fastened with hooks and eyes. On each end of the lace was a silver button on a tuft of white wool with a small fringe. The cuffs were also each decorated with two lace strips with a small tuft and fringe at the buttons. There was no lace on the collar. Shoulder straps were white with a crowned FWR monogram in gold lace. The feldwebel-lieutenants, sergeants and NCOs wore silver lace on collar and cuffs.

The parade and gala dress trousers were the same as before 1861, namely the white kersey gaiter trousers with integral spats, worn by the Foot Guards from 1815–43. They fastened on the side, below the knee down to the ankle, with white linen-covered buttons and secured under the instep with a strap, the "spat" part covering the top of the boots. Wide white cross-belts were worn, with an "Old Prussian" infantry sabre on the left hp and the large black leather cartridge pouch, decorated with the Guard star, on the right. On 15 October 1855, King Frederick William IV had decreed that NCOs with over 25 years service would carry the officers' degen as they would rank as feldwebel-lieutenants, sergeants or NCOs.

In undress the company wore a stiffened peaked mütze with red band and piping. The überrock worn by all had two rows of white-metal buttons with a red collar, and red piping on the cuffs and rear skirt lace. There were no shoulder straps. The collar bore NCO lace for those entitled. Grey trousers with red piping were worn in winter and white kersey ones in summer for undress. The sabre or sword with white shoulder belt was worn when on duty, but not on guard. For non-gala guard duty the same helmet as the 1st Foot Guards was worn with the überrock, complete with Guard eagle and star. Grey greatcoats were worn with white straps as for the tunic and red collar patches.

*Pensioners (*Invalides*)*

There were two pensioners' homes; one in Berlin, the other in Stolp. In addition there were one Guard company and six provincial companies.

Uniform

A peaked mütze was worn with a red band and piping with cockade. The coat was a *Litewka*, a short frock coat worn prominently by the German volunteer units in the Napoleonic Wars. It would make a comeback (somewhat redesigned) in the 1880s. The blue single-breasted litewka had a red patch on the square-cut collar but no piping. There were eight brass buttons down the front and two pockets on the side, fastening with a single button on each. The shoulder straps were white in the Life and Grenadier companies of the Pensioners' Home and the Guard Invalide Company. The Life Company bore the crowned FWR monogram in red and the Grenadier company bore the monogram surmounted by a grenade. The remaining companies wore blue shoulder straps with red piping. The Berlin Home had the letter B and the Stolp home an S in yellow Latin script on the straps and the remaining companies the Arabic number. NCOs wore silver lace on the collar only in Guard-pattern lace for the three companies mentioned above and plain for the rest.

The old Prussian infantry sabre on a black leather shoulder belt was worn by NCOs and the night watch on duty. The latter also carried a musket and wore a large black pouch on a black bandolier over the left shoulder. The senior NCO carried an officer's sword and knot. There were even musicians who wore red swallow's nests with white lace.

*Military academies (*Kadettenanstalten*)*

In 1861 there were five military schools or academies with classes divided into companies. The Berlin Academy had four cadet companies and there were two each at Potsdam, Kulm, Wahlstatt, and Bensberg.

The Berlin companies wore the helmet of the 2nd Foot Guards with a black plume for parades. The infantry-pattern tunic had six tombak buttons down the front. The red collar patches and Swedish cuffs bore two yellow camel-hair litzen on each and the shoulder straps were white. For officer cadets, the litzen were of gold intertwined lace with tassel. The trousers were as for infantry and the belt was of black leather with the infantry clasp. The infantry side-arm was worn by cadet NCOs only with white troddel strap and acorn. The slide and crown was white for the 1st Company and red for the 2nd, yellow for the 3rd and light blue for the 4th companies respectively.

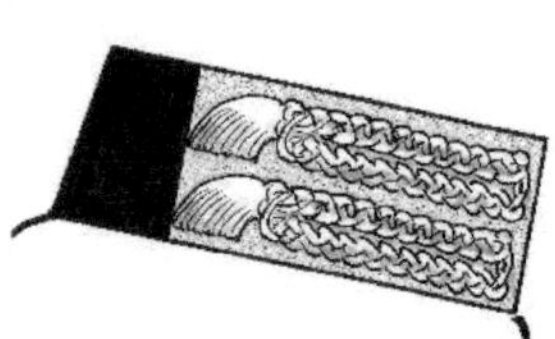

Collar and cuffs for officer cadets of the Berlin Military School.

The remaining companies did not wear a helmet, but the peaked mütze with red band and piping only. The collar patch on the tunic bore only a single litzen and the shoulder straps were red for Potsdam, white for Kulm, yellow for Wahlstatt and light blue for Bensberg. Cadet NCOs of these provincial schools did not have special lace on the collar. Instead they had a single yellow litzen with red centre on each shoulder strap (on the yellow straps of Wahlstatt, the litzen were red with yellow centre). The side arms by NCOs had troddel colours for 1st and 2nd companies only. The greatcoats were infantry pattern with shoulder straps the same as for the tunic.

Academy staff officers of the Berlin school wore the uniform of the 2nd Foot Guards with the black plume in the helmet. The provincial academy staffs wore regular infantry officers' uniforms. The silver/black sash was not worn.

*NCO schools (*Unteroffiziere-Schulen*)*

Two of these schools existed at this time; one in Potsdam, the other in Jülich, both with four companies.

The uniform was the same as for infantry of the Line. The school instructor NCOs wore a Guard eagle in brass with silver Guard star, the students' helmets bore the regular Line eagle. The tunic only differed from the Line infantry by having Brandenburg cuffs with a blue patch. The shoulder straps were white for Potsdam and red for Jülich. The sabre troddel was the same as companies 1–4 of an infantry battalion. Officers were seconded from their regular units and wore regimental uniform.

Infantry Instruction Battalion (Lehr-Infanterie-Battalion)

Soldiers attached to this unit, nominally incorporated into the Guard Army Corps, wore their regimental uniforms with black/white honour knots on the ends of their shoulder straps. The officers had no particular distinctions.

Officers of the army

These were officers detached from their regiments not attached permanently to particular units and for any reason, not entitled to a regimental uniform. The infantry uniform was worn by all with red collar patch and Swedish cuffs. The piping on the tunic of officers of foot troops (infantry, foot artillery, pioneers, train) had red piping down the front and skirts. Those of mounted troops (cavalry, horse artillery) had white piping. Foot officers wore the infantry helmet, while mounted troop officers wore the dragoon helmet. All active army officers wore white plumes for parade. Epaulettes had blue fields and red underlay. Buttons and lace were gold throughout. Grey or white trousers were worn.

Retired officers of the army

Officers on the retired list wore their regimental uniforms for functions that required they be worn. From 1833, the only indication of their status was the loops (*Passenten*) on the straps of their epaulettes which were of black/silver lace.

CHAPTER SEVENTEEN

Uniforms of the Royal Prussian Navy

DESPITE NEARLY FORTY YEARS OF existence, the Royal Prussian Navy was very much the junior service. By 1864 the total personnel of all branches amounted to fewer than 3,000 men. Until 1848 the uniforms followed army fashion of blue coats with red facings. Insignia included the anchor on most appointments. After about 1850 the facings became white and uniforms became standard when the infantry and artillery of the *Seebattalion* was created and they and the seagoing service separated. At the beginning of the Second Schleswig War, the only admiral in the navy was Prince Adalbert himself and there were only seventy or so sea officers. Eduard Jachmann, the officer who, with Adalbert was most associated with the creation of the navy, was promoted to rear-admiral in 1865. In 1866 the officer ranks of the Prussian navy were as follows:

Admiral
Rear-admiral (*Kontre-Admiral*)
Senior captain (*Kapitan-Zur-See*)
Captain (*Korvetten Kapitan*)
Lieutenant (*Lieutnant-zur-Zee*)
Ensign
Midshipman

Uniforms for officers

Headdress

The headdress worn for gala and official occasions was a low-crowned cocked hat made of black felt. For flag officers (admiral and rear-admiral) the hat was edged with broad gold lace. There was a large gold bullion loop on the right side that angled from the top front edge down to the centre of the hat. The upper part of the loop was secured by a large cockade and the lower by a button bearing the royal crown. The central part of the loop was plaited. For ranks below flag, the cocked hat had a wide black silk border and the loop had no central pattern.

Uniform

A dark-blue double-breasted coatee with plain tails was worn for full dress. The collar and Swedish cuffs were also blue. The top and front of the collar was edged with 1-cm (1/4-inch) gold lace as were the tops of the cuffs which had two buttons below the lace. For flag officers the collar and cuffs were decorated with the same oak-leaf pattern of gold lace worn by general officers of the army. The coatee had large white-faced lapels, which were worn open and edged with broad gold lace. Like their counterparts in the army, flag officers wore plaited gold lace shoulder cords with aiguillettes looped over the right breast. Plain horizontal pockets with square three-button flaps were worn at the waist in the rear. The dark-blue trousers had broad gold lace stripes down the sides, The belt was of black patent leather edged in gold lace and the sword was the army pattern *degen* with a lion's head pommel on which the right eye of the lion was green and the left red.

Officers under flag rank wore the same coatee except that instead of oak-leaf lace, the collar bore a wide band of gold lace. Below the buttons on the cuffs, medium-width lace was worn in the following combination: four bands for

Admiral gala dress coatee; cocked hat; lieutnant-zur-see gala

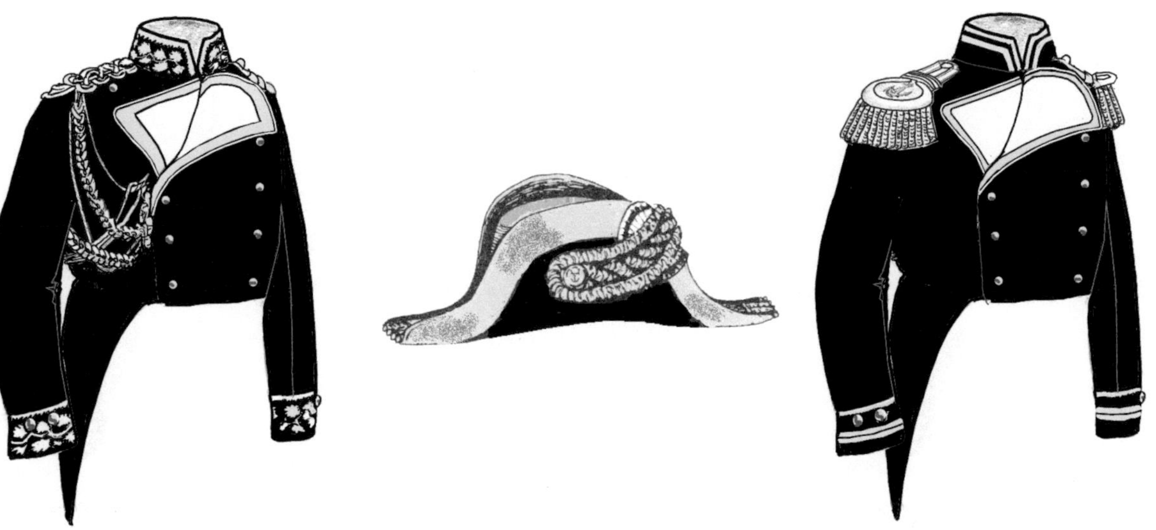

Kapitan-zur-See, three for *Korvetten-Kapitan*, three for *Lieutnants*, and one for the ensign. The white lapels had a thin gold lace edging and gold lace epaulettes with bullion fringes were worn. Each epaulette bore a silver fouled anchor. The trousers, sword and sword belt were the same as for flag officers.

Interim dress

For normal duties on both land and at sea a plain double-breasted blue frock coat was worn. For formal occasions not requiring gala dress, it was worn with the shoulder cords and aiguillettes by flag officers and epaulettes by other officers. The cocked hat was also worn. At this time there was no cuff lace worn (although an image of Prince Adalbert shows him with four rows of lace on his cuffs). A white shirt with wing collar and black tie was also worn. The trousers were plain blue. For sea duties and in port, the frock coat was mostly worn open and a plain blue peaked *mütze* with a gold lace band was also worn. The national cockade was worn on the band. A short dark-blue reefer jacket was also taken into wear for more arduous duties.

Midshipmen

Midshipmen wore a short blue waist-length double-breasted "monkey" jacket with four brass buttons down each side. It was generally worn open. There was a white loop secured by a button at the top on each side of the open collar. A blue waistcoat with six brass buttons was worn under the jacket and the white shirt with wing collar had a large black bow tie. The trousers were blue. For normal duties, the peaked mütze with gold band was worn. There was a provision for them to wear a plain blue felt cocked hat for formal occasions but it does not seem to have been worn.

Warrant officers and seamen

At this time warrant officers of the seagoing branch were known as *Deck Offiziere* to distinguish them from those of the dockyard branch. The warrant officer ranks were *Bootsmann* (boatswain/bosun) and *Stuermann* (coxswain). Petty officer (*Feldwebel*) ranks were *Obermaate* and *Maate.* As the Prussian navy and later Imperial Navy grew the rank structure expanded dramatically. By 1914 there were over forty rank levels for warrant and petty officers. Seamen ranks were *Obermatrose* and *Matrose.*

Warrant officers wore the same frock coat and jacket as officers with a brass or bullion fouled-anchor badge on the collar tabs. The white shirt and black tie were also similar and the blue peaked *mütze* had a black band with narrow gold lace on the top edge. Petty officers and seamen wore the short-waisted open double-breasted jacket in full dress over a white shirt and black tie. There were two sets of four brass buttons on each side. Rank badges in gold bullion were worn on the left sleeve. The *Obermaate* wore the badge of a fouled anchor with royal crown above, the *Maate* a fouled anchor and the *Obermatrose* a plain anchor. The only known branch insignia in 1864 were the crossed flags for signalers and crossed cannon for gunners. For parades a black lacquered hat was worn with slightly turned up brim. The black silk band around the crown bore the legend "KÖNIGLICHE MARINE" in gold Gothic letters. The band was tied at the back and the ends hung down. The trousers were blue. For undress and seagoing duty a dark-blue or white shirt was worn with large dark-blue square-ended naval collar. A soft cap with a black band carrying the same legend as the full dress hat was also worn. After the 1870 war the black hat was discontinued and a stiffer dark blue naval mütze with gold-lettered black silk tally was adopted. In addition, the collar was changed to medium-blue edged with three white stripes and was worn in all orders of dress including over the jacket in full dress.

Petty Officers' rank badges, above maate, and below obermatrose.

The See Battalion

When the *Marinier Korps* was raised in 1850 it consisted of two companies. On 13 May 1852 it was renamed the *See Battalion* and a third artillery company was added with a fourth company joining in 1859. The uniforms closely followed the style of the infantry in the Prussian army. It should be noted that as with the navy itself, there is little in the way of formal regulation governing the uniforms of the See Battalion at this time and almost no photographic evidence, so some speculation has been applied here.

Headdress

Until 1862 a *pickelhaube* with artillery-pattern ball finial was worn. The helmet plate was the standard Prussian eagle with a fouled anchor below. It was replaced by a French-style shako of dark-blue felt with leather band and peak. The front of the shako bore a bronze fouled anchor with a scroll across the middle with the motto "*Mit Gott für König und Vaterland*". It had a leather chinstrap. Officers'

See Battalion shako device.

shakos had gilt chin-scales and the plate was a gilt eagle with spread wings above a fouled anchor. This plate was adopted in brass by other ranks in 1875. There was no plume worn with this headdress.

Uniform

The tunic was dark blue with self-coloured collar and Brandenburg cuffs. The top and front of the collar and the tunic front were piped white. There was no piping on the cuffs or tunic flaps at the rear. There were eight tombak buttons down the front, three on the cuff flaps, three on each skirt flap and one on each shoulder strap. The shoulder straps were white decorated with a yellow fouled anchor. The artillery company had crossed cannon barrels instead. The trousers were dark blue with white piping down the side seams. NCO rank insignia was the same as in the army.

Officers' tunics and trousers were the same but of finer quality cloth. There were gold lace litzen on the collars and the cuff flaps were piped white on three sides. The epaulettes were white edged in gold lace with white straps and gilt crescents. The underlay was also white and the fouled anchor in gilt was worn. The blue trousers had white piping. The silver and black waist sash was the same as in the army as was the sword and sword belt. The naval sword was adopted by See Battalion officers in the 1870s.

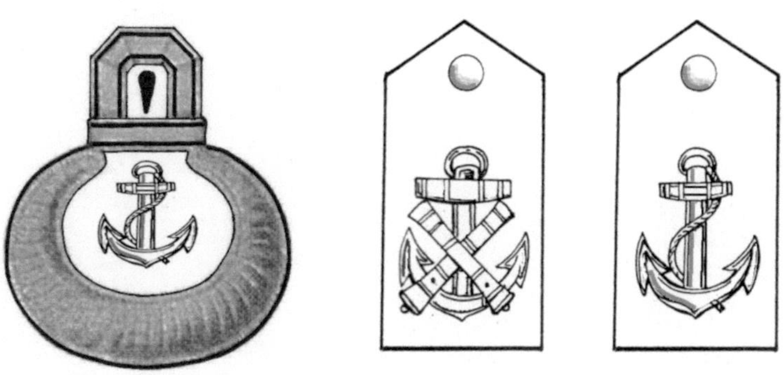

From left: epaulette for lieutenant of Seebattalion; shoulder strap for Seebattalion Artillery Company; shoulder strap for Regular Seebattalion Companies.

Undress

The mütze was dark blue and from 1860 was piped white on the crown and around the top edge of the band. The national cockade was on the front of the band. For fatigue duties, other ranks wore the coarse white jacket and trousers. Greatcoats were grey as in the army. Regulations dating from 1871 describe collar patches as dark blue with white edging. The dark-blue shoulder straps also had white piping and bore the same insignia as the tunic shoulder straps. It is not known if these insignia were in use during the period 1864–66.

Officers and senior NCOs had a stiffer cap with a peak. They wore the same undress uniforms as in the army. The dark-blue uberröck apparently had no piping at this time.

Weapons and equipment

In 1864 the See Battalion carried the rifled musket. It is possible that the needle gun was issued before 1866 but records are unclear. The belts, valise and side-arms were the same as in the army and the troddel colours were the same as for the first four companies of an infantry battalion. The artillery company's sidearm was the artillery pattern.

CHAPTER EIGHTEEN

Uniform Plate Commentary

Plate 1

(a) General of Infantry, King William I of Prussia, 1865
(b) Major, Aide-de-Camp to a Royal Prince, 1865

The youngest son of Frederick William III and Queen Louise, William was born on 22 March 1797. Although he was a sickly child, he was destined for a military career and was commissioned at the age of sixteen. He was with the army at Leipzig and when it entered Paris in 1814 and again in 1815, after winning the Iron Cross during the Hundred Days campaign. His rise in the army was meteoric; colonel at 20, major-general at 21 and commanding a division at 23. By the time he was a lieutenant general he was commanding the Prussian Guard Corps. He immersed himself in the military sciences and theory of the times and became an authority on the armies of Europe. When his elder brother, Frederick William IV, succeeded his father in 1840, William became heir to the throne. During the revolutions of 1848 he fled to London at his brother's request, but returned to lead the army in the suppression of the Baden revolt in 1849. When Frederick William IV became insane he assumed the regency in October 1858 and upon his brother's death in 1861, he became king.

A true "soldier" king, he threw himself into the reorganization of the army, appointing General von Roon to the task. He was politically astute enough to recognize Bismarck's talents and appointed him minister-president in 1862. His unshakeable sense of honour was to act as a foil to some of Bismarck's more excessive ideas in the early days, especially over Schleswig-Holstein. He was an intense believer in the authority of the crown and when the prospect of war with Austria loomed, he vested his government with the power to overcome all political opposition. Although the strategy and execution of the war was left to Von Moltke and the Prussian General Staff, he was at the head of his army when battle was joined at Königgrätz on 3 July 1866.

He is shown here in the mounted parade uniform of a general of infantry. Although he had reached the rank of field marshal in 1854, there was no specific uniform for this appointment higher than that of general. Generals did not wear the bullion epaulettes with this uniform but with all other orders of dress not worn in the field. He wears the sash of a knight of the Red eagle, plus many other orders and medals befitting his rank. At the battle of Königgrätz he wore his helmet without plume and his interim tunic underneath his dark-blue greatcoat, showing the poppy-red lapels.

The dismounted officer is an adjutant or aide-de-camp to a royal prince. The use of the title "adjutant" was widely used for many kinds of staff officers with a variety of responsibilities. This officer would have been the personal assistant to one of the royal princes serving with the army. Apart from some of the duties of private secretary, they were obliged to accompany their charges on campaign and had the authority to transmit their orders without hindrance. The full-dress tunic was somewhat unusual as it had the pointed, or "Polish" cuffs only worn by uhlans and the mounted Field Gendarmerie. He wears medals that include service in both Schleswig wars and the War Merit award.

Plate 2

(a) Flügeladjutant 1865

(b) Sergeant, Leibgendarmerie 1865

(c) Feldwebel, Schloß-Garde-Kompanie

By 1863, the Prussian General Staff system was the most developed in the world. The refinements added by von Roon and von Moltke firmly established Prussia as the most efficient military in Europe. Central to Prussian military doctrine was the study of *future* wars and planning and preparation for such conflicts were the main objectives of the General Staff.

However, the responsibilities of the entire staff structure of the Army were divided into three groups; The adjutants (Adjutuntur), the War Ministry (Kreigsministerium) and the General Staff (Generalstab) itself. War Ministry officials handled the day-to-day needs of the army such as supply, transport, ordnance and such. Flügeladutants (literally, wing-aides) were aides-de-camps on the staff at brigade or corps level. The approximate equivalent in the British Army was brigade-major.

This flügeladjutant ranks as a general and would have been on the staff of an army corps. He wears the same uniform as a general-á-la-suite except that a white horsehair plume would have been worn in parade dress instead of a feather plume and silver field and cipher on his epaulettes. His sword was also that of the line infantry.

The Leibgendarmerie was formed in 1820 as a personal escort to the king and consisted entirely of trusted NCOs. By 1860 it consisted of about thirty men under a senior NCO and served as both escort and couriers for the king and his suite. A royal decree of 1860 established the rank of commander of the escort who had gold instead of cloth lace on collar and cuffs. The uniform of the corps was almost the same as that for the cavalry staff corps (Stabswachen) attached to the Guards, the only difference being the Guard-star device on the helmet as worn by the Guard Jäger and Schutzen and the white plume.

The Palace Guard Company (Schloß-Garde-Kompanie) was raised in 1829 as the Guard-NCO-Company (Garde-unterofficier-companie) to provide ceremonial guards for the royal palaces and castles. It consisted of retired NCOs of good character and long service. It was renamed "Schloß-Garde-Kompanie" in 1861 with an establishment of one senior NCO ranking as feldwebel-lieutenant, two ranking as feldwebel-sergeants and five as feldwebel-unteroffizier with 62 NCOs.

This feldwebel-sergeant wears the full dress with the Grenadier cap, identical to that worn by the Grenadier battalions of the 1st Foot Guards except in silver instead of brass. He has the distinctive lace strips across his chest and lower skirts of the tunic and the old-fashioned cross-belts. The black ammunition pouch worn on the right hip had a Guard Star on the flap in silver. The trousers were fashioned as gaiters below the calf with white cloth buttons on the side and integral spats over the top of the black leather boots.

Plate 3

(a) Kaiser-Alexander-Garde-Grenadier-Regiment No. 1. Drummer, parade dress
(b) 1st Garde-Regiment zu Fuß. Grenadier, parade dress
(c) 4th Garde-Regiment zu Fuß. Captain, parade dress

In 1864 the infantry of the Prussian Guard Corps consisted of four Foot Guard regiments, a Guard Fusilier regiment, four Guard Grenadier regiments, a Guard Jäger and a Guard Rifle battalion and the infantry training battalion attached to the Guard corps for administrative purposes.

The Kaiser-Alexander-Garde-Grenadier-Regiment, raised in 1814, was the senior Grenadier regiment. It was in 3rd Guards brigade, 2nd Division of the crown prince's Second Army. After the short fight at Soor, they formed the advanced guard of their division arriving on the field of Königgrätz during the afternoon of 3 July. They supported the spearhead of the 1st Guard division in their assault on Horonowes and the bloody fighting around Chlum.

The drummer here is in summer parade dress with the red horsehair plume in his helmet and the white laced shoulder wings (Schwabelnaste, literally, "swallow's nests") worn by all drummers. The small white fringe on the wings was only worn by drummers in the Guard Corps.

The 1st Garde-Regiment zu Fuß was raised in 1688 and had its origins in the 6th and 15th Guard regiments of Frederick the Great's time. They were the spearhead of the Second Army enduring heavy losses as they fought their way up the heights of Chlum against the Austrian artillery. In the fight to secure the village of Rosberitz, the fourth company lost all but one of their officers.

The guardsman shown is wearing the unique uniform worn only for parades. The mitre cap (Grenadier mütze) was taken into use in 1824 (they were not a gift of the Russian tsar as legend has it). They were only worn by the 1st Battalion and a smaller version with minor differences in ornamentation, was worn by the Fusilier battalion from 1842. This headdress was supposed to be worn only with white trousers. For regular wear the Pickelhaube with silver guard eagle was worn as it was for the battle of Königgrätz.

The 4th Foot Guards were raised in 1860 and were part of the Army of the Maine in 1866 forming the right wing at Langensalza. The officer shown is in parade dress, his rank indicated by the half-moon epaulettes on each shoulder. He carries the officer's sword which fitted through a slot in his tunic skirt as it was supported on a belt under the tunic.

Plate 4

(a) 6th Rhenish Infantry Regiment No. 65. Regimentstambour

(b) 1st Garde-Jäger Battalion. 1st Lieutenant, überrock

(c) Princess Elizabeth Garde-Grenadier-Regiment No. 3. Field Officer, service dress

The Garde-Jäger Battalion, raised in 1744, was the senior light infantry regiment in Prussia and had been in continuous service since the War of Austrian Succession. It had served in Denmark during the Second Schleswig War of 1864 and was present at the storming of Alsen. During the Königgrätz campaign, it provided gallant service at Soor and in the desperate fighting around Chlum.

The central figure is a lieutenant of Garde-Jägers wearing the überrock or frock so popular with officers in undress. There was no mess dress as in the British Army so officers wore this for informal occasions. The basic colour is black with the red collar piped dark green. He wears his regimental undress cap (mütze) with peak in green with red band and piping.

The two other figures are from regiments raised during the army reorganization of 1860. The officer of the Princess Elizabeth Garde-Grenadier-Regiment No. 3 is a senior major in "Dienstanzug" or service dress meaning his day-to-day uniform without the sash. Among his medals is the Order of the Red Eagle third class and one for service with his regiment in Denmark in 1864. In 1866 one battalion served at Soor and Königgrätz with the 4th (Reserve) Guards Brigade of II Army Corps. The bulk of the regiment was in the Reserve Corps of the Army of The Maine.

The regimentstambour (drum major) of Infantry Regiment No. 65 is the impressive figure typical of his breed. Usually tall and of long service, in this case indicated by the medal on his chest, the drum major of the regiment was a distinguished individual. Unlike his peers in other armies like the British, Austrian or French, he wore no decorative baldric or shoulder sash. His only distinctions were the gold-laced swallow's nests with the staff musician's fringe, his NCO lace on collar and cuffs, his NCO sword with knot and his staff, or mace. Sometimes the mace was presented by some important personage and was more decorative, but in such a young regiment, the head on this was a plain brass one from the quartermaster's department.

Plate 5

(a) 2nd Silesian Jäger Battalion No. 5. Gefreiter, marching order
(b) 1st East Prussian Grenadier Regiment No. 1. Feldwebel
(c) 2nd West Prussian Grenadier Regiment No. 7. Grenadier, winter parade dress

The three regiments shown here were amongst the oldest in the Prussian infantry. The first twelve regiments in the order of precedence were grenadier regiments distinguished by special heraldic plates on the breasts of their helmet eagles and black plumes.

The feldwebel in the centre is from the most senior regiment from East Prussia raised in 1655. His rank is indicated by the lace on collar and cuffs with the buttons on either side of the collar. The officer's sword and knot is a further mark of his position. This regiment wore a special helmet plate which had a scroll with the date "1619" above the eagle. This commemorated their descent from one of the old Brandenburg regiments of the Thirty Years War. His white shoulder straps with the red number "1" along with the piping on his cuff patches place this unit in I Army Corps. His importance as the most senior non-commissioned rank in his battalion carried a unique mark of office in the form of a little black book tucked into his tunic beneath the first two buttons. The crimes and misdemeanours it carried can only be imagined and it would remain a "badge" of this office until modern times. He would affectionately become known as "Der Speiss" (daddy). His cuff patches have the first-class marksman's lace on the buttons and he wears the good conduct and long service medals. In 1866 the 1st Grenadiers fought in the advance guard at Trautenau and although gallantly taking the town, the miscalculations of their corps commander, von Bonin, allowed the Austrians to force them back out causing the only reverse of the whole campaign. Later, at Königgrätz they were in support of the Guards in the attack on Horonowes and Chlum.

The grenadier on his left is from the 7th Regiment (2nd West Prussian) formed in 1797 and wears his black plume as authorized for Winter Parade Order. His yellow shoulder straps and white cuff piping are from V Army Corps. The monogram on the shoulder strap is for Wilhelm I. The back view clearly shows his valise and canteen along with the sword at his belt with the company knot (troddel) on the hilt showing him to be in the 7th Company of the 2nd Battalion of the regiment. The side-arm knots were a much treasured distinction in the Prussian army and the system would survive through World War II. In the Prussian army at this time, the bayonet remained fixed to the rifle as there was no bayonet frog. The regiment was with Steinmetz' V Corps in the 1866 campaign and fought valiantly at Nachod, Skalitz and Königgrätz.

Jäger Battalion No. 5 was raised in Silesia in 1808 and distinguished itself in the Wars of Liberation. The corporal (gefreiter) shown here in about 1864 and is in winter parade order as he wears the black plume in his shako. This headdress replaced the helmet in 1854 and was shortened in height in 1860. Along with battalions 1, 2 and 6 it carries the FWR monogram on the front in brass. In 1865, all battalions were ordered to wear the heraldic eagle on the shako with bandeau as worn on the pickelhaube. The holly-green tunic with red collar patch and Swedish cuffs was common to all eight Jäger battalions. His rank is indicated by the button worn on either side of his collar. He wears the third-class marksman's lace on his sleeve above the cuff. A peculiar distinction of all the Jägers was the badger's head worn on the flap of the valise (see Plate 20). This battalion fought alongside the 7th Grenadiers in Steinmetz' V Corps during the 1866 campaign.

Plate 6

(a) Brandenburg Cuirassier Regiment, Tsar Nicholas I of Russia No. 6. Cuirassier
(b) Gardes du Corps. Guardsman, gala dress

There were ten Cuirassier heavy cavalry regiments in the Prussian Army at this time, two of which were in the guard. No new regiments had been raised since 1815.

The Gardes du Corps, raised in 1740, formed the official personal escort for the sovereign on important state and gala occasions (it is interesting to note that the Gardes du Corps was not designated to provide an escort for the king on campaign). In 1841, they were given the honour of providing the guard at royal palaces and residences for all official occasions. A guardsman performing this duty is shown here. Instead of the usual spike on his helmet, there is a brass-crowned Prussian eagle with wings spread. Cuirassier regiments wore no plumes except for the band and trumpeters which was of red horsehair. Replacing the cuirass is a red cloth "supraveste" with the guard star embroidered on the front. He wears the tight white kersey breeches and the long-jacked leather Brandenburg boots with spurs. His weapon is the 1852 heavy cavalry "Pallasch". In the 1866 campaign they were in the 1st Heavy Cavalry Brigade of the Guard Cavalry Reserve along with the Guard Cuirassier Regiment. They were mobilized on 7 May, joining II Army Corps on 16 June at Cottbus. They made their way to Glatz in Saxony by train and from thenceforth marched with their corps for the rest of the campaign. It was an arduous march according to the regimental history but they reached Königgrätz on 3 July relatively intact. Whilst forming a supporting manouvre before Chlum, they were shelled by the Austrian artillery and lost three men and four horses. The rest of the campaign was spent on garrison detachments and pursuit of the Austrians. There were also several deaths from cholera. The regimental history also paid tribute to the service of the horses, commenting on their hardiness and the fact that "a large quantity of horseshoes were used."

The mounted NCO of the Brandenburg Cuirassier Regiment is in parade dress. The regiment had its origins in an old corps raised in 1691 and also had the privilege of an honourary *Chef* in the person of the tsar of Russia whose monogram they wore on the shoulder straps. The facings were of Russian blue and among other distinctions that differed from the remainder of the Line Cuirassier regiments were the helmet and cuirass in brass instead of steel and the shabracque of red cloth instead of facing colour. The regiment was brigaded with the 7th Cuirassiers in the 2nd Heavy Cavalry Brigade of Major-General von Alvensleben's 1st Cavalry Division. At the start of the battle on 3 July, thc 1st Cavalry Division was transferred to support the Army of the Elbe, led by Herwarth von Bittenfeld, later angering Prince Frederick Charles who was unaware of the move. Their relative inactivity during the remainder of the battle justified his dismay.

Plate 7

(a) Neumärk Dragoon Regiment No. 3. Captain, überrock
(b) Pommeranian Cuirassier Regiment No 2. Officer, court dress
(c) Magdeburg Cuirassier Regiment No. 7. Gefreiter, waffenrock

Cuirassiers were the most fashionable regiments and attracted officers from the most aristocratic and prominent families. In the long era of peace prior to the 1860s, garrison life could be quite tedious and only relieved by balls and levées. Officers of Cuirassier regiments provided themselves with an array of uniforms unmatched by other arms. Shown here is a subaltern of the 2nd Queen's Cuirassiers, a historic regiment with a long pedigree including honours won at Hohenfriedburg in 1745, a distinction etched on a scroll on their helmet eagles. He is in court dress reserved for the most exclusive levées in Berlin or Potsdam. His substantially laced Koller is worn without the heavy cuirass and his elegant white trousers helped him cut quite a figure. The helmet was worn, or at least carried, on these occasions. His sword is the officer's pallasch still carried for all occasions. In later years cuirassiers would adopt the lighter cavalry dress sword for these functions. At Königgrätz the 2nd Cuirassiers were brigaded with the 9th Uhlans in von der Golze's 3rd Heavy Cavalry Brigade in reserve of the 4th

Infantry Division. As part of Prince Frederick Charles' First Army, they were among the first cavalry to cross the Bistritz and although suffering some casualties from Austrian artillery fire, partook in no major engagements.

The NCO of the 7th Magdeburg represents the other side of garrison life, which for a cavalry regiment meant constant attention to the horses. He is shown here in his working dress mütze and coat of coarse blue wool. Up until this time it was only meant to have a collar in facing colour but, beginning with the Garde du Corps it would develop into a troopers version of the officer's blue waffenrock with the regimental lace on collar and cuffs. Here it is shown at the time of the Schleswig War when photographs show some regimental liberties were being taken and plain yellow cuffs have appeared. Along with a cavalry bridle he is carrying the M1851 Cavalry percussion pistol used by all cuirassiers at this time. The 7th Regiment along with the 6th, in the 3rd Brigade of the 1st Cavalry Division saw little action at Königgrätz after their transfer to the Army of the Elbe.

The officer of the Neumärk Dragoons is wearing the überrock with helmet suggesting he was on some official duty at the garrison. The rose facings and piping were also worn on his trousers and epaulette underlay which was the custom in units with this colour facing. The Neumärk Dragoons had distinguished themselves during the Napoleonic Wars and were a renowned regiment in the Prussian Army. At Königgrätz, as part of the 2nd Cavalry Division, they were heavily engaged in the final cavalry battle at the end of the day which involved nearly 40 Austrian squadrons and 31 Prussian. They suffered badly at the hands of the Austrian cuirassiers but rallied with the help of the 4th Uhlans by which time the battle was won and the Austrians in general retreat.

Plate 8

(a) 2nd Guard Dragoon Regiment. Trumpeter, parade dress
(b) Rhenish Cuirassier Regiment No. 8. Officer, überrock
(c) 2nd Silesian Dragoon Regiment No. 8. Officer, levée dress

The 2nd Guard Dragoons had been formed in 1860 and adopted the same uniform as their senior regiment with gold rather than silver buttons and lace. This trumpeter is in parade dress with his red plume attached and as a Guard trumpeter, his swallow's nests have a short gold fringe. The trumpet that is slung over his right shoulder is the 1817 pattern which would survive until 1918 and the black and white trumpet cords were the same for all regiments. Königgrätz was to be their baptism of fire and the regiment was in the 2nd Light Cavalry brigade of the 2nd Cavalry division. They took part in the Prussian advance at Stresetitz in the afternoon and the pursuit that followed.

The officer of the Rhenish Cuirassiers is wearing the überrock with his undress cap. Unusually, although his regimental facings were green, the collar and cuff piping on this garment were white. This distinguished regiment, raised in 1815 as the 8th Dragoons, became Cuirassiers in 1819. They served in the First Schleswig War of 1848 and the suppression of the uprising in Baden the following year. At Königgrätz they were in the reserve cavalry of the 15th Division of the Elbe and were sorely plagued by the Austrian artillery at Problus, suffering many casualties.

The officer of the 2nd Silesian Dragoons is in levée dress, indicated by his cornflower-blue trousers with triple stripes. He is also the adjutant and therefore wears the silver sash with black stripes over his left shoulder and does not wear the pouch belt. Originally raised as the 7th Dragoon Regiment in May 1860 they "swapped" numbers with the 8th Regiment by a cabinet order of 5 July the same year, taking their facings with them! In 1866 they were part of von Wichman's Combined Cavalry Brigade in the crown prince's Second Army. They did some hard service in Bohemia, seeing action at Nachod and Skalitz before joining with general advance of the afternoon of 3 July.

Plate 9

(a) Pomeranian Hussar Regiment (Blücher Hussars) No. 5. Hussar, parade dress
(b) 1st Life Hussar Regiment No. 1. Officer, parade dress

In 1741 Frederick the Great raised two hussar squadrons with the name "Regiment of Black Hussars". This was the fifth hussar regiment he had raised and it fought in the War of Austrian Succession (1744–45) and the Seven Years War (1756–63), in which it distinguished itself at Zorndorf. It was the only Hussar regiment that survived the catastrophe of 1806 complete. In 1808 it was divided into two regiments; the 1st and 2nd Life Hussars (Leib-Husaren). The 1st fought at the great battle of Leipzig in 1813 and later entered Paris with the allied army. By 1817 the regiment was garrisoned in Danzig (now Gdansk in Poland) and was there when awarded this title in 1861.

The black uniform and the famous death's head badge worn by this and its sister regiment, 2 Leib-Husaren-Regiment No. 2, were given to the regiment in remembrance of Frederick William I and legend has it that the cloth used in the first uniforms was from his funeral drapes, which had hung in the Great Hall at Potsdam Palace. To distinguish the first regiment from the second, the first had red facings and the second white. The officer shown here is in mounted parade order. Officers and trumpeters of this regiment were known to ride white or grey horses. During the Seven Weeks War in 1866, the regiment was with Bonin's ill-fated I Corps at Trautenau and later in the day with von Clausewitz's 2nd Division at Königgrätz as it supported the advance of the Guards.

The 5th Hussar Regiment was raised as the 8th Hussars to serve in the Seven Years War and did so with gallantry at Zorndorf (1758) and later that year at Hochkirk. After the defeat at Jena and Auerstadt in 1806, the regiment surrendered at Ratklau. Reformed as the 5th Regiment in 1808, it served at Leipzig and Waterloo. When Prince Blücher commanded the regiment in 1794, it later took his name. In 1866 the title was restored.

The hussar shown here is in parade dress. The attila he wears is of a colour known as crab red and has been depicted in various shades of red. It is known that the officer's shade was considerably lighter than the men's. A curious feature of the officer's attila was the fringe in silver lace that framed the frogging on the front. At Königgrätz in 1866 the regiment was in the advanced guard of Prince Frederick Charles' First Army and was one of the first units across the Bistritz.

Plate 10

(a) 1 Garde-Uhlan-Regiment. Officer, levée dress
(b) Magdeburg Hussar Regiment No. 10. Officer, levée dress

At the beginning of the War of Liberation in 1813, a volunteer cavalry regiment named the Elbe Hussars was raised. As the Prussian Army became more organized it was taken into its service in 1814 as the 10th Hussars. It fought with the army at Waterloo and later entered Paris. It served on the French borders in 1830 and 1848 to contain the unrest in that country. The officer shown here is in the special gala or levée dress worn by hussars. The heavily laced tight pantaloons were usually in the bright colours of the busby bag or facings, in this case a dark pink known as pompadour red. Of interest too is his sabretache, which in other regiments would have been of the cloth of the facings or attila, but in this case a light blue in memory of the colours of the Elbe Hussars. In 1866 they fought in Major-General Fransecky's 7th Division of the First Army in Bohemia and later at Königgrätz where they must have watched with horror, unable to assist, as his infantry was decimated in the Swiepwald.

In 1745 Frederick the Great added a troop of "Bosniaks", Albanian cavalry armed with the lance, and attached them to the Black Hussars (see Plate 9). Later, in 1799 it was converted to the Regiment Towarczys as an Uhlan regiment based on the Polish Lancers. Later this unit would become the 1st West Prussian Uhlan Regiment from which all the uhlans would be modelled.

The 1st Guard Uhlans began as Landwehr cavalry in 1817. In 1821 the regiment was divided into two and re-designated as the 1st and 2nd Guard Landwehr Cavalry and both confirmed as Uhlans by March of 1826. By a High Cabinet Order of 2 October 1851, the regiment received its final title of "1 Guard Uhlan Regiment" which it retained until 1918. From September 1866 it was garrisoned in Potsdam.

The officer shown here, like his fellow hussar officer, is dressed for a levée. His dress blue trousers have the triple stripe in white with a red centre, which with his white plastron edged red was unique to this regiment. It was part of Alvensleben's Reserve Cavalry Corps at Königgrätz which unfortunately took little part in the battle.

Plate 11

(a) 1st Pomeranian Uhlan Regiment No. 4. Uhlan, parade dress
(b) 2nd Brandenburg Uhlan Regiment No. 11. Major, parade dress

Uhlan Regiment No. 4 came into being in March 1815 by combining squadrons from the West Prussian Uhlans, the East Prussian National Cavalry and the Pomeranian National Cavalry. It saw no action in the final months of the Napoleonic Wars and spent the next fifteen years garrisoned in various locations all over Prussia including Trier, Mühlberg and the Saxon duchies. In 1830 the regiment could be found on patrol along the Polish border and in 1848 on garrison duty in Brandenburg and Pomerania. They received this title in 1861.

The uhlan is shown here in parade dress. On service, his plastron would have been removed and an oilskin cover fitted over his tschapka. His lance pennant is white over black. At this time, NCOs of Uhlan regiments did not carry lances.

At Königgrätz, the regiment was in the advanced guard of Lieutenant-General von Bittenfeld's 4th Division. They were heavily engaged throughout the day capturing Sadowa and Mokrowous, taking much punishment as they did so.

By a high cabinet order of 4 July 1860 squadrons from the 6th and 7th Cuirassiers and the 3rd and 6th Uhlans, which since May had formed the cadre for a "3rd Combined Uhlan Regiment", were officially renamed 2 Brandenburg-Uhlan-Regiment No. 11.

The field officer of the regiment wears his full dress uniform for mounted parades. The last four numbered regiments of uhlans departed from the red facings with regimental colours on tschapka tops and epaulette fields worn by the other eight. Instead, they adopted individual facing colours for the entire uniform.

The 11th saw action early in its career in the assaults on Düppel and Alsen during the Second Schleswig War of 1864. At Königgrätz in 1866, they were involved in the final cavalry action at Stresetitz.

Plate 12

(a) Lower Silesian Artillery Brigade No. 5. Gefreiter, parade dress
(b) Garde Pioneer Battalion. Pioneer
(c) Pomeranian Train Battalion No. 2. Conductor

Each of the nine army corps had an artillery brigade, a pioneer battalion and a train battalion as part of its overall organization. The V Army Corps comprised the 9th and 10th divisions and formed the command of General von Steinmetz in the Bohemian campaign. The traffic jams in the mountains had caused the artillery brigade to come late to the battle of Skalitz where they found that the infantry had done most of the work. They would contribute decisively to the victory at Nachod, however. The gefreiter of the 5th Artillery Brigade wears the pickelhaube with the distinctive ball instead of spike. As a foot battery gunner, his black cuffs have a blue three-buttoned flap. He stands at ease armed with the standard artilleryman's side-arm. Foot gunners were not issued with firearms. The Guard pioneer is dressed identically to other pioneer battalions save for the white litzen on collar and cuffs and the white-metal Guard eagle on his pickelhaube. They provided valuable service in the Guard Corps during the Bohemian campaign.

The complicated logistics required of mid-nineteenth-century armies prompted the formation of a permanent train corps responsible for supply, transport, camp preparation and field bakeries. They were uniformed in the same manner as the rest of the Prussian army. The tunic facings reprised the light blue colour used by the train units of the Napoleonic Wars. Although the officers wore the pickelhaube, the other ranks wore the jäger shako. The conductor was the senior NCO in the battalion. The 2nd Battalion formed the supply train for the II Pomeranian Corps of First Army.

Plate 13

(a) Paymasters Department. Zahlmeister (paymaster) 1st Class, service dress
(b) Garnisonsvervaltung (Garrison Dept). Inspektor (inspector), überrock
(c) Ordnance Department. Proviantmeister (chief quartermaster), service dress

By the middle of the nineteenth century, the rise of mass armies had forced the creation of specific administrative services. The movement and storage of supplies for campaigns involving huge numbers of men and horses could no longer be entrusted to purely civilian contractors. In Prussia the growth of departments on a purely military basis had been steady since the early 1840s. By 1864, the separate administrative departments of the army numbered eighteen, including the medical and veterinary personnel. Despite the militarization of these ancillary services, the officers and men were classed as civilians and most positions lacked the distinction of a military rank. It is interesting to note that in Prussia, and later Germany, the civil status of the "Beamten" or military officials would always be distinct from the officers of combat units, never changing until after World War II.

Officials wore uniforms just as elegant as those of their combat counterparts. They tended to be piped in different colours than faced. The main distinction of the combat officer was the silver and black sash, which was not worn by officials. The paymaster, on the left, is wearing full dress. His sword, not seen, was the officer's degen with a silver and black sword knot. In addition to handling the soldiers pay, the zahlmeister's department dealt with the general finances of army administration from corps down to regiment. The officer in the überrock and cap is an inspector from the department that dealt with barracks and garrisons, ensuring that they were up to regulation standards. His cap bears a small eagle in brass above the cockade; a distinction of all the officers in the ancillary departments. The seated officer is a quartermaster whose job, as in any army, was to keep the troops supplied with clothing and equipment. He is wearing his full dress tunic and trousers.

The administrative personnel of the army were the first to operate in a major campaign that relied so heavily on railway transport. Although much vaunted in some accounts of the war, there were many difficulties. Trains broke down, were rerouted or never left their destinations. Supplies arrived where there was no one to unload or the wrong supplies ended up in the wrong places. The biggest problem was food, and many units went hungry in the field as fresh loaves of bread rotted in remote railway sidings in the middle of nowhere.

Plate 14

Second Schleswig War, 1864

(a) 7th Brandenburg Infantry Regiment. No. 60. Officer
(b) 6th Westphalian Infantry Regiment. No. 55. Private
(c) 4th Brandenburg Infantry Regiment. No. 24. Private

The war of 1864 in Schleswig was the first major campaign undertaken by the Prussian Army since the Napoleonic Wars. The action against the Danes and the suppression of the Saxon and Baden revolts in 1848 had involved little combat and were brief in duration.

This war began in winter and despite the relatively efficient supply of food and ordnance, the clothing situation left something to be desired. The issue greatcoat provided insufficient warmth for the average soldier exposed to the elements. Special hoods for the greatcoats were available and some arrived in time to be worn. But soldiers had to supply themselves with scarves, sweaters and other personal items to keep warm. Photographs and anecdotal accounts suggest that many soldiers, especially those on picket duty at night, found sheepskin coats to wear (similar to the "poshteen" worn by British troops on the Northwest Frontier of India). The condition that most impressed officers was the effect of deep snow, mud and wet. The trousers and footwear of the infantryman was no protection from this slushy mess. The men were forced to tuck their trousers into their socks, but the lace-up boots still let the wet in. After the war, foot soldiers were issued with knee-high jackboots, a uniform article that was to become as enduring a symbol of the Prussian/German soldier as the spiked helmet.

The three soldiers here were all involved in the assault on the fortress of Düppel on 18 April. The private of the 24th is shown as he would have looked earlier on in the campaign. His helmet carries a sprig of fir as an unofficial field sign (Feldzeichen). All invading troops in the campaign, including the Austrians, wore the white armband on the left arm. He also wears a homemade balaclava under his helmet; the official issue hood can be seen hanging on the hilt of his sidearm. In the battle, several companies of his regiment, part of the 12th Brigade of Major-General von Roder assaulted the Vth redoubt with heavy casualties.

The Westphalian infantryman of the 55th Regiment appears as he might have done at the siege. His greatcoat is worn en banderole around his valise, an item he would probably have left in his lines during the actual assault. Note the ubiquitous meerschaum pipe, an article without which most Prussian soldiers would have been unable to function. The 55th along with the 53rd, both from Lieutenant-General Winzingerode's 13th Division, stormed the IVth redoubt alongside the Brandenburgers, overwhelming it in 15 minutes according to records.

The officer of the 60th Regiment, part of the 11th Brigade of the 6th Division, is wearing an officer's greatcoat with, sensibly, the peakless cap of the lower ranks. His scarf is a regulation item. The wearing of beards was not unusual by soldiers on campaign. In fact, as photographs show, the "hirsute" look was predominant in all armies of the world at this time. As well as Düppel, the 60th also distinguished themselves in the seaborne invasion of the island of Alsen in June.

Plate 15

Second Schleswig War, 1864

(a) Brandenburg Pioneer Battalion No. 3. Pioneer
(b) Westphalian Dragoon Regiment No. 7. Dragoon
(c) Westphalian Artillery Brigade No. 7. Horse Battery. Sergeant

This plate again shows how troops adapted to the campaign conditions of a winter war. The dragoon from the 7th Regiment is in greatcoat and forage cap. This regiment was used mainly in reconnaissance tasks and as a reserve should there be a set-piece battle. In the war of 1866 the regiment served as the 15th Divisional cavalry under von Canstein in the Army of the Elbe. The sergeant of the Westphalian horse battery wears heavy thigh boots possibly acquired personally, but very useful in the siegeworks opposite the redoubts at Düppel. This unit formed the reserve artillery of the 1st Corps. The Brandenburg pioneer wears his trousers tucked into his socks like his infantry counterparts. He, like all other pioneers, carries an outdated rifled Minié carbine. This battalion acted with extreme bravery on the outset of the attack on the Düppel redoubts, blasting a path across the siegeworks to allow the infantry to pass through.

Plate 16

Second Schleswig War, 1864

(a) 1 See Battalion. Mann
(b) Marine Artillery Detachment. Gunner
(c) Königliche Marine. Leutnant Zur See
(d) Königliche Marine. Öbermaate

Despite a lengthy Baltic coastline, Prussia had made little effort to become a maritime power. By mid-century, most European navies, including those of the fledgling Kingdom of Italy were overwhelmingly larger than those of Prussia. The First Schleswig War of 1848 had exposed the inadequacy of Prussian naval forces even when operating as the Federal German Navy. Following that conflict, the expansion of the Prussian Navy became a more serious matter. Nevertheless, the onset of the Second Schleswig War found the navy still lacking in capability to confront the Danes at sea and despite a couple of skirmishes, the main naval action took place between the Danish and Austrian navies off Heligoland. In 1864 the Prussian Navy consisted of fewer than a dozen ocean-going ships, some of which were far away in foreign waters when the war began. The initial difficulty was that the Danish Navy had effectively blockaded the Prussian coast and the engagements that took place were to break the blockade; the main one being Captain Jachman's inconclusive action off Swinemünde. Although the navy had increased in size between the wars, it was given virtually no part in the campaign of 1866. Some gunboats were used in a riverine role, securing certain river port facilities in Hanover and on the Main during the campaign in the western theatre. Four years later the Franco-Prussian War saw little naval activity except the famous action between the Prussian gunboat *Meteor* and the French *Bouvet*. It would not be the Prussian but the Imperial German Navy that became the great seapower at the turn of the century; a status that would only survive until 1918.

Prussian naval uniforms were unsurprisingly similar to those of Great Britain. The officers' uniforms were almost identical in both dress and undress except for the usual differences in lace and how it was applied. The blue coatee had white lapels edged with wide gold lace as did the blue collar and cuffs, which varied according to rank. The blue trousers also had gold lace down the sides and a black, gold-laced cocked hat was worn. The leutnant zur see sitting on the capstan is wearing the undress plain frock coat with blue trousers. The peaked cap has a gold lace band with national cockade in front. The dress regulations for ordinary seamen in the Royal Navy had only been in existence since 1856, but those for the Prussian Navy had in fact been instituted earlier. The öbermaate is wearing a uniform reserved for parades or walking out. His short jacket (closed for parades) is worn open with four buttons on each side. His cuffs also have four small buttons. Regulations for rank badges are not so clear, but non-commissioned officers wore the fouled anchor in gold lace on the left sleeve, with a crown above for senior NCOs. The use of trade badges for signalling or other specialties are known to have existed but how they were worn is also not clear. His oilskin hat has a black silk band with the legend "KÖNIGLICHE MARINE" in gold on the front. In undress and for sea duty he would have worn a dark-blue jumper with wide blue collar and a soft cap with a black band and the same legend as the oilskin hat.

The See Battalion began life as the Marinier Korps in 1848 which in 1852 received its present title. It consisted of two infantry companies and an artillery company which by 1864 had become four and two respectively. The original uniform had conformed to the standard infantry pattern except that the cuffs and collar were blue and the tunic front and top of collar was piped white. The blue trousers were also piped white. The headgear was the artillery pickelhaube for all ranks, infantry or artillery, with the ball finial. In 1862 this was changed to a French-style shako bearing the Prussian eagle with outstretched wings above a fouled anchor in brass. This is the uniform worn by the sea soldier on the left. His accoutrements and side-arms are of standard infantry pattern. In 1864, the See Battalion had still not been issued with the needle gun but would receive them in 1865. The artillery NCO on his right is wearing the undress uniform with mütze piped white. His side-arm is of artillery pattern. The only distinctions between artillery and infantry were on the white shoulder straps. The infantry wore crossed anchors and the artillery crossed cannon barrels. The see battalions would be increased and flourish as the Imperial Navy grew in size. They would see action all over the world as the empire acquired colonial possessions in the latter part of the nineteenth century. The uniform would remain largely the same except for the adoption of the Jäger shako in 1872.

Plate 17

Seven Weeks War 1866

a) Minister-President Otto von Bismarck

b) General of Infantry, Chief of Staff of the Army, Baron von Moltke

c) General of Cavalry Crown Prince Frederick Charles of Prussia

All three of the men shown here spent most of the day of battle with the King atop a small hill known as the Roskosberg, near Dub. Bismarck (centre), stayed close to Moltke (right) for most of the day. His anxiety was considerable and he watched the chief of staff closely for any sign of concern. Moltke was not very forthcoming. Upon their arrival Bismarck had asked him how much of a grip they had on the towel that was the Austrian army, apparently making their stand. Moltke's reply was characteristically non-committal. The scene depicted shows an incident that occurred about midday when Bismarck proffered his cigar case to the general and, according to Bismarck, "He examined the contents very closely, before choosing the very best cigar that was in the case. At that point, I felt sure everything would be alright". Moltke himself, who had a cold that day and clutched a red handkerchief almost continuously, would try and assure the King and his staff that all would be well. They were often not assured, even when he made his famous announcement that the battle was won. At one point, he wandered off the hill and was seen watching an ox as it grazed, oblivious to the noise of battle around it.

Bismarck, who was a huge man, made quite an impression to all assembled on the Roskosberg. He wore the undress uniform of the 7th Landwehr Cavalry regiment. As this regiment was heavy cavalry it was styled as cuirassiers and he wore such a helmet with its spike and "lobster tail" neck guard. The collar of his blue frock coat (überrock) was yellow as was the piping on the cuffs. His grey trousers were tucked into cuirassier boots. He described the horse he rode that day only as "the chestnut" in a letter to his wife. This was the uniform he would wear, sometimes with the coloured peaked mütze, throughout the war with France and on most occasions during his chancellorship. When the battle was over, he rode along the lanes and through the villages where some of the fiercest fighting had taken place. As he looked upon the heaps of dead bodies, he could not help wondering if his son, Herbert who was serving as a cornet with the 1st Dragoons, was lying there, dead or wounded. (Herbert would be wounded at the battle of Mars La Tour in 1870.) Dusk came earlier than he expected and as he rode back to Horitz he could not find where his quarters were, so in the dark he stumbled into a barn and slipped into a manure pit. After struggling out he found a colonnade in the market place, fell on some straw beside it and with a carriage seat as a pillow, pulled his greatcoat over himself and went to sleep. He was fortunately rescued early in the morning by the Grand Duke of Mecklenburg who took him to his quarters for the rest of the night.

Moltke is wearing the undress uniform of a general of infantry in all respects according to the regulations. He is sometimes depicted as wearing heavy cavalry boots like Bismarck, but this is unlikely. Neither he, the king, nor most of the senior officers, wore long boots. Underneath his greatcoat, he would have worn the undress tunic of a general officer with its plain round cuffs and collar and its uniquely distinctive buttons and buttonholes all the way down the front, including the skirts. Unlike Bismarck, Moltke stayed with the king after the battle and, nursing a fever, rode straight to his quarters in Horitz and went to bed.

On the right stands the commander of 1st Army Corps and general of Cavalry, Prince Frederick Charles. Born on 20 March 1828 he was the nephew of King Frederick William IV and his brother the future King William I. Like his cousin, the crown prince he received a formal military education and later attended the University of Bonn (he was by no means as liberal as his cousin). His military mentor was von Roon who supervised his career as it progressed. In 1848 he was on Wrangel's staff in the First Schleswig War. As a major on the General Staff he was wounded in skirmishes with the revolutionaries in Baden a year later. His promotions were swift; colonel in 1852, major-general in 1854 and lieutenant-general in 1856. As general of cavalry, he commanded I Corps in the Second Schleswig War with Denmark in 1864. He was not considered by either his peers or later historians to have been a stellar military commander but he was brave and competent. Moltke considered him too cautious as evidenced by his anxiousness to try and overwhelm the Austrians with a frontal assault. Moltke wanted him to keep his nerve and hold the Austrians in place and wait for the arrival of Second Army before a general advance. As it stood, the Austrians had held the prince's troops in place after crossing the Bistritz and the bloody battles in the Sweipwald and Holawald were testament to that. The prince would leave the Roskosberg to lead his cavalry in what was supposed to be a glorious pursuit of the retreating Austrians, but the action on the plain at Stretetitz and the Austrian Artillery put paid to that plan. As the battle came to a close he rejoined the king and staff to take up quarters in Horitz. Four years later he would put in a solid performance during the Franco-Prussian War commanding Second Army and distinguished himself at most of the major battles. He died in 1885 at the young age of 57; a much honoured and decorated soldier.

Prince Frederick Charles was colonel-in-chief of the 3rd Brandenburg Hussars, whose uniform he wore during all the wars of German unification. It is specially laced on collar and cuffs for a general of cavalry and he always wore the undress mütze when on campaign.

Plate 18

Seven Weeks War 1866

a) General of Infantry Crown Prince Frederick William of Prussia

b) General of Infantry Karl Friedrich von Steinmetz

c) Major on the General Staff

Of the entire leadership of the Prussian military establishment, the crown prince of Prussia was by far the most liberal, both politically and socially. His military career was a foregone conclusion from his birth on 18 October 1831. Like his Hohenzollern forebears he started on this course at the age of ten being commissioned into the 1st Garde-Regiment zu Fuß but he confounded his father and pleased his liberal mother, Queen Augusta, by attending, like his cousin Frederick Charles, the University of Bonn when he was eighteen. Here the liberal ideas, that would be central to his thinking for the remainder of his life, were formed. His progression through the military system was as expected for the heir to the Prussian throne and he gained substantial knowledge of the general staff system under the tutelage of Helmuth von Moltke. He was 27 when his father became king and he became the crown prince. By that time he had been married three years to Princess Victoria, elder daughter of the British queen and completely in tune with her husband's liberal thinking. Frederick would spend much time in England. In 1864, while his cousin Frederick Charles commanded I Corps, he was attached to Wrangel's staff during the war with Denmark. Here he was able to observe combat for the first time and apart from the fact that he was unhappy that Prussia had even embarked on this campaign, he was a canny judge of affairs at headquarters and despaired at Wrangel's inefficiency. He was also in a good position to act as go-between when Moltke appeared on the scene. Two years later he was appointed to command Second Army in the war against Austria with General von Blumenthal as his chief of staff. His able handling of this army during the campaign earned him a *Pour le Mérite.* He would go on to greater glory in the war with France in 1870 leading III Army and winning victories at Wissemboug, Wörth and later at Sedan. His reign as emperor was tragically cut short at ninety-nine days in June of 1888, when he died of throat cancer. Much speculation has since been focused on the course that history would have taken had he lived longer.

The crown prince is shown dressed as most observers and artists have portrayed him during the 1866 campaign. His undress general officer's tunic is simple and unpretentious. He also wears the undress peaked mütze and his trousers are tucked into high-topped boots. The order of the Black Eagle is worn at his throat. He was well known for smoking his pipe on almost every occasion and it was never far from his hand. He would often puff on it thoughtfully before rendering a decision.

Karl Friedrich von Steinmetz was a Prussian general of the old school whose actions and demeanor were very similar to those of Blücher. Born in 1796 and educated at military school, he joined the army in the immediate confusion of Prussia's break with Napoleon in 1813 and the beginning of the War of Liberation. For two years he fought at most of the great battles (he lost his elder brother at Leipzig) and was wounded several times, winning the Iron Cross in the process. After the war he progressed through the system serving as an officer in Guard regiments of both Line and Landwehr, while studying at the War Academy. By 1839, he was a major commanding a battalion and later distinguished himself in the First Schleswig War of 1848, gaining the attention of Wrangel. For his courageous conduct he was awarded a *Pour le Mérite* by Prince William himself. In 1850 he was the military governor of Cassell and served later as colonel commandant of the Berlin Cadet School. He was a major-general in 1854 and in command of a Guards brigade in 1857. Promotion to lieutenant-general in 1858 gave him command of various cavalry establishments until in 1863 he was given command of II Corps. (He almost refused this and retired when he learned that von Bonin, his junior, had been given I Corps.) Later Crown Prince Frederick William took over II Corps and Steinmetz was given V Corps as well as being elevated to general of infantry in 1864. In 1866 his brilliant victories of Nachod, and Skalitz did much to assuage von Bonin's ignominious failure at

Trautenau and certainly paved the way for Second Army's advance to the Königgrätz battlefield. His actions during the Franco-Prussian War were not so meritorious with near calamities at Spicheren and Gravelotte after which he was relieved of command and sent home. Despite this, his reputation was never sullied and the "Lion of Nachod" died in 1877. During his life he was known as an outspoken and difficult man but one who would not suffer fools. His personal habits were rigorous as he avoided all the excesses so typical of military life such as alcohol and overeating and he was always physically fit.

Steinmetz was famous for wearing his old leather cap with peaks front and rear on campaign. Formal pictures show him in his regulation peaked mütze but anecdotal evidence show that more often than not, he wore the leather cap. He is shown here in the waffenrocke of the 37th Fusilier Regiment of which he was "chef" and would later bear his name. When in the field he probably wore the überrock for day to day wear.

Officers of the General Staff were assigned to the headquarters staff of the various army corps and kept army commanders informed of the overall strategy as envisioned by Moltke and were in communication with Royal headquarters as much as possible. The officer shown here wears his regimental uniform (the überrock was also common) with peaked mütze and butcher boots that were probably purchased privately.

Plate 19

Seven Weeks War 1866

a) 3rd Garde-Regiment zu Fuß. One-year volunteer
b) 1st Thuringian Infantry Regiment No. 31. Lieutenant
c) 2nd Upper Silesian Infantry Regiment No. 50. NCO Colour bearer

The 3rd Foot Guard Regiment was the senior guard infantry regiment raised in the 1860 reorganization. During the Danish War they were in the Combined Guards Division of III Corps with the 4th Foot Guards and served at the siege of Düppel. In 1866 they were part of the main body of Second Army's Guard Corps in the 1st Brigade of the 1st Division. They fought at the Battle of Soor during the advance into Bohemia. When First Army advanced on 3 July, they moved through Alvensleben's advance guard at Horonowes and then passed through the Swiepwald, now largely cleared of Austrians but littered with the carnage of the last few hours. They charged up the hill to Chlum which they would take with great loss and finally help extricate their comrades of the Guard Fusiliers from the village of Rosberitz. Among the officers of the 3rd Foot Guards present at that action was a certain Lieutenant Paul von Hindenburg.

It was not unusual for soldiers to discard their unwieldy helmets and put on their field caps (mütze) and the one-year volunteer Guardsman in the illustration is no exception. It seems also that most of his unit must have done so, which may explain the confusion of the commander of the Austrian Appiano Division facing them at Chlum, who lost valuable time insisting the approaching troops were Saxons. Most of the infantry by now had been issued with the new marching boots which this volunteer is wearing. They must have been much more comfortable. Some contemporary illustrations show infantrymen with their trousers un-tucked and the cuffs rolled up Danish style. Since his knapsack and other gear were stored in Köninginhof, he is wearing his greatcoat "en banderole" with his mess tin tied to it. His status as a One-Year Volunteer is indicated by the black and white piping round his shoulder strap. Beards and whiskers were not only fashionable in the middle of the nineteenth century, they were ubiquitous on campaign. Water was primarily reserved for drinking and then for washing. Shaving was not a priority and Prussian regulations allowed for the hirsute appearance well into the 1870s.

The 31st Infantry Regiment was raised in 1812 and had its origins in the old Russo-German Legion. It was initially a Rhine regiment but was designated the 1st Thuringian in 1860. In the 1866 campaign they were in Lieutenant General Von Horn's 8th Division forming the 15th Brigade with the 71st Regiment. During First Army's advance their first encounter with the Austrians was at Podol on the River Iser. At Königgrätz they were launched into the maelstrom of the Swiepwald where their losses were severe.

The lieutenant here (centre) is dressed in the regulation manner. It appears from contemporary illustrations and accounts that unlike their comrades in the Second Army, those in the Elbe and First Army were, for the most part, unable to stow their knapsacks, so they were generally worn during the battle by both officers and men. He likely carries a privately purchased percussion pistol and holster on his left side and the black leather pouch on his right hip is not a binocular case; it was for pistol ammunition and other sundries. This officer is wearing the field shoulder boards (*feldachselstücke*) ordered for wear on 7 June

1866. Not all officers were issued with them and many purchased them privately.

The 50th Regiment, raised in 1860, was in the 11th Division of Second Army's VI Corps. Under the command of Major-General Alexander Freidrich von Zastrow, this Silesian Division had been ordered to screen Josephstadt to prevent enemy reinforcements. However, his orders changed when he was directed to march to the sound of the guns at the junction of the Trotina river with the Elbe. His division, led by three battalions of the 50th, crossed the Trotina waist-high in the water then immediately bore down on the village of Racitz, ejecting its Hungarian defenders. Shortly later, the 2nd Battalion of the regiment under Major von Berken led the assault on Nedelist which also fell quickly.

The 50th Regiment was issued its silk colours in 1860 which were of the size and pattern set in 1828. The colour bearer (*Fahnentrager*) was usually a senior sergeant of the battalion. In battle he was flanked by a guard (*Fahnensektion*) of three NCOs and the whole group was situated in the centre of first rank of the reserve company. This sergeant (right) is dressed in the normal manner. There was no badge or device to distinguish colour-bearer NCOs at this time and he wears the colour case, made of oilskin-covered canvas, over his left shoulder, its brass top tucked under his belt. His cuffs display his marksman award. The good state of the colour itself is indicative of its recent manufacture. Frederick William III (1797–1840) instituted a rule that colours were "sacred" after the Wars of Liberation and therefore could not be replaced, so most of the older regiments carried very tattered colours.

Plate 20

Seven Weeks War 1866

a) Rhenish Fusilier Regiment No. 39. Gefreiter
b) Pommeranian Jäger Battalion No. 2. Colonel
c) Garde Schützen Battalion. Sharpshooter

The Pommeranian Jäger Battalion was in the First Army's II Corps and two of its companies formed part of Lieutenant-General von Werder's advance guard in the 3rd Division at the battle of Gitschin on 29 June. At Königgrätz the same two companies were in the advance guard of Lieutenant-Colonel Baron von Buddenbrock while the other companies remained with the main body. The mounted major wears the standard uniform of a jäger field officer and has replaced his epaulettes with *feldstücke*. In most other respects his uniform and horse furniture are as they would have been for a parade. Even though his company officers donned knee boots for the campaign, mounted officers did not generally follow suit.

It was in the western theatre of the war that the 39th Fusiliers first saw action. As part of Major-General von Beyer's combined division they were involved in the fighting at Hammelburg, during the wider Kissingen battle, chasing the retreating Bavarians across the Thulba river. Although the Bavarians put up a stout resistance in the town itself, it was soon taken by Major-General von Schachtmeyer's brigade, which included the 39th. After marching to Frankfurt they continued south, where they took part in one of the last actions at Helmstadt. The gefreiter shown (left) is wearing his trousers rolled up in the Danish style which was more popular among troops in the campaign south of the Maine as the weather was blazing hot during the first week of July. All battalions of fusilier regiments wore black leather equipment.

The Guard Sharpshooter (*Schützen)* Battalion was in the 2nd Guard Division of the crown prince's Second Army. They were in reserve at Soor and did see heavy fighting around Chlum and Rosberitz at Königgrätz. This soldier is typically equipped. He carries the Jäger version of the Dreyse rifle and on his belt is the bayonet scabbard issued only to riflemen. His uniform tunic is the standard holly green. The collar and cuffs were black piped red and the scalloped green cuff flap, unique in the Prussian Army, had three buttons. The collar bore the yellow litzen. His valise with its badger-head flap was a distinction for all Jäger and sharpshooter troops.

Plate 21

Seven Weeks War 1866

a) Silesian Cuirassier Regiment No. 1. Cuirassier

b) Westphalian Cuirassier Regiment No. 4. Trumpeter

c) Brandenburg Dragoon Regiment No. 2. Dragoon

The 1st Cuirassier regiment was raised on 16 October 1807 from the remnants of several cavalry units surviving the Battle of Jena. They were given the title on 7 September the following year although the regimental history claims their ancestry to 1674. They were in the Heavy Cavalry Brigade of Second Army's cavalry reserve under Major-General Hartmann. Unfortunately, they were caught in the traffic jam behind von Bonin's artillery during Second Army's advance on 3 July. Major-General von Blumenthal would later complain that the whole division had completely "disappeared" during the course of the battle. They would have their chance at action after the battle as part of the advance guard following the retreating Austrians to the Danube. The cuirassiers fell upon the rearguard of the fleeing army at Rokeinitz and Tobitschau on 15 July, capturing many guns. The 1st Cuirassiers was one of the few regiments issued with the high jackboots just before the campaign. In fact only three squadrons received them in time. It is not clear, but likely that trumpeters did not wear them. In all other respects, this cuirassier's uniform is regulation (left).

The Westphalian Cuirassier regiment came into being on 25 March 1815, raised from squadrons taken from the three existing regiments standing at the end of the Napoleonic wars, plus parts of Saxon Cuirassier regiments absorbed into the Prussian Army at the time. Like many of its sister Wesphalian units, it had served in the Schleswig campaign of 1864 and would find itself in the Army of the Maine in 1866. It formed the cavalry element of Major-General von Treskow's reserve brigade in Lieutenant-General von Goeben's division on its march to Frankfurt in the western theatre. It saw action at Aschaffenberg and Tauberbischofsheim toward the end of the campaign. The trumpeter (centre), is in regulation dress. He wears no cuirass, revealing the piping on the back seams of his tunic as well as the back of the sleeves. The distinctive orange facings also appear on his collar, cuffs and swallow's nest shoulder wings as well as the lace on the front of the tunic, collar and cuffs.

The antecedents of the Brandenburg Dragoons rested in the 1st Dragoon regiment raised in 1690. It was present at some of the most prominent battles of the eighteenth century including Oudenarde (1709), Malplaquet (1710), Hohenfriedburg (1745) and Leuthen (1757), distinguishing itself in the latter two. Enough remained of the regiment after Jena to form the cadre of the 5th Dragoons, which by 1815 had become the Brandenburg Regiment No. 2. The black facings remained a feature of the regiment since the beginning. They began the 1866 campaign as the cavalry element of von Manstein's 6th Division of the First Army. Despite being the divisional cavalry they found themselves mixed up behind the infantry on the way into Gitschin and only came into action later in the battle. On 2 July, they were transferred (with the 3rd Uhlans) to the 2nd Cavalry division of

Major-General von Weyhern, (part of Prince Albrecht's Cavalry Corps) and were in reserve during the cavalry action at the end of the battle. The dragoon soldier's dress and accoutrements are typical of this branch of cavalry (right). Like hussars they were classified as light cavalry and carried the Dreyse carbine.

Plate 22

Seven Weeks War 1866

a) Lithuanian Uhlan Regiment No. 12. Uhlan
b) Guard Hussar Regiment. Hussar
c) 2nd Silesian Hussar Regiment No. 6. Sergeant

The three cavalry regiments here were all in Crown Prince Frederick's Second Army. The 12th Uhlans, raised in 1860, were part of Colonel von Bredow's Reserve Cavalry Brigade in I Corps. The only serious action that the regiment saw was during the advance to Brünn at Tobitschau. The uhlan is fully dressed for campaign. His tunic plastron (*paraderbatter*) has been removed and shows only piping and his cap (*tschapka*) has an oilskin cover, with all cap lines removed.

The Guard Hussar Regiment was raised in 1815 from the war-raised East Prussian National Cavalry and the Hussar squadron from the Guards Light Cavalry. They formed the cavalry element of Major-General Alvensleben's 2nd Division in Hiller von Gartringen's 1st Guard Division. They took little part in the first action after emerging from the mountains at Soor on 28 June, until it was time to pursue the retreating Austrians. Two squadrons from the regiment were part of the advance guard at Königgrätz and became involved in the heavy fighting during the assault on Chlum. The commanding officer of the Guard Hussars, Colonel von Krosigk, personally captured an Austrian gun in the earthworks before the village. As the Guards began to move past Chlum to Rosberitz, a squadron saw off an element of the Austrian 7th Hussars attempting to stall the advance and it was an NCO of the regiment who helped carry the mortally wounded Hiller back to the rear after he was struck by shrapnel. Like most of the hussars during the war, the Guard Hussars made few adjustments to their dress on campaign. The Hussar cap (*colback*) with its distinctive star was not covered and although the plume was removed, the cap lines were retained. In all other respects, the uniform was the same as if on parade.

Hussar Regiment No. 6 was raised in 1808 as a new regiment, mostly from remnants of other cavalry units, and known as the 2nd Silesian Hussars. It served valiantly during the War of Liberation. In 1866 it served as the 12th Division cavalry of Lieutenant General Conrad Wilhelm von Prondzynski. It supported the advance of Mutius VI Corps down the west bank of the Elbe and was involved in several clashes with the retreating enemy. It suffered heavy casualties toward the climax of the battle near Rosberitz when trying to pursue Austrian cavalry retreating from a mauling received from the infantry of the 11th Division. Having failed to send scouts ahead, they galloped into a hidden gully and many of the horses fell along with their riders. As they tried to regroup, a squadron of the Austrian 11th Hussars fell among them and put them to the sword. The 2nd Silesian Hussars retained the same uniform colours of green and red with yellow lace that they wore when first raised. This sergeant is dressed as he would have been while supervising the de-training of horses at the railhead. His attila has a strip of extra lace on the collar and cuffs, under the Austrian knot. He also wears his mütze with its red band.

Plate 23

Seven Weeks War 1866

a) Medical Department. Surgeon
b) Guard Horse Artillery. Gunner
c) Field Hospital Corps. Krankentrager

By the standards of later wars, the medical arrangements available in 1866 to deal with mass battlefield casualties were still closer to Napoleonic standards. Although public awareness about the inadequacies of medical care for soldiers at war had risen dramatically after the Crimean War, little had been done to drastically improve things. The founding of the Red Cross after the battle of Solferino had laid the groundwork to improve care for the wounded and medical services had expanded in most armies. Uniformed stretcher-bearer units now existed to collect battlefield casualties and often wore the red cross brassard to protect them from hostile fire. With close to 450,000 men engaged in the battle of Königgrätz it was one of the largest battles to date. The casualties were also considerable with nearly 10,000 Prussians and 45,000 Austrians killed or wounded. It was beyond the capabilities of any nation's military medical services to deal with such numbers efficiently. The Prussian Medical Branch was certainly much more advanced than the Austrian, but as is always the case the victor's services bore the brunt of medical care for all. Fortunately, at Königgrätz a large number of volunteers from the Order of the Knights of St John of Jerusalem, revived since 1831 and devoted to hospital work, were present to assist with the wounded.

The main field hospital (*Lazarett*) had been established in Horitz, but there were others, often hastily set up, in most of the villages. By the end of the battle there were wounded soldiers in almost every building that was still standing. It would be more than a month before all the dead were buried and the wounded treated and moved to other locations. Returning villagers related that the stench of death was still in the air in September.

Each army corps had a complement of surgeons, assistants and hospital orderlies, most of whom were mobilized from civilian life when the war started. They were then assigned to the hospital trains which followed the army on the march. Photographic evidence is sparse, but that which does exist indicates that most of the surgeons wore the überrock which was piped red on the front and top of the collar. The surgeon illustrated wears his regimental uniform without the belt, sash and sword.

His tunic has red piping on the blue velvet collar and cuffs which also bear silver litzen. His cap has a blue velvet band piped red. Where possible, some surgeons were in the field, but mostly they were hard at work in the lazarett in shirtsleeves with a leather apron in conditions probably difficult to describe.

There were three stretcher-bearer (*Krankentrager*) companies to an army corps, each numbering about 60 men. This stretcher-bearer is attached to the 6th Silesian Corps. His tunic has crimson collar patches and piping on the cuffs. He wears the red-cross brassard on his left arm. The sidearm is standard infantry pattern. The Landwehr Cross on the peaked cap was worn by all stretcher-bearer companies except those in the Guard Corps as they were mobilized directly through the Landwehr. The Guard Corps krankentrager had crimson shoulder straps, collar patches and cuffs, the latter two with *Gardelitzen.*

The wounded soldier is from the Guard Horse Artillery and probably served in one of Prince Hohenlohe's batteries supporting the assault on Chlum. He seems to have fared somewhat better than most of his valiant opponents in the Austrian artillery. His uniform is entirely regulation with the *Gardelitzen* on collar and cuffs. His battered helmet bears the Guard eagle.

Plate 24

Seven Weeks War 1866

a) Landwehr Uhlan Regiment No. 6. Uhlan

b) Landwehr Infantry Regiment No. 28. Feldwebel

c) Infantry Staff Corps. Field Police. Private

The Landwehr, which had been completely reorganized in 1859/60, was again under a process of change in 1866 when the war broke out. The Landwehr cavalry was to be replaced by a reserve cavalry system incorporated into each army corps organization. When the war against Austria began there were twelve Landwehr cavalry regiments (five Uhlan, five Hussar and two Cuirassier regiments) which were apportioned out to the reserve cavalry divisions of the various army corps. The 6th Landwehr Uhlan Regiment was in the reserve cavalry corps of the Elbe Army. Both the Landwehr uhlans and hussars wore uniforms that resembled their regular army counterparts with the exception of their headgear. While the Hussar units wore their distinctive mirletons (dating back to the 1840s) the Uhlans wore the dragoon pickelhaube.

The infantry of the Landwehr were to provide for the vast number of rear area troops used to garrison the towns and cities of Saxony and Bohemia in the wake of the main armies. This is not to say they weren't involved in any of the combat, especially in the western theatre. Landwehr troops fought at Langensalza, where their indifferent performance was criticized, as well as many other battles on the march to Frankfurt. One battalion of the 28th Landwehr Infantry Regiment served in the formation of troops (which included units from Waldeck and Schwartzburg-Rudolstadt) that garrisoned Frankfurt and Wiesbaden. Landwehr infantry wore regular infantry or Guard uniforms with the exception of the jäger shako, which bore the Landwehr cross in a circle on the front. Guard Landwehr shakos had the cross on the Guard star. Knee boots were not issued.

Although the appellation "Military Police" was not in use at this time, the Infantry Staff Corps of the Prussian Army certainly performed this function during the war of 1866. Like their mounted brethren, they were used to convey orders and dispatches between units, but they were also used to man checkpoints, direct traffic at crossroads and generally ease the congestion of an army on the march. This was not an easy task and the constant rain during the campaign must have hampered their efforts. They performed duties in the rear areas and in the bivouacs when there were unruly or drunken soldiers to deal with. Typically they would involve NCOs and officers of the units concerned to restore discipline where necessary as there was only one detachment per army corps and apparently there were no powers of arrest. The soldier shown in the illustration is typically dressed in the green tunic with cornflower-blue collar and cuffs with red piping. The distinctively wide cornflower-blue stripes with the red centre piping on his trousers must have made him quite visible when he needed to be. He wears the undress green mütze with cornflower-blue band and red piping. His pickelhaube was decorated with the eagle (as in the line infantry) with spike and other fittings in brass.

PLATE 1

(a) General of Infantry, King William I of Prussia, 1865

(b) Major, Aide-de-Camp to a Royal Prince, 1865

PLATE 2

(a) Flügeladjutant 1865

(b) Sergeant, Leib-Gendarmerie 1865

(c) Feldwebel, Schloß-Garde-Kompanie

PLATE 3

(a) Kaiser-Alexander-Garde-Grenadier-Regiment No. 1. Drummer, parade dress

(b) 1st Garde-Regiment zu Fuß. Grenadier, parade dress

(c) 4th Garde-Regiment zu Fuß. Captain, parade dress

PLATE 4

(a) 6th Rhenish Infantry Regiment No. 65. Regimentstambour

(b) 1st Garde-Jäger Battalion, 1st Lieutenant, überrock

(c) Princess Elizabeth Garde-Grenadier-Regiment No. 3. Field officer, service dress

PLATE 5

(a) 2nd Silesian Jäger Battalion No. 5. Gefreiter, winter parade dress

(b) 1st East Prussian Grenadier Regiment No. 1. Feldwebel

(c) 2nd West Prussian Grenadier Regiment No. 7. Grenadier, winter parade dress

PLATE 6

(a) Brandenburg Cuirassier Regiment, Tsar Nicholas I of Russia No. 6. Cuirassier

(b) Gardes du Corps. Guardsman, gala dress

PLATE 7

(a) Neumärk Dragoon Regiment No. 3. Captain, überrock

(b) Pomeranian Cuirassier Regiment No 2. Officer, court dress

(c) Magdeburg Cuirassier Regiment No. 7. Gefreiter, waffenrock

PLATE 8

(a) 2nd Guard Dragoon Regiment. Trumpeter, parade dress

(b) Rhenish Cuirassier Regiment No. 8. Officer, überrock

(c) 2nd Silesian Dragoon Regiment No. 8. Officer, levée dress

PLATE 9

(a) Pomeranian Hussar Regiment (Blücher Hussars) No. 5. Hussar, parade dress

(b) 1st Life Hussar Regiment No. 1. Officer, parade dress

PLATE 10

(a) 1 Garde-Uhlan-Regiment. Officer, levée dress

(b) Magdeburg Hussar Regiment No. 10. Officer, levée dress

PLATE 11

(a) 1st Pomeranian Uhlan Regiment No. 4. Uhlan, parade dress

(b) 2nd Brandenburg Uhlan Regiment No. 11. Major, parade dress

PLATE 12

(a) Lower Silesian Artillery Brigade No. 5. Gefreiter, parade dress

(b) Garde Pioneer Battalion. Pioneer

(c) Pomeranian Train Battalion No. 2. Conductor

PLATE 13

(a) Paymasters Department. Zahlmeister (paymaster) 1st Class, service dress
(b) Garnisonsvervaltung (Garrison Department). Inspektor (inspector), überrock
(c) Ordnance Deptartment. Proviantmeister (chief quartermaster), service dress

PLATE 14

Second Schleswig War, 1864

(a) 7th Brandenburg Infantry Regiment. No. 60. Officer
(b) 6th Westphalian Infantry Regiment. No. 55. Private
(c) 4th Brandenburg Infantry Regiment. No. 24. Privat

PLATE 15

Second Schleswig War, 1864

(a) Brandenburg Pioneer Battalion No. 3. Pioneer

(b) Westphalian Dragoon Regiment No. 7. Dragoon

(c) Westphalian Artillery Brigade No. 7. Horse Battery. Sergeant.

PLATE 16

Second Schleswig War, 1864

(a) 1 See-Battalion. Mann

(b) Marine Artillery Detachment. Gunner

(c) Königliche Marine. Leutnant Zur See

(d) Königliche Marine. Öbermaate

PLATE 17

Seven Weeks War 1866

a) Minister-President Otto von Bismarck

b) General of Infantry, Chief of Staff of the Army, Baron von Moltke

c) General of Cavalry Crown Prince Frederick Charles of Prussia

PLATE 18

Seven Weeks War 1866

a) General of Infantry Crown Prince Frederick William of Prussia

b) General of Infantry Karl Friedrich von Steinmetz

c) Major on the General Staff

PLATE 19

Seven Weeks War 1866

a) 3rd Garde-Regiment zu Fuß. One-year volunteer

b) 1st Thuringian Infantry Regiment No. 31. Lieutenant

c) 2nd Upper Silesian Infantry Regiment No. 50. NCO Colour-bearer

PLATE 20

Seven Weeks War 1866

a) Rhenish Fusilier Regiment No. 39. Gefreiter

b) Pomeranian Jäger Battalion No. 2. Colonel

c) Garde Schützen Battalion. Sharpshooter

PLATE 21

Seven Weeks War 1866

a) Silesian Cuirassier Regiment No. 1. Cuirassier

b) Westphalian Cuirassier Regiment No. 4. Trumpeter

c) Brandenburg Dragoon Regiment No. 2. Dragoon

PLATE 22

Seven Weeks War 1866

a) Lithuanian Uhlan Regiment No. 12. Uhlan

b) Guard Hussar Regiment. Hussar

c) 2nd Silesian Hussar Regiment No. 6. Sergeant

PLATE 23

Seven Weeks War 1866

a) Medical Department. Surgeon

b) Garde Horse Artillery. Gunner

c) Field Hospital Corps. Krankentrager

PLATE 24

Seven Weeks War 1866

a) Landwehr Uhlan Regiment No. 6. Uhlan

b) Landwehr Infantry Regiment No. 28. Feldwebel

c) Infantry Staff Corps. Field Police. Private

Appendices

APPENDIX A

Order of Battle for the Royal Prussian Army

Denmark 1 February 1864

ALLIED ARMY HEADQUARTERS

Commander in Chief	Field Marshal Baron von Wrangel
Chief of Staff	Lieutenant-General Vogel von Falckenstein

ROYAL PRUSSIAN COMBINED ARMY CORPS
(I PRUSSIAN CORPS)

Commander in Chief	H.R.H. Prince Frederick Charles
Chief of Staff	Colonel von Blumenthal
Commandant of Artillery	Colonel von Colomier
Commandant of Engineers	Lieutenant-Colonel von Kriegsheim

6th (Brandenburg) Division — **Lieutenant-General von Manstein**

11th Brigade — Major-General von Canstein

Fusilier Regiment No. 35
Infantry Regiment No. 60

12th Brigade — Major-General von Roder

Infantry Regiment No. 24
Infantry Regiment No. 64

Divisional Troops

Uhlan Regiment No. 11 (4 Sqns)
Artillery Brigade No. 3 (3rd Foot Arty Div.)
Pioneer Bn. No. 3

13th (Westphalian) Division Lieutenant-General von Winzingerode

25th Brigade Major-General von Schmid

Infantry Regiment No. 13

Infantry Regiment No. 53

26th Brigade Major-General von Goeben

Infantry Regiment No. 15

Infantry Regiment No. 55

Divisional Troops

Jäger Bn. No 7

Dragoon Regiment No. 7 (4 Sqns)

Artillery Brigade No. 7 (1st Foot Arty Div.)

Pioneer Bn. No. 7

Combined Cavalry Division Lieutenant-General Count von Münster-Meinhovel

6th Brigade Colonel Flies

Cuirassier Regiment No. 6 (4 Sqns)

Hussar Regiment No. 3 (4 Sqns)

13th Brigade Major-General von Hobe

Cuirassier Regiment No. 4 (4 Sqns)

Hussar Regiment No. 8 (5 Sqns)

Artillery

Artillery Brigade No. 7 (2nd Horse Arty Div.)

Reserve Artillery

Artillery Brigade No. 3 (2nd Foot Arty Div.)

Artillery Brigade No. 7 (1st Horse Arty Div.)

Combined Guards Division Lieutenant-General von der Mülbe

Comb. Foot Guards Brigade Major-General Count von der Goltz

3rd Foot Guards Regiment

4th Foot Guards Regiment

Comb. Guard Grenadier Brigade Colonel von der Bentheim

3rd Guard Grenadier Regiment

4th Guard Grenadier Regiment

Cavalry

Guard Hussar Regiment

Artillery

Guard Artillery Brigade (2 batteries)

Units arriving March 1864

5th (Combined) Division	Lieutenant-General von Tümpling
10th Brigade	Colonel von Kamienski
Brandenburg Grenadier Regiment No. 8	
Brandenburg Infantry Regiment No. 48	
20th Brigade	Colonel von Kettler
Posen Infantry Regiment No. 18	
Brandenburg Infantry Regiment No. 52	
Divisional Troops	
Guard Artillery Brigade (3 Foot batteries)	

Units arriving April 1864

21st Silesian Brigade	Major-General von Bornstedt
Grenadier Regiment No. 10	
Infantry Regiment No. 50	
Westphalian Artillery Brigade No. 7 (5th Horse Artillery Battery)	

APPENDIX B

Order of Battle for the Royal Prussian Army June 1866

ARMY HEADQUARTERS

Commander in Chief	His Majesty the King
Chief of Staff	General von Moltke
Inspector General of Artillery	Lieutenant-General von Hindersin
Inspector General of Engineers	Lieutenant-General von Wasseschleben

FIRST ARMY

Commander in Chief	H.R.H. Prince Frederick Charles
Chief of Staff	Lieutenant-General von Voigts-Rhetz
Quartermaster-General	Major-General von Stülpnagel
Commandant of Artillery	Major-General von Lengsfeld
Commandant of Engineers	Major-General von Keiser

II ARMY CORPS

General Commanding	Lieutenant-General von Schmidt
Chief of Staff	Major-General von Kamecke
Commandant of Artillery	Major-General Hurrelbrink
Commandant of Engineers	Lieutenant-Colonel Leuthaus

3rd Division	Lieutenant-General von Werder
5th Brigade	Major-General von Januschowsky
Grenadier Regiment No. 2	
Infantry Regiment No. 42	
6th Brigade	Major-General von Winterfeld
Infantry Regiment No. 14	

Infantry Regiment No. 54

Cavalry

Hussar Regiment No. 5

4th Division Lieutenant-General von Herwath

7th Brigade Major-General von Schlaberndorf

Grenadier Regiment No. 9

Infantry Regiment No. 49

8th Brigade Major-General von Hanneken

Infantry Regiment No. 21

Infantry Regiment No. 61

Cavalry

Uhlan Regiment No. 4

Corps Troops

Jäger Battalion No. 2

Pioneer Battalion No. 2

Artillery Brigade No. 2

III ARMY CORPS

General Commanding *None*

5th Division Lieutenant-General von Tümpling

9th Brigade Major-General von Schimmelman

Grenadier Regiment No. 8

Infantry Regiment No. 48

10th Brigade Major-General von Kaminsky

Grenadier Regiment No. 12

Infantry Regiment No. 18

Artillery

2 Light Foot batteries from Artillery Brigade No. 3

1 6-Pounder Foot battery from Artillery Brigade No. 3

1 12-Pounder Heavy battery from Artillery Brigade No. 3

Pioneers

1 Company from Pioneer Battalion No. 3

6th Division	Lieutenant-General von Manstein
11th Brigade	Major-General von Gersdorf
	Fusilier Regiment No. 35
	Infantry Regiment No. 60
12th Brigade	Major-General von Kotze
	Infantry Regiment No. 24
	Infantry Regiment No. 64
	Jäger Battalion No. 3
Artillery	
	2 Light Foot batteries from Artillery Brigade No. 3
	1 6-Pounder Foot battery from Artillery Brigade No. 3
	1 12-Pounder Heavy battery from Artillery Brigade No. 3
Pioneers	
	1 company from Pioneer Battalion No. 3

IV ARMY CORPS

General Commanding	*None*
7th Division	Lieutenant-General von Fransecky
13th Brigade	Major-General Gross von Schwarzhoff
	Infantry Regiment No. 26
	Infantry Regiment No. 66
14th Brigade	Major-General von Gordon
	Infantry Regiment No. 27
	Infantry Regiment No. 67
Cavalry	
	Hussar Regiment No. 10
Artillery	
	2 Light Foot batteries from Artillery Brigade No. 4
	1 6-Pounder Foot battery from Artillery Brigade No. 4
	1 12-Pounder Heavy battery from Artillery Brigade No. 4
8th Division	Lieutenant-General von Horn
15th Brigade	Major-General von Bose
	Infantry Regiment No. 31

Infantry Regiment No. 71

16th Brigade — Major-General von Schmidt

Infantry Regiment No. 72

Jäger Battalion No. 4

Cavalry

Uhlan Regiment No. 6

Artillery

2 Light Foot batteries from Artillery Brigade No. 4

1 6-Pounder Foot battery from Artillery Brigade No. 4

1 12-Pounder Heavy battery from Artillery Brigade No. 4

Pioneers

2 companies from Pioneer Battalion No. 4

CAVALRY CORPS

General Commanding — General of Cavalry Prince Albrecht

1st Cavalry Division — Major-General von Alvensleben

1st Light Cavalry Bde — Major-General von Rheinbaben

Guard Dragoon Regiment No. 1

Guard Uhlan Regiment No. 1

Guard Uhlan Regiment No. 2

Artillery

Guard Horse Artillery Battery No. 2

2nd Heavy Cavalry Bde — Major-General von Pfuel

Cuirassier Regiment No. 6

Cuirassier Regiment No. 7

Artillery

Guard Horse Artillery Battery No. 1

2nd Cavalry Division — Major-General von Weyhern

2nd Light Cavalry Bde — Major-General Duke of Mecklenburg

Hussar Regiment No. 3

Uhlan Regiment No. 11

Guard Dragoon Regiment No. 2

3rd Light Cavalry Bde — Major-General Groeben

Dragoon Regiment No. 3
Hussar Regiment No. 12

3rd Heavy Cavalry Bde — Major-General von der Goltz

Cuirassier Regiment No. 2
Uhlan Regiment No. 9

FIRST ARMY ARTILLERY RESERVE

General Commanding — Major-General Schwarz

4 4-Pounder Light Foot batteries from Artillery Brigades No. 3 & 4
4 6-Pounder Foot batteries from Artillery Brigades No. 3 & 4
8 Horse Artillery batteries from Artillery Brigades No. 3 & 4

ARMY OF THE ELBE

Commander in Chief	General of Infantry Herwarth von Bittenfeld
Chief of Staff	Lieutenant-General von Schlotheim
Commandant of Artillery	Major-General von Rozynski-Manger
Commandant of Engineers	Major-General von Forell

VII ARMY CORPS

General Commanding — *None*

14th Division — Lieutenant-General von Münster

27th Brigade — Major-General von Schwarzkoppen

Infantry Regiment No. 16
Infantry Regiment No. 56

28th Brigade — Major-General von Hiller

Infantry Regiment No. 17
Infantry Regiment No. 57
Jäger Battalion No. 7

Cavalry

Uhlan Regiment No. 5

Artillery

2 Light Foot batteries from Artillery Brigade No. 7
1 6-Pounder Foot battery from Artillery Brigade No. 7
1 12-Pounder Heavy battery from Artillery Brigade No. 7

15th Division	Lieutenant-General von Canstein
29th Brigade	Major-General von Stuckradt
Fusilier Regiment No. 40	
Infantry Regiment No. 65	
30th Brigade	Major-General von Glasenapp
Infantry Regiment No. 28	
Infantry Regiment No. 68	
Cavalry	
Dragoon Regiment No. 7	
Artillery	
2 Light Foot batteries from Artillery Brigade No. 7	
1 6-Pounder Foot battery from Artillery Brigade No. 7	
1 12-Pounder Heavy battery from Artillery Brigade No. 7	

VIII ARMY CORPS

General Commanding	*None*
16th Division	Lieutenant-General von Etzel
31st Brigade	Major-General von Senden
Infantry Regiment No. 29	
Infantry Regiment No. 69	
Fusilier Brigade	Major-General von Wegerer
Fusilier Regiment No. 33	
Fusilier Regiment No. 34	
Cavalry	
Uhlan Regiment No. 7	
Artillery	
2 Light Foot batteries from Artillery Brigade No. 8	
1 6-Pounder Foot battery from Artillery Brigade No. 8	
1 Horse battery from Artillery Brigade No. 8	
Pioneers	
1 Company from Pioneer Battalion No. 8	
1st Cavalry Brigade	Major-General von der Goltz
Hussar Regiment No. 7	
Hussar Regiment No. 11	

Reserve Cavalry Brigade	Major-General von Kotze
Cuirassier Regiment No. 8	
Landwehr Heavy Cavalry Regiment (Pomeranian)	
Artillery Reserve	Major-General von Bülow
4 Light Foot batteries from Artillery Brigade No. 8	
4 6-Pounder Foot batteries from Artillery Brigade No. 8	
4 Horse batteries from Artillery Brigade Nos. 7 & 8	
Reserve Cavalry	Lieutenant-General von Mülbe
Reserve Landwehr Div	Major-General von Gruscynski
1st Landwehr Cav Div	General Rosenberg
2nd Light Cavalry Div	
Reserve Cavalry Div	Major-General Dohna

SECOND ARMY

Commander in Chief	Crown Prince Frederick William
Chief of Staff	Major-General von Blumenthal
Inspector General of Artillery	Major-General von Jacobi
Inspector General of Engineers	Major-General von Schweinitz

I ARMY CORPS

General Commanding	General of Infantry von Bonin
1st Division	Lieutenant-General von Grossman
1st Brigade	Major-General von Pape
Grenadier Regiment No. 1	
Infantry Regiment No. 41	
2nd Brigade	Major-General von Barnekow
Grenadier Regiment No. 3	
Infantry Regiment No. 43	
Cavalry	
Dragoon Regiment No. 1	
2nd Division	Lieutenant-General von Clausewitz
3rd Brigade	Major-General von Malotki
Grenadier Regiment No. 4	

	Infantry Regiment No. 44
4th Brigade	Major-General von Buddenbrock
	Grenadier Regiment No. 5
	Infantry Regiment No. 45
Cavalry	
	Hussar Regiment No. 1
Corps Troops	
	Jäger Battalion No. 1
	Artillery Brigade No. 1
	Pioneer Battalion No. 1

Reserve Cavalry Brigade	Colonel von Bredow
	Cuirassier Regiment No. 3
	Uhlan Regiment No. 12
Artillery	
	1 Horse Artillery Battery

V ARMY CORPS

General Commanding	General of Infantry von Steinmetz
9th Division	Major-General von Loewenfeld
17th Brigade	Major-General von Below
	Infantry Regiment No. 37
	Infantry Regiment No. 58
18th Brigade	Major-General von Horn
	Grenadier Regiment No. 7
Cavalry	
	Dragoon Regiment No. 1
10th Division	Lieutenant-General von Kirchbach
19th Brigade	Major-General von Tiedemann
	Grenadier Regiment No. 6
	Infantry Regiment No. 46
20th Brigade	Major-General von Wittich
	Infantry Regiment No. 47
	Infantry Regiment No. 52

Cavalry

Uhlan Regiment No. 1

Corps Troops

Jäger Battalion No. 5

Artillery Brigade No. 5

Pioneer Battalion No. 5

VI ARMY CORPS

General Commanding — General of Cavalry von Mutius

11th Division — Lieutenant-General von Zastrow

21st Brigade — Major-General von Hanenfeld

Grenadier Regiment No. 10

Infantry Regiment No. 50

22nd Brigade — Major-General von Hoffman

Fusilier Regiment No. 38

Infantry Regiment No. 51

Cavalry

Dragoon Regiment No. 8

12th Division — Lieutenant-General von Prondzynski

Brigade — Major-General von Cranach

Infantry Regiment No. 22

Infantry Regiment No. 23

Cavalry

Hussar Regiment No. 6

Corps Troops

Jäger Battalion No. 6

Artillery Brigade No. 6

Pioneer Battalion No. 6

Reserve Cavalry — Lieutenant-Colonel von Wichmann

Hussar Regiment No. 4

GUARD CORPS

General Commanding — Prince Augustus of Württemberg

1st Guard Division — Lieutenant-General Hiller von Gartringen

1st Guard Brigade	Major-General von Obernitz
1st Regiment of Foot Guards	
3rd Regiment of Foot Guards	
2nd Guard Brigade	Major-General von Alvensleben
3rd Regiment of Foot Guards	
Guard Fusilier Regiment	
Cavalry	
Guard Hussar Regiment	
Divisional Troops	
Guard Jäger Battalion	

2nd Guard Division Lieutenant-General von Plonski

3rd Guard Brigade	Major-General von Budritzki
1st Guard Grenadier Regiment	
3rd Guard Grenadier Regiment	
4th Guard Brigade	Major-General von Loen
2nd Guard Grenadier Regiment	
4th Guard Grenadier Regiment	
Cavalry	
3rd Guard Uhlan Regiment	
Divisional Troops	
Guard Schützen Battalion	

Corps Troops

Guard Artillery Brigade	
Guard Pioneer Battalion	
Guard Cavalry Reserve	Major-General Prince von Albrecht Jr.
Gardes du Corps	
Guard Cuirassier Regiment	

II Army Corps Cavalry Reserve Major-General Hartmann

Light Cavalry Brigade	Major-General von Witzleben
Hussar Regiment No. 2	
Uhlan Regiment No. 10	
Heavy Cavalry Brigade	Major-General von Schoen

Cuirassier Regiment No. 1

Cuirassier Regiment No. 5

Landwehr Cavalry Bde — Colonel von Franckenberg

1st Landwehr Hussar Regiment

2nd Landwehr Hussar Regiment

ARMY OF THE MAINE

Italics denote North German Prussian allied units

Commander in Chief — General of Infantry von Manteuffel

Chief of Staff

Inspector General of Artillery

Inspector General of Engineers

13th Division — Lieutenant-General von Goeben

25th Brigade — Major-General von Kummer

Infantry Regiment No. 13

Infantry Regiment No. 53

26th Brigade — Major-General von Wrangel

Infantry Regiment No. 15

Infantry Regiment No. 55

Lippe-Detmold "Fusilier Battalion Lippe"

Cavalry

Hussar Regiment No. 8

Artillery

2 Light Foot Batteries

1 6-Pounder Foot Battery

1 12-Pounder Heavy Foot Battery

ombined Reserve Brigade — Major-General von Tresckow

Infantry Regiment No. 19

Cavalry

Cuirassier Regiment No. 4

Artillery

1 Horse Artillery Battery

	1 Pioneer Company
Combined Infantry Division	Major-General von Beyer
32nd Brigade	Colonel von Woyna
	Infantry Regiment No. 30
	Infantry Regiment No. 70
Brigade	Major-General von Schachtmeyer
	Infantry Regiment No. 20
	Infantry Regiment No. 32
	Fusilier Regiment No. 39
Cavalry	
	Hussar Regiment No. 9
	10th Landwehr Hussar Regiment (2 sqns)
Combined Infantry Division	Lieutenant-General von Flies
Brigade	Major-General von Freyhold
	Fusilier Regiment No. 36
	Infantry Regiment No. 25
Brigade	Major-General von Korth
	Grenadier Regiment No. 11
	Infantry Regiment No. 59
	Saxe-Coburg-Gotha Infantry Regiment (2 bns)
Cavalry	
	Dragoon Regiment No. 5
	Dragoon Regiment No. 6
Artillery	
	1 Horse Artillery Battery
	5 Foot batteries
Oldenburg & Hanseatic Brigade	Major-General von Weltzien
Infantry	
	Oldenburg Infantry Regiment (2 bns)
	Hamburg Infantry Regiment (3 bns)
	Lübeck Light Infantry Battalion
	Bremen Fusilier Battalion
Cavalry	
	Oldenburg Cavalry Regiment

Hamburg Dragoon Regiment

Artillery

2 Oldenburg Foot Batteries

Frankfurt-on-Main / Wiesbaden Brigade

Landwehr Infantry Regiment No. 17 (5 bns)

Landwehr Infantry Regiment No. 25 (2 bns)

Landwehr Infantry Regiment No. 28 (1 bn)

Landwehr Infantry Regiment No. 30 (1 bn)

Waldeck Fusilier Battalion

Schwartzburg-Rudolstadt Fusilier Battalion

1 Combined Jäger Battalion

Cavalry

10th Landwehr Hussar Regiment (2 sqns)

Hussar Regiment No. 7 & Hussar Regiment No. 11 (1 combined sqn)

Artillery

3 batteries of 4 guns each

SECOND RESERVE ARMY CORPS

General Commanding	Grand-Duke Frederick Francis
Prussian Division	Lieutenant-General von Horn
Combined Guards Infantry Bde	Colonel von Tresckow
Combined Infantry Brigade	Colonel von Schkopp
Combined Mecklenburg-Schwerin Division	
	Major-General von Bilgner
Mecklenburg Brigadc	Colonel von Jasmund
Brunswick/ Saxe-Altenburg Brigade*	
	Colonel von Girsewald

*The Brunswick element was completely unprepared for deployment, remaining in barracks and never joining the 2nd reserve Army Corps.

APPENDIX C

Ships of Royal Prussian Navy

January 1864 – August 1866

Name	Guns	Launched/Purchased	Tons
SCREW CORVETTES			
Arcona	28	Launched Danzig May 1858	1,900
Gazelle	28	Launched Danzig Dec 1859	1,900
Nymphe	17	Launched Danzig June 1859	1,100
Hertha	28	Launched Danzig Oct 1864	2,100
Medusa	17	Launched Danzig Oct 1864	1,100
Vineta	28	Launched Danzig Jan 1864	2,100
Augusta	14	Purchased from France May 1865	1,800
Victoria	14	Purchased from France May 1865	1,800
SCREW GUNBOATS			
Camäleon	3	Launched Danzig June 1860	350
Comet	3	Launched Danzig June 1860	350
Cyclop	3	Launched Danzig June 1860	350
Delphin	3	Launched Danzig June 1860	350
Basilisk	3	Launched Danzig Jan 1862	350
Blitz	3	Launched Danzig Jan 1862	350
Drache	3	Launched Danzig Jan 1862	350
Meteor	3	Launched Danzig Jan 1862	350

Name	Guns	Launched/Purchased	Tons
OTHER VESSELS			
Rover (brig)	16	Purchased from Great Britain Nov 1862	510
Musquito (brig)	16	Purchased from Great Britain Nov 1862	510
Gefion (frigate)	48	Ex-Danish (1849), refit 1852	960
Niobe (frigate)	26	Purchased from Great Britain Nov 1862	1,300
Thetis (frigate)	36	Purchased from Great Britain May 1855	1,500
Prinz Adalbert (ironclad ram)	3	Ex "Cheops" purchased from France May 1865	1,400
Arminius (monitor)	4	Purchased from Great Britain May 1865	1,600
Loreley (paddle steamer)	2	Launched Danzig May 1859	430
Preussicher Adler (paddle steamer)	4	Purchased from Postal Service July 1862	1,200
Hela (schooner)	6	Purchased March 1854 (later brig)	270
Grilile (yacht)	2	Purchased from France June 1858	350

In addition there were 15 second-class gunboats of 240 tons each mounting two guns and 32 smaller vessels such as sloops and yawls.

Bibliography

History and Biography

Carr, William, *The Origins of the Wars of German Unification*. London & New York, Longmans, 1991

Clemente, Stephen E., *For King and Kaiser! The making of a Prussian Army Officer 1860–1914*. Greenwood Press, 1992

Craig. Gordon A., *The Battle of Königgratz*. Philadelphia, Lippincott, 1964

Craig. Gordon A., *The Politics of the Prussian Army*. Philadelphia, Lippincott, 1964

Crankshaw, Edward, *Bismarck*. New York, Viking Press, 1981

Embree, Michael, *Bismarck's First War. The Campaign of Schleswig and Jutland 1864*. Solihull, Helion & Company, 2006

Eyck, Erich, *Bismarck and The German Empire*. New York, Norton, 1964

Gillespie-Addison, A. D., *The Strategy of The Seven Weeks' War 1866* Solihull, Helion & Company, 2000

Hall, Walter Phelps and Davis, William Stearns, *The Course of Europe Since Waterloo*. New York, Appleton-Century-Crofts (3rd ed), 1947

Hozier, Sir H. M., KCB, *The Seven Weeks War. Its Antecedents and its Incidents*. London, Macmillan & Co. Ltd, 1908

Jakl, Jan, *The Battle of Königgratz 1866* (English translation). Solihull, Helion & Company, 1999

Ludwig, Emil, *Bismarck, The Story of a Fighter*. New York, Little Brown, 1927

Maguire, T. Miller, *Notes on the Campaign Between Prussia and Austria in 1866*. Solihull, Helion & Company, 2000

Seaton, Albert, *The Army of the German Empire 1870–1888* (Men-at-Arms 4). Oxford, Osprey Publishing, 1973

Showalter, Dennis, *The Wars of German Unification*. London, Hodder Arnold, 2004

Showalter, Dennis, *Railroads and Rifles*. London, Hodder Arnold, 2004

Sondhaus, Lawrence, *Preparing for Weltpolitik. German Sea Power Before the Tirpitz Era.* Annapolis, Naval Institute Press, 1997

Von Brühl, F., *The History of the Prussian Garde du Corps during the Campaign of 1866*. Solihull, Helion & Company, 2000

Voss, Wilhelm, *Illustriete Gesichte des Deutches Eingungskriege 1864–1866*. Stuttgart, Union Deutsche Verlagsgesellschaft, 1914

Wawro, Geoffry, *The Austro-Prussian War. Austria's War with Prussia and Italy 1866*. Cambridge University Press, 1996

Uniforms, Organization, Weapons & Insignia

Brown, F. W., *Unit Organizations and Orders of Battle of the Great Armies of Europe 1853–1870*. Minneapolis, Absinthe Press, 1994

Fosten D. S. V., *Cuirassiers and Heavy Cavalry 1900–1914*. Almark Publishing Co. New Malden, 1973

Grancher, Jacques, *Casques à Pointe et Coiffures Prestigeuses de L'Armeee Allemande 1842–1918,* 2 vols. Paris, Collection Uniformes, 1983

Hagger, D. H., *Hussars and Mounted Rifles 1900–1914*. Almark Publishing Co. New Malden, 1974

Hammer, F. W., *Das Königlich Preußische Heer (1861–1865) in Seiner Gegenwärtigen Uniformirung*. Berlin, 1865

Hicks, Maj. James E., *German Weapons, Uniforms & Insignia 1841–1918*. La Canada James E. Hicks & Son, 1937

Knötel, Herbert and Lezius, Martin, *Deutsche Uniformen. 1864–1914* Vol 1 (cigarette card album). Dresden, Sturm Zigaretten GmbH, 1934

Knötel, Knötel & Sieg, *Handbuch der Uniformenkunde*. Stuttgart, W. Speman Verlag, 1956

Knötel, Richard, *Uniformenkunde*. 18 vols. Berlin, Rathenow & Babizon, 1904

Kube, Jan K., *Militaria – Ein Bilderbuch für Sammler und Freunde alter Helme und Uniformen*. Freiburg, Podzun-Pallas Verlag, 1987

Lehrbach, Werner, *Uniforms of the Austro-Prussian War 1866* (Vol 1 Prussia & Allies) USA, Hand Carved Books, 2002

Marrion, R. J., *Lancers and Dragoons 1900–1914*. Almark Publishing Co. New Malden, 1975

Pietsch, Paul, *Die Formations und Uniformierungs-Gesichte des preußischen Heeres 1808–1914*. 2 volumes. Hamburg, Verlag Helmut Gerhard Schulz, 1963

Schulz, Hugo F., *Die Preußischen Kavallerie-Regimenter 1913–1914*. Freiburg, Podzun-Pallas Verlag 1985

Smith, Nigel J., *1866. The Uniforms and Armies of the Austro-Prussian and Austro-Italian Wars*. Privately published UK, 1989

Solka, Michael, *German Armies 1870–71 Prussia* (Men-at-Arms 416). Oxford, Osprey Publishing, 2004